COUNTDOWN
TO VICTORY

BARRY TURNER

COUNTDOWN TO VICTORY

The Final European Campaigns
of World War II

Hodder & Stoughton

Copyright © 2004 by Barry Turner

First published in Great Britain in 2004 by Hodder and Stoughton
A division of Hodder Headline

Maps by Martin Collins

1 3 5 7 9 10 8 6 4 2

A CIP catalogue record for this title is available from the British Library

ISBN 0 340 82202 3

Typeset by Palimpsest Book Production Limited,
Polmont, Stirlingshire

Printed and bound by
Mackays of Chatham Ltd, Chatham, Kent

Hodder Headline's policy is to use papers that are natural, renewable
and recyclable products and made from wood grown in sustainable forests.
The logging and manufacturing processes are expected to conform to
the environmental regulations of the country of origin

Hodder and Stoughton Ltd
A division of Hodder Headline
338 Euston Road
London NW1 3BH

'As fighting all over the globe reaches a climax of fury, we on the home front must back our fighting men and women to the limit. That is our supreme duty . . . I shall not now make any prediction concerning the length of the war. My only prediction is that our enemies will be totally defeated before we lay down our arms.'

Franklin D. Roosevelt
January 9th, 1945

In memory of
Morris Crawford Fulton MD MC
one of the many for whom the war changed everything

Contents

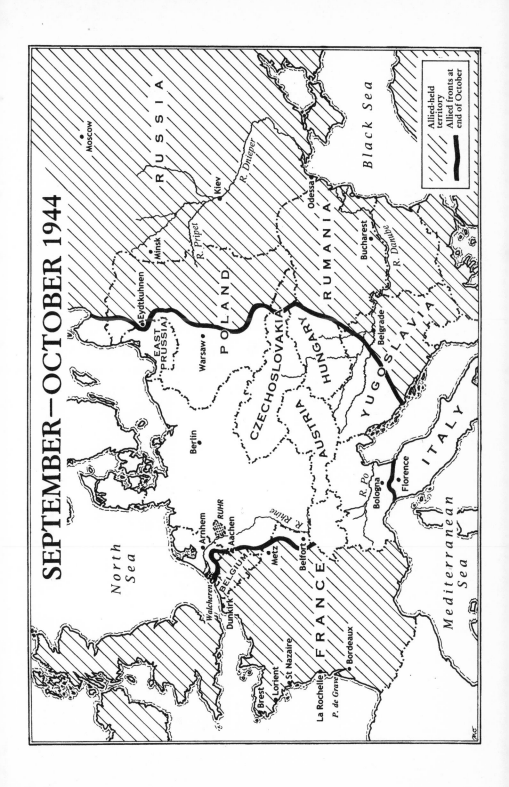

SEPTEMBER–OCTOBER 1944

Allied-held territory

Allied fronts at end of October

Black Sea

Moscow

RUSSIA

R. Dnieper

Kiev

R. Pripet

Minsk

Eydtkuhnen

EAST PRUSSIA

POLAND

Warsaw

Odessa

RUMANIA

Bucharest

R. Danube

Belgrade

YUGOSLAVIA

CZECHOSLOVAKIA

HUNGARY

AUSTRIA

Berlin

ITALY

R. Po

Bologna

Florence

Mediterranean Sea

North Sea

Arnhem

RUHR

Aachen

R. Rhine

Walcheren

Dunkirk

BELGIUM

Metz

Belfort

FRANCE

Brest

Lorient

St Nazaire

La Rochelle

P. de Grave

Bordeaux

Picture Acknowledgements

Hulton Archive/Getty Images: 5 top. Imperial War Museum, London: 1 top (EA49926), bottom left (EA12429), bottom right (FRA200371), 2 top left (MH12850, top right (EA38785), bottom left (MH12850), bottom right (AP69738), 3 bottom (EA48337), 4 top (EA47947), bottom (EA47959), 5 bottom (BU2154), 7 top (EA68875), 7 bottom (OWIL64545), 8 top (BU5207). Landesarchiv Berlin: 8 bottom, 9, 11, 12, 13, 14, 15 bottom, 16. Museum of Danish Resistance 1940–1945, Copenhagen: 6 top. Private Collections: 3 top, 10 photos by Carl Weinrother, Berlin, 15 top photo by Stevens, Haarlem. Svenska Dagbladet, Stockholm: 6 bottom.

Chronology

1944

December 16 After a quiet spell on the western front, the Germans launch a powerful counter-attack in the Ardennes. In what became known as the Rundstedt offensive after Field Marshal von Rundstedt or, more popularly, the Battle of the Bulge, American positions are overrun.

December 19 Field Marshal Montgomery is made commander of all Allied forces north of the bulge created by the German offensive. General Bradley commands all Allied forces to the south.

December 20 Ten thousand GIs taken into captivity. Strategic towns St Vith and Bastogne under pressure. German troops penetrate as far as Stavelot.

December 22 Bastogne under siege but American resistance stiffens. St Vith falls but Stavelot retaken by Allies.

December 24 German advance reaches its limit at the Belgian village of Celles.

December 25–26 Relief of Bastogne by US Third Army.

December 29 Battered by Soviet advance in the east, Hungary changes sides and declares war on Germany.

December 31 Allies recapture Rochefort.

1945

January 1 Luftwaffe mounts its last bombing raid with attacks on Allied airfields and on Brussels.

January 2 Allied counter-attacks in the Ardennes gather pace with the recapture of several towns.

January 3	US First Army launches counter-attack north of the Ardennes salient towards Houffalize.
January 9	US Third Army counter-attacks south of the bulge towards Houffalize.
January 17	US First Army, commanded by Montgomery throughout the Battle of the Bulge, reverts to Bradley's Twelfth Army Group. Red Army advance destroys all German defences along River Vistula.
January 20	President Roosevelt inaugurated for fourth term in office. US Third Army enters Brandenburg. French First Army launches attack in the Vosges.
January 22	Russians reach River Oder.
January 23	US First Army recaptures St Vith.
January 24	SS leader Heinrich Himmler appointed by Hitler to take command on the eastern front.
January 27	German forces retreat from all territory taken in the Battle of the Bulge.
January 29	US Third Army crosses River Our.
January 30	US and British Chiefs of Staff meet in Malta to prepare for the Big Three Allied conference in Yalta.
January 31	US First Army crosses German frontier east of St Vith, two miles from the Siegfried Line.
February 1	French forces break into Colmar and begin closing the gap between Colmar and Mulhouse, a move calculated to cut off German forces in southern Alsace. In Holland, the Hunger Winter takes hold with sugar beet and tulip bulbs now part of the subsistence diet.
February 2	British Second Army crosses River Maas.
February 3	Colmar captured by French and US forces. Berlin suffers its worst air raid of the war.
February 4	Big Three meet at Yalta in the Crimea. US First Army captures first of seven Roer dams.
February 6	Russians cross River Oder southeast of Breslau.
February 7	Germans destroy Roer dams, putting areas round Düren and Jülich under water.

February 8 Operation Veritable. Canadian First and British Second Armies launch offensive southeast of Nijmegen.

February 9 British and Canadian forces pierce outer defences of Siegfried Line in sight of the Rhine.

February 10 US First Army captures last of Roer dams.

February 11 US Third Army takes Prüm, east of St Vith. West bank of the Rhine from Swiss border to north of Strasbourg now in Allied hands. Red Army crosses River Oder northeast of Breslau.

February 12 British and Canadian forces enter Cleve.

February 13 Whole of Reichswald now cleared of German forces.

February 13–14 RAF and USAAF raid on Dresden.

February 14 Budapest surrenders to Red Army after eight-week battle. Canadian and British forces reach Rhine opposite Emmerich.

February 17 US Third Army breaks through Siegfried Line on an eleven-mile front. To the south, the US Seventh Army advances towards Saarbrucken.

February 22 Canadian and British forces take Goch. In Operation Clarion, 9,000 aircraft attack communication links in the area of Emden, Berlin, Dresden, Vienna, Mulhouse.

February 23 Russians capture Poznan after four-week siege. US First and Ninth Armies cross River Roer between Jülich and Düren.

February 25 Jülich and Düren captured.

February 26 Operation Blockbuster. British and Canadian troops attack towards Calcar and Xanten.

February 27 Canadians take Calcar and reach the Rhine.

March 1 US Ninth Army captures München-Gladbach.

March 2 US Third Army captures Trier and US Ninth Army reaches the Rhine at Düsseldorf.

March 3 British air attack on German V2 rocket sites in Holland goes wrong with bombs landing on The Hague, causing heavy casualties.

March 5 US First Army enters Cologne. German conscription extended to fifteen-year-olds.

March 6	US Third Army reaches Rhine northwest of Koblenz.
March 7	US First Army captures Rhine railway bridge at Remagen.
March 8	British troops enter Xanten.
March 9	US First Army takes Bonn. Remagen bridgehead troops capture Erpel.
March 10	Kesselring arrives from Italy to replace Rundstedt as C-in-C West.
March 11	Air attack on Essen destroys vital rail junction.
March 14	US Third Army crosses Moselle southwest of Koblenz.
March 16	Remagen bridgehead extends to twenty-five miles.
March 17	Remagen bridge, badly damaged in air and ground attacks and overloaded with traffic, finally collapses. Russians capture Brandenburg in East Prussia. US Third Army takes Koblenz.
March 18	Four thousand tons of bombs dropped in central Berlin.
March 21	British precision air attack on Gestapo headquarters in Copenhagen.
March 22–23	US Third Army crosses Rhine south of Mainz.
March 23–24	Operation Plunder. British and Canadian Twenty-First Army Group crosses Rhine at four points between Rees and Wesel. Operation Varsity. Airborne assault follows infantry. US Ninth Army attacks between Wesel and Duisberg.
March 25	US First Army breaks out of Remagen bridgehead to advance six miles. British and Canadian Twenty-First Army Group Rhine bridgehead now over thirty miles. Entire west bank of Rhine in Allied hands. Churchill visits troops on Lower Rhine.
March 26	US Seventh Army establishes bridgeheads over Rhine near Worms.
March 27	Last V2 rocket to reach England drops on Orpington in Kent.
March 28	Twenty-First Army Group advance now fifteen miles beyond the Rhine.

March 29	US Seventh Army takes Mannheim. US Third Army captures Frankfurt.
March 30	German front collapses opposite Twenty-First Army Group.
March 31	French First Army crosses Rhine at Karlsruhe, making for Stuttgart.
April 2	Twenty-First Army Group advance now over one hundred miles north and northeast of the Rhine.
April 5	Canadian forces begin clearing German occupiers from western Holland.
April 7	Russians fighting in Vienna.
April 10	British forces capture Hannover.
April 11	US Third Army captures Weimar. US Ninth Army takes Essen. Canadians attack Deventer.
April 12	Death of President Roosevelt. Vice-President Truman sworn in as successor. Belsen and Buchenwald liberated.
April 13	Red Army captures Vienna.
April 15	British and Canadian forces capture Arnhem. In Italy, the US Fifth Army and British Eighth Army break through into the Po Valley to take Bologna.
April 16	US Seventh Army reaches Nuremberg.
April 18	German resistance in Ruhr ends. British Second Army reaches Lüneburg. US forces enter Czechoslovakia. US Ninth Army takes Magdeburg. US First Army enters Düsseldorf.
April 19	British Second Army reaches Elbe.
April 21	Soviet troops in outskirts of Berlin.
April 22	US Third Army begins advance down Danube Valley.
April 24	Himmler offers surrender to western Allies. British and Canadian forces enter Bremen.
April 25	Russian and US forces meet at Torgau on the Elbe.
April 26	Bremen surrenders. Russians capture Stettin.
April 27	Himmler surrender offer formally rejected by US and Britain.
April 28	Mussolini and supporters captured and shot by partisans. Operation Manna, the airlift of food into Holland, begins.

April 28–29	Hitler marries Eva Braun and appoints Admiral Doenitz his successor.
April 29	Dachau liberated.
April 30	Hitler commits suicide. US Seventh Army takes Munich. Russians in the centre of Berlin.
May 2	British and Canadian spearheads reach the Baltic to take Wismar and Lübeck. Hamburg surrenders. Berlin surrenders to Red Army. German armies in Italy surrender.
May 3	Innsbruck falls to the Americans.
May 4	All German forces in Holland, northwest Germany and Denmark surrender unconditionally to Montgomery on Lüneburg Heath.
May 7	At Eisenhower's headquarters at Reims, all German forces surrender unconditionally to western Allies and Russia.
May 8	VE Day.
May 9	Final surrender document ratified in Berlin.
May 23	Doenitz government dissolved. Doenitz and his ministers arrested.

Introduction

My memories of war in Europe are of a small boy. Knowing nothing of the luxuries of peacetime and living some way apart from any serious action, I took to the conditions of conflict as part of the natural order. While my parents studied maps cut from newspapers and fretted over Allied performance in battle, I was impervious to any sense of danger. The flotilla of aircraft on its way to a bombing raid over Germany was no more than an exhilarating aerial display. Convoys of armoured vehicles held more fascination than the town carnival. And when American troops were passing through there was always the bonus of a handout of chewing gum or chocolate. The biggest excitement in my young life was to be put to bed under the heavy dining room table whenever there was an air raid warning.

One might have expected a more realistic view of warfare to come with puberty but for me and my generation, fed on a cultural diet of gung-ho books and movies, it took a long time to grow out of the fantasy that war, or at least the 1939–45 war, was one big adventure. The politicians and generals who had led the Allied cause were presented as spotless heroes while the serious fighting was portrayed almost exclusively in terms of victory for the righteous. Men had died but bravely and honourably, without observable pain unless they were the enemy, in which case they were liable to turn into snivelling wrecks. Atrocities were assumed to be a German speciality. The change in the popular conception of the war started when the self-serving memoirs of the military greats and the popular histories based on them gave way to the less enchanted recollections of front-line soldiers and of the civilians who had happened to get in the way of the action. In recent years, with intimations of mortality, there has been a rush of American, British,

Canadian and German first-hand accounts of the fighting. They are spread across museums and library collections and on a host of websites. Together, they give a fresh and honest picture of that great European drama that ended sixty years ago. Most particularly, and in the context of this book, the war as seen by fighting men and civilians from both sides reverses the popular conception of the last six months of the war, a period in which it was supposed to be all over bar the victory parades. The reality could not have been more different. If the German forces had broken through at the Battle of the Bulge, more of a possibility than the Allied generals could ever bring themselves to admit, the fighting might have continued for months, even years or ended in a negotiated peace. As shown by the evidence here, much of it published for the first time, some of the most desperate battles on the western European front took place in this last phase. Those who were there saw the chaos and the tragedy, great acts of courage and as many cruel excesses. Their stories finally put to rest the easy assumption of inevitable victory. For myself, I still find it hard to believe that it is in my lifetime that Europe got so close to realising a death wish.

I
Misreading Hitler

The party was over almost before it started. In August 1944 there were short odds on the war being over by Christmas. A month later, all bets were off. That the Third Reich would fall, few doubted. But when? It could take weeks or months; maybe even years?

The success of the Normandy landings, by no means a foregone conclusion, had been a great morale booster. In June the biggest ever invasion force had broken through German defences to sweep across France and Belgium. Caught in a pincer movement between American forces curving round from their advance south and Canadian and British troops moving down from Caen, the German Fifth and Seventh Armies had been trapped and destroyed. On August 20th, General George S. Patton led his Third Army on an assault across the Seine, creating a bridgehead at Mantes-Gassicourt nearly thirty miles to the northwest of Paris. Four days later, the French Second Armoured Division entered the capital. Meanwhile, to the east, the Soviet summer offensive had annihilated three Germany army groups to forge bridgeheads over the Narew River, north of Warsaw and the Vistula, south of the Polish capital.

But an advance of such speed and ferocity could not be sustained. On both fronts supply lines were dangerously extended. There was a desperate shortage of fuel and an equally desperate shortage of human energy. Battle-weary troops were in need of a respite. On the Polish frontier, Soviet forces dug themselves in at the river barriers, secure against Panzer counter-attacks. At the other side of Europe, the forward rush of three US armies was halted some sixty-four miles short of the Rhine. The Fifth Armoured Division of Patton's Third Army liberated Luxembourg, penetrating over ten miles into Germany. But then, in early September, even Patton's battle express ran out of steam.

Hopes of an early breakthrough were not easily abandoned. Operation Market Garden, a combined ground and airborne attack across sixty miles of enemy-held territory, was conceived by Field Marshal Sir Bernard Montgomery as a speedy conclusion to the war. The airborne troops would be dropped at Arnhem where they would secure a Rhine crossing. An infantry follow-up by Thirty Corps, led by General Brian Horrocks, was scheduled within forty-eight hours of the first landings. After that it should have been full speed to the great industrial cities of the Ruhr. In the event, the tanks of Thirty Corps fell easy victim to German gunners and Allied supplies failed to get through. The plan foundered. After nine days of close fighting, which virtually wiped out the British First Airborne Division and inflicted heavy casualties on the American parachutists, the operation was called off.

The ability of the Wehrmacht to challenge the odds was proved again eighty miles south of Arnhem, at Aachen, the first German city to fall to the Allies but at terrible cost to American forces. It had all seemed so easy. As the US Seventh Corps, led by General 'Lightning Joe' Collins, crossed open country towards Aachen, the defences showed every sign of crumbling. While Nazi officials were packing their bags, the commander of the 116th Panzer Division was also preparing to move out. He left behind him a letter to his American opposite number asking him to 'take care of the unfortunate people [of Aachen] in a humane way'. But then an altogether tougher commander took over. Determined to fight to the last man, Colonel Gerhardt Wilck forced Collins to abandon his plan to take Aachen 'on the run'. Instead, while the First Infantry, the 'Big Red One', America's finest infantry division, was fighting from house to house in the city suburbs, Collins' main force bypassed Aachen to enter what became known as the Hürtgen Forest or, as the GIs called it, the 'Green Hell of Hürtgen'. The objective was to achieve a pincer that would cut off the defenders of Aachen from the rest of the Wehrmacht. It worked but few would argue that it was worth the effort and the death toll. By mid-October, when Aachen finally passed to the attackers, American losses were close to 60,000 or, to put it another way, a casualty rate over six months higher than that for the six years in Vietnam. This was no way to win a war.

It was the same story in Italy, the only other front where progress might reasonably have been expected. After the capture of Rome in June, the Allied forces moving north had bumped up against a stubborn German defence of the Po Valley. As winter approached it was clear that the stalemate would not be broken easily. Everywhere the Allied advance was on hold. The emphasis now was on the build-up to a massive winter or spring offensive carrying the war well into 1945.

Preparation for a full-scale assault on the formidable West Wall or Siegfried Line defences along the German frontier were hampered by the destruction of past battles. The French railway system had been devastated first by Allied bombing and then by the Germans in retreat, while many of the Channel ports had been shelled or sabotaged beyond immediate use. Nonetheless, American and British forces captured Gelsenkirchen on the edge of the Ruhr conurbation, the heartland of German industrial power, and overran the outer defences of the Siegfried Line without much difficulty. It was when they struck at the main defences with networks of pillboxes and minefields that had to be cleared step by step, that the real horror started. Reporting for the BBC, Frank Gillard spoke of mile after mile of trenches across the countryside.

> They zigzag along the edges of the roads and behind the embankments, and I saw one particularly well-prepared system alongside a sunken railway track. Most of these trench systems had culs-de-sac branching out at right angles, leading across fields, up to little bumps of rising ground or out towards other tracks. Obviously, at the ends of these limbs the Germans had listening posts and observation points and machine-gun positions. The main trenches were inter-communicating so that you could pass from one system to another and cover wide stretches of the front without once coming above ground.[1]

And the weather didn't help. After the heaviest November rains for many years, the swollen rivers of France and the Low Countries turned the countryside into marshland. For the forward infantry, unprepared for such conditions, it was a watery version of hell. A Canadian infantry officer, broadcasting in the last week of November, asked his listeners:

> Do *you* know what it's like? Of course you don't. You have never slept in a hole in the ground which you have dug while someone tried to kill you. It is an open grave – and yet graves don't fill up with water. They don't harbour wasps and mosquitoes, and you don't feel the cold, clammy wet that goes into your marrow. At night the infantryman gets some boards, or tin, or an old door, and puts it over one end of his slit trench; then he shovels on top of it as much dirt as he can scrape up near by. He sleeps with his head under this, not to keep out the rain, but to protect his head and chest from airbursts. In the daytime he chain-smokes, curses, or prays – all of this lying on his belly with his hands under his chest to lessen the pain from the blast. If it is at night, smoking is taboo. If there are two in a trench they sit at each end with their heads between their knees and make inane remarks . . . such as, 'Guess that one landed in 12 Platoon.'[2]

Trenches had to be chiselled out of frozen earth. Blankets and clothing were like wet cotton wool. Trench foot and frostbite were commonplace. When litter-carrying jeeps bogged down in snow-drifts, the wounded had to be carried on stretchers to the aid stations, often half a mile or more away. Baths were a rarity, though Captain Howard Sweet with the US 908 Field Artillery Regiment took comfort from the thought that 'it has been so long since I had my clothes off – or at least the bottom two layers – that I *can't* be dirty. Dirt just *can't* penetrate through as many layers of clothing as I wear!'[3]

Wilbur McQuinn from Kentucky, a platoon sergeant in the 331st Regiment, staved off frostbite by toe- and finger-clenching exercises to keep the blood circulating. But he and his men learned some other tricks, too.

> Some of the men took off their overshoes and warmed their feet by holding them near burning GI heat rations [fuel tablets] in their

foxholes. Others used waxed K ration boxes, which burn with very little smoke but a good flame. Both GI heat and K ration boxes are also fine for drying your socks or gloves. I also used straw inside my overshoes to keep my feet warm while we were marching. Some of our other men used newspapers or wrapped their feet with strips of blankets or old cloth.[4]

Everyone agreed that keeping their feet warm was the worst problem. It was particularly bad for those stuck for long periods in tanks. 'We wore as many pairs of socks as we could obtain and wore overshoes to cover the socks. At least once each day we would remove the socks and put the sweaty pair on the outside and the dry pair next to the feet.'[5] Not everyone had it quite so bad. Three-quarters of a mile back from the front line, troops who whiled away the day writing letters home, brewing tea or coffee and hanging out the washing had only desultory shell or mortar fire to remind them that there was still a war on. Not that this was any comfort to those who took the brunt of the punishment.

As one of a forward signal platoon, Sergeant Walter Caines of the Fourth Dorsets recalls ammunition and other supplies had to be manhandled by carrying parties.

This took hours, and the whole time the Battalion area was under heavy fire from German artillery. The field behind the wood was littered with vehicles stuck in the mud. Rain fell heavily. All of us were soaked to the skin, with absolutely no cover whatsoever. Trenches we had taken over from the 5 Dorsets were half full of water, and some were not even completed. The majority had no head cover, except the Command Post. The signals carrier with all the stores on board was lost in the woods and there was no communication except runners. Wireless could not be relied upon, as batteries were run down and all sets became waterlogged. I spent the night sitting in a trench half full of water, with rain trickling down my neck, it was bloody miserable. In fact the only remedy was a swig at the bottle.[6]

For Captain J.J. Moore, of the First Battalion Oxfordshire and Buckinghamshire Light Infantry, settling in on the Dutch-Belgian border near the villages of Neeritter and Ittervoort, the miserable climate was less of a worry than his company's exposure to counter-attack. Identifying a weakness that the Germans were soon to exploit only too thoroughly, he noted that Allied defences were so scattered that no one company linked up with another and that even within companies, platoons were often cut off from each other. No wonder, he complained, so many German patrols were crossing his lines undetected. The risks of getting caught unawares were vividly and uncomfortably illustrated when Captain Moore was sent forward to check out an apparently unoccupied farmhouse. And so it turned out except that close by on the banks of a canal, the patrol came across a heavily armed German force guarding what was presumed to be a troop-crossing.

> I reported this back to Company H.Q. I was told to attack the Germans on my side of the canal, using half of the platoon. With this in mind I took Cpl Cooper and Sgt Wilkins into the farmhouse. At the gable end of the farmhouse was a hayloft to which we climbed by ladder and then, loosening one or two pantiles on the roof, we could see the canal bank quite clearly, but we did not see it for long.
>
> Without warning, hundreds of Spandau machine-gun bullets hit the house, shattering the pantiles on the roof and tearing into the hayloft. Instantly we leapt down the ten foot drop and scurried into a room in the middle of the house from which doorways led into the yard at each side. Hundreds of bullets tore across the yards, tearing up the ground and chipping off the brickwork of the farm and outhouse. I tried to return to the abri but as I left the doorway the ground flew up just in front of my feet with a hail of bullets. I stepped back into the house. It was chaotic: there were, it seemed, six Spandau machine-guns firing from points forming a semi-circle almost round the farm. One was firing at the side of the farmhouse, seemingly from the house further down the track beyond the farmhouse. We were trapped.

Just as suddenly the machine-gun fire stopped. The besieged watched and waited. Captain Moore felt certain it was the end. 'I imagined with great clarity the white cross on my grave and even checked the lettering, "256396 Capt. J.J. Moore, 1st Oxf & Bucks L.I. aged 23. K.I.A. 3rd Nov. 1944".'

His fatalism was unwarranted. Advancing in line across a field towards the farmhouse, the Germans had been met by flanking fire and fearing a trap had pulled out. Knowing that he could expect another attack as soon as it was dark, Captain Moore led a dignified withdrawal before getting some rest in a slit trench. 'I fell fast asleep; I had not slept for two days.' The following morning there was excitement of a different sort.

Well after dawn, in the bright daylight, our sentries were amazed to see a German soldier leap to surrender. I was impressed by his imagination and patience. He was brought into the yard and he told us there was another German soldier, wounded, further down the track. A small party was sent out and a German soldier was brought in on a stretcher, a terrible, pitiful sight, for he was clearly dying of stomach wounds. We made him as comfortable as possible and he was taken away but there seemed to be little hope. I was singularly impressed by the German who had given himself up, for he must have stayed to comfort his wounded comrade, waiting until it was clearly light before giving himself up so that his friend could get medical attention.

I walked back with the prisoner to Company H.Q. He was cold, wet and shivering. I sat by a stove and got warmer. The prisoner looked quite scared, so I gave him a cigarette and ordered some food – a spare tin of Irish stew – but, suspecting something, he would not eat it. However, when I ate half of it, he ate the rest and became quite talkative. He was then taken off to the Intelligence Officer.

I listened to the official War Communique on the radio and discovered that there had been some 'local minor patrol activity' on the previous day. I wondered in what comfort the Staff Officer who wrote that was living and I wished him in hell.[7]

Luck was with the Allies on the taking of Antwerp. With critical support from the Belgian resistance, the city had fallen to Montgomery's Eleventh Armoured Division with its harbour virtually intact. The second largest port on the continent, Antwerp was within easy reach of the northern half of the front. Moreover, supplies could be moved forward on Belgian railways which had suffered relatively little damage. The Germans now set about trying to remedy that omission.

Some 6,000 V1s and V2s, pilotless missiles known in Britain as doodlebugs or buzz bombs, fell on Antwerp. Over 4,000 citizens died, 567 of them when, in December 1944, a V2 landed on a crowded cinema.

Richard Hough, a fighter pilot with 197 Squadron who was stationed briefly in Antwerp, witnessed the German effort to wipe out a vital communications centre. Finding an undamaged house was an achievement in itself. Hough's billet for several weeks was no worse than that endured by the civilian population.

> There were holes in the roofs and gaps in the walls, while the last remnants of an extinguished domestic life – one or two smashed pictures on the walls, a three-legged sofa downstairs, a chest of drawers with a single child's sock in one drawer in my 'bedroom' – all added to the poignancy. It was bitterly cold and when not on standby we pilots spent most of our time collecting firewood, sawing up the less needed floorboards, the banisters, anything that would burn in the open grates.
>
> Outside in the streets, Belgian citizens showed in their faces and their walk the price of more than four years of German occupation. Women in black and their children picked over the railway tracks for an unlikely lump of coal which had escaped so many eyes before. Antwerp itself had a haunted air. Liberation had brought only temporary relief and, ironically, had led to more deaths than under the Germans. We were discouraged from going into the city at all, and it was hardly an attraction anyway, with nothing in the shops or restaurants, and the wretched people sunk in disillusionment.[8]

Adding to the general feeling of depression, evidence started to emerge of just how far the occupying forces had been prepared to go to keep civilians in line. On a cold, wet day in mid-November Sergeant Richard Greenwood of the Ninth Battalion, Royal Tank Regiment, was one of a group taken six miles south of Antwerp for a guided tour of Fort de Breendonck, a former headquarters of the Geheime Staatspolizei (state secret police) otherwise known by its acronym, Gestapo.

First we saw some cells measuring about 6 ft x 8 ft in which 5 or 6 prisoners had to sleep: there were no windows to the cells, and the inmates had to live in complete darkness: there was no doubt about the intensity of the darkness, the walls being of reinforced concrete about 10 ft thick. We were told that prisoners usually spent four days in these cells. We saw other cells, much smaller, each made to hold one man. And we saw the dirty and insanitary sleeping quarters of the Jews.

At the rear of the fort, we saw ten wooden pillars erected vertically in the ground – about 30 ft from the wall of the fort and 6 ft apart. To these pillars used to be strapped the bodies of the men who had been condemned to be shot: a few bullet marks were quite visible in the wall behind. We were told that 400 Belgians were shot in this manner at this particular prison. Close to this shooting 'gallery', there was a crude gallows – consisting of a low stage with a trap door, and a beam overhead to carry the rope. We were told that three Belgians had been hanged on this contraption. Not having seen the underground torture chamber, I cannot describe it. But I believe the Germans destroyed most of their implements before departing. We were told that everything has been thoroughly photographed and filmed, so no doubt the world will be made aware of this frightful place.[9]

Sergeant Greenwood had a change of mood when his battalion crossed into Holland. For one thing, the standard of accommodation improved markedly.

Saturday 18.11.44 – Indoors all afternoon – too comfortable in these billets to bother about going out. We are being well looked after – waited on hand and foot. Fires, tidying up, etc all done by civvys. Unfortunately, none of the people in the house speak English, but we manage to 'converse' somehow. It is really amazing how much 'conversation' is carried on by means of a few words, signs and pantomime.

That evening there was a party.

> Each member of the troop invited a lady friend, making about thirty
> of us in all. Unfortunately, we only had a portable gramophone for a
> 'dance band' – it was more or less useless, but the dancers managed
> somehow. Refreshments were surprisingly good – the lads having been
> scrounging and buying for a couple of days beforehand.[10]

For the really lucky ones, there was the prospect of weekend leave
in Brussels. Undamaged and now a busy leave centre, Brussels,
recalls Richard Hough, was doing a 'roaring trade in nightclubs,
restaurants and brothels, and of course the black market'. But the
zenith of comfort and relaxation that Brussels had to offer was a
hot bath. Captain Holdsworth wrote:

> I had four and they were among my most treasured memories of those
> 48 hours of leave: great steaming baths lasting an hour at a time,
> sweating out the aches and pains, cleansing the sores and cuts, and
> forcing out the dirt accumulated since D-Day. The evidence of the
> need for these baths was plainly to be seen after the water had drained
> away. They were blissful, energy-sapping, and time-consuming, they
> did me more good than any other diversion.[11]

Arnhem, Aachen and Antwerp were evidence enough of German
determination to fight on. While there were signs of a collapse of
morale in the civilian population hit hardest by the Allied advance,
it was equally clear that the military was holding firm. While
Germany was a nation in fear of its future it was a long way from
accepting the inevitability of defeat. Fed on warnings of the night-
mares to follow unconditional surrender, optimism was kept alive
by the promise of new weapons of unprecedented destructive power
soon to be unleashed. The success of the V2s, capable of reaching
an altitude of fifty miles, the very edge of space, and of reaching
a target nearly 124 miles away in six minutes, gave some credence
to the propaganda. It is hard to know the extent to which Joseph
Goebbels, Hitler's propaganda minister, believed his own wild
fantasies but he took seriously the imminent deployment of a
mysterious new compound. 'One jet of it will be enough to burn

a man to death. It will penetrate the tiniest gaps in the armour of tanks and will make superiority in armour useless.'[12]

Hitler's own secret weapon was his capacity to surprise. With the Allies held down at the Siegfried Line, he had time to reinvigorate the Wehrmacht and he did so with ruthless energy. Reserves of manpower were discovered by the simple expedient of lowering the recruitment age while roping in those hitherto let off as too old or unfit to wear uniform. It was an awesome thought that a battered Germany, beset on all sides by powerful enemies, still had ten million men in uniform, two-thirds of them in an army backed by formidable military hardware.

But Hitler had something more ambitious in mind than a defensive war. There were few that he trusted to share his plans. After the July plot on his life he was wary of declaring himself openly, even to his senior commanders who had no inkling of Operation Watch on the Rhine (later Autumn Mist), until October 22nd, barely a month before the intended start date. It was then that Hitler called together the Chiefs of Staff of Field Marshal Karl von Rundstedt, recently recalled from retirement to take up his old job as Commander-in-Chief West and of Field Marshal Walther Model, commander of Army Group B which straddled the western front. The strategy, to sweep through the Ardennes forest on a sixty-mile front along the Belgian and Luxembourg frontiers and then, having crossed the Meuse, make straight for the Channel coast to take Antwerp, was nothing if not audacious. If successful it would disrupt the Allied troop supply, extend German control of the Netherlands and split the British and Canadian armies in the north from the Americans in the south, allowing both to be encircled. With Antwerp recaptured there would be no Allied escape by sea. Three armies were to be thrown into the assault. After a breakthrough by the infantry, the tanks would follow at speed, bypassing strongly held towns and villages, a tactic which had been used to great effect on the eastern front.

But there were glaring deficiencies. Many of the troops were fresh to battle and inadequately trained, essential equipment had still to come on stream and air support was minimal. Only a quarter of the fuel needed could be guaranteed, advancing units were expected to capture supplies from the enemy. Moreover, fighting conditions in winter over a heavily wooded and mountainous region were hardly propitious. But Hitler was adamant. Even if he could not destroy his enemies, cutting them off from their supply lines via Antwerp would, he calculated, weaken Allied resolve and even conceivably lead to a negotiated peace on the western front so that Germany could concentrate on the threat to the east.

Rundstedt and Model did their best to persuade him otherwise. The two field marshals were not on the best of terms. Rundstedt, a general since 1927, was of the old school of German military elite. He had led the invasion of France in 1940 and the defence against the Allied landings in Normandy four years later and was considered by Eisenhower to be 'the ablest of the German generals'. In fact, Model, sixteen years Rundstedt's junior, was the more able strategist. His Commander-in-Chief could not see this. For him, Model was a middle-class upstart whom he once described as having 'the makings of a good sergeant-major'. The class prejudice carried over to the Allied side where who you were in the military still had the edge over what you were. But for all their differences, Rundstedt and Model agreed on one thing: Autumn Mist had all the makings of a disaster. The plan, said Model when he first heard of it, 'hasn't got a damned leg to stand on'. Both were prepared to argue their case with Hitler but at sixty-nine and in poor health, Rundstedt was not the best spokesman for the opposition. However, he did try.

> When I was first told about the proposed offensive in the Ardennes, I protested against it as vigorously as I could. The forces at our disposal were much, much too weak for such far-reaching objectives. I suggested that my plan against the Aachen salient be used instead, but the suggestion was turned down, as were all my other objections. It was only up to me to obey. It was a nonsensical operation, and the most stupid part of it was the setting of Antwerp as the target. If we had reached the Meuse we should have got down on our knees and thanked God – let alone try to reach Antwerp.[13]

The two leading commanders in the field, the diminutive (at 5 ft 2 in) General Hasso von Manteuffel who led the Fifth Panzer Army and the burly General Sepp Dietrich of the Sixth Panzer Army, also voiced their fears. Summoned to Army Group head-quarters in early November, Manteuffel assumed that the conference was routine:

> but a glance at the document that was now passed round quickly showed that this was to be an unusual meeting. Each officer present had to pledge secrecy: should any officer break this pledge, he must realise that his offence would be punishable by death. I had frequently attended top secret conferences presided over by Hitler at Berchtesgaden or at the 'Wolf's Lair' both before and after 20 July 1944, but this was the first time I had seen a document such as the one which I now signed.[14]

However, he was not so unnerved by the occasion as to remain silent. His objections were overruled.

If anyone had a better chance of getting Hitler to change his mind it was Sepp Dietrich. Dismissed by the traditionalists as a red-necked Bavarian, Dietrich was one of Hitler's earliest followers who had proved his leadership qualities and personal bravery on the Russian front. A blunt talker and one to whom Hitler usually gave attention, he knew he had been handed an impossible task.

> All I had to do was to cross the Meuse river, capture Brussels and then go on and take the port of Antwerp. And all this in December, January and February, the worst three months of the year; through the Ardennes where snow was waist deep and there wasn't room to deploy four tanks abreast, let alone six armoured divisions; when it didn't get light until eight in the morning and was dark again at four in the afternoon and my tanks can't fight at night; with divisions that had just been re-formed and were composed chiefly of raw untrained recruits; and at Christmas time.[15]

But Dietrich too had little chance to voice his objections.

> I told Hitler that I wasn't ready to attack and that we didn't have the ammunition or food to carry it through successfully. The generals

were all in line waiting to speak to Hitler and I had only a minute to tell him this before the line moved on. He said that I would have everything I needed.[16]

Rundstedt and Model continued to push their alternative plan, an attack that stopped well short of Antwerp, a 'little slam' instead of a 'grand slam' as Manteuffel put it, but it was a lost cause. Hitler's orders were 'irreversible'.

With so much professional opinion against him it would be easy to assume that Hitler had nothing going for him except a misguided faith in his own genius. Not so. Though now judged to have been an act of desperation, the Ardennes offensive was not without its merits. In 1914 and again in 1940 the Ardennes had given cover to a lightning surprise attack. Hitler convinced himself that it could be done again. His only concession to his generals was to postpone the attack until December 16th when poor weather was expected to offer protection against aerial bombing. The Wehrmacht started with another advantage. The strategy adopted by the Allied Supreme Commander, General Dwight Eisenhower, of advancing on a broad front inevitably left some sectors light on manpower. In the Ardennes, General Omar Bradley's Twelfth Army Group straddled eighty miles of Belgian-German border with just one armoured and three infantry divisions. Two of these had lately arrived fresh from the States and the other two were exhausted by their recent bruising encounter with the enemy in the Hürtgen Forest. Though perilously overstretched, his troops, many of them fresh arrivals, were encouraged to think that a weakened enemy was unlikely to mount a winter campaign in such unfavourable territory.

Recruited into the 106th Division of the 422nd Regiment, Jack Brugh crossed the Atlantic in early November. Less than a month later he was on his way to the Schnee Eifel in the northern sector of the Ardennes with the assurance of his colonel that 'it had been very quiet up here, you'll have the opportunity to learn the easy way.'

The Ardennes Front was known by the GIs as the 'Ghost Front' – a cold, quiet place where artillery was seldom heard and patrols probed the enemy lines just to keep in practice. Within rifle range of each other, the German observers watched the Americans, and the Americans watched the Germans. Both sides rested and watched and avoided irritating each other.[17]

That was not quite true. Much was happening, it was just that no one on the Allied side seemed to know what to make of it. It says much for the quality of the German military machine that, despite the obvious defects of Autumn Mist, it came close to inflicting a major defeat on the Allies. So laid-back were the army chiefs that front-line warnings of tanks and other heavy equipment moving into position opposite the weakest sector of the Ardennes front were discounted. 'The German crust of defence is thinner, more brittle and more vulnerable than it appears to the troops in the lines,' Bradley was assured less than a week before the guns blazed.

A German general captured by the French let slip the intention to use the Sixth Panzer Army for a single large-scale counter-attack at the end of December. He was ignored.[18] The collective wisdom of intelligence chiefs held that at worst Dietrich's forces were preparing for a defensive battle in anticipation of an Allied assault. 'Don't be so jumpy,' said one intelligence officer when he was asked to explain rumours of troop movements. 'The Krauts are just playing phonograph records to scare you newcomers.' In fact, three German armies with twenty divisions, including twelve Panzer divisions, up to 300,000 men, were gathering for the onslaught. The price of lax intelligence was the loss of a unique opportunity to use air supremacy to annihilate elite German forces concentrated on a small area. Of all the Allied generals, it was Patton alone who was suspicious. Even the cautious Montgomery was planning to spend Christmas at home. While others relaxed, Patton revised his planned advance to allow for a dramatic switch north ready to help out the raw recruits who had supposedly been given the soft option of holding the centre ground of the Ardennes front.

Musing on the wisdom of fifty years' hindsight, Noel Annan, formerly of military intelligence, later provost of King's College,

Cambridge and vice-chancellor of London University, acknowledged that their greatest failure was to get inside Hitler's mind
and think like him.

The problem was insoluble: how could one persuade the Chiefs of
Staff that Hitler would take decisions that were the despair of his
finest strategists. Here was a man who seemingly understood the new
tactics of armoured warfare, yet in reality he was enslaved by his
memories as a front-line soldier in the First World War, refusing to
fight a battle of manoeuvre and insisting that every inch of territory
conquered must be held. In the Ardennes we made the mistake of
asking ourselves: 'What would an experienced commander like
Rundstedt do?' It was not Rundstedt we should have thought of, but
Hitler. Hitler did what no one expected him to do. And yet, was it
not in Hitler's character to recall that it was he who had backed
Manstein's plan to break through the Ardennes in 1940? Should we
not have guessed that he could hear destiny calling him once again
to choose the Ardennes, seize Antwerp and encircle with his three
Panzer armies the British as he had done in 1940? None of us could
rise to such a flight of imagination.[19]

The German build-up was allowed to continue without hindrance.
Hans Hejny, of the Fifth Panzer Army, was in a forward position
close to the border with Luxembourg.

Orders were quiet and lights out. Only a thin ray of the night advance
device made the road track barely visible. It was hard to see the roads
and we had to concentrate to avoid falling into ditches. There were
no tanks in sight. The road was empty, nobody was ahead of us in
the dark.
We reached the top of a hill and could see the vague outlines of
Luxembourg. The road extended from a forest into a plain and there
were tail-lights from the column ahead of us gliding downwards and
disappearing into the woods.[20]

Hejny's confidence would have been all the greater had he known
what little was being done by way of an Allied reception. Military
matters had low priority. With Christmas approaching the emphasis

was on home comforts to cheer up the troops – an extra ration of chocolate, supplies of woollen socks and gloves, even luminous watches. When Gene Curry and friends of the Twelfth Armoured Division got tired of army food, they took a few sticks of TNT and threw them in the river. 'We had all the fish we could eat. The local people had plenty too.'[21] Those billeted in farms fed well on domestic produce. Beef was plentiful. 'We had steak almost every day because of all the cattle killed in the fields.'[22] And conveniently frozen in the snow.

The desperate need for basic training does not seem to have been met with any great sense of urgency. An often repeated memory of army veterans is of fresh-faced recruits having to be taught how to load a rifle. Some of the best advice came not through formal instruction but by listening to those who had first-hand experience of fighting over inhospitable countryside. Newcomers to the Ardennes were too inclined to think that trees offered protection against enemy fire until it was pointed out that you could just as easily be killed by a shower of splintered wood as by getting hit by shrapnel. 'Whenever you dug a foxhole and planned on being there a while, it was a good idea to put some logs over the hole. The Germans used what were known as time fire or proximity fused shells which went off while still in the air.'[23]

Mines and booby traps left behind as the Germans backed up towards the Siegfried Line were varied and frequently lethal. Yet, too often, the dangers were ignored by the uninitiated.

The regal mine was about three feet long, eight inches wide and eight inches high. I saw what was left of a jeep-load of French soldiers after they'd driven over one. There were some pieces of uniforms hanging in the trees and the biggest part of the jeep that was left was the engine.

This same regal mine caused a lot of noise in a town I was in. The people had just finished putting the tiles back up on their roofs when I heard a big blast. It came from in front of the house we had just moved into. I thought the Germans had fired in a large shell. Some engineer outfit had dug up a lot of these regal mines and put them on the side of the road. They had been marked real well with red ribbons. Along came a crane, mounted on the back of a truck. The streets were narrow in Europe, so the driver was looking back at the crane's boom. He drove right over the pile of mines and set them off. The truck didn't have a top on it, so the driver was blown about fifteen feet over a fence and killed. The crane operator was trapped in the cab. He'd had most of his head blown off.[24]

More threatening to limb than to life was the shoe mine, encased in wood so that it was next to impossible to pick it up on a detector. It was powerful enough to take the feet off anyone who stood on it, hence its name.

The Germans had another rotten weapon that they'd bury in a trail or walkway. When a G.I. stepped on it, it fired a bullet into his leg. This weapon was shaped like a pencil and about the same size. They'd bury it just barely under the dirt, with the bullet end up. It had a firing pin on top of a spring. When you stepped on it the spring would pop up and set off the shell. It made one hell of an ouch.[25]

A persistent worry among troops was that if it did come to a full-scale battle in winter conditions, their olive drab uniforms made them sitting targets against the snow. The point had already occurred to the German commanders who themselves took the precaution of equipping their front-line soldiers with an overlay uniform of white leggings and anorak. The Twelfth Army chose improvisation. Those closest to the enemy were each given a square yard of white cloth to cover their helmets. GIs came up with their own solution to adapting wool-lined leather gloves which were too bulky for firing a rifle. Civilians who acquired cast-off gloves took time to work out why, so often, the covering for one finger had been cut off.

Towards the end of the second week in December, the warning signals of a battle about to start were clearer and more frequent. Local people with relatives or friends on the other side of the line were the best sources of information. Many were prepared to speak out but more eloquent were those who said nothing while they packed a few belongings, loaded a cart and made off down the road. Each night brought fresh reports of distant rumbling noises that might – or might not – be tanks and artillery on the move. Was that the wind in the trees, or the rustle of men edging through the undergrowth? The received wisdom held firm. Whatever the rumours and imaginings of a cold night, the Germans simply did not have the capacity to mount a serious offensive. The morning of December 16th proved just how wrong received wisdom could be.

At 0530 hours, German artillery opened up a forty-five-minute barrage, destroying communication links between Allied comm-anders and their forward observation points. When the guns stopped searchlights pierced the night sky, the beams bouncing off the clouds to create artificial moonlight. Made ghostly by their white combat gear, the ranks of infantry, fourteen abreast, rushed the American lines. The surprise was total.

Harry Martin was still trying to get his hearing back after the artillery pounding when a wild figure crashed through the door of his hut, screaming, 'The Germans are coming! The Germans are coming. We'll all be killed.'

Those words are etched in my brain for the rest of my life. Thoughts raced through my head: this had been a quiet sector for almost three months. We had only been here for five days so why are the Germans attacking us? We grabbed our rifles and steel helmets and got out of the cabin as fast as we could. Bill and I were assigned to the open foxhole on the extreme left flank. The rest of the platoon went to the log bunkers directly in front of them.

Seconds later I could see hundreds of shadowy heads bobbing up and down coming over the crest of the hill just before dawn. They acted like they were drunk or on drugs. They came over the hill screaming and shrieking. Their shrill screams went right through my head. I was terrified. They had already out flanked our company and now they were coming to finish us off.

Being on the extreme left flank with nothing on our left and out of sight of our platoon on the right it felt almost like we were against the entire Germany Army . . . There was no way of stopping all of them. I had a feeling of utter hopelessness of surviving the attack.

I was panic-stricken. I felt that my entire life force had left my body. I was already dead and I was fighting like a zombie.

Then in the middle of this terrifying battle I head a very confident calm voice inside my head say, 'Squeeze the trigger.' I instantly calmed down, took careful aim at one of the charging Germans through my gunsight and squeezed the trigger. He flung his arms up over his head and fell down dead, shot through the head. I felt a sensation surge through my whole body. I was no longer a zombie. My life force had come surging back. I was alive and for the first time I felt that I had a chance to come out of this battle.[26]

But soon American forces had crumbled across the entire eighty-mile front. By the time the high command realised that they were not dealing with localised attacks but a full-scale offensive, the German push had extended fifteen miles into Allied lines. Fifteen thousand GIs had been captured, thousands more lay dead or wounded in the snow, while others wandered aimlessly, cut off from their own lines and having no idea how to find them. After a night trying to get some sleep in the shelter of the forest, Jack Brugh and some twenty other GIs decided to head east, hoping to put distance between themselves and the German front.

As we came upon a cleared area, we discovered a deserted German field kitchen. The Germans did not leave anything of value, but there were about ten loaves of stale bread and some potatoes in what I think was the garbage heap. We split up the spoils. Raw potatoes are not too tasty, but they will help to keep you going. All day long, we wandered and did not see anyone. The night was spent in the woods again.

On December 18th, we met up with five infantrymen from the 28th Division. They too were completely lost. They joined our group and in the afternoon we were sighted by a German patrol. We went into the woods and they followed. They fired into the forest, but for some reason, they did not pursue us. We never returned their fire and they finally left.

Again, we spent the night in the woods. The Germans knew where we were and late that night the patrol (or possibly another patrol) returned and came within 200 feet of where we were and fired shots over our heads. They were using tracer bullets, and it was a scary feeling looking up and seeing the tracers streaking overhead. After about 15 minutes, they left. It seemed they were taunting us.

The sun broke through the clouds on December 19th, the first time I had seen the sun since I had been on the front lines. We were all hungry and tired, having had nothing but bread and potatoes for three days. We were very concerned because we knew the Germans knew where we were. We had the feeling they were watching and waiting for us to make a move. Unfortunately, we had wound up in a patch of woods that would be difficult to escape from without coming out in the open.

We realized we were trapped, so we decided to stay where we were . . . It remained quiet until about 3:00 pm, when three German tanks pulled up in the open field in front of the forest where we were hidden. They each fired several shots into the woods, and then stopped firing. They then opened the turrets and stood up. One of the tank commanders who spoke English yelled to us to 'Surrender! Surrender!' We all knew that there was nothing we could do but lay down our rifles and come out with our hands in the air. It was a most humiliating and sickening experience.[27]

Leon Setter was one of a mass round-up of GIs near St Vith where the 106th Infantry Divison, the Golden Lions, had been in the line for just five days. None of its senior officers had ever been in action, except for the regimental commander who had served in France for a few days in 1918. Inexperienced and hopelessly outmanoeuvred, the 106th was caught in a pincer movement and encircled.

As I finished digging my foxhole, my squad leader came to me and told me that the entire 42nd Infantry Regiment had been ordered to surrender to the enemy by Colonel Deschenaux and that we were ordered to destroy our weapons. Needless to say I was confused. This had been my first day in actual combat. At first I felt relieved. Soon another kind of fear set in, a fear of the unknown. What was going to happen next?

I dismantled my carbine, throwing the parts in all directions. I walked toward the assembly area where a couple of enemy soldiers lined us up in a column of fours to march us down the hill.

It took about 40 minutes for the column to get into Schonberg where we were put inside a Catholic church. As soon as the church was filled, the rest of the prisoners had to sleep outside on the ground. On the morning of December 20th we were marched into Germany.[28]

Finding an abandoned farm, Joe Tatman and six companions hid for the night in the hayloft, only to discover the next morning that a German company headquarters had been set up in the house.

We were trapped. We ran out of food and water. One of the boys had a D ration Bar and we all nibbled on it. Imagine 7 of us on a 2 inch square bar! After 5 days and nights things began to get rough and cold. We talked about Christmas and home.

Around 4:00 pm Christmas Eve, German soldiers appeared at the top of the ladder to the hay mow. He shot up through the barn roof and yelled at us to come down. As we were lined up he called for his superior officer. He came out from the house near by, a smile on his face, a big hand shake and greeted us like brothers. He had been a lawyer in New York and had returned to his home land to settle his father's estate.

He spoke very plain English, and asked no questions. He took us into their kitchen, where the cooks were preparing for a Christmas party. They gave us milk and hot donuts. He talked and joked about the war and hoped it would soon be ended, so we could all be back home again.[29]

A few of the 106th managed to break out of the trap. Most did not. Some 10,000 GIs were taken into captivity, the biggest surrender ever of American forces on foreign ground. German propaganda made the most of it with cinema newsreels showing streams of ragged and weary soldiers being led away to spend the rest of the war behind barbed wire.

We were all weak from the lack of food and sleep, but Will was especially weak. We were really concerned about him. We walked through open fields and woods and seemed to be headed out of the mountains to the valley below. We came to a road that had been churned up by tanks and trucks. Although Will was really struggling, he managed to keep going. He knew that if he fell out, he would be left in the snow to die.

It was about 2.00 a.m. on December 20th when we came to a small village where we joined hundreds of other American POWs, many of whom were from our ill-fated 106th Division. They kept us there for about three hours, and during that time, other POWs were brought into the village . . . When we left at about daylight, again lined up four abreast, the column stretched out for nearly one-quarter of a mile.

We walked about four miles and reached the town of Prum. Will had made it the entire march, but just barely. We were marched to the railroad station where we were to be loaded in boxcars. There was an English speaking German guard with us, and one of the POWs asked him where we were going. His answer was Siberia, and he said, 'You will be there forever, because the German Army has taken Antwerp and is moving through France to Paris.'[30]

Bradley was at Eisenhower's HQ when the attack started. He was reminded by General Bedell Smith, Eisenhower's Chief of Staff, that he often wished for the Germans to come out of their pillboxes to fight in the open.

'You've been wishing for a counter attack; now it looks as though you've got it.'

'A counter attack, yes,' replied Bradley, ruefully. 'But I'll be damned if I wanted one this big.'[31]

After the 106th was escorted from the battlefield, the focus was on St Vith itself, a road and rail junction that was vital to the German assault plan in an area where communications were minimal, bordering on primitive. GIs with experience of London traffic jams dubbed the town, Piccadilly Circus. St Vith held out for a week of house-to-house fighting. Leaving it to the last moment, General Bruce Clarke led 22,000 of his men to safety, an achievement for which he was given scant credit by superiors who were more in need of victories than withdrawals, however skilfully managed.

The Allied pull-back from east Belgium was a heart-breaking business for those who had so recently been welcomed as liberators. James Cassidy of NBC was in one of the front-line towns. The evacuation was, he said, an experience he would never forget – the experience of conquest in reverse. 'Most civilians stood around in silent groups in the streets watching the mud-spattered army trucks moving. American flags were removed from some of the shop windows. As I left I wondered how long it would be until Nazi banners would once again adorn those windows which for three months have displayed the Stars and Stripes.' Not far away, Robert Barr stood on a crowded street as a convoy of infantry prepared to move out.

> There was handshaking and many questions. How near were the Germans? Did we think they'd come to their town again? Was it true that German tanks were just over the hill? There were awkward silences. The GIs couldn't answer that question. A truck driver tying a tarpaulin over his loaded truck swore quietly and said, 'I never thought this would happen to us.' We had been planning a Christmas party for the local children; a GI took the notice down, looked at it, and tore it up. The Belgian people watched it all. Whatever you did, wherever you went, their eyes followed you.[32]

Jack Belden of *Time* magazine had a gut feeling of terrible guilt 'that seems to come over you whenever you retreat. You don't like to look anyone in the eyes. It seems as if you have done something wrong.' It got worse.

> A middle-aged woman grabbed me by the arm and began pouring out words of broken English in a pleading, tortured voice. She wanted us to take her children, a boy aged ten and a girl aged twelve, with us. 'Just a little way on the road,' she said, 'then you can drop them off. My husband, he's been in the resistance movement. He'll have to get out. The collaborators will report him. It doesn't matter about me. But only take my children with you.' Her eyes were red and I realized she would have been crying if her need for saving her children had not

been stronger than her grief. A French photographer finally agreed to take her in his civilian car.[33]

Along with the convoys of American troops moving west went the refugees: 'carrying suitcases and blankets and tablecloth packs, plodding slowly and painfully along the shoulders of the road. Some of the more fortunate ride bicycles with their packs balanced on the handlebars. Others push carts loaded with lamps and favorite chairs and loaves of bread and sacks of potatoes. A baby too young to walk sits on a sack of potatoes and smiles at everything.'[34]

Despair for the Americans equalled jubilation for the Germans whose morale rose to giddy heights. In a letter home, Lieutenant Rockhammer shared his delight at being once more on the winning side.

This time we are a thousand times better off than you at home. You cannot imagine what glorious hours and days we are experiencing now. It looks as if the Americans cannot withstand our push. Today we overtook a fleeing column by taking a back-road through the woods to the retreat lane of the American vehicles; then, just like on manoeuvres, we pulled up along the road with sixty Panthers. And then came the endless convoy driving in two columns, side by side, hub on hub, filled to the brim with soldiers. And then a concentrated fire from sixty guns and one hundred and twenty machine-guns. It was a glorious bloodbath, vengeance for our destroyed homeland. Our soldiers still have the old zip. Always advancing and smashing everything. The snow must turn red with American blood. Victory was never as close as it is now.

Hans Hejny of the Fifth Panzer Army entered Clervaux, a small town halfway in to Luxembourg.

Leaving the protection of the woods behind us, the street led us among the first houses. A huge fire raged in the middle of the roadway obstructing any passage. Dense clouds of smoke floated above our heads. Because of the dark smoke I could not make out what was burning until a gust of wind for an instant provided sight of the street. About 50 metres away, an American Sherman tank was fully aflame. Behind it some Americans sought cover, but these poor devils had no escape left. There was no possibility of flight. There were too many eyes, too many rifle barrels waiting tensely for them to step forward.

Dense smoke clouded the scene almost completely and the enormous heat exploded the ammunition inside the tank. Now certainly the Americans could not last too long behind the tank and would have to leave the worst cover in the world. A massive detonation wave shook the street. Whole pieces of steel were hurled into the air. The windowpanes of neighbouring houses burst with loud cracks. A terrible gust of fiery wind threw me back, choking and coughing.

Then I saw for the first time an American soldier and he was jumping for his life. Inside, I crossed my fingers for him, somehow perhaps he could make it and that would save me. But no sooner did he make his daring leap, than rifle and machine pistol shots whipped the pitiful guy. Mortally wounded, he fell to the ground. A comrade took off to help him, risking his life. As he bent down to the fallen one, he too was dropped by murderous bullets.[35]

Confused and frightened, their officers trying to reconcile conflicting orders or to cope without any orders at all, whole units of 'fresh, green and utterly untested' GIs were thrown into panic. Told to defend Malmédy on the River Our against the soon to become infamous First SS Panzer Division, Colonel David Pegrin of the 291st Combat Engineer Battalion was like Gary Cooper in *High Noon*, appealing unsuccessfully for help as convoys of American troops headed out of town. He was left to do his job with some hundred or so lightly armed engineers.

'The Americans are on the run,' wrote a German soldier to his wife. 'We cleared an enemy supply dump. Everybody took things he wanted most. I took only chocolate. I have all my pockets full of it. I eat chocolate all the time, in order to sweeten this wretched life . . . Don't worry about me. The worst is behind me. Now this is just a hunt.'

2

Comeback

Once Eisenhower realised the power of the German drive, he pulled in reinforcements, including two airborne divisions. It was not enough. It took a change of command at the highest level for the Allies to regain the initiative. With the risk of the German advance cutting off Bradley's headquarters in Luxembourg, on December 19th, Eisenhower handed over the northern front, including the Ninth and First Armies, to Montgomery's Twenty-First Army Group leaving Bradley to concentrate on the southern sector.

It did not go down well with Bradley. Eisenhower had to work hard to persuade his friend that it was a temporary and emergency measure forced on him by problems of communication.

Montgomery was asleep when Eisenhower telephoned. His first move was to summon his liaison officers or 'gallopers'.

They consisted of hand-picked, intelligent, tough young staff officers who lived at his tactical headquarters. Every day they were dispatched to the different formations fighting the battle. In the evening after dinner each in turn would report to Monty on what he had seen or heard. As a result of their reports Monty was probably the only man who had a completely up-to-date picture of the whole battle front.[1]

On this occasion, Montgomery's gallopers were sent out to contact the various American corps commanders to find out what was going on before meeting up at Lieutenant General Courtney Hodges' First Army headquarters the following day. Montgomery then went back to bed.

Meanwhile the liaison officers were going through a series of wholly unusual adventures. Any trip in a jeep over those ice-bound foggy roads was a considerable experience, but the chief difficulty occurred

27

when the British officers entered the American lines. They knew no passwords and several of them were promptly arrested as spies and parachutists. Others found that the American corps to which they were assigned had been cut off in the night. Somehow by various means they managed to get themselves out of arrest, to drive on to their destination, to gather the news and then make their way back. All succeeded in making their rendezvous with the commander-in-chief at 1 pm.[2]

Their reports confirmed what Montgomery already suspected, that Rundstedt was aiming to strike across the Meuse around Liège.

Barring the way to Antwerp, Montgomery threw the bulk of the American First Army and much of the Ninth into the battle area. British and Canadian forces were used as a backstop to hold the line of the Meuse. There were sound reasons for this, not least the wish to avoid the administrative complications of thrusting the British troops into the centre of an American army. But it was a decision that was to damage Montgomery's reputation with his US colleagues who resented his boast of a British victory achieved, as they said, on the backs of American casualties. Of more than thirty Allied divisions engaged in the struggle, nine-tenths were American.

The highpoint of German success was Manteuffel's breakthrough to within striking distance of the Meuse and his encirclement of General McAuliffe's 101st Airborne Division, known as the Screaming Eagles, who had raced to protect Bastogne, another of the road junctions that could determine the outcome of the campaign.

It was now that the Germans made their first serious mistake. Slow to get to Bastogne, faulty intelligence and mud-sodden roads combining to lose precious hours in the race with American re-inforcements, Manteuffel was justified in asking for support from Dietrich's Sixth Panzer Army. In truth, this was asking a lot of Dietrich. Hitler's masterplan called for the Sixth Panzer to make the decisive breakthrough across the Meuse and on to Antwerp. For this reason Dietrich had been allocated the strongest reserves, five divisions at full fighting strength. But the advance of the Sixth Panzer had slowed to a crawl while Manteuffel's Fifth Panzer Army was still making good progress. Giving full backing to Manteuffel could have changed the outcome of the battle for Bastogne and thus of the entire Ardennes offensive. But Dietrich held back. Maybe he still believed that the final victory would be his; maybe he was unwilling to change his orders without approval from Hitler. Whatever the reason, the opportunity to keep up the momentum of the German advance was lost irretrievably.

Ed Peniche with the 502nd Parachute Infantry Regiment was dug in at the edge of the village of Longchamps, three miles north of Bastogne. He had a clear view of the valley sloping down between Longchamps and another village, Monaville, to the right. On Wednesday, December 20th, the weather turned colder and snow began to fall. Two days later:

> A heavy blanket of snow covered our entire sector and we were surrounded by the enemy. It was incredibly cold; the water in our canteens was freezing. We also had to rub each other's feet to prevent frostbite. From our foxholes, despite the horrible weather, it was fascinating to gaze at the wintry scenery, the snow was pretty deep and very white. The wind had picked up; it was much, much colder – I was terrified by the thought of freezing to death; being a 19-year-old soldier from the Yucatan in southern Mexico, I had never experienced snow on the ground, much less standing and sleeping on frozen ground.[3]

But coming under heavy artillery fire there was not much opportunity to worry overmuch about the cold. Martin Roeder, a teenage New Yorker, was also dug in on the outskirts of the town. 'The Germans quickly pinned us into a ditch with machine-guns. We had no air cover because of the fog, so we just couldn't move. Half of me was under water for three days.'

With the growing strength of German artillery within range of the town, McAuliffe was given two hours to surrender or face 'total annihilation'. Knowing that Patton's Third Army was charging to the rescue, he held his nerve, rejecting Manteuffel's invitation to capitulate with an emphatic 'Nuts', a response which lost something in translation.

The Third Army's race north, up from Luxembourg, was a spectacular demonstration of mobile warfare. More than 130,000 tanks and trucks, in double banked columns, took part in the 'round-the-clock trek' over icy roads. They were kept going by six new supply points holding 235,000 rations and 300,000 gallons of petrol. 'The troops in heavy great coats still caked with the mud of the Saar were huddled against the wintry cold that knifed through their canvas topped trucks while the tank commanders, their faces wrapped in woollen scarves, huddled in the turrets of their Shermans.' Along the way, they met up with remnants of the divisions that had taken the brunt of the German attack. There was a certain wariness in greeting battle-jaded stragglers. Reports had come in of fifth columnists operating behind American lines. In the event, the numbers were small but that they were there at all added to the nervousness of already anxious GIs.

'We were suspicious of everyone we did not know personally,' recalls a Bulge veteran. 'Passwords were of little value so a series of questions were asked such as the names of baseball players and movie stars.'[4] This was effective in so far as most Germans, even those who spoke good American and knew the States, would not be up to date with the latest sport and Hollywood news. Trouble was, neither were many GIs. It was not uncommon for Americans to be 'captured' by other Americans when they were unable to come up with the right answers.

'One soldier asked me what was the longest river in America and I, like a fool, answered correctly, "the Missouri". He nearly blew my head off until I changed my mind and said "Mississippi".'[5]

Never the easiest commander to satisfy, the Third Army's progress did not match up to Patton's expectations. What he wanted was a hell-for-leather tank attack that would cleave a way through to Bastogne. But German resistance was both stubborn and calculating. Leading the attack, the Fourth Armoured Division soon found that villages captured by armoured assault were invariably retaken by German infantry once the tanks had roared on. Each little community in the battle path had its stories. Bob Shine left his son, Dan, with memories of the assault on Grandmenil, 'a village so small that it could be crossed by foot in less than five minutes – unless, of course, the village was filled with waiting German soldiers – and it was.' Dan Shine continues his father's story:

Item Company was to attack the village with the support of Sherman tanks. Two of Shine's friends huddled behind one of the tanks, seeking shelter from the German small arms fire. As Shine watched, a shell landed and exploded near to the two and flung their bodies against the tank. They were killed instantly; there were almost no visible wounds, but the concussion from the explosion left the two dead Americans looking like lumps of bread dough thrown and flattened against a wall.

The Sherman tanks advanced up the village streets first, firing their cannons point-blank into the occupied houses. Then the riflemen followed. First they threw hand grenades into the houses; immediately after the explosions, they sprayed the insides of the houses with rifle fire. Shine and another young soldier entered one house. Inside the house, a dazed German reached for his gun. There was no time to ask him to surrender; the soldier with Shine quickly raised his Colt automatic pistol and fired. The .45 calibre bullet hit the German soldier squarely in the forehead, and the top of his head was blown off.[6]

The Germans fought desperately; the Americans were forced to take Grandmenil one house at a time. At day's end, Item Company had driven the Germans from Grandmenil, and had dug their foxholes in a defensive line along the edge of town. Twenty-four hours earlier, none of them had ever seen battle; now they were veterans.

In what he called a 'typical foray to the front' Michael Moynihan of the *News Chronicle* described what he saw at the 'bleak upland' village of Samree.

The footsteps are fresh in the snow and the burned wrecks of tanks lie stark in the ditches. Two hours of furious fighting in the cold light of dawn have left their trail of blood and debris. From Amonines to Dochamps and on to Samree the icy road that overhangs the valley, where there is scarcely room for two cars to pass, is flanked with burned-out German vehicles and American tanks that have been blasted or have lost their grip to crash down the steep slope . . .

From the deep snow of a ditch the legs of a German soldier protrude. A charred and shrivelled body lies by a burned-out half-track, unrecognisable as human, black in the snow like a monkey. In deeper drifts parts of frozen bodies stick out. Not until the thaw sets in will the snow give up its gruesome burden.

Frostbite and exhaustion accounted for many casualties, wrote Moynihan, adding:

the cruellest fighting is hidden in the half-light of the forest through which the infantry advances, guided through the maze by the air bursts of our artillery. In parts of the forest, dark and forbidding like something out of a Grimm's fairy tale, the snow is dyed red with blood where German and American infantry came to grips. Dead bodies are being ploughed from six-foot snowdrifts. The snow slopes are turning pink in the sun. Beauty sits strangely in the frozen valleys of death.[7]

Increasingly desperate for action, Patton resorted to divine intervention, ordering his chaplain to lead a communal prayer.

Almighty and most merciful Father, we humbly beseech thee, of Thy great goodness, to restrain these immoderate rains with which we have had to contend. Grant us fair weather for Battle. Graciously hearken to us as soldiers who call upon Thee, that armed with Thy power, we may advance from victory to victory and crush the opposition and wickedness of our enemies and establish Thy justice among men and nations.

It is hard to know if he was serious or if this was Patton's idea of a joke.

Meanwhile, the American paratroopers inside the Bastogne perimeter fought and waited. The occasional radio message hinted at a certain impatience. Just before midnight of December 24th, one of McAuliffe's staff sent a reminder to Fourth Armoured command post: 'There is only one more shopping day before Christmas.'[8] It was one of the many ironies of a Christmas Eve in the middle of the battle zone that when the Luftwaffe put in one of its rare appearances to bomb Bastogne, American servicemen and German prisoners were in unison with 'Silent Night'.

On Christmas Day, the German mounted a strong attack on the northwestern sector of the Bastogne perimeter. Ed Peniche remembers:

> Suddenly, around 03.00 a.m. the first barrages crashed against our positions, a few German planes droned over regimental headquarters and dropped bombs. Minutes later, wearing snow suits, the first grenadiers crept forward against our lines, supported by a few tanks. The fire fight in our left flank intensified. As the ground shook under the impact of the heavy shelling, the snow-covered battlefield soon became a spectrum of bright flares and deafening explosions and machine-gun tracers. Mortar rounds exploded in front and behind me while our machinegunners were delivering flanking fire. To me, this was a defining moment in my life and as an American, to see well-disciplined soldiers following orders under the most hellish of circumstances without hesitation. Everyone seemed to know what had to be done and they DID IT![9]

Four days after the Third Army started its 130-mile 'fire call' run, the tanks of the Fourth Armoured Division were in Bastogne.

> Two Shermans with the armored infantrymen wiped out an entire company of Krauts. Tankers set fire to a barn on the edge of town with machine-gun tracers. Wind drifted the smoke through the center of the village and gave the doughs of the 51st a perfect screen to mop up half the town at a time. They fought Christmas Eve and knocked off for cold turkey while artillery and mortar fire crashed in. A tank destroyer took a direct hit on the engine compartment and flamed in the night. German soldiers died wholesale, but those who lived held on. The hillside town of Chaumont was to change hands three times before the rubble heaps were taken.[10]

Martha Gellhorn was one of the first war reporters to see what was left of Bastogne:

> You can say the words 'death and destruction' and they don't mean anything. But they are awful words when you are looking at what they mean. There were some German staff cars along the side of the road: they had not merely been hit by machine-gun bullets, they had been mashed into the ground. There were half-tracks and tanks literally wrenched apart. There were also, ignored and completely inhuman, the hard-frozen corpses of Germans.[11]

One of those young Germans who died was Corporal Helmut Spindler who was hit by shrapnel. His parents heard the news from his senior officer, Captain Rudolf Schueppel, almost two months after the event.

> Your son hadn't been in my unit for very long. Before he joined he had been through a lot of difficulties and in the short time I knew him showed himself from only his best side. He was hardworking, willing and dutiful, always cheerful and a good comrade for his fellow soldiers. It is more than a shame about his young life. His battery and I grieve with you and will constantly honour his memory. Please accept our deepest sympathy, from myself and my battery. The main dressing station wrote to us that your son would be buried in a hero's grave in Ortho. Unfortunately I am not in the position to send you the personal possessions he was carrying on him. The main dressing station will take care of this.[12]

When it was all over, General McAuliffe found it hard to wind down from the bullish optimism he had maintained throughout the siege.

> Now I, and everyone else in the 101st, resent the implication that we were rescued or that we needed to be rescued. When General Taylor arrived on the 27th the first thing he asked me was what kind of shape were we in. I told him, 'Why, we're in fine shape: we're ready to take the offensive.' The fact is we were thinking about what a tough time the Kraut was having.[13]

The Screaming Eagles now adopted a new name – the Battered Bastards of the Bastion of Bastogne.

Overall, Montgomery's strategy for repulsing the Rundstedt offensive was successful, though any suggestion that the Allied response was closely targeted would be misleading. Fighting conditions over heavily wooded and frozen terrain made that all but impossible. There was little or no intelligence feeding through to front-line units to tell them what was happening. Contemporary warfare assumes constant and uninterrupted communication at all levels of command. Sixty years ago it was not so easy. Radio contact was hard won and easily lost through bad weather or faulty equipment or a hundred other reasons all of which seemed to conspire to confuse in December 1944. The fighting in the Ardennes was as near chaos, at least on the Allied side, as any battle of the Second World War.

To help out with the relief of Bastogne, General Matthew B. Ridgway flew over from his English base to join his Eighty-Second and 101st Airborne Divisions assembled at Reims for refitting after their two-month tour of duty in Holland. His progress gives a fair notion of the hazards encountered along the Ardennes front. Even getting to it was an adventure.

> As the last planes took off, a pea-soup fog rolled in from the Channel and we were the last planes to leave England for forty-eight hours. We flew in that soup across France to Reims. Fortunately, my own personal pilot, Colonel J.G. Brown, a magnificent airman, was at the controls. By a miracle of navigation, or sixth sense or something, for we had no ground contact, and no radio aids to speak of, he hit Reims on the nose. It lay under a blanket of low-hanging cloud, and as we broke through the cloud cover, I looked out of the window to see the spire of a church steeple flash by. It was considerably higher than we were.

It got worse.

> We landed on a deserted strip and I immediately set out for the bivouac areas of the 101st and the 82nd. The 82nd had already moved out and the last elements of the 101st were clearing the area

as I arrived. I waited until the last battalion had cleared, and moved on up the road myself. It was not a pleasant ride. The only transportation available was some ancient Gl sedans. We couldn't see out of these things. The fog was thick as heavy smoke, a cold, drizzling rain was falling, and the chances were good that a German patrol might loom suddenly out of the murk to take us by surprise. Just about dark, we found the command post of General Troy Middleton's VIII Corps. The gloom inside that headquarters was thicker than the fog outside. Middleton knew that some of his units had been overrun. He knew the German attack had opened a great gap in his lines. But nearly all his communications with his forward elements were out, and he had no knowledge of where his forces were, nor where the Germans were, nor where they might strike next.[14]

In conditions that challenged the fundamentals of humanity, atrocities against civilians who simply happened to be in the way were not uncommon. In Stavelot, Ster, Parfondruy and Renardmont over one hundred Belgians were shot by units of the First SS Panzer Division. The evidence of one random massacre was discovered by a unit of the Third Armoured Division on December 20th, 1944.

Ten or twelve completely burned bodies, charred black, were seen where a small shed had once stood . . . in the adjacent house, there was the body of a middle-aged woman who had been stabbed with a knife and then shot. Bodies of two boys between the ages of six and ten were seen with bullet holes in their foreheads . . . One old woman had been killed by a smash over the head, probably with a rifle butt . . . Near a foxhole were bodies of a 13-year-old boy and a 15-year-old girl who had been shot, apparently as they tried to escape.[15]

On the afternoon of December 22nd, the Second SS Panzer Division, accompanied by Gestapo interrogators, entered Bande. Thirty-five young people were lined up against a wall and shot one by one.

It was the turn now of Léon Praile to go. The German put his hand on the prisoner's shoulder, like he had done to all the others, when, suddenly the Belgian noticed that the Feldwebel was weeping. He decided to risk everything to save his life. When they were both about two yards from the sinister house Betrand, Léon Praile gathered together all his strength and with his right fist gave the German such a punch full in the face that the soldier taken aback fell to the ground and the lad, taking advantage of the obscurity, ran away. He ran for about fifty yards then crossed the Route, quicker than lightning, and found himself on the banks of the Wasme. This he crossed and ran again into the fields on the other side of the river. The Germans were firing on him all the while but did not touch him once. He spent the night in the woods and tried to get to the American lines, but owing to German patrols this was not possible; so he was obliged to go back to Bande where he took refuge in the barn of his uncle's house.[16]

When Bande was freed by Belgian paratroopers on January 11th, Léon Praile led them to the scene of the execution where the bodies were piled up in a cellar.

While both sides were responsible for sporadic acts of savagery, the worst excesses were linked to the lead unit of the Sixth Panzer Army, the battle-hardened First SS Panzer Division also known as the Blowtorch Battalion after it had burned its way across Russia. Its commander was Lieutenant Colonel Jochen Peiper, at twenty-nine a brave and charismatic leader but one, it was said, who was bereft of ordinary human emotions. On December 17th, an observation unit of the US Seventh Armoured Division on its way to help relieve St Vith was diverted through Malmédy. As they passed through Five Points crossroads near Bauges they were confronted by Peiper's leading tanks. The convoy of American jeeps and trucks were no match for heavy armour. The occupants piled out of their vehicles and were herded into a field. What happened next is unclear in detail but after Peiper and most of his division had gone on their way, the SS troops left in charge of the prisoners opened up with machine-guns. Later, eighty-one bodies were recovered. Of the seventeen who escaped, Ted Flechsig was saved by a fatally wounded soldier who covered him as he fell. 'After the machine-gunning ceased, the SS men walked among the fallen, shooting

37

those who showed signs of life.' With wounds in his leg, arm and hand, Ted held his breath.

When Ted didn't stir, the soldier moved on. Eventually the troops got into their tanks and half-tracks and moved out. Ted and another survivor left in the direction of Stavelot, some six miles to the south. On the way they met two Belgian civilians on bicycles. Seeing that Ted was having difficulty walking, one of the Belgians put him on his bicycle and pushed him the rest of the way to Stavelot where he was taken to hospital.[17]

Peiper was among those eventually brought to trial for the worst single atrocity against US troops in the entire European war. He escaped the death penalty, claiming that he had no direct knowledge of the massacre but his moral responsibility followed him to his death in 1976 when his house in Treves was firebombed by former French resistance fighters.

The Malmédy Massacre stands out as a gruesome example of what can happen in war rather than as a typical instance. Edward Bautz, a professional soldier who, post-war, retired as a general, is among those who speaks up on behalf of front-line German soldiers.

> They fought very well and they were tough . . . I didn't see any atrocities . . . In fact, going up to Bastogne, near the Bigonville area, Lt. Cook, one of our platoon leaders, was wounded, and his tank was knocked out, and his people couldn't get to him right away, and he was a prisoner. He became a prisoner of the Germans and they took care of him. They wrapped him up . . . kept him warm, gave him some food, and positioned him so that he could be found when they were leaving. So, you know, there are all sorts of horror stories you hear but my experience was that the frontline troops were capable and disciplined.[18]

Conversely, there were those on the Allied side who were not greatly troubled by the Geneva Convention. As news of the Malmédy Massacre spread, so too did the incidents of retaliation. Roy Brown, who was part of a force rounding up German prisoners, had a hard job trying to persuade front-line troops to cooperate. 'I would get word that a prisoner or two had been captured but before I could get there, I'd hear a rat-tat-tat and these tough looking guys would get out of their tanks and say, "Oh, they tried to get away."'[19]

At least one war reporter confirms that reaction to Malmédy was immediate and often savage:

> Before an attack scheduled for the following day an order was issued to infantrymen of one American brigade stating, 'No S.S. troops or paratroopers will be taken prisoner but will be shot on sight.' During a battle in the village of Chegnogne, a house whose cellar was being used as a first-aid post by the Germans was set on fire, causing the 21 wounded soldiers in it to emerge, the first carrying a Red Cross flag, only to be mown down by machine-gun fire at the doorway.[20]

There were those like Nathan Shoehalter who could never forget the horror of mindless revenge. 'A terrible thing happened . . . My captain, in our battalion aid station, had two or three youngsters, Germans, sitting in our aid station. We were bringing in casualties. The captain said, "Take them out and shoot 'em. Take them out and shoot 'em," and they did. It was awful. He murdered them.'

The counterbalance was the experience of Horst Lange, of the German Fifth Parachute Division, who was captured at Bigonville. It was not the best time of his life but it could have been much worse.

> First of all papers, like my pay-book, were taken. Also personal papers, like family letters and photos were taken and thrown away. The few German marks that I had were of no more use to me anyway. I didn't need the steel helmet any more now, but I would have liked to keep my forage cape, for it was bitter cold. The camouflage flying-jacket, which could still offer some protection against the cold, was also taken away from me. So all I had left, finally, was a dirty handkerchief and my life. We were then guarded for more than an hour by four or five GIs. We waited around with our hands clasped behind our heads. One of the soldiers was, for some reason, sympathetic to me. He also tried to have a conversation, and told me he was from Chicago. I replied, 'I am from Hamburg.' That was

my first school-English that I was able to put to use. He gave me a cigarette and lit it for me, for I still had my hands behind my head. At around noon we were brought behind the American lines, about 30 of us in all. At that time, fierce fighting was still raging in Bigonville. We had a difficult march in the cold and the snow until we reached the American artillery position. Here we stood in formation, about 100 German prisoners of war. Most of us were from the 5th Parachute Division. Anyone wearing American shoes had to take them off, despite the icy cold. I took off my sweater, tore it up, and wrapped it around my feet. After about two hours, an American officer saw this and everybody got shoes.[21]

The Rundstedt offensive reached its limit on Christmas Eve. In the Belgian village of Celles, a swastikaed tank serves as a monument to mark the Germans' point of return. For one German soldier it was the end of the war and almost the end of his life.

We were divided into two groups. Our two guards spoke Polish as they took us into a yard behind a building. When they told us to climb onto a manure heap of a pig sty and stand with our faces to the wall, we understood what they were planning to do. We had survived all the infernos of the war but suddenly we were closer to death than ever before. I remember every detail of that moment on the manure heap in Bigonville. Every sound, the pigs running around, the grey wall in front of me, the smell around us, all of it comes back to me every year on Christmas Eve.

Suddenly we heard an American voice: 'What are you doing there?' He told us to turn around and step down from the manure heap. We saw an officer with a gun in one hand and a grenade in the other. I was taken to a badly damaged house and ordered to climb into a cellar. There I found a woman and her baby. She had given birth during the shootings. The lieutenant had found her and had been looking for someone who could help him find some milk for the baby. We tried to find a solution together but communication was a struggle as my school English was not particularly good. However, I had noticed that he had hung his grenade on his belt again and his gun was now laying next to him. Suddenly I heard the sound of a cow. I grabbed a bucket and ran to find it. My guard followed me. Soon I found a stable with a beautiful black and white cow. It had not been harmed by the gunfire but it had stood in its stable for two days without being milked because of it. I had learnt how to milk a cow from our neighbours in my summer holidays so I began straight away.

We boiled the milk in the cellar and I found an old, dirty milk bottle. The man who had been my enemy only this morning and I watched the 'Festival of Milk'. Only the child did what children do when they are thirsty. She drank what we had provided.

I never found out what became of the two of them. The town register did not record a baby born on the 23rd or 24th of December. Maybe the mother lost her life in the aftermath of the war, alone or along with her child. However, I did manage to find the cellar two years ago. The building had been modernised but it was still recognisable. Above it was a restaurant. We went in and ordered fish. I did not bother with the milkshake on the menu.[22]

In Berlin, a meeting called at the Reich Chancellery, to prepare the way for the restoration of German administration of Belgium, was cancelled. As Patton broke through to relieve Bastogne, American forces in other sectors were pushing the Germans back over territory they had so recently occupied. Clear skies opened German supply lines to intensive air attack. Five thousand Allied bombers took to the air to set ablaze the roads from Bastogne and St Vith, all the way to the Siegfried Line. Rundstedt urged a withdrawal to strong defensive positions but Hitler, still seeing attack as the best defence, ordered a diversionary offensive in the north of Alsace. Operation North Wind would, he calculated, divert Patton from his Ardennes counter-attack, freeing Manteuffel to resume his advance towards Antwerp, the great prize that Hitler refused to accept was now beyond reach. North Wind began on New Year's Day. It failed utterly.

On January 3rd, the US First Army counter-attacked towards Houffalize nine miles from Bastogne on the German escape route to the east. Six days later, the US Third Army launched its own attack on Houffalize. After heavy bombers erased the town, Third Army bulldozers 'swept the charred rubble of Houffalize into the gaping bomb craters'. War correspondent Michael Moynihan met the survivors:

> It was in the low-ceilinged dank crypt of the church that we found the 70 inhabitants of Houffalize who had lived through the deluge of bombs. For ten days it had been their home, their sanctuary. They covered every inch of floor space, young children, mothers, old men and women. As they told us of their experiences their voices warmed into animation, as might the voices of people waking slowly from a nightmare.
>
> For ten days they had lived on small supplies of potatoes and the flesh of cows killed in the bombing. Four old women had died from shock and privation. In other parts of the town nearly two hundred fellow-villagers had been killed. But Germans had died too. 'If you had not bombed,' said a young woman, 'the Germans would still be here.' Many of the inhabitants had found refuge from the bombing in neighbouring villages. They will be returning to find nothing left of their town. Its 15 hotels, to which tourists flocked for winter sports and the summer beauty of the hills, are impossible to locate amongst the heaps of crumbled brick and stone. But the Germans have gone.[23]

As German forces slowly gave way, there came news of a renewed Russian offensive across the Vistula. Veteran troops, including Dietrich's Sixth Panzer Army, were sent east, leaving the remnants of Command West to make what best way they could back to their original start line. The Battle of the Bulge, as it was described by an Associated Press reporter and, more famously, by Churchill, was over.

Six weeks of fighting brought heavy casualties to both sides. Of the Allies, the Americans suffered most with 9,000 killed and 70,000 wounded or captured. Nobody knows the true extent of the German losses but between 80,000 and 120,000 of the Wehrmacht's finest were put out of action. More serious still, at a strategic level, was the destruction of military hardware, much of it blown to pieces, as armour and trucks queued nose to tail on icy and pitted escape roads.

For the Luftwaffe there was no prospect of recovery. Against expectations, not least those of the attacking infantry and armour, the German air force gave strong support, mounting surprise attacks on Allied airfields in northern France, Holland and Belgium. The most successful attack was on the airfield at Eindhoven, just as the Typhoons of 438 and 439 Squadrons of the Royal Canadian Air Force were taxiing out for a bombing raid. The Germans came in skimming the ground with cannon and machine-guns blazing. Nearly all the Allied planes were destroyed or badly damaged.

On January 1st, Major General Sir Francis de Guingand, Twenty-First Army Group Chief of Staff, was holding a morning conference at his headquarters in Brussels when he was rudely interrupted:

I heard a certain amount of air activity around the building as I was talking, but this was nothing unusual. A few heads turned towards the window, but still no one really guessed what was happening. Then suddenly, as one aircraft flew roof-top high past the Headquarters, a shout went up, 'Christ, it's a 190!' Bombs and cannon fire were to be heard, and the air was full of German aircraft circling round and round, and then diving down to shoot up the aircraft on the Brussels airfield. Later that day I went out to see the damage. It was very great – I should hate to have costed the value of the aircraft that had been written off that day. Both Montgomery's Dakota and my own lost their lives! But although a great deal of damage had been sustained, we could afford it, whilst the enemy could not stand the cost of his audacious attack. His losses amounted to over two hundred aircraft, which meant a great enemy defeat.[24]

For those who had been in the line longest it was time to relax and to enjoy the greatest luxury known to the fighting soldier.

We were taken back in trucks several miles to an open field where the engineers had set up a portable bath house. This unit consisted of a tent and duck boards to stand on with a series of showers powered by a generator and we had honest-to-gosh hot water. Also included was a change of long underwear and clean socks. If you have never had to do without one you cannot imagine our delight in having a fresh bath.[25]

It was only now that the home front in America and Britain was let in on the traumatic events of the past weeks. In an age when wars are treated to blanket coverage in print and on screen, it may seem outrageous that reporters were told to keep quiet about what was happening in the Ardennes. But however culpable the Allied commanders were in bringing the near disaster upon themselves, an attack from the rear by armchair theorists could have achieved nothing. On the contrary, it could have made matters worse by causing panic across liberated Europe. In the event Paris and Brussels remained calm.

The Ardennes offensive drove home the reality that massed armour was no match for an opponent who had command of the air. It was an expensive lesson. As General von Manteuffel observed, 'Our precious reserves had been expended and nothing was available to ward off the impending catastrophe in the east.' But the Allied response had to be put on hold for six weeks and, while the Germans had suffered devastating losses, nobody now imagined that crossing the Rhine would be any easier than breaching the Channel defences. Germany was down but by no means out. Hitler's last stand threatened to be one of the most closely fought battles of the entire war.

3
The Best of Enemies, the
Worst of Friends

Not everyone assumed there would be a last stand. Hitler himself remained convinced that his luck would turn. Arriving in the early hours of New Year's Day at the Führer's headquarters near Bad Nauheim, armaments minister Albert Speer was surprised to find that the mood in the circle of the faithful was still buoyant.

> There seemed to be a general feeling of thankfulness that we could begin anew at least on the calendar. Hitler made optimistic forecasts for 1945. The present low point would soon be overcome, he said; in the end we would be victorious. The circle took these prophecies in silence. Only Bormann enthusiastically seconded Hitler. After more than two hours, during which Hitler spread around his credulous optimism, his followers, including myself, were transported in spite of all their scepticism into a more sanguine state. His magnetic gifts were still operative. For it was no longer possible to produce conviction by rational arguments. We ought to have come to our senses when Hitler drew the parallel between our situation and that of Frederick the Great at the end of the Seven Years' War, for the implication was that we faced utter military defeat. But none of us drew this conclusion.[1]

What is missing from this account was Speer's own endeavours to keep alive the hope that all would eventually turn out for the best. Despite the attentions of the US Army Air Force and RAF (nearly 700,000 tons of bombs were dropped in Germany in 1944), Speer's armaments and production ministry had been adept at disguising the scope of the damage and, on occasion, at improvising a seemingly miraculous recovery. In early 1944 every known aircraft plant in Germany was hit and assumed to be put out of action. Yet in that year the Luftwaffe was reinforced by nearly

40,000 new aircraft of all types, compared to under 16,000 in 1942 before any of the plants suffered attack. The explanation had to wait until after the war when it became clear that Allied bombs were more effective in destroying buildings than the machine tools inside. In answer to the bombing campaign, the Speer ministry had set up Jägerstab or Fighter-Staff, teams of technicians and managers who created a network of small specialised production units which were virtually immune to attack. The paradox was the inability of the Luftwaffe to take full advantage of its change of fortune. Many of the new aircraft were grounded for lack of fuel or trained pilots.[2]

Nonetheless, overall, German industry and enterprise proved remarkably resilient, causing Allied concern that the Reich, still in control of most of Europe, had the capability of rejuvenating its military machine. The fear was reinforced by clear evidence that U-boat construction, protected by huge concrete 'pens', was on the increase and that new, more powerful models were coming into service. With boosted diesel engines, they were capable of moving faster under water than their escorts above. Moreover, they were able to recharge their batteries, courtesy of the new Schnorkel air-tube, without exposing themselves to surface radar. By the end of 1944, eighteen of the new submarines, ocean-going Type XXI and the smaller coastal Type XXIII, were being launched each month. The strength of the German U-boat force rose from 432 in December 1944 to a peak of 463 three months later. In January, U-boats sank seven supply ships in the English Channel; in February, eleven; in March, ten.

Even more of a threat to the Allied supply chain was the motor torpedo boat or E-boat which, operating from the Dutch coast, sank thirty-one ships between January and May. The main defence against them was Coastal Forces with its own motor torpedo boats based mostly at Great Yarmouth and Felixstowe on the Suffolk coast. As a fledgling war correspondent, Tom Pocock saw them in action.

Ferocious battles took place at high speed and close range. It was a curiously old-fashioned form of warfare, fought with dash by both sides. In the balance of the weaponry there was a touch of medieval trial by combat. E-boats and MTBs were about the same size; wooden boats of little more than one hundred tons with a crew of thirty-odd, but their armament and capabilities were as different as those of gladiators with trident and net, or sword and armour. Armed with torpedoes, or mines, and few guns, the E-boats could make more than forty knots, whereas the British, heavily armed with torpedoes, depth charges and perhaps a dozen guns, could not manage thirty. If the E-boat came within range of the MTB it could be instantly shot to pieces. Since it could not be caught in pursuit, the British would lie in wait with engines stopped – as we were that night in the North Sea – in the hope of interception.[3]

If new types of naval craft might throw the balance of the war at sea, how long would it be before German jet fighters put at risk Allied air supremacy? By January 1945, work on jets, especially the ME-262, the most advanced plane in the world, was progressing well. By May 1945, 1,400 jets had been produced. That they did not deliver the expected punishment was less to do with shortages than Hitler's ill-timed directive to convert the ME-262 to a fighter bomber. The consequent delay in getting the prototype off the drawing board robbed the Luftwaffe of its last chance for a comeback.

Few outside the Allied senior command understood the potential, or even knew of the existence, of jet aircraft. But in Britain, practical experience introduced a large part of the population to the awesome potential of unmanned rocketry. Having come through the blitz and beaten off the threat of invasion, the all but exhausted citizens of a small island were now kept on edge by the prospect of being blown to bits by a Vergeltungswaffe or V1, soon known on the receiving end as a flying bomb, doodlebug or buzz bomb. These long-range missiles were all the more terrifying for their erratic aim. A long-drawn-out screech announced their arrival. When the sound stopped, it was only a matter of seconds before they nose-dived to the ground, shattering whatever was in their path.

Over seven months until March 1945, 2,511 Londoners were killed and 5,869 seriously injured in rocket attacks. One of the worst single incidents was at Deptford in south London when a rocket hit a Woolworth's crowded with Saturday morning shoppers. The 160 who died and the hundred seriously injured were mostly housewives with young children.[4] The human cost was small by comparison with the bombing of Germany but that did not stop the war-weary citizens of London and other cities worrying about what else they might have to endure.

The answer came with the first launching of the V2. Though it had the same destructive capacity as the V1, its advantage over the earlier model was its speed. Flying at 3,600 miles an hour, it was too fast to be destroyed by anti-aircraft fire. When nearly a hundred of the V2s had done their worst, German radio reported that London 'was devastated' by the weapon, a claim that was quickly denied, though there was no disguising the fear that, even at this late date, rocketry was a serious threat to Allied hopes of a speedy victory. At a remote settlement on the island of Usedom in the Baltic Sea, the presiding genius, the thirty-four-year-old Dr Wernher von Braun, was already at work on a V2 with a booster rocket that would take it across the Atlantic.

Those at the front had no need to be persuaded of the awesome potential of German technology. Their tanks were far superior to anything on the Allied side and in capacity if not in numbers were getting better all the time. In early March after the US 117 Infantry overran the town of Oberembt, a captured Tiger tank was found to have the heaviest calibre weapon so far encountered in any of the fighting, a 380-millimetre howitzer, with a seven-foot barrel. 'It fired projectiles apparently rocket propelled, five feet long and fifteen inches in diameter, weighing 800 pounds. A hoist was used to load the huge gun.'[5]

Fresh recruits who had been encouraged to think they had the best equipment of any of the combatants were soon disillusioned. Many discovered the hard way that among the most effective weapons of the war was the German 88 cannon. Relatively small and manoeuvrable, it could be used as an anti-tank, anti-personnel or even as an anti-aircraft weapon. The 88, which was usually mounted on a tank, had other merits.

It had a flash arrester for one thing. But not only that, but it had a lower trajectory than our shells. Higher velocity, lower trajectory. They were deadly accurate.

German machine-guns were also judged to be superior.

Our machine guns were firing at the rate of 600 rounds a minute, theirs were at 1,300 rounds a minute. Brr! And if they were under continuous fire, every half a minute or every minute, they would have to replace their barrels; their barrels would be red hot. So red that you could see 'em at night time.[6]

Wild stories circulated of weapons so powerful as to negate all the assumptions of conventional warfare. German propaganda was only too ready to feed the rumour network suggesting, for example, that American and British bombers would soon be made ineffectual by a mysterious searchlight beam that would paralyse their engines.

Quite apart from helping to demoralise the enemy, the purpose of such fantasies was to persuade the German people to keep faith with military technology. As long as they believed that deliverance was at hand, if not this month, then the month after, the longer they would be ready to hold out against the invaders. Given enough time, argued Goebbels, who successfully fed the line to Hitler, divisions would open up between the Allies allowing for a negotiated settlement that would favour the Reich or at least ensure its survival.

There was something in this. Each of the powers lined up against Germany had an agenda that was at odds with consensus. Most obviously, the Soviet Union had little in common with the democracies except a desire to win the war against Germany. Stalin knew that victory on the eastern front, which only he could deliver, was vital to the Allied cause. But he remained deeply suspicious of the other two war leaders who, in other circumstances, would have fought against everything he stood for. Churchill, in particular, was rabidly anti-Communist, a reputation he had made as early as 1919 when, as Secretary of State for War, he had sent troops to Russia to try to frustrate the Bolshevik revolution. Stalin must have wondered if Churchill was tempted to promote a separate peace with Germany, much as he, Stalin, had done in 1940, but on this occasion to use the Reich as a means of destroying the threat of Soviet domination. In reality there was no risk of this; Churchill was too far committed to Hitler's unconditional surrender. But as the war entered its final phase, the conviction grew on him that once victory had been achieved, Stalin's territorial demands would take over where Hitler's had left off. He saw his best hope of preventing this in treating Stalin as a blunt, no-nonsense fixer who could do business with another like-minded character, i.e. Churchill.

This led to the infamous 'naughty document' agreed at their Moscow meeting in October 1944. On a half sheet of paper Churchill had set out mutual spheres of interest in contested Europe – 50/50 in Yugoslavia and Hungary, 75/25 in Russia's favour in Bulgaria, 90/10 also in Russia's favour in Rumania and the same division but weighted towards the Anglo-Americans in Greece. The deal did not go down well in Washington, as Churchill soon came to realise. His good friend, as he liked to call Franklin D. Roosevelt, was of another school of diplomacy. Having served his political apprenticeship in the first German war, he was imbued with the idealism of Woodrow Wilson. The failure of the League of Nations, Wilson's brainchild, only made him more determined to bring his own skills to bear on creating a new world order based on mutual trust. This was a world away from Churchill's old-fashioned view, practical or cynical according to taste, that the only way of keeping the peace was to engineer a balance of power between nations, enabling each to satisfy their territorial ambitions without allowing any one country to become strong enough to overwhelm the others.

This fundamental difference in their approach to world politics had been heavily disguised in the early stages of the war when Roosevelt had recognised that Britain was indispensable to the Allied war effort and Churchill had known that his country's survival depended on American support. But now, as victory in Europe edged closer, mutual dependency was no longer an issue. The military and economic muscle exercised by the US was so mighty as to dwarf all other combatants except Russia. In early 1945, the Americans had nearly twelve million men in arms, the British only five million. And there were those who believed that the raw numbers understated the imbalance. Writing from London, US Ambassador John G. Winant conveyed a dismal picture.

> Remember that Great Britain has been fighting for five years and that they are at the bottom of the barrel as regards manpower. Men from 16 to 65 are conscripted, and women from 18 to 50. The country has been on short rations for this entire period. I live on them and know what this means. The British Army is older than our Army. The British Navy is older than our merchant seamen. Only the Royal Air Force has been able to continue to recruit the youth of the country. In the Battle of Britain it saved Britain. In the intervening years its continuous operation has done much to save life in the other serv- ices, but it has taken a frightful toll of the youth of the country.[7]

With American power came the freedom to dictate policy. The 'naughty document' was so called because Roosevelt did not approve and was not slow in making his views clear. Churchill was equally prompt with his excuses, arguing that his percentage carve- up of a large part of Europe agreed with Stalin was no more than a guide. Later, he doctored the official record to make his actions seem less machiavellian. But this was just one indication of a widening gulf between Washington and London.

Roosevelt's advisers urged him to keep his distance from the wily Churchill. Even Harry Hopkins, an Anglophile if ever there was one, who was closer to the President than most, counselled against one-to-one Anglo-American meetings for fear that Stalin would resent being left out in the cold. If such a meeting was deemed essential, 'it would be much better to have him [Churchill] come to you instead of you going to him'.[8]

Churchill kept his own feelings well disguised but the giveaway on the cooling of the relationship on which Churchill had set such store was his failure to attend Roosevelt's funeral. Between now and the President's death in April much else, including differences over military strategy against Germany and reaction to Soviet double-dealing, was to drive the two leaders further apart. But for a seasoned traveller like Churchill to pass up the opportunity to be chief mourner at the Presidential wake does suggest more an estrangement than 'differences between friends'. In his biography of Churchill Roy Jenkins concludes that 'the emotional link between Churchill and Roosevelt was never as close as was commonly thought. It was more a partnership of circumstance and convenience than a friendship of individuals, each of whom was a star of brightness which needed its own unimpeded orbit.'[9]

But while Roosevelt and Churchill at least made an effort to gloss over differences, their generals, less practised in the art of gentle persuasion, were increasingly disposed to fight each other as hard as they fought the enemy. It was no secret that the American and British military did not get on as well as the official hand-outs suggested. Antagonism was born of chauvinism. To the Americans, the Brits' easy assumption of superiority was based on an imperial tradition that was less glorious than its apologists had been brought up to believe. The contrary opinion held that the Americans, arriving late as usual, behaved like white knights to the rescue, at once patronising and arrogant. The significance of both unreliable generalisations was heightened in war. With their tendency to uncompromising opinion, often ill-informed, senior commanders were walking parodies of national prejudice.

The two polar extremes were General George Patton Jr and Field Marshal Bernard Law Montgomery. Both were inspired, both were possessed of an unshakeable belief in their own judgement, both were blessed with the gift of attracting talent and winning loyalty and each had a hearty dislike of the other.

Patton was the more flamboyant of the two. His famous pearl-handled revolvers were of dubious practical value but they symbol-ised his bravado and his irresistible urge to shoot first and ask questions later. A bold and imaginative tank commander who believed that armour should lead not follow the infantry, Patton got his kicks by gambling against the odds. Most of the time he succeeded, roaring ahead of his supply lines, for example, but still managing to keep going by raiding enemy fuel dumps or, not infre-quently, purloining reserves allocated to other sectors of the advance. While Montgomery was a 'showboat', as one GI described him, Patton 'could put Barnum and Bailey to shame'. But then, 'he was ideal for the war we fought. He had a feeling for the terrain, he was the most aggressive of all the generals.'

British war reporters could not abide Patton who riled them with unflattering comments about their heroes. Cyril Ray described him as 'tall, slim, under sixty and a foul mouthed bully who looked like a rural dean'. And, he might have added, sounded like one too, for Patton had a high-pitched voice that was quite out of harmony with his macho image. But he had a way of endearing himself to his troops as Edward Bautz, who rose to the rank of general to serve in Vietnam, recalls:

> There was a new weapon, a half-track with a flame-thrower, and there was this demonstration. There was a Chemical Corps captain in charge of the demonstration and then, Patton rolled up in his jeep . . . you know, shiny boots, all creased, nice, with his pearl-handle pistols, just the picture you see of him all the time, and he stomped right into that mud and this captain went through a little spiel about it, and then he said, 'Now, we're going to demonstrate it. Now, if everybody would just step back.' At that point, you know . . . everybody started taking a step back, except Patton, and he said, 'What do you mean, step back? Don't you have any confidence in this weapon?' 'Well, yes, sir, I do.' 'Well, you damn well better have. You're going to stand right next to that thing and I'm going to stand right over here, too.' And, of course, everybody else stood there, too, and the weapon, you know, he fired it and it worked.[10]

Montgomery, whose star rose in North Africa where he had rallied the exhausted Eighth Army to defeat Rommel at Alam Halfa and El Alamein, first came up against Patton in the Allied invasion of Sicily. Montgomery led the Eighth Army, Patton the Seventh Army. Whatever judgement is made of the wisdom, at this stage of the war, of trying to neutralise Italy, it is undeniable that the rivalry between Montgomery and Patton culminating in their race to their prime objective, the port of Messina, damaged relations between the two Allies. Patton got there first, a triumph, as he claimed, for his aggressive style of leadership as contrasted with the cautious Montgomery, the 'silly old fart' who was too slow and ponderous for a modern army. This was to overlook their joint failure in frustrating Field Marshal Kesselring's classic withdrawal of over 40,000 German and 60,000 Italian troops to the Italian mainland. But by now strategic gains and losses were secondary to the cause of self-justification.

To say that Montgomery was hard to get on with is putting it mildly. In a recent assessment, one that takes account of all that has been said previously of this extraordinary character, General Sir David Fraser concedes the flaws of personality. Montgomery was 'obsessively conceited' in the manner of 'a bumptious schoolboy – immature, insensitive, often rather ignorant'. He treated other commanders badly 'unless they served him and he could gain some reflected light'.

However, his human touch showed in his devotion to his men and in his ability to inspire confidence. Like Patton he had a high-pitched, squeaky voice but overcame this disability by sheer force of personality. But in contrast to the hard-driving Patton, his battles were:

> largely – and by no means unwisely – affairs in which massive bombardments by air and/or artillery would be followed by the well-organised advance of greatly superior forces. For manoeuvre, opportunism, speed and ingenuity he had little instinct. He believed, like Ludendorff, in the big battalions – if you need a division for a job, use three and thus win more cheaply and more certainly; if you haven't got three, wait until you have. His victories were gained by the orthodox and some would argue ponderous deployment of numerically predominant force, intelligently used.[11]

If Patton and Montgomery were two extremes, national rivalries were apparent at every level in senior command. This is hardly surprising. War lords through the ages have had monstrous egos. How could it be otherwise? The expenditure of lives for whatever cause demands an unshakeable belief that what is done has to be done. Victories are vindication of superior talents, defeats are excused or denied and regrets are confined to letters of condolences.

But if it is accepted that generals on the same side may regard each other less charitably than they might judge the enemy, somehow they have to be made to work in harness. From 1942, this awesome responsibility fell to the Combined Chiefs of Staff, consisting of the military Chiefs of Staff in Britain and America with the personal Chiefs of Staff to the Prime Minister and the President. Since these geographically diverse entities could meet only infrequently, the Combined Chiefs of Staff had its base in Washington with a British Joint Staff Mission alongside to represent British views. Until his death in November 1944, the voice of the Joint Staff Mission was that of Field Marshal Sir John Dill, an outstanding diplomat who understood and appreciated what the Americans were trying to achieve and who got on particularly well with Roosevelt's Chief of Staff, General George C. Marshall. Dill's successor, Field Marshal Sir Henry Maitland Wilson, was not in the same league but also had a more difficult job in that, as the balance of power shifted, Washington was less inclined to accommodate British interests. Increasingly, the job of keeping the British on side fell to the senior officer at the front, General Dwight D. Eisenhower.

The Supreme Commander's greatest quality was his talent for getting on with people. 'There was something about his warm, friendly personality which always did me good,' said Lieutenant General (later Sir) Brian Horrocks, himself no mean judge of character. Eisenhower was a politician in uniform. Those who knew him best – Patton among them – surmised that Eisenhower had set his sights on the presidency. It was a fair guess. If all went well on the battle front he would return home to a hero's welcome worth millions of votes. A Gallup Poll in December gave him 24 per cent approval as a presidential candidate, ahead of all others who had not previously held public office with the exception of General Douglas MacArthur, the dominant Allied figure in the war in the east, who scored 26 per cent. At fifty-three, Eisenhower had more than enough time to build a political base that would transform popular support into executive power. The risk was in meeting failure in battle. So far, Eisenhower had been lucky. His gamble on the weather proving favourable to the Normandy landings had paid off magnificently and Eisenhower, rightly, took much of the credit for the first sweep across occupied Europe. But the German counter-offensive over the Ardennes had taken the gloss off his reputation. His critics argued that it was his strategy of advancing on a broad front that had overstretched his manpower, handing the advantage to a concentrated German attack. So it was that while the Battle of the Bulge ended in defeat for the Wehrmacht, it opened up divisions in the Allied command that caused headaches for Eisenhower and gave comfort to Berlin.

The trouble started with what Jack Colville, Churchill's private secretary, described as a 'triumphant, jingoistic and exceedingly self-satisfied' press conference, stage-managed by Montgomery. Self-promotion was second nature to Montgomery and there can be little doubt that he wished to stake his claim to the leading role in defeating Rundstedt ('one of the most interesting and tricky battles I have ever handled'). But he was also keen to show that American troops served well under his command, thus proving to Eisenhower that he was every bit as capable as General Omar Bradley of leading the forthcoming assault on Germany. He started well with a paean of praise for the American serviceman.

> He is a brave fighting man, steady under fire, and with that tenacity in battle which stamps the first-class soldier; all these qualities have been shown in a marked degree during the present battle.
>
> I have spent my military career with the British soldier and I have come to love him with a great love; and I have now formed a very great affection and admiration for the American soldier. I salute the brave fighting men of America; I never want to fight alongside better soldiers.[12]

But in the way it came over to the assembled journalists, there were two likely storylines. 'I am proud to have led such fine Americans, says Monty' or 'Americans can do wonders when I am in charge'. Knowing what their readers wanted, the British press gave the headlines to Monty, the war leader who, with a little help from his American friends, had saved the Allies from a humiliating defeat.

The crisis in Anglo-America relations, for it was no less, came as a godsend to German propaganda. Indeed it was with German radio, in the guise of Radio Arnhem, which claimed to 'promote the reconciliation of people of all nations', that much of the misunderstanding and confusion originated. Described as 'the only truly innovative and effective operation the Nazi propagandists created in the Second World War',[13] Arnhem Radio mixed intercepted BBC transmissions with fake news bulletins. Thousands of troops, American and British, tuned in regularly, unaware or unconvinced that they were being duped. Radio Arnhem's greatest coup was an alleged BBC broadcast which gave all the credit for the Ardennes recovery to Montgomery. German intelligence had intercepted a report by the British journalist Chester Wilmot, passed it on to Radio Arnhem where a willing prisoner of war and a good mimic read a doctored version of the script. It was convincing enough to wound American sensitivities and to provoke a press backlash with headlines like, 'Monty Gets Glory – Yanks Get Brushoff'. Official denials were ignored or disbelieved.

Montgomery came to think that the press conference – it was, after all, his idea – had been a great mistake. How right he was. The whole thing was seen by the Americans as a renewal of his campaign to be made sole commander of all land forces in Europe. Stung by the implied insult, Bradley, whose Twelfth Army Group had taken the brunt of the punishment in the Battle of the Bulge, relieved his anger on Eisenhower. He was egged on by Patton whose Third Army came under Bradley's command. Any suggestion that Eisenhower was about to advance Montgomery's cause would result in the resignations of two of America's best-loved generals and the inevitable calls back home for the return of American troops or their transfer to the Pacific where their efforts would be better appreciated.

It was left to Eisenhower to pacify his warring generals. His relationship with Montgomery had always been edgy. The veteran of the Great War with wounds to prove it was not easily won over by a leader who was a relative stranger to active service. In his dealings with the Supreme Commander, Montgomery adopted a condescending tone known to lower ranks as dumb insolence. The hero of El Alamein made no secret of his conviction that he was alone capable of leading the Allies to victory in Europe. He took the same line with Bradley.

As the grand conciliator, Eisenhower did well in hiding his impatience, at least in public. He was not fond of the teetotal, anti-smoking Montgomery – it was impossible to imagine the two of them settling down to a convivial chat – but he recognised his strengths, primarily his faith in meticulous planning and in building an overwhelming force before committing himself to battle. But, in truth, there was no chance that Montgomery would be elevated over Bradley. Apart from mutual regard between the two American generals who had been at West Point together, Bradley was too high profile at home not to have a prominent role in the culmination of the war.

Eisenhower thought he had already given enough assurances to his colleague that he would not be leapfrogged by Montgomery but Bradley was still edgy. Eisenhower's first move therefore, after Montgomery had done his worst with the press corps, was to telephone Churchill to ask his help in quelling the 'riotous sentiment of the Twelfth Army Group'. The Prime Minister ('I fear great offence has been given to the American generals') responded with a speech to the House of Commons in which he emphasised the American sacrifice ('they have lost sixty to eighty men for every one of us') and warned against the British army claiming 'an undue share of credit for what was undoubtedly the greatest American battle of the war'.

Eisenhower knew also that he could count on qualified support from Field Marshal Alan Brooke, Chief of the Imperial General Staff and Montgomery's mentor. Brooke was not a natural ally of the Supreme Commander. An Ulster martinet with a strict Puritan conscience, he was the antithesis of the laid-back Eisenhower whose love of golf and female company too easily diverted him, in Brooke's view, from the task in hand. There was another, more critical, point of difference. Brooke, like Montgomery, doubted the capacity of Eisenhower, 'a second rate player' after the Ardennes, to perform a double role, as Supreme Commander and as commander of the three army groups preparing to invade Germany. On the other hand, with his sensitivity to practical politics, Brooke realised that there was only the remotest chance of Montgomery realising his dream to be Eisenhower's chief action man. His solution was for Bradley to be 'made commander of land forces, with [Air Marshal Arthur] Tedder as the air commander working closely with him. The front should then be divided into two groups of armies, one north of the Ardennes under Monty, one south under Patton, whilst Ike returns to the true duties of Supreme Commander.'[14]

It was not a suggestion that appealed to Eisenhower but it did help to put Montgomery in his place. There was support too from Montgomery's Chief of Staff, Major General Francis de Guingand who 'sensed that a difficult stage in Anglo-American relations had been reached'. He flew to Eisenhower's headquarters in Reims to talk directly with his opposite number, Lieutenant General Walter Bedell Smith.

> Later, we both went and had a long talk to the Supreme Commander. He was more worried than I had ever seen him, and we discussed the problem in all its aspects. I told him I thought the matter could be put right, and asked him to let me see what could be done to help.
>
> The next morning I flew to Montgomery's headquarters which then was just north of Hasselt and explained to him the full meaning of the dangerous situation that was arising. His reaction was characteristic of the man. 'Give me a writing pad,' he said. And then he proceeded to draft a really generous signal to Eisenhower saying that he would do anything to help. After a cup of tea I drove back to Brussels as it was now too dark to fly, where I had arranged to meet the war correspondents committee, of which Alan Moorehead was the chairman. I arrived there about 8 p.m. and found them waiting for me in my office. I at once explained the dangers if the present trend of press comment persisted, and gave what I hoped was a fair appreciation of Montgomery's and Bradley's part in the Ardennes battle – and also the reasons for Eisenhower's recent re-grouping of First and Ninth US Armies. I also stressed the drawbacks if by any

chance the Supreme Commander had restrictions imposed which would limit the flexibility of his command.[15]

Bradley was pacified, for the moment, but Eisenhower was not yet in the clear. The shock of the Ardennes counter-offensive had caused alarm in Washington where Army Chief of Staff General George Marshall, who was as close to the President as Brooke to his Prime Minister, was beginning to doubt the broad front strategy as against the mighty single thrust and to wonder if Eisenhower was up to carrying through either. At the same time he was opposed to anything that lifted Montgomery's profile at the expense of Bradley. On both sides of the Atlantic there was talk of bringing in a soldier deputy for Eisenhower to replace Tedder whose talents did not extend to fighting a ground war.

Eisenhower made much of the apparent weakness of the single thrust. It gave the enemy advance notice of Allied objectives, he argued. Also, there was a risk that enemy pockets left behind would recover sufficiently to strike across Allied communications. How much more sensible it would be to 'defeat the enemy west of the Rhine as a necessary preliminary to the defeat of Germany on the Western Front'. It was at the West Wall that the enemy could be decisively beaten 'and it was here that his organisation together with a large part of his forces could be destroyed'.

Eisenhower held fast to the strategy agreed in broad terms in December 1944.

> In planning our forthcoming spring and summer offensives, I envis-aged the operations which would lead to Germany's collapse as falling into three phases: first, the destruction of the enemy forces west of the Rhine and closing to that river; second, the seizure of bridgeheads over the Rhine from which to develop operations into Germany; and, third, the destruction of the remaining enemy east of the Rhine and the advance into the heart of the Reich.

While Bradley's Twelfth Army Group kept up their pursuit of the German forces in the Ardennes region, Montgomery, with the US Ninth Army under his command, was to launch a major offensive between the Maas and the Rhine north of Düsseldorf, through the

Reichswald Forest where the Battle of the Bulge had left a concentration of Allied forces. The attack would make straight for Germany's industrial heartland. It was the sector where Hitler's forces could least afford to give way but where they were also most vulnerable.

Montgomery again! Why him? Bradley demanded to know. If the broad front strategy was still in place it surely made sense to use the First and Third Armies to push straight ahead across the Siegfried Line and then, having bridged the Rhine at Bonn, launch a major thrust south of the Ruhr. At a succession of meetings Eisenhower gave Bradley reason to think that his arguments were getting through but the appeal of letting Montgomery take the lead had too many advantages. Eisenhower was thinking of the next stage in the grand plan when Montgomery would stage a set piece crossing of the Rhine to strike at the centre of Germany's industrial power. For Bradley, and even more for the eager Patton, this was to hand Montgomery the golden chance to be the first in Berlin. Once he had crossed the Rhine and outflanked the industrial Ruhr, the plains of north Germany, perfect for tanks, opened the way to the capital. As it happened, Montgomery's hopes and Bradley's fears were unfounded. The prize would go elsewhere.

Meanwhile, however, Eisenhower had to persuade Bradley that he was not being deliberately upstaged. He did this by stressing that Bradley would not simply be following in Montgomery's tank tracks, that the push by the Twelfth Army Group in the centre of the Allied line between Düsseldorf and Koblenz, supported by a converging attack by the US Third and Seventh Armies up into the Mainz-Karlsruhe sector, was in no way subsidiary but essential to a grand pincer movement that would trap the enemy and vindicate the broad front strategy. Bradley was not convinced but for the time being had more than enough to do in driving the Germans out of the Ardennes.

4
Bleak Midwinter

For the ordinary soldiers who had to endure the harsh European winter of 1944, the lowest ebb was at Christmas, a celebration that, just a few weeks earlier, many had confidently expected to be sharing with their families at home. Instead here they were, in the cold and the wet, pipe-dreaming the festive spirit. Even those not caught up in the Battle of the Bulge found little to be thankful for.

The men were taking their leggings and shoes off for the first time in weeks. The linoleum floor, which was like ice to touch, became one large bed as soon as the blankets were spread out. It was going to be a tight squeeze for all of us to lie down. We tried it, stretching out in a double row. Our feet met in a line down the centre of the room and there was just enough space to lie flat, shoulder to shoulder. Once that was settled, everyone sat up, the drink came off the stove and was passed around, poured into the canteen cups. It tasted like scorched lighter fluid, but it was burning hot, revivifying. Cigarettes were lighted, and out of the din of chatter and laughter singing began. The mournful *I'm Dreaming of a White Christmas, Silent Night, Jingle Bells, O Come All Ye Faithful, Hark! the Herald Angels Sing, O Little Town of Bethlehem, White Christmas* again, and then, growing more secular, the Army favourites: *I've got Sixpence, Someone's in the Kitchen with Dinah, For Me and My Gal, When You Wore a Tulip, There's a Long, Long Trail, I'm Going to Buy a Paper Doll that I Can Call My Own, Roll Me O-ver in the Clo-ver* . . .

. . . After a half hour of singing, *Silent Night* began again, wavered and stopped half-way. Most of the others were going to sleep. More than half the men, as everywhere in the Army, slept with their heads under the blankets. The lantern went out, leaving a small warm ruby glow in the darkness from the open bottom door of the stove.

And in the morning:

'Mass! Anyone here going to Mass? Fall out!' The church bells were ringing. It was odd to see the door of a badly smashed house open and a little boy and girl, dressed in Sunday clothes, run out, followed by a neat woman in an old-fashioned fur-collared coat, beaver hat and gloves. The children raced ahead to laugh and talk with other children, comparing, I supposed, what they had received for Christmas. There were men in overcoats, felt hats turned down all the way around, and stiff, high, polished shoes. None of the girls or women wore makeup. The civilians all kept to the sidewalk, while the soldiers roamed, talking, up the middle of the street.

The church was surrounded by a wrought-iron fence. All the stained-glass windows were blown out and the still air was icy and damp. There were crystal-and-brass chandeliers and a worn, patterned marble aisle. Civilians sat on one side, we on the other. An organist played unfamiliar hymns. Out of the corners of their eyes the civilians watched us and we watched them.

When the bell rang for the start of Mass, the parish priest came out in handsome white vestments, the two altar boys in red cassocks, starched white lace-edged surplices and white gloves. Blasts of frigid air blew in. The children sang hymns in French, but when the priest – stocky, middle-aged and dark – ascended the pulpit, the long sermon, surprisingly, was in German. He had a fine voice, deep and clear. Occasionally he gestured towards us, and the children all turned to look, then he gestured towards the crèche.[1]

R.M. Wingfield and his comrades spent the last Christmas Eve of the war in slit trenches hard up against the River Maas. Inevitably there was talk of that famous Christmas in 1914 when British and German troops played football in no-man's-land. And then:

Tom gripped my arm. 'Listen!'

Faintly, from across the river, came the sound of voices singing *Stille Nacht, Heilige Nacht*.

'Their forward patrols,' said Joe.

'Shut up, Joe, and listen!'

The age-old carol gained in strength as it floated to us on the frosty air. The first verse ended. After a short silence the second verse began – from *our* side of the river. We listened to the voices alternating the verses back and forth across the river. At the end faint greetings could be heard intermingled: 'Happy Christmas!' – '*Fröhliche Weinacht!*'[2]

Noel Ryan was part of a draft lately arrived from Canada. Joining his platoon of the Black Watch he was handed his 'balmoral headdress with the famous blood red Hackle feather fastened into the headband on the right' and told to bunk down with others in a requisitioned farmhouse, somewhere (he wasn't quite sure where) near the River Maas. The first priority was to construct a makeshift heater.

First off, you needed a friend in the motor pool, for used engine oil and empty gas cans. It took two cans to make a stove. The bottom one was the fire chamber and the upper the heat chamber. They were anchored together somehow with a large hole between them to let the heat and smoke go into the one on the top, and then into some sort of chimney and out of the window. There was also a tin cylinder to hold the motor oil. This had a piece of copper tubing soldered to the bottom with a petcock to adjust the flow of oil down the tube and into the fire chamber. The tube would go in through the side of the bottom can and make a little circle around the middle, ending up pointing downwards about four inches from the bottom in the middle. Finished.[3]

For some in the Black Watch, Christmas dinner had to wait until January 5th. 'An excellent menu was provided, the *piece de resistance* being the rum egg-flog. A good time was had by all and even a few shells landing in the near vicinity failed to put a damper on the party.'[4] Light reading came courtesy of the German propaganda ministry which had within its ranks at least one writer with a sense of the ridiculous.

As I sit on the banks of the MAAS
I reflect that it's really a FAAS
At my time of life
And miles from my wife
To be stuck in the mud on my AAS.

Most pitiful of all was the plight of families caught up in the front-line fighting along the German border. As Captain William Morgan of the US Army Corp of Engineers recorded, these people were deranged by misery, not knowing which way to turn to escape the heavy artillery exchanges that were daily battering their villages.

Many families had piled their few belongings onto old carts and wagons, but each vehicle carried a small Christmas tree lying among the pots and pans. While mostly pro-German, they nevertheless wanted to get out of the danger zone, behind the army which seemed to be winning. Until 18 December, these poor people were streaming westwards along the mud-soaked roads toward our rear areas. However, on that day, word of the German surprise attack to the north plus the fast removal of many of our units must have suggested to them the possibility of an American withdrawal, because many of these shabby vehicles with their little Christmas trees were soon observed headed the other way, back towards their homes or what was left of them.[5]

Some of the hardest fighting early in the year was in Alsace where Hitler launched the Nordwind offensive, a diversionary tactic intended to relieve pressure on the Ardennes front. The thinly stretched US Seventh Army positions took most of the punishment, falling back towards their supply base at Haguenau. Suddenly it looked as if Strasbourg was at risk of recapture. This was bad news for the French provisional government, eager to build its prestige on the euphoria created by the liberation. Allowing any part of France to fall back into German hands was, for General Charles de Gaulle, tantamount to a devastating defeat. When Eisenhower showed no inclination to play the German or, for that matter, the French game by rushing troops from the Ardennes to prop up Strasbourg's defences (indeed, some units had been withdrawn to help shore up the Ardennes front farther south), de Gaulle came hot foot to the Supreme Commander's headquarters at Versailles. Touchy at the best of times and ever sensitive to French honour, de Gaulle demanded that Strasbourg be held at all costs. If the city fell by American neglect, the French First Army under General de Lattre de Tassigny would refuse to take orders from any but its own officers. In practical terms this was not much of a threat. Relying on US arms and supplies, not to mention five divisions of General Devers' US Seventh Army, the undermanned French First Army, with its heavy weighting of Algerian and Moroccan recruits, had fought itself into the ground in Italy and North Africa. Charged with clearing German positions in and around Colmar to the south of Strasbourg, it had soon got bogged down. Some thought it had lost its fighting spirit, though this was not the impression of BBC reporter Wynford Vaughan Thomas who had nothing but praise for the dash and élan of the French military.

> I've never heard any French officer issue any other order except *En Avant*, 'Forward'. No French command post seems to be anywhere except slightly ahead of the front line. When a French colonel invites you to visit the front – he means the Front. And the first thing you know is a sudden shower of shells as the gallant officer points to the farmhouse a hundred yards away – 'Les Boches?' you ask nervously. 'Ah! there they are, les Salauds,' he says. And you prepare immediately to take off rapidly to the rear. For you know exactly what the next order will be: 'Forward – *en avant*.' And forward they do go against the toughest resistance. This new army of France has got something to avenge – something which makes it dare the impossible. It's got nothing in common with the disillusioned armies that went down to defeat in 1940.[6]

What was undeniable was the absence of joint planning between the Americans and French. Linguistic differences may have had some bearing but French resentment at constantly being told what to do in their own country was also a factor. Eisenhower was determined to break the deadlock. While resenting de Gaulle's assertion that any deficiencies of the French First Army could be traced back to half-hearted American support, he was prepared to accept that all forces, American and French, charged with clearing the Colmar pocket needed gingering up. A sharply worded message was sent to General Devers ordering him 'in no uncertain language' to get on with the offensive with the aim of clearing Alsace up to the Rhine. At the same time Marshal Alphonse Juin, Chief of Staff of the French National Defence Committee under de Gaulle, was summoned to Versailles to be told that 'now is the time for the French to fight like fury'.

This brought the inevitable protest from de Gaulle and another demand for reinforcements and a warning that if Strasbourg should fall, and here he played his strongest card, the shame and humiliation would almost certainly bring an end to his provisional government. Eisenhower could see a political gulf opening before him. At the same time it was vital that the German threat in Alsace be neutralised before the next big push to clear all enemy forces west of the Rhine. De Gaulle got his reinforcements. On January 23rd, Bradley heard the unwelcome news that five divisions were to be moved from the Ardennes to Alsace, a reduction in his strength that he took to be a deliberate slap at his hopes for upstaging Montgomery in the final thrust into Germany.

The reallocation of forces had the desired effect. On February 1st, de Lattre's troops broke into Colmar. Then, attacking from north and south, they began closing the gap between Colmar and Mulhouse, intending to cut off the three German divisions that remained in southern Alsace. By the 5th, US forces were within a mile of Neuf Brisach on the Rhine where the bridge was still intact. But not for long. Like so many Rhine crossings it was reduced to a waterlogged heap of stone and metal by the retreating German Nineteenth Army. By February 11th, the west bank of the Rhine from the Swiss border to the north of Strasbourg was in Allied hands.

The destruction of the Nineteenth Army achieved a reconcilia-tion between French and American commands but at troop level differences persisted, not least American incomprehension at their ally's apparent inability to cope with mechanised vehicles.

A French tank, an American Sherman with French markings came along, and he was moving very slowly because of the ice. But he came to a slight downgrade right in front of us and the darned thing started to slide on the icy road and he must have hit the brakes and locked the tracks. It kept right on sliding. It wasn't a hill, it was just a grade, and there was a T-shaped intersection at the bottom. The tank went through the side of the house at the foot of the grade, and the floor wouldn't support the weight of the thirty-five ton Sherman, so it dropped right through into the cellar. I was standing there watching this craziness.[7]

An admirer of all things French, even Wynford Vaughan Thomas had to agree that driving was not their strongest quality, as he told his BBC listeners.

Speed is the first impression you get when you are out with the French. No one seems to travel at less than sixty miles per hour, and my memory of a French convoy is of a mile-long pandemonium – lorries coming bumper to bumper one way, lorries meeting them head on coming from the other, jeeps weaving in and out. And everyone hand-weaving, tying themselves into knots and backing into each other's vehicles with the greatest of goodwill in the world.[8]

A famous cartoon in the American service paper, *Stars and Stripes*, summed it up. It showed a line of disconsolate American lorry drivers being addressed by their lieutenant before departure. 'Men,' says the lieutenant, 'some of you may never come back. There's a French convoy on the road.' If there was more good humour in Franco-American relations, Anglo-American rivalry showed no signs of letting up. While Montgomery added the finishing touches to his plan (code-named Veritable Grenade) for putting his troops on the banks of the Rhine, Bradley continued to work on Eisenhower to persuade him that it was the Ardennes, his own sector, that was the key to ending the war. Patton's Third Army had already penetrated the outer fringe of the Siegfried Line below the forest hills of the Schnee Eifel; what could he not achieve if he was given his head? But Patton was the inspired maverick in an army group that otherwise showed all the signs of exhaustion after the heavy fighting of recent weeks.

The climactic meeting between Eisenhower and Bradley came on the last day of January. The presence of American and British staff officers in no way deterred Bradley from speaking his mind. He wanted to know why it was that the Americans who 'were doing all the fighting and dying in Europe with 61 divisions in the field next to 15 understrength British divisions, were forever obligated to give and give'. Eisenhower reminded his friend that in a pretty well continuous process of consultation, Bradley had approved the broad strategy, including the decision to put the Ninth Army under Montgomery. What had changed?

As the discussion heated up, it became clear that Bradley was still smarting from the press verdict on his handling of the Battle of the Bulge. He was determined to 'retrieve the integrity of the US command'. That meant putting Montgomery in his place. While the Field Marshal had been collecting his thoughts, he (Bradley) had advanced his front by six miles in two days, despite heavy snowfalls and biting temperatures. Eisenhower was suitably impressed but pointed out that this did not amount to a break-through. Meanwhile, it was paramount to close the Rhine north of Düsseldorf with all possible speed: '"I can't be responsible to the American people if you do this," Bradley snapped. "I wish to resign at once." Eisenhower turned pale, then red. "Brad," Eisenhower resumed, "I, not you, am responsible to the American people. Your resignation therefore means absolutely nothing." After a long silence, Bradley backed down.'[9]

When the encounter was over, Eisenhower did what any good politician would do. He covered his tracks by making it known to Montgomery that one peep out of him suggesting that he had won out against the American command would put him back on the start line taking orders from Bradley.

If some generals were showing signs of impatience, across the entire front there were many ordinary soldiers, on both sides, who had had more than enough.

In the bitter, cold dusk a soldier approached me uncertainly. When he was close I saw that his eyes, pale in a dark-complexioned face, were fixed and dilated. He was talking in French, as if in a daze, then, half whispering, half aloud, drawing the word out, he said, 'Noi-i-se! The noi-i-se!' His eyes became even larger and he started plucking at my sleeve.

A distant shell exploded. He moistened his lips, then harkened, one finger raised. I could think only of a moving-picture actor giving a not wholly convincing performance. I asked, 'Would you like a cigarette?'

'Yes,' he said. 'The noise . . . The noise, you know.'

I gave him a light from the tip of mine. He bent towards it, his hands covering mine, and in the act his face was absorbed; it had lost its vacancy of expression. There was a heavy college ring on his finger. Once the cigarette was going, he said, 'The noi-i-se!'

I remained silent and he stood a short distance away, his collar turned up. About five minutes later I heard the captain saying, 'take this man over to Battalion Headquarters and tell them I said to let him rest up a few days. He'll be all right.' The man, who was about twenty-four, was led out past me by a medic, whispering, 'The noi-i-se. The noi-i-se!' The two figures went down the road and disappeared into the gloom.[10]

Signs of battle fatigue were becoming all too apparent. There were reports of whole units disintegrating under pressure. This had certainly happened in the Battle of the Bulge. The mass surrender of the 106th Infantry had caused a few tremors at Supreme Headquarters. Everywhere there were stories of self-inflicted wounds – the million-dollar injury, as the GIs called it then – a shot through the foot or a deliberately clumsy fall off the tailback of a truck which could easily break a bone or two. There were some ingenious excuses for faked accidents.

Bathroom facilities were a slit trench, you'd dig a slit trench and you'd straddle it if you had a bowel movement. Now, a very obvious way if you were going to the slit trench and you had your carbine in your hand and, by mistake you pulled the trigger, you would shoot yourself in the calf of the leg. So some enterprising guy worked out that sequence as his excuse for what happened when actually what he did was just shot himself in the calf of the leg.[11]

Desertion was also common, as James Graff of the 134th Infantry recalls:

> A deserter by the name of Smith from Sandoval, Illinois rejoined us. He had run off several times before and he was told not to try it again or it would be too bad. When we fell out next morning he was gone. They caught him a few days later and he was court-martialed. These kind of cases were not unusual we were to find out. Many men would do anything to get out of the front line.[12]

No less demoralising for those who were reconciled to seeing out the war were the occasions when orders were flatly rejected.

> As we proceeded to move out, Landrum called out telling us to saddle up (put on our equipment). As I was getting mine on I said to Sgt. Buchanan to get ready. His reply was, 'I told those SOBs I wasn't going to fight anymore as I have been wounded twice and that's enough.' I told Bob and he said he would talk to Buchanan. I said okay, but that I would cover him as I knew he (Buchanan) carried a German pistol. They talked and Landrum then took Buchanan's weapons and turned him over to the regimental MPs who took him away. We saw him later guarding GI prisoners after we had crossed the Rhine. The regimental officers had taken his stripes away and busted him to a private, but in consideration of his past service had not court-martialed him but gave him a job in the rear area.[13]

The treatment of genuine cases of breakdown was generally sympathetic, the Americans leading the way in taking note of psychiatric advice.

> I remember two or three people who were really, really battle fatigued, and they would start wandering around, like a dream world, or start walking the wrong way, and doing this and that. We had to get people like that back. There were some medics who after a point began to crack. I don't know how long I would have taken it, frankly, if the war had gone on and on. I'd have needed some help. That's why they had R and R, rest and recuperation, for battle fatigue cases. They were casualties, really. So, we had to lead them back to shelter.[14]

But there were senior commanders who were more inclined to take a hard line. It comes as no surprise to find that Patton got into serious trouble, even risking his career, by slapping a GI who was in battle trauma. On the other hand, though not given to impetuous conduct, General Ridgway was also one who was less than sympathetic to weaker vessels.

> In another hour, on that same spot, another incident occurred which I remember with regret. In the fierce fighting, Manhay changed hands several times. The Germans had brought up some flat trajectory guns, and they started shelling our little group. Fragments whizzed everywhere. One struck an artillery observer, who was standing by me, in the leg, and another punctured the tank of his jeep. As this shell exploded an infantry sergeant standing nearby became hysterical. He threw himself into the ditch by the side of the road, crying and raving. I walked over and tried to talk to him, trying to help him get hold of himself. But it had no effect. He was just crouched there in the ditch, cringing in utter terror. So I called my jeep driver, Sergeant Farmer, and told him to take his carbine and march this man back to the nearest MP, and if he started to escape to shoot him without hesitation. He was an object of abject cowardice, and the sight of him would have a terrible effect on any American soldier who might see him.[15]

It was an incident he remembered 'with regret', though whether it was his own behaviour or that of the sergeant that caused him remorse is not clear.

What of Eisenhower? As far as is known, he never came in direct contact with battle weariness but he did know its effects. One of his biggest worries was what he saw as a degeneration of the fighting spirit of his front-line troops, compared to that of the Germans. There was a degree of inevitability about this. The Germans were fighting for survival and within a cultural context that praised military valour above all else and permitted savage reprisals against those who believed otherwise. Young Americans were at the other extreme. Raised in a democracy that championed individual freedom, they tempered patriotism with a resentment at being pushed around. The British, with their European and Common-wealth Allies, came some way behind, part of a class structure that emphasised respect for authority but, as post-war politics were to prove, an authority that was losing its grip. Nowhere in the anti-Nazi coalition was there fear of lynch law parading as justice. But by the same token, everywhere the question could be asked often and openly, if we are so close to winning this war, why should I risk getting killed?

It was the fear of a collapse of morale, and of the military conse-quences, that pushed Eisenhower to a decision he would have given much to avoid. At the height of the Ardennes offensive, when the Germans had forced a salient fifty miles deep and sixty miles wide, the Supreme Commander signed four execution orders. Three were for German fifth columnists who had been captured wearing American uniforms. The fourth was for Private Eddie Slovik, G Company, 109th Infantry, Twenty-Eighth Division. Slovik was a serial deserter whose confidence in getting away with it may well have contributed to the poor discipline throughout the Twenty-Eighth. But in the past six months across the western front there had been more than 40,000 desertions. Of these, 2,800 had been tried by general court-martial, with punishment in every case well short of the death penalty. This was not surprising, since there had not been a single execution of an American soldier for a battle-field offence since 1865. Moreover, Slovik had simply run away; he was not accused of the more serious offence of assaulting an officer or comrade. And he had appealed for another chance to 'be a good soldier', though he had refused to go back to the Twenty-Eighth, a unit that had taken a heavy battering in the first wave of the German attack. Whichever way the case is examined, Slovik comes across as no worse than most of his fellow offenders and better than some. That he had to die as an example to others is a measure of Eisenhower's pessimism on the general state of morale.

It was a measure too of his awareness of the awesome battles still to come. Fast forward a few weeks to the point where victory west of the Rhine had pushed the Wehrmacht back across their last great natural defence. Reflecting on the achievements of the soldiers under his command, Lieutenant General Horrocks concluded:

> The strain to which the soldier of today is subject is far, far greater than anything experienced by his grandfather or his great-grandfather. This battle was a particularly good example. The 53rd Welsh Division and, farther south, the 51st Highland Division were fighting their way through that sinister black Reichswald Forest. Their forward troops would very often consist of two young men, crouching together in a fox-hole, both of whom had long since come to the conclusion that the glories of war had been much over-written. They were quite alone for they might not be able to see even the other members of their own section and all around them was the menace of hidden mines.
>
> It is this sinister emptiness that depresses them most – no living thing in sight. During training, officers and NCOs had been running round the whole time, but they cannot do it now to anything like the same extent, or they won't live long. Our two young men are almost certainly cold, miserable and hungry, but they are at least reasonably safe as long as they remain in their fox-hole. But they know that soon they will have to emerge into the open to attack. Then the seemingly empty battlefield will erupt into sudden and violent life. When that moment arrives they must force themselves forward with a sickening feeling in the pit of their stomachs, fighting an almost uncontrollable urge to fling themselves down as close to the earth as they can get. Even then they are still alone amidst all the fury; carrying their loneliness with them.[16]

Meanwhile, the sentiment of the fighting man on both sides of the line was best expressed by a young German soldier writing home: If you actually saw me you would lift your hands in dismay. I am ragged and filthy. I have had the same underwear on for five weeks. If one doesn't get lice it's a miracle. If only the war were over soon; it has lasted long enough already.'[17]

5
United in Hate

While Hitler was proclaiming his resolution to Hold Hold Hold the
west bank of the Rhine, his three antagonists – Roosevelt, Churchill
and Stalin – congregated for their last meeting of the war. The place
was Yalta, a one-time summer resort of the Tsars on the Black Sea,
now little more than a ruin. 'If we had spent ten years on research,'
Churchill told Harry Hopkins, Roosevelt's confidant, 'we could not
have found a worse place in the world.' Yalta was 'good for typhus'
and 'deadly on lice which thrive in those parts'.[1]

Roosevelt had even better reasons for resisting the Crimea.
Struck by polio and paralysed from the waist down at the age of
thirty-nine, his fitness to travel had been a cause of worry
throughout his presidency. Now, in early 1945, his medical advisers
were seriously worried that he might not survive an arduous
journey. It was bad enough for Churchill, at seventy the oldest of
the Big Three, who had survived a recent heart attack and a bout
of pneumonia and almost always got ill when he went abroad, but
at least he was not permanently on the danger list. Shortly before
Roosevelt set off for Yalta, preparations were made for the likely
succession of Vice-President Harry Truman who was told bluntly
that 'the President might go at any time'.[2]

On the other hand, Roosevelt was not a man to give up easily
on his ideals, one of which was to reach an accommodation with
the Soviet Union that would carry over to the second half of the
century. If Stalin wanted to meet at Yalta, and he was emphatic on
this point, then, said Roosevelt, Yalta it had to be. Churchill tried
harder for an alternative. In Jerusalem there were 'first class hotels,
government houses etc. . . . and Stalin could come the whole way
by train' (the Soviet leader had a mortal dread of flying)[3] but this
idea fell flat after Lord Moyne, the British minister of state in the

Middle East, was assassinated by Jewish terrorists outside his house in Cairo. Churchill gave way with reasonable grace. 'I daresay Stalin will make good arrangements ashore,' he wrote to Roosevelt but, just in case, he ordered accommodation on a British destroyer with a generous stock of whisky.

Churchill must have wished that everything else at Yalta could be fixed so easily as his domestic comforts. But with victory over Germany within sight, the gulf between the two English-speaking allies was getting wider, with no early prospect of it contracting. Disagreements on the conduct of the war were exacerbated by the US rejection of blanket financial support for post-war Britain. While it was assumed that some form of lend-lease would continue to aid Britain's post-war recovery, the terms were the subject of heated debate.

When, in late 1944, the prospect of a loan to Britain of three to five billion dollars was put to American voters by way of a Gallup Poll, only 27 per cent voiced their approval, 13 per cent were 'don't knows' and the rest, 60 per cent, were most emphatically against. The general feeling seemed to be that America was already doing enough. With twelve million men in arms, as against five million British, the US was producing close on half the Allied weaponry in all theatres of war. It was payback time. On the US side, a minimum demand was the relaxation of Imperial Preference, the mutually favourable trade deal Britain had with the Commonwealth countries which prejudiced American exporters. The British reaction was to question the US commitment to free trade when, for example, powerful interests lobbied against competition on air routes monopolised by American companies.[4]

The wider discussion on how far America was prepared to support economic rejuvenation on mainland Europe was even more fractious. There were those, like Harry Hopkins, who recognised that there could be 'no recovery and no peace and no democracy in Europe if its people did not have enough to eat and the tools and materials with which to get back to work'.[5] But beset by ill-health, Hopkins' influence with the President was fading, leaving Admiral Leahy, who favoured a tougher, self-help approach, to fill the vacuum. Two years ahead, under a new President, America was to launch the Marshall Plan, a programme of regeneration for Europe to rival the New Deal, but in the closing months of the war neither politicians nor public were ready for further European entanglements, believing with Leahy that 'involvement of America in European politics would inevitably bring us into another European war'.[6] Even the military presence was projected to scale down dramatically. In 1943, Roosevelt was confidently predicting to his Chiefs of Staff that after victory in Europe, he expected to field an occupation force of 'about a million American troops . . . for at least one year, maybe two'.[7] At Yalta, the estimate was down to one or two divisions for a year at most.[8]

Instead of the military acting as firefighters at every political flashpoint, Roosevelt had a grander vision of world harmony. Conscious of his own frailty, he was determined to crown his presidency by inaugurating a new start in international affairs. This was to have the US and Russia, as the two most powerful countries, working in partnership to support a United Nations framework for peace.

Churchill tried to warn his friend against an impossible dream but Roosevelt, a sick man in a hurry, was in no mood to listen. Prompted by Henry Wallace, his Vice-President until Truman took over on Roosevelt's re-election for a fourth term in 1944, and his politically myopic ambassador in Moscow, Joseph E. Davies, not to mention the rosy view of Soviet intentions in literary and intellectual circles, Roosevelt held to the illusion that Stalin's notion of 'democracy' and 'anti-imperialism' was in line with American values. Stalin was happy to go along with Roosevelt's self-deception, while sharing with him a jeer at Britain's old-fashioned loyalty to monarchy and empire. While not unaware of Stalin's intention in Europe of setting up a protective barrier of friendly, i.e. Communist-led states, Roosevelt nonetheless believed he could bring Stalin round to his formulae for post-war co-existence and had no intention of allowing Churchill to frustrate his efforts. At the Quebec Conference he had been 'brutally frank' with the British Prime Minister, telling him, 'I can handle Stalin better than either you or your Foreign Office.' Recognising that it was only with Russian help that the war could be ended before signs of war-weariness at home and in the forces became only too apparent, Churchill was conciliatory, while continuing his efforts to edge Roosevelt his way.

One of the irritations for the President in the last year of his life was the persistent reminders from Churchill that it was he, not Stalin, who should be sitting at his right hand. Holding to the traditional faith in the balance of power as the best way of keeping the peace, he lobbied for a restoration of European frontiers much as they were before the war with a revitalised France and a reformed Germany helping to put the brakes on Russian expansion. The new element in his thinking was the need for a strong Anglo-American alliance to act as a guarantor of international good behaviour. Roosevelt disagreed on just about every point. He had no confidence in France making it back into the league of world powers and, far from wanting to help Germany, he was more inclined to favour its destruction, once and for all, as an industrial economy. As for a closer association with Britain, the President was not at all sure that the two countries had much in common except language, more or less, and a concept of democracy in the broadest sense.

In the early days of the war Roosevelt and Churchill had both made superhuman efforts to keep the alliance in smooth working order – Roosevelt because he despised Fascism and realised that America was not immune to attack, Churchill because he knew there was no hope of victory over Germany without American backing. So important was the American connection, by late 1942 Britain had over 9,000 representatives in Washington. Whether they were the best 9,000 is another question. Born of imperial splendour, British diplomats were not well attuned to their American cousins who were less experienced in world affairs. 'Completely dumb and appallingly slow' was how General Dykes, acting for the British Chiefs of Staff in Washington, described his opposite numbers.[9] Relations improved with experience but there remained an underlying suspicion in American political and diplomatic circles that the British were for ever trying it on in their devious and patronising way.

This suspicion, resurfacing in the last months of the war, showed up most obviously at Yalta where Churchill – who presented himself as an equal partner with Roosevelt – was left in no doubt that he was, in reality, a junior associate. Churchill had hoped for a one-to-one meeting with Roosevelt in Malta by way of a preliminary to the Yalta Conference. No time, said the President, although he was prepared for the Combined Chiefs of Staff to gather in Malta to discuss Eisenhower's plans for the final assault on Germany from the west and for himself to stop off for a brief rest before proceeding to the Crimea. His travel schedule was thus Virginia to Malta, 4,884 miles by sea, followed, after a short break, by 1,375 miles by air from Luga airfield across the Aegean and Black Sea to Saki in the Crimea, followed by a six-hour drive through the mountains to Yalta, in all a challenge to the strongest constitution.

Transport was adapted to give him every convenience such as onboard lifts to cope with his wheelchair but the biggest worry of his staff was for the President's safety when he was out of their control. A security reconnaissance of Saki airfield revealed it to be thick with anti-aircraft batteries manned by trigger-happy gunners who might all too readily shoot down a VIP plane, assuming it to be a German attacker. The best that could be done to prevent such a catastrophe was to post a US air force sergeant with every emplacement, a concession that the Russians acceded to most reluctantly.

On the British side, administration was in the hands of Joan Bright Astley, a young lady of metal who had joined a typing pool of a Territorial Army unit at the time of the Munich crisis. She had since risen to be a leading figure in the Prime Minister's Special Information Centre, reporting to General Ismay, Churchill's Chief of Staff and Whitehall mediator. Joan left England on January 25th, 'the long lists in my handbag weighing heavily against the latest message from Moscow that the People's Commissariat of Foreign Affairs was much perturbed at the extent of overcrowding' at Yalta.[10]

Two days later, she joined a group of American delegates for the last leg of the flight to Saki airport, seventy miles outside Sevastopol.

At 1.30 p.m. precisely the Skymaster's wheels touched down and crunched through mud and slush. We climbed out and trudged across to a huddle of buildings, over which hung a listless flag, watched by a standing group of Russian guards . . . I was greeted by Wing-Commander Harpham, who was adjutant and interpreter for Group-Captain Pickard, officer commanding the dreary airfield of mud, slush and wooden buildings. It was extremely cold. 'Harpie' took me into a dark and cheerless dormitory with eight beds in it and introduced me to a Russian Army girl called Sima. She was fascinated by me, and followed me everywhere, stroking my arm, touching me, staring at my clothes. When I changed and washed in a basin that evening she and another girl watched my every move.

Because Pickard was only a group-captain, the Russians paid no attention to him; the Americans had wisely imported a selection of brass-hats which included admirals and brigadier-generals, and were being treated respectfully. Pickard had no car and had been unable to push ahead with his ground preparations. We decided to build me up into a powerful figure. 'Harpie' telephoned to General Ermshenko, who was in command for the Russians, and told him that the 'Administrative Officer to the British War Cabinet who held the rank of major-general had arrived and wished to pay her respects to him; the British Government expected General Ermshenko to do all in his power to help.' The General said he would call later that evening. He never came, but a car did, next morning, which broke down in front of the mess; all we saw of it was the bottom of the driver and much of the engine lying on the ground beside him.[11]

It got better. Another car, a long black Zis limousine, carried the English party the rest of the way to Yalta where they were to prepare for Churchill's arrival on the SS *Franconia*, a 20,000-ton liner requisitioned from Cunard. 'The road was rough and full of slush as our racy driver bumped us along. It was worrying to think of President Roosevelt, who had looked so sickly at Quebec, being driven over such surfaces, but that was just one worry among so many.'[12]

Yalta had been knocked about by the retreating Germans. But two magnificent buildings, the Livadia and the Vorontzov Palaces, previously occupied by the German high command, were in reasonable order. The Americans were allocated Livadia, the British were put in the Vorontzov, the two headquarters being about half an hour's drive apart. The Vorontzov was the less spacious but the British delegation was more than happy with the accommodation.

> The site was lovely. On one side the Black Sea a few hundred feet below us and less than five minutes' walk, and on the other a buttress of mountains rising steeply to a height of several thousand feet. The Villa was a fantastic mixture of bogus Scottish castle and Moorish palace; but the rooms were well enough proportioned and, thanks to enormous log fires, warm and comfortable. It had been the head-quarters of General Manstein during the German occupation of the Crimea and been left a shambles when they were driven out.[13]

Getting the rest of Yalta into working order was, said Joan Bright Astley, 'a monument to Russian efficiency'.

> A thousand or more soldiers had restored roads, replaced broken windows and planted gardens. Hundreds of railway trucks had made the long slow journey from Moscow bringing furniture, carpets, bedding, pictures, food and the wherewithal to cook and eat it, drink, glasses, chefs, waiters, housemaids. Moscow hotels had been emptied of staff. Many of them had been aroused secretly during the night, told to pack their bags and leave their homes, with what misgivings it can be imagined.
>
> In the Vorontzov, as at Livadia, the modern Communists, our hosts, had turned the clock back to the days of the Tsars. Our walls were hung with pictures from Moscow art galleries, our fireplaces crackled with burning logs, our waiters were immaculate, our maids in black dresses with white aprons.

Security was thorough.

Besides its own guards, each house was completely ringed by sentries, who were doubled at night, with the addition of dog patrols. Around these rings another, and another round that. The water supply for Vorontzov which came from a natural spring was guarded for the whole of its length. Every ten yards of the roads between Sevastopol, Saki, Yalta and Alupka, there were men and women guards.[14]

While preparations were underway for the reception of the VIPs at Yalta, the Combined Chiefs of Staff were in session in Malta. They had much to occupy them. The western front in the wake of Rundstedt's Ardennes offensive was a disappointment waiting to be corrected. The clearing of German positions west of the Rhine, Operation Veritable Grenade, had yet to make its impact. As Churchill told the House of Commons, victory 'is no longer in doubt' but it was still distant and 'will certainly be costly'. The imperative for the top brass was to improve on Churchill's prediction. They were spurred on by unfavourable comparisons with progress on the eastern front.

From the autumn of 1944, after a period of relative inactivity, the Red Army had scored some mighty victories starting with a breakthrough to the Baltic coast which had cut off the entire Army Group North in the Courland Pocket between the Baltic and the Latvian capital of Riga. Thereafter the news from the east had been uniformly good, if a little galling for those who were still getting to grips with the Rhine crossing. In November and December, Soviet offensives in the Baltic region and Hungary had sucked in German forces from the critical Warsaw-Berlin axis.

The assault on Budapest had been sustained throughout a month of drenching rain which slowed the Russian tanks to a crawl. But by the end of November, the Germans had been forced back to the Danube. On the night of December 5th an attack was launched across the river thirteen miles below Budapest. The German defences on the west bank were pierced and by dawn a ten-mile bridgehead had been established. Simultaneously, Russian forces north of the city smashed through what remained of German defences on the east bank of the Danube. Budapest now came under heavy attack from north, east and south. Counter-attacks delayed the surrender of Budapest until mid-February but by then its survival as a German outpost had lost all significance. Changing sides, Hungary declared war on Germany on December 29th, in the process depriving the German war machine of oil from the Balaton fields and food from the Hungarian plain.

Attention had then switched to the main Russian objective which was to strike at the heart of the Reich across the Polish frontier into east Germany and from there to Berlin. This critical central sector of the eastern front, from the Baltic to the foothills of the Carpathians, with Warsaw midway, was ominously quiet for all of the tail end of 1944. There were good reasons for this. Having demonstrated to Hitler, and Napoleon for that matter, the painful consequences of overstretching an army's supply lines, the Russians had no intention of making the same mistake. Their summer offensive had carried the Red Army across the vast stretch of territory between the Upper Dnieper and the Vistula, stopping just short of Warsaw and the borders of East Prussia. To have gone further at that time would have been to risk a repeat of Stalingrad but with advantage to the Wehrmacht.

Dug in behind the Vistula, one of the strongest natural defences guarding the eastern approaches to the Reich, the Germans in retreat had shortened the distance to their centres of war production, including the industrial cities in Silesia which were beyond the reach of Allied bombers. Sensibly, Marshals Zhukov and Konev urged patience while their army groups massed the weapons and resources needed for a resumption of the offensive. Calling for a greater weight of artillery and for a sufficiency of tanks to mount an all-embracing armoured sweep across the open Polish plain, their intention was to frustrate the classic withdrawal and regroup technique perfected by the Wehrmacht. Time and again the Germans had been able to outdistance their pursuers long enough to rally in new defensive positions. It was not to happen again.

The offensive was to begin at dawn on January 12th, earlier than originally planned to help take the pressure off the western front. It was a favour for which Churchill expressed his undying gratitude, though he might have pointed out that Stalin had cause to be grateful for Anglo-American resolve in holding off the Ardennes offensive. Crack German troops that might otherwise have moved east had been held down at the Rhine. Ignoring all the signs of a catastrophic defeat, Hitler refused to give the Soviet threat the priority it deserved. Never one to hide his contempt for the Red Army (a 'useless rabble' he called them in one of his less excitable moods), he nonetheless credited his co-dictator with a tendency to act rationally – a case of the pot failing to recognise that the kettle was equally black. Military logic suggested that Stalin's first priority would be to sweep up the 200,000 German troops in the Courland Pocket. Thereafter, it was East Prussia that Hitler thought to be most at risk.

General Heinz Guderian, Chief of the General Staff of Land Armies together with his closest advisers, believed otherwise though, with first-hand experience of the Red Army, they were inclined to hedge their bets. The likeliest prospect was seen as an attack to the south towards Vienna. This way was barred by five redoubts between the Vistula and the Oder. The way their generals worked it out, the Russians had five great battles ahead of them to get within striking distance of Berlin. Failure at any stage would be the signal to begin the rollback. But it was a strategy that took no account of the reality – an attack over a wide front of such massive power (over two million men and 6,000 tanks against a force little more than half the strength) that all calculations were scattered to the winds.

When the Russian artillery opened up in the early hours of January 12th, the shock waves reverberated all the way back to Hitler's headquarters. Speer and others witnessed a furious row between Guderian who demanded an immediate evacuation of the Courland Pocket and Hitler who refused to authorise a withdrawal to the Baltic ports. Hitler had the last word, though for the first time Speer saw the symptoms of a disintegrating authority. 'Matters had come to an open quarrel in the larger circle. The novelty was almost palpable. New worlds had opened out. To be sure, Hitler had still saved face. That was a great deal. But at the same time it was very little.'[15]

Hitler did at last agree to the transfer of troops from the west. But to Guderian's dismay, they were to be sent to Hungary to force the Russians back across the Danube. The aim was to recapture the oil fields essential for a German counter-offensive. Such high-flown intentions were soon to be an irrelevancy in a battle for survival. But Hitler and his intimates failed to get the point. They 'were only too anxious to believe what they wanted to believe', said Guderian. 'Ostrich politics were combined with ostrich strategy.'[16]

The Russian artillery barrage lasted from 1.30 a.m. through to dawn. On a twenty-five-mile front, 7,000 guns shattered the German defences. At first light Marshal Konev's First Ukrainian Army Group braved a heavy fog and a snowstorm that took the breath away to attack across the upper Vistula towards Cracow and Silesia. The first two lines of German defences were overrun in a single day; the third and strongest line, protected by a deep belt of minefields, was crossed a day later. In forty-eight hours the Russians had advanced twenty-five miles on a thirty-seven-mile front. After another day, the front was over seventy miles and Cracow was within striking distance. It was at this point that the First Belorussian Army Group under Marshal Zhukov launched a double attack from two narrow bridgeheads across the Vistula to break through twelve miles of deep defences, before fanning out to sweep round Warsaw, opening the way to the Oder and Berlin. Long since left behind, the German forces in Courland, Hitler's sacrificial victims, were pinned down to await their fate.

Warsaw, a decimated city, people and buildings crushed by Nazi vengeance, was taken on January 17th. The first Russian generals to enter Warsaw guessed that upwards of 300,000 civilians had been killed in ninety days. Doubtless they reflected how different it could have been had the Red Army given air support to the Polish Home Army when it had risen up against the German occupiers back in August. Instead, ignoring appeals from Washington and London and refusing to allow American and British bombers to land on Russian airfields east of Warsaw for refuelling and repair, Stalin had allowed the slaughter to continue unabated. Why interrupt what the Germans were doing so effectively to prepare the way for Russia to install its puppet government?

Two days after the fall of Warsaw, Cracow and Lodz were captured. The plains of western Poland were now wide open. The Russian tide rolled forward at up to forty miles a day.

Meanwhile, to the north, General Chernyakhousky led the way into East Prussia making for Koenigsberg on the Baltic coast while, in a flanking move, Marshal Rokossovsky attacked from the southeast. With each of the Russian army groups far superior in strength to that of the whole German force in East Prussia, the envelopment of the province was only a matter of time. Within days, even German commentators were conceding that the war had reached a decisive stage. Hitler's response, on January 23rd, was to place his interior minister, Reichsführer Heinrich Himmler, in command of the new Army Group Vistula with orders to stop the Russians from severing East Prussia from Germany proper. The madness of desperation was all too obvious. Himmler's appointment was short-lived. His failure to mount an effective counter-offensive marked the beginning of the end for Hitler's SS chief.

Three weeks after launching their winter offensive, the Russian spearheads were 300 miles west of their starting point. The Germans had been swept from Poland, except for the neck of the corridor leading to Danzig. There was no prospect of a German counter-offensive from East Prussia which was now enveloped and crushed by Russian forces moving in from north and south. By the end of January, the great industrial region of Silesia, with its tank and aircraft factories little touched by Allied bombing, was in Russian hands. But all this paled against a single, awe-inspiring reality, that from the bridgehead on the Oder near Küstrin, Berlin was little more than sixty miles away.

For the Anglo-American Chiefs of Staff meeting in Malta, the knowledge that the Russians had moved so far, so fast, had a mixed reception. On the plus side, it was encouraging that the Red Army was draining the strength of the Wehrmacht, making it impossible for it to switch forces to the western front. But equally it was embarrassing, to put it mildly, that the balance of achievement was so much weighted on the Russian side. The Germans had been thrown back across the Ardennes, but at this stage in the war the Siegfried Line was still intact and the Rhine, as a prime objective, was more distant than Berlin to the Russians.

The question for the generals was how to speed up the western advance without spending lives on a scale tolerated by the Russians. The debate centred on the old argument between the supporters of Eisenhower's broad front strategy and those who favoured the single thrust aimed at cutting through the German forces and then encircling them before they had time to recover. Opinion divided along national lines with Brooke promoting the single thrust, while Marshall and Bedell Smith backed Eisenhower, who had decided wisely that he would be better occupied elsewhere while the table-thumping went on. It was, by all accounts, except that of the official minutes, a first-class row. 'The arguments reached such a point that Marshall, ordinarily one of the most restrained and soft-spoken of men, announced that if the British plan were approved by the Prime Minister and President he would recommend to Eisenhower that he had no choice but to ask to be relieved of his command.'[17]

In the end, there was no contest. When Marshall gave vent to his anger, as he did most volubly whenever Montgomery's name came up as a possible rival to his American opposite numbers, Brooke had no option but to concede before working off his frustration with a characteristically tart entry in his diary. ('Marshall clearly understood nothing of strategy and could not even argue out the relative merits of various alternatives.'[18]) Montgomery, the great war hero in Britain, had few friends in the States. Portrayed as one of the 'down to the last shoelace' school of generals, the American press attributed a longer than expected war to his excessive caution, a view heartily endorsed by the military establishment.

The one major point of agreement was to move five divisions over from Italy to strengthen Eisenhower's forces in the imminent battle for the Rhine. This finally put paid to one of Churchill's favoured diversionary tactics, to advance up through Italy to strike as deep as possible into eastern Europe to pre-empt any attempt by Russia to create satellite states answerable to Moscow.

The scene shifts to Yalta. There the Chiefs of Staff had little to do except watch over their political masters, hoping that their painfully laid military plans would not be disrupted by extraneous affairs of state. The omens were not good. Roosevelt was weak and getting weaker, prompting worries that he was not best able to represent American interests. His own staff noted a 'serious deterioration'[19] and Churchill's doctor reported that he 'was an utterly changed man . . . not only looking 20 years older but scarcely able to speak'.[20]

Allowing for the diagnosis of a known pessimist, it does seem to have been true that at best Roosevelt was capable of 'talking situations to a superficial conclusion'. Though in a better state than Roosevelt, Churchill too was frequently bed-ridden after a strenuous journey. Stalin alone was buoyant, taking pleasure in the certainty that Russia was winning the war and that the conference at Yalta was, above all, a Russian show. It started with the six-hour car journey from Saki airfield to Yalta, 'a boneshaking and extremely cold drive . . . over a mountain road with its rough surface and innumerable hair-pin bends'.[21] The purpose was to show at first hand the damage inflicted by the war in the east, something that could not be done from the air.

> The sight of wasted villages, fields littered with tanks and transports, gutted factories – the remnants of the two campaigns fought through the area that had claimed two and a half million lives in the Crimea alone – was a reminder of the devastation of Russia, the basis of Stalin's demands in Eastern Europe. Roosevelt and Churchill were moved by the panorama of destruction which, according to Stalin, was mild compared with what could be seen in the Ukraine.[22]

There followed the inevitable dinners, speeches and declarations of undying friendship washed down with prodigious quantities of vodka. There was a loose agenda for the formal sessions. The paramount objective was to agree to agree, to show the world that the Big Three were still as one in their determination to crush the

Third Reich. In consequence many key questions were glossed over by fair-sounding but unrealistic compromises. Poland was a case in point.

It has been described as the unsolvable problem. Britain had a clear commitment to do what it could to create a free Poland, secure from the attention of avaricious neighbours. It was, after all, why the country had gone to war in the first place. But Russia too had legitimate or, at least, irresistible demands to make on Polish territory. Never again must the Polish plain be open to an invader. There were two ways of preventing this. The first was to move the Russian frontier into eastern Poland, a modification that could be compensated by Poland encroaching on Germany. Since Stalin had made clear his territorial demands as early as 1942, when he had also laid claim to the Baltic states of Lithuania, Latvia and Estonia, nobody could say that they had not been warned. Stalin's second guarantee of security was more problematic. This was to have a government in Warsaw sensitive to Moscow's wishes. Interpreted by the London-based Polish government in exile to mean subservience to Moscow, opposition to Soviet interference was stubborn. With little support from Roosevelt, who seemed to think that the affairs of eastern Europe could be safely held over until Germany's surrender, it had been left to Churchill to try to find some accommodation between Stalin and the London Poles.

It was a hopeless task. Whenever a settlement was in sight one side or the other raised objections. By the time of Yalta, when Roosevelt was at last giving some attention to eastern Europe, it was too late for compromise. Given Russia's overwhelming military presence in Poland, Roosevelt and Churchill had no choice but to accept the 'provisional government now functioning', i.e. the handpicked Communists based in Lublin, as the core of the new regime. Stalin nodded through a concession that other Poles, including the exiled leaders in London, would be involved and that the Provisional Government of National Unity would soon hold 'free and unfettered elections'. Roosevelt believed him.

He was not alone. Usually perceptive observers found Stalin deeply impressive. In the British delegation, Harold Nicolson felt that Stalin could be trusted to keep his word, while Sir Alexander Cadogan, Churchill's private secretary, was fulsome in his praise for Uncle Joe.

> He is very quiet and restrained. On the first day he sat for the first hour and a half or so without saying a word – there was no call for him to do so. The President flapped about and the P.M. boomed, but Joe just sat taking it all in and being rather amused. When he did chip in, he never used a superfluous word, and spoke very much to the point. He's obviously got a very good sense of humour – and a rather quick temper! I have never known the Russians so easy and accommodating. In particular Joe has been extremely good. He *is* a great man.[23]

Confident that Stalin was 'gettable', Roosevelt remained convinced that the newly created United Nations would provide the framework for active cooperation with the two superpowers, plus Britain, China and, more dubiously, France able to sort out their problems and those of the rest of the world in an atmosphere of mutual regard. But even Roosevelt must have taken a deep breath when he signed up for the Declaration on Liberated Europe which, in theory, committed the Big Three to helping the freed nations 'to destroy the last vestiges of Nazism and Fascism and to create democratic conditions of their own choice'. The President lived just long enough to recognise the depth of cynicism measured by these words. In late March, sixteen Polish resistance leaders were lured to Moscow on the pretence of discussing the agreed broadening of the Lublin administration. Instead they ended up in the Lubianka prison where they were tortured into confessing to fabricated charges, including Poland's participation in a British-organised anti-Soviet bloc. Wounded feelings in Washington that Stalin could act so blatantly against the spirit of Yalta were aggravated by news that a puppet government had been set up in Soviet-occupied Rumania. But by then the diplomatic climate in Washington was changing fast. With Roosevelt's death and the advent of the Truman administration, unity between east and west was recognised as a sham; an artificial creation born of anti-Nazism which quickly disintegrated once Nazism had been eliminated.

Apart from the high-sounding declarations on the future of Europe, the talks at Yalta followed an agenda set by previous Allied conferences. For the military in attendance, it was a frustrating experience. 'I cannot recall that anything was achieved which could not have been equally well settled by the Combined Chiefs of Staff machinery in Washington, and the British and American Missions in Moscow,' wrote General Ismay.[24] All the hard strategic work had been done in Malta which is the way Roosevelt liked it since, in contrast to Stalin and Churchill, he had little to contribute on military matters beyond that fed to him by Marshall and other professional advisers. But this is not to say that the political decisions were of no military consequence. The Three gave formal approval to an existing plan for carving up a defeated Germany into occupation zones. Significantly, the Russian zone included Berlin, though the city itself was to be put under joint control. The President's acceptance that the Russians would be first into Berlin was not lost on Eisenhower who followed proceedings rather more closely than some of his generals who were still set on beating the Russians to the German capital.

For the rest, Russia signed up for the war in the Far East in return for territorial and other concessions that, for the time being, were kept under wraps. (Not quite the open diplomacy that Roosevelt was said to favour.) On the vexed question of reparations, the general principles were laid down that removals were to take place from the national wealth of Germany within two years of the end of the war so as to destroy its military potential; that there should be annual deliveries of goods from Germany 'for a period to be fixed'; and that German labour should be used in the reconstruction of war-devastated lands. A detailed plan was to be drawn up by a three-power Allied Reparations Commission sitting in Moscow, though this was never able to reconcile the conflict between the Soviet determination to milk Germany dry in order to make up Russia's war losses and British and American reluctance to pump assistance into western Germany to keep life going there while reparations went out on the other side to Russia. However, in the teeth of British resistance, Stalin secured a basis for reparations of a total sum of twenty billion dollars with 50 per cent going to the USSR. Was this a definite commitment? Russia later said it was. Britain and America denied it.

Churchill had his successes. He saw off without too much trouble Roosevelt's renewed attempt to incorporate the British Empire into the Atlantic Charter. It had taken some time for him to realise that when Roosevelt talked of nations having the right to choose their own government, he was including countries under British rule. When the truth dawned Churchill immediately crossed India off the agenda, acknowledging it as the country most vulnerable to Roosevelt's rhetoric. There was a sharp reaction too when Washington mooted the desirability of handing Hong Kong back to the Chinese. At Yalta, Churchill was able to take strength from Stalin's interpretation of the Atlantic Charter that did not preclude his own territorial ambitions. The breathtaking hypocrisy of Stalin speaking in support of an American proposal that all dependent territories be placed under international trusteeship allowed Churchill to hold forth in righteous indignation.

Churchill was on a hiding to nothing in standing up for French demands. De Gaulle had expected to use Yalta as a platform for national rehabilitation. But neither Roosevelt nor Stalin was ready for that. Both were dismissive of French claims to big power status and Roosevelt had a strong antipathy to de Gaulle as a devious and ungrateful ally. Churchill too was liable to lose patience with the assertive French leader ('Really, France has enough to do this winter and spring in trying to keep body and soul together, and cannot masquerade as a Great Power for the purpose of war.') but stood by his belief in a European future where a strong France balanced a German revival. Attracted to any idea that reduced the pressure on America to take care of a post-war Europe, Roosevelt agreed to France having its own German-occupation zone and to become the fourth member of the Allied Control Council for Germany. That was good enough for Churchill but not for de Gaulle who found it hard to imagine that any concession was anything but part of an anti-French plot hatched up by the Anglo-Saxons.

The publicity circus that elevated Yalta to a triumph of Allied unity was a masterpiece of self-deception. Roosevelt received floods of messages telling of the enthusiastic response to the publication of the Yalta communiqués in the United States. One of the cables quoted Herbert Hoover as saying, 'It will offer a great hope to the world.' William L. Shirer called it 'a landmark in human history'. The majority leader in the Senate regarded it as 'one of the most important steps ever taken to promote peace and happiness in the world'.

Churchill too was lauded with Lord Beaverbrook, the newspaper tycoon and close political associate, telling him, 'You now appear to your countrymen to be the greatest statesman as well as the greatest warrior.'[25] Even the normally sober-minded Harry Hopkins was moved to paeans of praise.

> We really believed in our hearts that this was the dawn of the new day we had all been praying for and talking about for so many years. We were absolutely certain that we had won the first great victory of the peace – and, by 'we', I mean *all* of us, the whole civilized human race. The Russians had proved that they could be reasonable and farseeing and there wasn't any doubt in the minds of the President or any of us that we could live with them and get along with them peacefully for as far into the future as any of us could imagine. But Hopkins did have one worry. I think we all had in our minds the reservation that we could not foretell what the results would be if anything should happen to Stalin. We felt sure that we could count on him to be reasonable and sensible and understanding – but we never could be sure who or what might be out the back of him there in the Kremlin.

It did not take long for other doubts to set in. There were sharp exchanges between Washington and Moscow over reports of Russian ill-treatment of liberated American POWs. The complaints were brushed aside as unworthy of further inquiry. The refusal to allow American relief planes to land in Poland showed how much store the Russians put on the Yalta promise of joint action to help liberated countries. But even more disturbing was Russia's sabotage of negotiations in Italy where there were strong hints that the Germans were ready to surrender. The unequivocal ruling from Moscow was that no talks could be held if the Russians were not directly involved even, apparently, in a region where their interests were minimal. The counter-warning to the Americans not to meddle in affairs that were strictly Soviet suggested that Moscow wanted and expected to have it both ways.

Judged at sixty years' distance, the exhilaration at Yalta at the prospect of an imminent German collapse was understandable, as too was the Allied need to persuade the Germans that there was no chance of a divide and negotiate settlement. But the representation of Yalta as the high tide of Allied unity was a nonsense. The reality was, at best, the cobbling together of a bunch of fair-sounding compromises which were dumped overboard before the Potsdam meeting of the three powers in July and August. At worst, Yalta created more problems than it solved. Ismay put it succinctly: 'From the gastronomical point of view, Yalta was enjoyable; from the social point of view, unnecessary; and from the political point of view, depressing.'[26]

With hindsight, there is no doubt that America could have been tougher without putting at risk an alliance that was every bit as important to Russia as to the western allies. The Red Army was still dependent on American handouts though it was hard to know it, such was the absence of any show of gratitude. Yet Roosevelt and, to a lesser extent, Churchill put themselves out to be accommodating, even knowing that Stalin saw it as weakness. In a sense, they were victims of their own national propaganda which had metamorphosed Stalin from a brutal dictator into warm and cuddly Uncle Joe, everybody's best pal. A month after the German surrender, a Gallup Poll survey found that 45 per cent of Americans felt that Russia could be trusted to cooperate with the US. By September, the proportion had risen to 54 per cent.[27] But public sentiment might just as easily have switched the other way if press criticism of Soviet objectives, not to mention Soviet atrocities in eastern Europe, had been as free as it was over Churchill's intervention in Greece. When he sent in British troops to help frustrate a Communist takeover, the American newspapers were quick to accuse him of imperialist ambitions.

Aside from an ill-defined hope that America and Russia might together bring in the age of peaceful co-existence, Roosevelt had two other reasons for trying over-hard to keep Stalin on side. The first was the worry that, if antagonised, Stalin might follow the precedent of 1940 and sign a separate peace. How he might have done this without incurring the wrath of the Red Army, now on the verge of taking revenge on a demonised enemy, is hard to say. A second more practical reason was the assumption that Russian help would be needed in that other American war, against Japan. The toll of the island-hopping campaigns in the Pacific convinced the American army that a powerful ally was required to defeat the Japanese in their Manchurian vassal empire and in the Japanese home islands.

What is intriguing is that the solution to ending the war with Japan, the one that was eventually adopted, was already known to Roosevelt. As early as 1938, when Hitler invaded Austria, putting the world on red alert, two German chemists, Otto Hahn and Fritz Strassmann, found evidence that a uranium nucleus could be 'fusioned' by the impact of a diminutive neutron, releasing ten million times more energy per gram of material than any chemical reaction. Shortly afterwards Leo Szilard, a Hungarian physicist, suggested that if the fusion of one uranium nucleus shook loose several neutrons in addition to the two large fusion halves, then each of these new neutrons could fusion another uranium nucleus nearby, setting in motion an explosive chain reaction. It was Einstein who made Roosevelt aware of the awesome military possibilities, warning him that a practical demonstration of atomic theory was a matter of urgency unless he was prepared for the Germans to get there first. The result was the setting up of the secret Los Alamos laboratory in the desert of New Mexico.

Britain, too, was aware that the creation of an atomic bomb was only a matter of time. Churchill's first instinct was to compete with the US on equal terms but it was soon made clear that any attempt to operate independently would cause a 'major dislocation in war production'.[28] Instead, in June 1942, he proposed to Roosevelt a joint research plan. No minutes were kept of this discussion but Roosevelt gave informal approval to a 'sharing of results as equal partners'.[29] The subject came up again at Casablanca in January 1943. By now Churchill was worried by the American interpretation of sharing which seemed to suggest that the results of British research should be handed over on demand but with little in the way of return. The blame was put on the US War Department which had taken over responsibility for the last stages of design and production of an atomic bomb. The need for security was given as the not altogether convincing excuse for keeping the British out of the picture. Roosevelt accepted the justice of the British complaint. A new deal was struck whereby no secrets were to be withheld from either side and, significantly, no communication made to third parties except by mutual consent.[30]

By the time the leaders gathered in Yalta, the US was on the verge of perfecting an atomic bomb with an explosive power equivalent to at least 30,000 tons of TNT. But while Roosevelt had shared this knowledge with Edward Stettinus, his Secretary of State and chief adviser at Yalta, swearing him to secrecy, he does not seem to have thought through the implications. True, the A Bomb was still untested but while nothing could be taken for granted enough was known to suggest that America would soon have the capacity to knock Japan out of the war without Soviet assistance. On the other hand, if Japan why not Germany? If Stalin got to know of the A Bomb, would he not have insisted that it be used against the Reich, achieving at once the end of Nazism, the destruction of Germany as an industrial economy and the prevention of further sacrifice of Russian lives? Here was reason enough for Roosevelt to keep silent on the A Bomb. To venture weaponry of such destructive power in central Europe was to court unacceptable risks. How strange then that towards the end of the formal session at Yalta, the President 'in a casual manner spoke of revealing the secret to Stalin'.[31] His reasoning was yet more curious, that if de Gaulle got to hear about it, he 'would certainly double cross us with Russia'. Churchill was adamant. The A Bomb was an Anglo-American affair and should be kept that way as long as possible. Though too polite, or too cautious, to say so openly, Churchill must have wondered at the President's judgement. Was he too ill to function?

The official business over, Churchill was keen to get away from Yalta. He had in mind a brief rest on the *Franconia*, waiting for him at Sevastopol, before flying to Athens where the government helped to power by British forces was beginning to get a grip. The next stop after that was London. But his plans were changed when, on the day the conference broke up, he was 'flabbergasted'[32] to hear that Roosevelt was intending a high-powered incursion into the Middle East, a region where Britain was used to having the last word.

Three successive meetings had been arranged between Roosevelt and the Kings of Egypt and Saudi Arabia and Emperor Haile Selassie of Ethiopia. Churchill now decided that he too would go to Cairo to confer with the Arab sovereigns. The official story was that he wanted an opportunity for a concluding chat with Roosevelt but he was more interested in discovering if, as he suspected, there was a deep-laid American plot to supplant Britain in the Middle East. As it turned out he had good reason to be worried, although it took some time for him to realise that a great commercial prize was about to be snatched away.

Having flown from Saki across the Black Sea to Egypt, the President and his advisers settled in on board the *Quincy*, anchored in Great Bitter Lake, near Cairo, and prepared to receive their royal visitors. Fleet Admiral William D. Leahy, Roosevelt's Chief of Staff, was in the official welcoming party.

> King Farouk of Egypt was the first to arrive, and I met him at the landing on February 13th. He was accompanied by several of his chief advisers and the United States Minister to Egypt, S. Pinckney Tuck. King Farouk was a young man of twenty-five who spoke perfect English and, in the uniform of an Admiral of the Fleet, looked like an Englishman.[33]

Little of consequence was discussed and Leahy was left with the impression of a 'friendly social visit' which was later sealed by a symbolic declaration of war by Egypt on Germany and Japan. As an early warning that following the American lead could be dangerous for Arab politicians, the Egyptian Prime Minister, Ahmen Maher Pasha, who made the official announcement, was shot dead by an assassin who confessed that the crime was committed in the cause of Fascism.

Next on board the *Quincy* was Emperor Haile Selassie of Ethiopia. 'The "Lion of Judah" was a very dignified, small, black man who speaks and understands French and English, but who talked with the President in Amharic through an interpreter. I was told that the ruler of Abyssinia expected to be addressed as "His Imperial Majesty".'[34] This meeting had more substance. 'Roosevelt told me later that Haile Selassie discussed with him the possible disposition of captured territory, particularly Italian possessions in North Africa.'[35] But all these sessions, with all the accompanying pageantry, were but a preliminary to the real purpose of Roosevelt's diversion to the eastern Mediterranean.

On the morning of February 14th, the President's daughter Anna Boettiger, who had been with him for the entire trip, was sent ashore to go shopping in Cairo. This was not by her wish. King Abdul Aziz Ibn Abdul Rahman al Faisal al Saud of Saudi Arabia was expected and he had made it known that no women could be seen in his company. The reason why Roosevelt was happy to abide by what he would normally have dismissed as an archaic custom could be told in one word – oil. The American connection with Saudi Arabia had started in 1933 when the Standard Oil Company had won the concession to begin exploration. By 1938 the area covered by the deal had increased to 440,000 square miles. At this point there was little indication of how much, if any, oil was under the desert. But it was not long before Standard knew that it had chanced on a major find. So colossal were the estimated reserves that three other American oil companies were encouraged to join a consortium which in 1944 became known as Aramco.[36] By now the American government was taking a strong interest. If the experience of modern warfare proved anything it was the dependence of the fighting machines on a plentiful supply of oil.

According to Leahy, in mid-September 1943 the American Joint Chiefs were 'anxious that everything possible be done to give the US access to the Saudi Arabian oil', emphasising 'that in the unhappy event of another war in Europe, possession or access to Near Eastern oil supplies were essential to any successful campaign by the Americans'.[37] Roosevelt despatched America's most eminent geologist, Everette Lee De Golyer, to the Middle East to assess the energy potential not just in Saudi Arabia but also in Kuwait, Iraq and Iran. His report was dramatic. 'The centre of gravity of world oil production is shifting from the Gulf-Caribbean area to the Middle East and the Persian Gulf area and is likely to continue to shift until it is firmly established in that area.'[38]

There were token protests from London at interference in a British sphere of influence but there was no question that the Americans were in the best position to exploit the opportunity and when Roosevelt took a strong line the British government went quiet.[39] Accommodating King Saud was a more delicate matter. Ibn Saud had only recently assumed royal authority. A member of the Wahhabi sect, a puritanical branch of Islam, he had led a conquest of tribal territories neighbouring his own province, the Najd. In 1932 these were forged into a unity called Saudi Arabia. The oil was irrelevant to King Saud except as a source of revenue for his hard-pressed exchequer but if his devotion to pure Islam was no deterrent to dealing with western companies, there were strict limits to his tolerance, as Roosevelt waiting for his guest for lunch on the *Quincy* was about to discover.

King Saud and his forty-two-strong retinue, all dressed in white, made a grand spectacle. Flanked by ten sabre-armed guards chosen from the leading tribes of Saudi Arabia, he was accompanied by the Royal Fortune-teller, the Royal Food-taster, the Chief Server of the Ceremonial Coffee and the Royal Purse-bearer. It was, noted Leahy, 'like something transported by magic from the Middle Ages'.[40]

Did Roosevelt realise what kind of man he was entertaining? Not according to Harry Hopkins who thought that the President had failed to take into account the monarch's antipathy to the

Jews. The Palestinian question was introduced by Roosevelt almost as an afterthought to the main business of sealing the agreement on oil.

> When the President asked Ibn Saud to admit some more Jews into Palestine, indicating that it was such a small percentage of the total population of the Arab world, he was greatly shocked when Ibn Saud, without a smile, said 'No.' Ibn Saud emphasised the fact that the Jews in Palestine were successful in making the countryside bloom only because American and British capital had been poured in in millions of dollars and said if those same millions had been given to the Arabs they could have done quite as well. He also said that there was a Palestine army of Jews all armed to the teeth and he remarked that they did not seem to be fighting the Germans but were aiming at the Arabs. He stated plainly that the Arab world would not permit a further extension beyond the commitment already made for future Jewish settlement in Palestine. He inferred that the Arabs would take up arms before they would consent to that and he, as religious leader of the Arab world, must, naturally, support the Arabs in and about Palestine. The President seemed not to comprehend what Ibn Saud was saying to him for he brought the question up two or three times more and each time Ibn Saud was more determined than before.[41]

Still Roosevelt seemed unable to understand. Promises were made on guaranteeing the security of the Saudi dynasty as long as the oil flowed westwards. There was talk of a vast public works programme to help raise living standards in the region. Roosevelt made no objection to King Saud's autocratic rule. However, when the President returned to the subject of Palestine, expressing the hope that the Arabs and the Jews would get along together:

> Ibn Saud politely but firmly gave the President a lesson in the history of Palestine from the Arab point of view. The King, with great dignity and courtesy and with a smile, said that if Jews from outside Palestine continued to be imported with their foreign financial backing and their higher standards of living, they would make trouble for the Arab inhabitants. When this happened, as a good Arab and a True

Believer, he would have to take the Arab side against the Jews, and he intended to do so.[42]

So it was that a deal was struck that was to have repercussions far outlasting all the agreements at Yalta. The oil that was to fuel the Cold War was guaranteed but at the long-term expense of peace in the Middle East.

We can only speculate on Churchill's reaction had he known how far Roosevelt had compromised US foreign policy. In his own meeting with King Saud, Churchill put in a word for the Jews but was rebuffed. Since he did not press the point, it can be assumed that he, like Roosevelt, was prepared to take a chance on Jewish immigration into Israel, hoping that the Arabs would eventually be reconciled to the creation of a Jewish state. The question was not discussed when he lunched with Roosevelt on the *Quincy*. Joined by members of the two families, 'It was a pleasant social gathering in the President's cabin, and I do not recall that affairs of state intruded into the conversation.'[43]

On March 1st, Saudi Arabia declared war on Germany and Japan. The newspapers barely gave it a mention.

6

War in the Air

As Roosevelt and Churchill celebrated their departure from Yalta, 1,500 tons of high explosive and a corresponding weight of incendiaries fell on Dresden.

The sirens started wailing across the city at just after 9.40 on the evening of February 13th. Twenty minutes later, flares lit up the sky and ten minutes after that the first explosions rocked the huddled buildings and narrow streets of the old town. Then the fires started. There followed fourteen hours of carefully orchestrated attacks which razed a medieval city with its theatres and museums to a heap of cinders and rotting corpses. Nobody knows how many thousand civilians were burned, blasted or suffocated to death. When whole families were incinerated, including many who had lately arrived in the city seeking refuge from the blood-bath in the east, a census of the dead was all but impossible. First guesses put the casualty total at over 200,000. This was later reduced to around 50,000. But who knows? Whatever the true figure it is too clinical to convey reality. The real measure of the horror only comes across in the testimony of those like Margaret Freyer who witnessed and survived.

> Because of the flying sparks and the fire-storm I couldn't see anything at first. A witches' cauldron was waiting for me out there: no street, only rubble nearly a metre high, glass, girders, stones, craters. I tried to get rid of the sparks by constantly patting them off my coat. It was useless. I stopped doing it, stumbled, and someone behind me called out, 'Take your coat off, it's started to burn.' In the pervading extreme heat I hadn't even noticed. I took off the coat and dropped it.
>
> Next to me a woman was screaming continually, 'My den's burning down, my den's burning down,' and dancing in the street. As I go

on, I can still hear her screaming but I don't see her again. I run, I stumble, anywhere. I don't even know where I am any more. I've lost all sense of direction because all I can see is three steps ahead.

Suddenly I fall into a big hole – a bomb crater, about six metres wide and two metres deep, and I end up down there lying on top of three women. I shake them by their clothes and start to scream at them, telling them they must get out of here – but they don't move any more. I believe I was severely shocked by this incident; I seemed to have lost all emotional feeling. Quickly, I climbed across the women, pulled my suitcase after me, and crawled on all fours out of the crater.

To my left I suddenly see a woman. I can see her to this day and shall never forget. She carries a bundle in her arms. It is a baby. She runs, she falls, and the child flies in an arc into the fire. It's only my eyes which take this in; I myself feel nothing. The woman remains lying on the ground, completely still. Why? What for? I don't know, I just stumble on. The fire-storm is incredible, there are calls for help and screams from somewhere but all around is one single inferno. I hold another wet handkerchief in front of my mouth, my hands and my face are burning; it feels as if the skin is hanging down in strips.[1]

Emerging from the nightmare, Margaret spent the next day searching for her fiancé.

I looked for him amongst the dead, because hardly any living beings were to be seen anywhere. What I saw is so horrific that I shall hardly be able to describe it. Dead, dead, dead everywhere. Some completely black like charcoal. Others completely untouched, lying as if they were asleep. Women in aprons, women with children sitting in the trams as if they had just nodded off. Many women, many young girls, many small children, soldiers who were only identifiable as such by the metal buckles on their belts, almost all of them naked. Some clinging to each other in groups as if they were clawing at each other.

From some of the debris poked arms, heads, legs, shattered skulls. The static water tanks were filled up to the top with dead human beings, with large pieces of masonry lying on top of that again. Most people looked as if they had been inflated, with large yellow and

brown stains on their bodies. People whose clothing were still glowing
. . . I think I was incapable of absorbing the meaning of this cruelty
any more, for there were also so many little babies, terribly muti-
lated; and all the people lying so close together that it looked as if
someone had put them down there, street by street, deliberately.[2]

This was terror bombing on a scale beyond ordinary imagination. What happened that night of February 13th and in the early
hours of the 14th has come to symbolise the inanity of total war.
How did such a monstrous error of judgement come about?

The Anglo-Americans at Yalta were keen to prove to Stalin that
Russian sacrifices on the eastern front were not the only means
of promoting the Allied cause. There had been hard fighting up
to the Rhine but the promised offensive across the river was still
in preparation. What could be done meanwhile to lighten the pressure on the Red Army? The obvious answer was to intensify air
attacks on German supply lines. With the Luftwaffe no longer a
credible fighting force, British and American bombers had a free
range of targets with only sporadic enemy flak to trouble them.
One of the least depressing statistics to come out of Dresden was
that less than 1 per cent of the 1,200 aircraft that took part in
the raid fell victim to German defences.

On questions of air strategy, Britain held the initiative. This
followed from the difference between the American and British
command structure. The RAF was able to keep itself apart from
its two sister services, giving it the edge over the American air force
or rather the American Army Air Force, which came into play not
so much as an independent arm, capable of taking on the enemy
on its own terms, but as a support for ground operations. So it
was that for the war in the air Britain was able to exert an influence out of all proportion to its real strength, an influence made
yet stronger by the dominance of Arthur 'Bomber' Harris. A flying
veteran of the Great War, and from February 1942, Commander-
in-Chief of Bomber Command, Harris was convinced that the war
could be won from the air. He was not alone.

Devastation raining down from swarms of flying machines had

been the stuff of science fiction since the turn of the century. H.G. Wells had predicted *The War in the Air* in 1908 and in his *Things to Come*, published two years before the Hitler war, a city called Everytown was destroyed by a fleet of giant bombers. Fiction became reality when, in April 1937, the Luftwaffe bombed Guernica on behalf of the Spanish Nationalists. It was, said the American ambassador in London, 'a practice for the bombing of London and Paris'.[3] The deeper implications were not lost on the military mind. 'The object of raids like this,' wrote Basil Liddell Hart, 'is to smash at a blow the morale of a population . . . The spirit of the population is the military objective.'[4] The experts exchanged increasingly dramatic estimates of the likely civilian casualties caused by mass air attacks on big cities. A secret report from the Committee of Imperial Defence suggested that an initial air raid on London would last sixty days and kill 600,000. This and other doomsday predictions raised the inevitable question, what if we got in first?

Of the air strategists who argued that in any future war squadrons of bombers could deliver the decisive blow Harris was the most forceful. In blunt language he made his points. Troops deprived of essential supplies were liable to become disaffected with their leaders; likewise civilians driven from their burning homes. With the collapse of authority, peace would soon follow. There were those who saw in this neat formula a none too subtle attempt by the junior service to have a bigger say in overall military strategy. Others opposed unrestricted aerial bombardment as an abomination that would destroy European civilisation. Two weeks after the declaration of war with Germany, Prime Minister Neville Chamberlain promised: 'Whatever the lengths to which others may go His Majesty's Government will never resort to the deliberate attack on women and children, and other civilians for purposes of mere terrorism.' Chamberlain's successor, of necessity many would argue, took a more pragmatic view. Churchill's government 'reserved the right to themselves of taking any action they considered appropriate'.

But what was appropriate? The Battle of Britain (September 1940 to May 1941), in which 40,000 civilians were killed and two million homes destroyed, provided verifiable evidence of the effects of terror bombing. It was not what Harris and his friends expected. Solly Zuckerman, one of Churchill's scientific advisers, carried out the first systematic study of air raids. His Bomb Census of Luftwaffe targets such as Hull and Coventry led him to conclude that blanket bombing could not win a war. As an instrument of battle it was ineffective, even against industrial centres where production, as in Coventry, might be cut as little as 5 per cent after suffering an air attack averaging fourteen tons of bombs per square mile. Zuckerman advocated specific objectives such as transportation centres to maximise the disruption of military planning.[5]

Harris, an undoubtedly charismatic war leader, but a man of few refinements and even less subtlety, was not persuaded. He dismissed Zuckerman, a biologist who had carried out research on baboons at London Zoo, as a student 'of the sexual aberrations of the higher apes', a boffin who clearly had no role to play in the business of war. More to his liking was the advice offered by another Churchill confidant. Professor Lindemann (later Lord Cherwell) recommended a 'barn door' offensive against the working-class districts of eighty-eight German towns of over 100,000 population.

Since, later, Harris took the brunt of the criticism for the wholesale destruction of German cities (of all the senior wartime commanders, he had to wait longest for official recognition of his services), it is only fair to acknowledge that for much of the war the distinction between precision and saturation bombing was largely theoretical. When it came to attacking industrial centres, already established policy when Harris took over Bomber Command, he had no choice but to target urban concentrations with all the attendant risks of civilian casualties.

> The Command had had no radar navigational aids, though the first of these was just being issued, to enable the bomber crews to navigate or find the target without seeing the ground, and it had become glaringly obvious that the average crew in average weather could not find their way to the target by visual means alone. It had also become obvious to all who had studied Bomber Command's previous

operations that it would be necessary to concentrate the force in time and space, both for its own protection against enemy defences, and to ensure the destruction of the target. But the tactical and technical problems involved in achieving such a concentration had scarcely been tackled, nor was it realised what degree of concentration was necessary; it was hoped eventually to reach a total of a hundred aircraft over the target per hour. There was also a serious deficiency of trained crews.[6]

Harris was further hampered by the aircraft at his disposal. The Wellingtons and Blenheims which made up the bulk of Bomber Command were lumbering heavyweights which by day fell easy victim to German air defences. Forced to attack by night, the chances of hitting anything of direct military importance were remote. But even with more effective bombers like the Avro Lancaster and technological breakthroughs such as the electronic beam for night navigation, there was still a wide overlap between precision and saturation bombing. A pilot setting out with a specific brief but unable, as happened all too often, to find his target was told to off-load his bombs anyway. What, if anything, was hit was often a matter of chance.

At the start, Churchill was among Harris's strongest supporters. It seemed to him that Harris offered the only practical way of showing that Britain was capable of fighting back. With a land war in Europe still a distant possibility, the one hope of reversing German fortunes was by launching 'an absolutely devastating, exterminating attack by heavy bombers on the Nazi homeland'.

With the backing of Air Marshal Charles Portal, Chief of British Air Staff, Harris mounted a succession of raids against targets in northern Germany, concentrating on the heavy industrial centres of the Ruhr. 'We are going to bomb Germany incessantly,' declared Harris. 'The day is coming when we will put over such a force that the Germans will scream for mercy.'

Still reeling from the blitz on London, the British public warmed to the chance of getting some of their own back. In late May 1942 Harris staged what the press headlined as 'The Greatest Air Raid in History'. Over a thousand bombers released 1,500 tons of high explosive and incendiaries over Cologne, all but wiping out the city centre. But aside from boosting morale at home, the bombing of Cologne and other soft targets did not achieve their objective. There was no hint of a battered population turning on its leaders or even of any appreciable impact on Germany's war production.

The lesson was not lost on the Americans. From August 1942 the US Eighth Air Force under General Carl Spaatz was operational from Britain with its B-17 Flying Fortresses and Liberators. But any hopes that Harris might have had of enlisting American support for saturation bombing were soon disappointed. Attacks on defence-less civilians were not well received in Washington. While the USAAF favoured daytime raids on identifiable military targets, Harris held to his conviction that city bombing was the only means of forcing Germany to submission. Churchill stayed loyal. Really, he had no choice. To have fired Harris would have been to slap the face of public opinion and its cheerleaders in the popular press. A sure sign of what would happen if Harris was taken down a peg came when Vera Brittain, a radical thinker who had converted to pacifism after her fiancé and only brother had been killed in the First World War, published *Massacre by Bombing*, a plea to the Allies to stop mass bombing. She was denounced in the House of Commons, in the press and from the pulpit. Even Roosevelt found time to put in a bad word.[7] Of other opinion leaders who stepped in, only Bishop George Bell openly sympathised with Vera Brittain but he was already on record as an opponent of carpet bombing and he too was pilloried as a traitor. But maybe something of what they said got through to the people who mattered.

After Roosevelt and Churchill met at Casablanca in January 1943, their directive for a joint bombing programme gave comfort to both Spaatz and Harris. Precision targets such as oil refineries and transportation centres were to be given priority but there was still the explicit aim of 'undermining the morale of the German people to a point where their capacity for armed resistance is fatally weakened'. Harris chose to take this to mean a free hand in mounting a concerted offensive against German cities. When Spaatz demurred, Harris argued that the USAAF alternative of mounting daytime raids against military targets was no alternative at all.

To reduce losses the Americans developed the combat box, a formation of fifty-four bombers able to direct firepower in any direction. Having frustrated the attention of the German Messerschmitts, the trick was to trigger a simultaneous release of the collective bomb load. But wasn't this area bombing by another name?

Meanwhile, Harris raised the stakes. In late July 1943, Hamburg became the first victim of a new development in aerial warfare – the fire-storm. Operation Gomorrah had the RAF drop thousands of incendiaries to create a tornado-like column of hot air, two miles high. The devastation was total. Air raid shelters built of solid concrete were no protection. The heat generated inside them was so intense that all that remained of the occupants was a layer of grey ash.

By now Harris was beyond argument. 'War is a drug . . . peddled by mythmakers,' writes Chris Hodges in a recent book. 'Even with its destruction and carnage, it can give us what we long for in life. It can give us purpose, meaning, a reason for living.'[8] Harris had discovered his reason for being and he was not about to give it up. Hamburg was followed by Berlin. Harris vowed to destroy the capital 'from end to end' but though damage was extensive Bomber Command did not deliver the knockout blow Harris had promised. With German air defences much stronger than anticipated, he was forced to call off the offensive. He now had vociferous critics close to the Prime Minister. Moreover, Portal was beginning to have doubts. Too many mistakes were being made. The raid on Nuremberg in March 1944 showed just how badly things could go wrong. Of the 782 Lancasters and Halifaxes that took off, ninety-five were brought down, many before they had even crossed the Rhine. Those that did get through were blown off course by high winds and were further confused by low cloud. The result – Nuremberg escaped virtually unscathed while towns and villages up to sixty miles away took the punishment.

By late 1944 US Eighth Air Force, now under the command of General James Doolittle, had the planes and the technology to support the American strategy of selective bombing. Operating out of East Anglia were 2,000 heavy bombers, two-thirds of them 13-17 Flying Fortresses which could carry fourteen 500-pound bombs. When flying at full strength the procession of bombers was an awesome sight extending seventy miles, all the way from the east of England to the Dutch coast.

> British Bomber Command did all the night bombing and the Americans did the day bombing. Their aeroplanes were Flying Fortresses – very large machines indeed. It was quite a sight to watch the Americans marshalling their forces for a bombing raid on Germany. You could look all around and from north, south, east and west the Flying Fortresses would rise from the aerodromes in flights, squadrons and wings. They would rise like a swarm of insects and orbit their airfields whilst more and more rose into the sky. After about an hour when the airfields would have hundreds of circling aircraft over them they would all merge together in one vast swarm, perhaps a thousand aeroplanes, and move out over the North Sea. They didn't fly out in a stream; it was one great black cloud of aero-planes. It was very quiet after they had gone. Some hours later they would return, some flying on three or even two engines with black smoke trailing behind. They would disperse to their various airfields and commence the orbiting procedure prior to landing.[9]

In support were long-range Mustang fighters. Once over enemy territory, the recently introduced radar bombsight gave a better than evens chance of hitting the designated target.

Allied air supremacy was now pretty well an accepted fact, on both sides. The Luftwaffe was exhausted of men if not machines. Having been in combat almost continuously from Britain to the Soviet Union and from North Africa to Norway, there were no longer any human reserves to draw on. Most of the veteran pilots were dead and their replacements, hurriedly and inadequately trained, lacked the skill to make best use of the new fighters coming off the production line. By mid-1944 the life expectancy of a German pilot fresh out of flying school was just thirty days.

German air defences were still capable of inflicting damage but even where there were no guns to throw up the deadly radar-controlled flak, ways were found to divert or fool the enemy. Seen from the air, the 'scarecrow', a gush of flare and smoke to simulate a bomber being shot down, was often enough to make an inexperienced pilot turn for home. With railways a priority target, train drivers were under orders to call a halt whenever an Allied plane was spotted, the hope being that a stationary train would be assumed to be empty and not worth attacking. Another ruse was for smoke canisters to be let off to fool the bombers that they had made a direct hit. Many Allied bombs were wasted on dummy factories, military installations and refineries. But it was a measure of the desperation now felt by the German command that Field Marshal Model, head of Army Group B, put his name to an order, couched more like an appeal, for the men of the Wehrmacht to play their part in combating the threat from the skies.

TO ALL DRIVERS AND PASSENGERS.

WHOEVER CAMOUFLAGES LIVES LONGER!

CARBINES AND MARCH DISCIPLINE VERSUS STRAFING!

10 DAYS SPECIAL FURLOUGH FOR SHOOTING DOWN ENEMY STRAFER!

The Anglo-American ground-attack aircraft are the modern high-waymen. They are searching not only for columns of traffic, they are hunting down every gasoline truck, every truck with ammunition.

Our fighters and anti-aircraft have had considerable success during the days of the great winter battles. But fighters and anti-aircraft cannot be everywhere.

. . . EVERY SOLDIER CAN AND MUST JOIN IN THE FIGHT AGAINST GROUND ATTACKERS! . . .

SPECIAL FAVOURS WILL BE SHOWN SUCCESSFUL GUNNERS AND UNITS. EACH SOLDIER WHO KNOCKS DOWN AN ENEMY STRAFER WITH HIS INFANTRY WEAPON RECEIVES 10 DAYS SPECIAL FURLOUGH! UNITS WHICH HAVE BEEN PARTICULARLY SUCCESSFUL IN SHOOTING DOWN ENEMY GROUND-ATTACKING AIRCRAFT WITH INFANTRY WEAPONS WILL RECEIVE SPECIAL RATION ALLOTMENTS!

Therefore: SEEK COVER FIRST,

Then: FIRE AWAY![10]

Differences between Harris and his superiors were exacerbated by Eisenhower's deputy, Air Marshal Sir Arthur Tedder, who urged a combined American and British bombing campaign to deprive the German war machine of its remaining oil supplies. Harris was dismissive but when outvoted tried to have it both ways, agreeing reluctantly to attack the Ruhr and its oil refineries while continuing to hammer German cities.

While the US Eighth Air Force and the US Fifteenth Air Force operating out of northern France went after the German industrial lifeblood, Harris still had his sights on the big targets. In October 1944, Bomber Command gave its attention to Duisburg, described by briefing officers in emotively exaggerated terms as 'the largest inland port in the world and an arsenal of the Reich'. It was the greatest single attack against a German city since the start of the war. Four thousand five hundred tons of bombs were dropped and, as Harris proudly pointed out, it was done in broad daylight. BBC reporter Richard Dimbleby saw it happen:

> A year ago it would have been near suicide to appear over the Ruhr in daylight – a trip by night was something to remember uncomfortably for a long time. To-day as the great broad stream of Lancasters and Halifaxes crossed the frontier of Germany, there was not an aircraft of the Luftwaffe to be seen in the sky, only the twisting and criss-crossing vapour trails of our own Spitfires and Mustangs protecting us far above and on the flanks.

After it was over Dimbleby was left thinking, 'that not only in the smoke and rubble of Duisburg, but deeper in the heart of Germany, there must be men charged with the defence of the Reich whose hearts to-night are filled with dread and despair'.[11]

A fortnight later it was the town of Cologne – again. The press was told that an all-out attack was justified to remove 'the most important forward base and collecting point for the German army in the field', a dubious proposition since Bomber Command had all but wrecked the city in 1942. Ah, but Cologne was only forty miles ahead of the US First Army so, it was argued, it had to be taken out once and for all. The Pathfinders whose job it was to pinpoint the attack by dropping red, green and yellow flares did so over the city centre.

> Cologne has been shattered and set on fire not only by British heavy bombers, but by American Flying Fortresses and by our own little Mosquitoes carrying big bombs. To-day, after last night's attack, the city is a shambles. This week I've been seeing large-scale photographs of Cologne. There is acre upon acre of complete devastation, street after street where life has died and the powdered rubble that was a house has been swept aside and banked up to leave a passage clear. From one end of the city to the other, you can count the buildings that have not been shattered on your fingers. Whole blocks have vanished; whole suburbs lie tumbled to the ground. There is nowhere to live and hardly anywhere to work in Cologne, any more.[12]

The wonder of it all was that the 700-year-old cathedral, though heavily scarred, remained standing, a tribute to medieval builders.

In all Cologne suffered 262 air raids. Over 90 per cent of the city was laid waste, half a million citizens were evacuated and 20,000 died. Forty years after the end of the war Cologne's Historisches Archiv collected together the memories of those who had come through the bombing to witness the entry by Anglo-American troops into what was left of the city.

To keep himself relatively sane, JK, a fifty-year-old gas worker, kept a simple diary.

> Thursday 8.3.45
> We have had no radio for weeks, no newspaper for a week, no-one really knows what's happening, whether the front is on the west or east side of the Rhine. As usual lots of rumours, a great confusion. No civilian administration, lootings, etc. There is nothing in the shops, not even with food tokens, rarely is there something and then as usual I don't get anything – I am life's stepchild.

> Friday 9.3.45
> Last night was fairly quiet. Isolated artillery fire during the day. The Americans are supposed to have crossed the Rhine somewhere between Bonn and Koblenz. No-one really knows where the front is

here. Nobody would have missed me if I had died in an air raid or some other way in the past few weeks. Not even now – away from the family, away from home. Up to now I've been writing on a piece of cardboard. My writing reflects my constitution.

Saturday 10.3.45
I'm writing my report as long as I can because I can't write anyone a letter and I want to keep track of the days. Today someone said they'd heard Goebbels on the radio, saying all that's left of Cologne is the red mob and the rabble . . . Should my life be blown out in some way and you find these scribblings, then you will have a rough idea of how I spent my final hours. I have been feeling absolutely miserable. My wife and children are gone, I don't know if the Russians are already here . . .

Sunday 11.3.45
Last night was relatively calm . . . Did some washing and cleaning yesterday – it was about time for it. I'd like to dig the garden and put some potatoes in. We could use them next year, provided I'm still around . . .

Wednesday 9.5.45
Today, at one minute past midnight, the ceasefire began. After almost six years of murder. Now it's as if we are all criminals. Now we are guilty for the crimes committed by the top ten thousand. We – especially – we should have known what was going on. It's always the little people who are to blame.[13]

At whatever age, staying in Cologne was to risk being rounded up for military duties. One young teenager manned an anti-aircraft gun in the Cathedral Square for forty-eight hours without a break and would have gone on longer had not his mother shamed him in public by demanding of the officer in charge that he should allow her son some respite. Others who challenged authority, particularly when the Gestapo was involved, risked their lives. The firing squads were active in the cathedral bunker and an exhibition hall was turned into an execution shed where, it was said,

350 supposed deserters were hanged. 'In the last weeks of the war, they searched all the cellars in our district for people in hiding. To make matters simpler the Nazis simply fired into the cellars to chase people out. After the war I found one of their bullets in our cellar, embedded in an old cardboard box.'

But somehow in the midst of destruction, new life emerged. Margaret Muhr had not intended to get pregnant but it was too late to think about that.

Despite all the dangers we still somehow carried on, although there was suddenly neither water nor light anymore. Necessity is the mother of invention and our men tapped into a water pipe in the garden and made a little pump which provided us with enough of the precious wet stuff. Warned of water shortages, we filled empty vessels with sterilised water, so we would at least have some for the impending birth.

When the contractions really started, at regular intervals, something had to be done. They moved me from the communal room and bedded me down in the potato cellar. Uncle Peter told us that in the Russian camp of the Bayer company there was a woman who had assisted at several births – we had to find her. Father ordered 16-year-old Christa to accompany him on her bike. Sleepy and reluctant, she followed his order . . . Two hours later the two of them returned with the Russian. Aunt Mimi was boiling water and she sterilised the scissors from the sewing basket. While I made my last efforts tea-towels and bedsheets were torn up. Then you were born – and you were quite normal, which I hadn't expected. The vicar christened you in the safest corner of the church, safe from the bullets.[14]

Even with much enhanced chances of survival, Allied crews could be forgiven the gut fear of every new raid. 'Every time my plane roared down the runway I wondered if I would ever see that runway again,' recalls an American gunner. A comfort pack went some way to calm nerves.

Each airman carried on his person a map of all of Europe made of rice. If you were caught, just wad it up and eat it. We were even told that if we were shot down over Vienna and Munich what streetcar to catch in order to get in touch with resistance people. In the back-pack of each parachute was 50 $1.00 bills, a block of chocolate, fishhooks & line, and a new 45 calibre automatic pistol. But the two things you must not forget were your dog tags and a razor. If you were caught without tags, you would be executed as a spy and to be unshaven would get you caught real fast.[15]

Flak came in two kinds:

Two minutes from target, as the formation swung left to line up properly, I looked out left side of the plane and ahead. What I saw was what looked like an angry thundercloud. I had not seen anything like it before, so I called the navigator on the intercom and asked what it was. I will never forget his answer. He said you will know in a couple of minutes. It was flak being fired by 88 and 105 guns. The 88s caused shells to explode at a predetermined altitude. It formed a box which we had to fly through. The 105mm were shooting for a direct hit. You could see the 105s bursting above us because the shell burst was white instead of black from the 88s. We flew through the thickest and most destructive fire I had experienced up until that day.[16]

Flak was not the only distraction. Conditions inside an aircraft could be just as dangerous.

We were assigned the aircraft factory [in Vienna] as target this day. After we grouped and climbed to 33,000 feet, we encountered an almost unbearable condition. Our planes were not pressurized. In plain words, it was open. The outside and inside temperature was 55 degrees below zero. We had been on pure oxygen since approxi-mately 15,000 feet and the moisture we breathed out froze inside our oxygen masks making it necessary to hold your breath long enough to remove the mask, crush the ice inside, shake it and reapply it to your face. In an effort, everyone called in every 10 minutes over the intercom to repeat this procedure. Everyone checked in except the ball turret underneath the plane. He did not answer. Myself and another waist gunner went on portable oxygen. We had to disengage the ball turret so the door to it could be put in a position to open it and get him out. We administered pure oxygen and artificial respiration all the way back to base – nearly four hours – but he was pronounced dead on arrival. He was a replacement flyer. This was his second mission. We all rode with death every day we went out.[17]

There were occasions, seldom touched on in early post-war memoirs, when the strain of combat became too much. One way out was to fly to a neutral country such as Sweden or Switzerland where sanctuary was rarely if ever refused. In April 1944, fifty-two Eighth Air Force planes and their crews were lost in this way and dozens more followed in the next few months. That the RAF had fewer problems with deserters can be partly explained by the cultural differences between the Allies. While Britain was still gripped by a class structure which paid due respect to authority however misguided or incompetent, America was a much more open society where individuals of whatever rank felt free to express their views, and their fears. Stories like the following were told by stiff upper lip Brits to show that they had the martial edge on their transatlantic cousins. But with the passing of more than half a century, the underlying message does not quite ring true.

I was in Norwich on one occasion with three other chaps from 125 Squadron: Vernon Key, Alfie Crouch and George Irving. Now George Irving had somehow managed to get something in his left eye which made it very inflamed and painful. He had also acquired a nasty boil on his left wrist. The M.O. had given him a patch to put over his eye, held round his head by a tape, and had also put his left arm in a sling. Looking at him on his left side George Irving was the picture of a wounded hero.

We went into a café for afternoon tea and got a table near the wall. George sat next to the wall but turned sideways so that his bad left side was against the wall and his good right side to the table. I sat on what would have been his right side if he had been facing the table and the other two had the other two chairs. There was a party of American airmen at a nearby table – some seven or eight of them. They were drunk and completely demoralised. They were sprawled across their table or draped over their chairs and talking in loud voices. We kept hearing the phrase 'This goddam war'.

One of them came swaying across the room towards us and spoke to me. They had had enough of this goddam war and were not going to fly any more. I was invited to join their mutiny.

I was absolutely horrified at the thought of what punishment the American Air Force might inflict on American airmen who, not only were mutinous, but had invited British Officers to join them. I decided the best thing was not hear what was said so I sat still and didn't let on. Also I thought it was up to Vernon Key to take the lead if necessary, he being a Squadron Leader was the senior officer present. Having failed with me, the American then tried Alfie Crouch with the same negative result and then approached Vernon Key. During this incident George Irving had sat still with his good right side to the table. He now turned round and showed his bad left side. The American was struck dumb at this sudden appearance of a wounded hero all bandaged up. He ceased his diatribe and one of his friends then came over and took his arm and led him back to his own table. Thereafter, they continued with their mutinous plots in very subdued voices and with many a backward glance at us.[18]

Maybe it did happen just like that but to describe booze-induced talk as a 'mutinous plot' is going it a bit and may reveal more about the inhibitions of the British than of the indiscipline of American airmen. The fact was, anyone who took off in a military aircraft had every cause to be nervous. For those who were fighting far from home for a cause that was not obviously their own, the tension and fear were all the greater.

One way to bolster the confidence of young airmen who were beginning to regret their impetuous decision to sign up for missions precarious was to dish out a plentiful supply of what nowadays are called 'go pills'. Though rarely mentioned in official documents, the use of amphetamines to counter weariness or stress with a 'sense of high energy, a release of social inhibitions and feelings of cleverness, competence and power',[19] was common practice not just in the air forces but in all branches of the military.

The most common form of amphetamines was Benzedrine which could become addictive. 'I have been feeding on Benzedrine,' declared a much decorated pilot in a letter home. Side effects such as heart problems, anxiety and even paranoia were known but seldom admitted. A nurse with the Queen Alexandra's Nursing Service reported having to treat soldiers suffering double vision brought on by 'the prolonged use of Benzedrine'. The pills could keep weary aircrews awake but there was no evidence that they improved life-or-death judgements.

Where no encouragement to dare-devilry was needed was in the period of training when young recruits, fresh out of high school, were only too eager to show off their prowess. Accidents caused by over-confidence were commonplace. 'Dusty' Miller, head of training at Atcham in Shropshire, recalls: 'We were losing pilots on sector reconnaissance. The squadron instructors would take up a group of pilots and just fly around Shropshire to show 'em the lay of the land and we'd start losing pilots on these flights – flying into the ground. Then we started losing them spinning out of cloud. Silly accidents.'[20]

In rural East Anglia, which had the highest concentration of Allied aircraft, damage to life and property was more likely to be caused by friend than foe. The break-up of formations on the home run 'all the ships jerkily diving into and out of their right places' led to frequent mid-air collisions. In November at Bury St Edmunds, two Flying Fortresses, one above the other, crashed when the lower aircraft put its nose up rather too sharply. A month later, in poor weather, a newly arrived crew came to grief in a similar incident. Ernest Langholz, an instructor navigator, lived to tell the tale.

We were flying along smoothly when suddenly there was a bump and a 'bucking' of the aircraft. I somehow sensed it was time to get out, and tried to get to the forward escape hatch; however, before I could make it, a ball of flame came out of the bomb bay area. The next thing I was aware of was falling through the air with pieces of wreckage going by me. Fortunately, I had obtained a back-pack type parachute which came through the wreck intact. But when I put my right hand up to get the ripcord handle on the left shoulder, all I had was a thumb. Four fingers had been rather neatly amputated, probably by a prop or heavy piece of metal. I got the 'chute open with my left hand and floated down into the middle of a beet field, where two elderly men working there came up to me and escorted me out to the road. Some people at the base near Bury St Edmunds had seen the accident and had a jeep on the road waiting to take me to the base clinic. From there it was the 65th General Hospital near Diss for skin graft and then to the Walter Reed Hospital in Washington. Only three of the ten crew on board survived.[21]

15 DECEMBER 1944

Rotterdam
R. Lek
Arnhem
R. Waal
R. Maas
St Hertogenb'ch
Duisberg
Düsseldorf
RUHR
Antwerp
GERMANY
Brussels
R. Roer
Cologne
BELGIUM
Maastricht
Aachen
Liège
Namur
R. Meuse
Malmédy
Coblenz
Dinant
Marche
St Vith
Prüm
R. Rhine
Bastogne
R. Moselle
Neufchâteau
Trier
Arlon
LUXEM-
BOURG
Sedan
FRANCE
R. Saar
Metz
Saarbrücken

Allied front line
German counter attack
Area of greatest
German penetration

7

The Unstoppable War Machine

The Allied bombing campaign against German oil installations, agreed in the face of opposition from Harris, was more successful than anyone had dared hope. It was, as Harris grudgingly conceded, the one 'panacea' that actually paid off. His American counterparts were not satisfied with that. They pointed to their success in taking out rail centres, bridges and canals, causing transport chaos. 'The decline in carloadings and marshalling capacity in the chief industrial areas spelled catastrophe for the Germans.' But it was the shortage of oil that most worried the Wehrmacht. With production down by 70 per cent, supplies for the Ardennes offensive fell to five days of continuously heavy operations, not nearly enough to keep up the momentum of a blitzkrieg to Antwerp. Thanks largely to the US Fifteenth, by the end of December all the major refineries were out of action, as too were most of the sympathetic petroleum plants.

Holding his corner, Harris pointed to the formidable armoured force put together by the Wehrmacht for the Ardennes. This surely confirmed his scepticism as to the effectiveness of attacks on armaments factories and ordnance depots. But, as he very well knew, this was not quite the point. Even if, oil excepted, strategic bombing had not lived up to expectations, neither had saturation bombing achieved its objective. Not only had Harris failed to destroy Germany's industrial capacity but his penchant for wholesale destruction was building up to a human disaster of such magnitude that it was becoming hard to imagine what would happen to Germany after the fighting was over. Who was to govern this ruined state and how? Where, in an impoverished Europe, were the resources to bring Germany back to life? It was a question soon to occupy Churchill. But meanwhile, while there was a war still to be won, Harris himself, if not his targets, remained fireproof. Shrugging off directives to concentrate on military targets, Harris intensified his assault on German cities. On average some 1,400 bombers went in on the attack every day in the winter of 1944, carrying the war to urban centres thus far untouched by war. To support this effort, Harris now had 230,000 personnel serving under him. Bomber Command was a mighty war machine that would be hard, some said impossible, to wind down before unconditional surrender had been achieved.

In early December, Heilbronn, near Stuttgart, came under air attack. When the first bombs fell, Feuerwehr-mann (Fireman) Flein was just sitting down to dinner.

> I immediately set off in the direction of Haigern . . . where I had a good view over the city. I cannot begin to describe what I saw there, it was simply too terrible. A great sea of fire. All you could hear was the roar of the mass of planes and the bang of the exploding bombs. The ground was a seething mass of fire. Everywhere explosions, which looked like little fountains of fireworks, and then larger explosions in between . . . What I saw filled me with dread. I thought about the thousands of people, including children, exposed to this sea of fire, and what would happen to them. This was no longer war, this was total destruction. This was what mankind was capable of. It was clear to me that our help was urgently needed so I went back to my family in the cellar and said I would be moving to Heilbronn immediately. I was imagining the worst scenes as I approached Beethovenstrasse. Then I was so shocked, I was rooted to the spot. Two drunken soldiers with girls came from the burning city, howling and shouting, as if they'd come straight out of the lunatic asylum. They laughed when they saw me: 'Ha! – a fireman! What good does he think he can do?!' I couldn't believe it. They came from the burning city and were totally oblivious. Could it be possible that people had become so desensitised to such destruction?[1]

Hans Martin was caught up in the raid as he was making his way home.

The Kilian church was badly hit, Fliener and Kirchbrunnenstrasse were still passable. I was heading for the cellar of the monastery, but the air pressure of a bomb propelled me into the Klarastrasse, where I lay winded in some ruins, but without any serious injury . . . I found a small cellar where I climbed down and met 12 elderly people. However, as smoke crept into the cellar I didn't stay long there either. I warned the people there of the danger and they came with me to the big shelter next to the St Peter's church. On the way there we came across some hideously burned people who had not managed to escape. In the cellar I was in now there were 130 people . . . The situation was getting dangerous here too due to the burning building, the iron exit door had started to glow . . . We went upstairs and managed to escape through an opening in a side wall. I was exhausted . . . and made slow progress. Some of the streets were blocked by burning rubble. Electrical wires, some of them glowing, were particularly obstructive. About 60 metres in front of the Goetzentrum I fell and my leg went into a manhole. Stuck and caught up in the wires, I saw the moment coming where I would be killed by burning rubble. But someone had seen me and my cries for help were answered by the winegrower Wilhelm Seitz who freed me (he lost his life on January 21st). As I reached the Goetzentrum . . . I was near fainting. After a short breather I tried to get to Sontheim along the river bank. It was burning terribly on the other side of the Neckar. In the darkness I fell into a bomb crater filled with water and had my difficulties getting out again. Covered in mud and freezing, I set back upon my path. As I reached the Sontheimer strasse by the Knorr factory, I saw firemen I recognised, although they didn't recognise me. I was totally exhausted. After a long rest they got me back on my feet with a schnapps, and I was able to set off on the way home to Sontheim.[2]

The end of the attack was marked by sudden stillness. It was just after 7.45 p.m.

We got up but were all still in such a state of shock that we didn't think of leaving the cellar. We understood that the people there were in danger . . . We two men took picks and knocked down the dividing wall. Twenty-five people burst in, women, children and four men.

The fear of death was written on all of their faces. They flooded in, along with the smoke and stifling air of their cellar with its burning wooden stairs.[3]

A year after the war ended, pupils of a boys' school in Nuremberg were asked to write down their memories of the night when their town disintegrated. The essay title was 'The Day I Will Never Forget'. Here are a few lines chosen at random.

It was two o'clock in the morning as the sirens went off. We went to the air raid shelter. As we were halfway there we heard the roar of the planes, and started to run faster and faster. When we reached the shelter I realised I didn't have my coat on my arm anymore. I told my mother and she started to give me a right telling-off . . . When we got home I was expecting a smack from her because of the coat, but it was on the table. I was overjoyed that I had my coat back.

It was midnight and I was fast asleep. All of a sudden shooting began. My mother woke me up and said 'get up, they are firing already.' I murmured, 'it won't be too bad today, we can lay here for a little while longer.' Bang, a bomb fell into the neighbouring house. My mother shouted, 'into the cellar – now!' I quickly got dressed and went downstairs . . . The bombs were flying. One hit and our house was destroyed. Rubble piled through the cellar window and our door was blocked with rubble. It took the fire brigade six hours to uncover us.

The raid lasted for two hours and after it was over we stayed for another three hours in the cellar . . . The next day we had no school because everywhere was still burning. People's fingers were lying around, and then a burned head rolled out. I will never forget such things in my whole life.[4]

Six thousand died in the raid on Heilbronn and more than two-thirds of the city went up in flames.

Heilbronn was wiped out, a dead city, the rubble glowing hot. We went back to the Lixstrasse to see if anything was left of our house.

The cellar was full of hot ash and our cat Peter was lying dead along with the 11 dead members of the Baumann family. The large wine barrels in the cellar had partly burst and Trollinger was glugging out. The air was hot and dry. You could breathe a little bit . . . We helped a neighbour to search for his family and found them sitting in the cellar – dead. They were sitting together, as if sculpted of marble. The mother with her arms wrapped protectively around her two children, holding them to her, the other two had buried their heads in her lap. The mother was looking straight ahead, as into the distance. They had died of carbon monoxide poisoning from the fire.

Herr Scheufler, our grocer from the Wollhausstrasse, came running towards me. He shook me, trembling all over his body and shouted 'Get my wife out of the cellar, my family – Hitler, Heil Hitler!' I felt very uncomfortable, he had obviously lost his mind.

Then I sat down next to the Braun children, who I had always played with. They were lying in the front garden, their faces blue. I cried bitterly for the first time. The burned-off branches of the trees roared in the dark night.[5]

On January 11th, an attack on the Rhine city of Krefeld set alight the south of the city. After the all-clear sounded there were funerals to arrange. An anonymous war diary tells of one such event.

We buried Mrs R, our former neighbour. The family were in the cellar and Mrs R ran back upstairs to fetch something she'd forgotten and a dud bomb fell. A second one threw the poor woman through a cupboard and crushed her into the wall. They had to get the corpse out piece by piece, the hand with her wedding ring wasn't found until after the funeral.

The funeral was at 9 a.m. and at 9.30 . . . an air raid siren went off, then low-flying bombers boomed along and we heard them letting off fire. The women started to panic, the men yelled 'don't run outside! keep off the streets! everyone stay in the church!' The vicar interrupted the service and said it would be continued when the all-clear siren went off. This happened after ¾ hr and the service went on as normal.[6]

There was just a shared longing for the torment to end.

> Yesterday half a dozen English planes were circling south and south-west above the railway. I didn't take my eyes off the brothers. Then Juliane came home – she'd had to throw herself to the ground three times on the way to avoid the aerial fire . . . Her talking took my mind off it a bit, then all of a sudden there was a screaming above us and a plane flew so low we could have sworn it would take the tops off the trees . . . then more heavy droning followed by continuous bombing . . . we thought our last hour had come. Anna was on her knees praying loudly. The three of us huddled together so at least we could die together. Juliane was terribly brave, as always.[7]

War memories of Bonn, another Rhine city hit badly from early January on, were collected in the 1980s. The Swiss consul, Franz-Rudolf von Weiss, recorded events as they happened.

> 10 January 1945 – . . . The city is still without light and gas and an acquaintance of mine who was on his way to fetch permission for a candle, was killed on the way. The emergency has reached such proportions in Bonn that the aid trains have been stationed over half an hour from the city centre. Every inhabitant who needs food has to make this long journey, of course there are no more trams running in the city.

The raid of January 6th was one of the most devastating.

> As the air raid warning sounded, my parents wanted to go straight into the air raid shelter in the courthouse. A man who knew my parents was standing at the courthouse shouting 'Quick, quick, get in here!' but a friend they'd just met advised them not to go into the courthouse but the shelter in Theatre Street. They were barely inside when the bombs began to fall. This shelter remained intact, as did all the other bunkers. Yet almost all the 230 people who had sought shelter in the courthouse were killed. The noise was so awful that for days afterwards my mother felt like she was being hammered over the head.[8]

Franz Lanser also had a lucky escape but remembers others who were less fortunate.

As I heard the sirens I took my bike and headed for the air raid shelter in the courthouse. I had a look for friends on the way, but finding none I went back out and took shelter in the theatre bunker. I found two colleagues there. I put my bike outside – it remained intact, but other people who had left things outside the shelter lost almost everything. Then a bomb hit the courthouse and exploded in the cellar. Seine the carpenter was in the courthouse cellar with his wife and daughter, when his wife said she had left the dinner on! – 'run home quick, and turn it off.' That's when the bomb fell. The man was saved, but his wife and daughter lay dead in the court-house.[9]

Another town that was virtually wiped from the earth was Pforzheim, between Karlsruhe and Stuttgart. Soon to be mayor of a rejuvenated community, Friedrich Adolf Katz noted the deaths of friends and colleagues.

Fritz S was at a meeting and managed to escape with his life but his wife and only son are dead, the factory reduced to rubble . . . Herr Oswald is dead, whose Jewish wife was taken away just a few days ago. The director of the Reichsbank, Blume, is dead. There is a huge bomb crater where the Reichsbank once stood. The whole family of Richard Kraft is dead, with whom I often discussed the hopelessness of the situation, and Herr Luplow, who felt so safe under his seven layers of reinforced concrete nine metres under the ground, is also dead. Who could possibly have known that the phosphorous would run everywhere and burn everything, that the bombs would go straight through six layers of concrete?

But what surprised and encouraged the writer was the ability of some of his fellow citizens to transcend the horrors.

Now I've experienced for myself how an unbelievable will to live can rise from death and destruction. As long as the attack lasted, people sat with their heads bowed. However, as soon as it was over, people breathed out, freed of an enormous pressure and full of energy and vigour. Of course I met many completely broken people, who were utterly distraught by the loss of their family and their entire possessions, and could only cry and complain, but I spoke to just as many who were making determined plans for rebuilding everything and getting back on their feet. This will slowly dwindle as the grey everydayness returns. But what is distinctive is this powerful flame of life. I have never before seen how life and death belong together, how life grows out of death.[10]

It was not what Bomber Harris would have wanted to hear. More to his liking would have been the man out of his mind who stood on a street corner screaming, 'Now come here, Mr Goebbels and take a look at this – come really close so you can see everything. Come here, come here, quickly! Why is this war carrying on, after it's lost its purpose? We are just waiting for it to end, we have lost all hope.'

But these were the extremes – hope and despair. In between were those who just kept going, almost as if they were on automatic drive.

I was in town again, this time to search for father. The rescue team gave me seven men with picks and shovels. As we climbed onto the piles of rubble, we saw a bomb crater at both ends of the arched cellar. The heat was still intolerable. The end wall of the cellar was torn away, the rubble lay a metre deep in the cellar. There was nothing to discover there. No remains, no bones, nothing. The dead bodies had to be buried under the rubble. But it was still too hot to get them out. Empty-handed, we left again. The whole town was engulfed in a sickly sweet smell. The typical corpse smell. Cellars are still being emptied, the dead unearthed. The dead bodies of 117 work girls lie on the Enzland. One keeps meeting people pushing wheelbarrows with dead bodies inside. My brother-in-law's foot was buried today.[11]

At the pre-Yalta meeting of the Chiefs of Staff in Malta on January 30th, the Allied air forces in the west were given a pivotal role for the last stage of the war. While the armies gathered strength for the Rhine offensive, the bomber fleets would go in to support the Russian advance in the east. Oil targets were still the first priority but transportation centres came a close second. It was here, yet again, that American and British air force chiefs, finding themselves at odds over objectives, somehow patched together a compromise which left Harris free to pursue his own agenda. When the Big Three began their talks at Yalta, they had before them a Chiefs of Staff proposal for a three-pronged bombing campaign against synthetic oil plants, cities like Berlin, Leipzig and Dresden 'where heavy attack will cause great confusion in civilian evacuation from the east and hamper reinforcements' and against communications in the Ruhr to deter the Germans from withdrawing forces from the west to bolster the eastern front. The first communication targets were located south and east of Berlin, starting with 'rail assembly areas and bottlenecks for eastward movements'.

It was here, in the small print, that Spaatz, now USAAF commanding general, and Harris imposed their own conflicting interpretations. For Harris the distinction between military and general targets was entirely spurious. Holding to his belief in a more humane form of warfare, Spaatz believed that at least an attempt should be made to spare civilian lives. But Spaatz had no way of controlling Harris. Their differences, more important now than at any other time in the war, were glossed over at Yalta where a show of force to back up the Russians was quickly approved. Any doubts were silenced by intelligence reports of three German infantry divisions moving east with others soon to be on their way, including the armoured divisions of the elite Sixth Panzer Army. It was more serious than that, the Russians argued. Many more German divisions were on the move, including eight from Italy and three from Norway. The threat was so great, claimed the Soviet Chiefs of Staff, that if the Allies 'were unable to take full advantage of their air superiority, they did not have sufficient superiority on the ground to overcome enemy opposition'. The threat was less serious than presented, though in the circumstances the Russians can be forgiven an exaggeration.

In giving their backing to the military or, rather, in failing to raise pertinent questions as to the real need to take out cities like Dresden, the Anglo-American leadership was committing a grave mistake. It has been argued that Churchill in particular should have known that with Harris giving the orders Bomber Command could not be trusted to act with discretion. Warning signals against annihilation bombing at this late stage in the war could well have been passed down the line. But the peculiar circumstances at Yalta go a long way in mitigation. It was not just that the Anglo-Americans were under pressure to help the Russians. They were all, in their various ways, in triumphant mood. The imminence of victory after so long a struggle put sympathy for the enemy, albeit innocent civilians, low on the order of priorities. Stalin, in particular, would have had no time for sidetracks into sentimentality and since the demonstration of Allied unity was the prime objective of Yalta, what Stalin did not want to talk about was a guarantee of it falling off the agenda. At the time Dresden must have been seen, if it was seen at all, as a dot on the canvas of world affairs. It was soon to grow.

But first in line for the Yalta treatment was Berlin. The capital, which had gone for two months without a major bombardment, was given precedence as immediate testimony to Stalin that the Anglo-Americans were as good as their word. To hit Berlin was to strike at marshalling yards and rail stations, government offices and industries that were all vital to the German war effort. Moreover, the Sixth Panzer Army was said to be moving through the city on its way to the eastern front. The mission went to the US Eighth. Spaatz and Doolittle stuck to their line that they would not bomb indiscriminately but as 1,000 Flying Fortresses and 400 Liberators took off for Germany on February 3rd, observers must have wondered who was kidding whom. Visibility was good and there was no trouble from Luftwaffe fighters but flak brought down twenty-one bombers and may well have caused others to unload well short of their targets. Rail transport was disrupted often beyond early redress and there were hits on the Reich Chancellery, Air Ministry and Gestapo headquarters. However, these objectives were all heavily urbanised which meant a correspondingly high level of civilian casualties. Estimates of the number of deaths started at around 25,000. Harris could have been excused a wry 'I told you so' but it was one thing to try and fail, quite another not to try at all.

No one in Dresden could have imagined themselves entirely immune to attack though there was comfort in the rumour that the city had been spared on the understanding that Oxford, an equally venerable city, would be spared the attentions of the Luftwaffe. Another rumour had it that Churchill protected Dresden because his aunt lived there. More realistically, the absence of vital industries reasoned against an air strike. But Dresden was another link in the rail and road network, much used by troops on the move and by February a focal point for the mass of refugees fleeing the Russian advance. An attack on the city, Harris promised, would cause maximum disruption and a hysteria of imminent defeat that would quickly spread across what was left of the Reich. Dresden was the culmination of his campaign of mass destruction. Hitherto fire-storms had been an unforeseen 'bonus'. This time the fire-storm, centred on the medieval part of the city, was integral to the strategy. Of the 1,252 aircraft despatched by Bomber Command over Germany on the night of February 13th, no fewer than 805 made for Dresden. The first wave carried the load of incendiaries. By the time the second wave arrived the city was burning uncontrollably – an illuminated sitting target.

Technically, the attack was a brilliant success. As Harris's latest biographer, Henry Probert, puts it:

> Harris's plan worked perfectly. The weather did exactly what the fore-casters had said it would, the enemy defences were fooled by the three-hour delay between the first and second phases of the attack, as well as by a separate attack on the oil refinery at Böhlen, the crews of the 800 aircraft involved demonstrated great skill, no more than six Lancasters failed to return, and the heart of the city was destroyed in a fire-storm unparalleled in the European war other than in Hamburg.[12]

However, Probert goes on to say that 'it was a truly horrifying event'. And so it was. Prompted by German propaganda, Dresden was seen by the international press, including the American papers, as an official endorsement of terror bombing, incontrovertible evidence that the Allies were determined to destroy Germany beyond redemption.

Some of the pilots who flew on the February 14th raid were inclined to agree. They took to calling their mission the St Valentine's Day Massacre. 'Dresden burning fiercely as we left the target area,' wrote one; 'consider we hit the jackpot. Fires visible when 150 miles away.' The following day when American bombers carried out strikes on the rail yards (the railway bridge that served as an aiming point escaped unscathed) the fires were still raging. Subsequently, there was a feeling among aircrews that they had been misled as to the true purpose of their mission. It was reasonable to describe Dresden as a rail centre (No. 1 Army briefing), even a Germany army headquarters (No. 3 Group) but those squadrons told that Dresden was a Gestapo headquarters or accommodated a poison gas plant were seriously, and probably deliberately, misinformed. What they did not hear was that Dresden's peacetime population had more than doubled with the influx of refugees from the east, a helpless mass of humanity packed into cellars and subways. It was a social disaster in the making even without the help of fire bombs.

Of the most vivid reminiscences the diaries of Victor Klemperer strike a peculiarly poignant note for he and his wife Eva were two of the few remaining Jews in Dresden. Moreover, just a few hours before the bombs fell, a friend had warned them of a final round-up of Jews that would almost certainly despatch them to the death camp. The couple had just sat down for coffee when they heard the humming of approaching aircraft.

> The light went out, and explosion nearby . . . Pause in which we caught our breath, we knelt head down between the chairs, in some groups there was whimpering and weeping – approaching aircraft once again, deadly danger once again, explosion once again. I do not know how often it was repeated. Suddenly the cellar window on the back wall opposite the entrance bursts open, and outside it was bright as day. Someone shouted: 'Incendiary bomb, we have to put it out!' Two people even hauled over the stirrup pump and audibly operated it. There were further explosions, but nothing in the courtyard. And then it grew quieter, and then came the all-clear.

I had lost all sense of time. Outside it was bright as day. Fires were blazing at Pirnaischer Platz, on Marschallstrasse, and somewhere on or over the Elbe. The ground was covered with broken glass. A terribly strong wind was blowing. Natural or a firestorm? Probably both. In the stairwell of 1 Zeughausstrasse the window frames had been blown in and lay on the steps, partly obstructing them. Broken glass in our rooms upstairs. In the hallway and on the side facing the Elbe, windows blown in, in the bedroom only one; windows also broken in the kitchen, blackout torn in half. Light did not work, no water. We could see big fires on the other side of the Elbe and on Marschallstrasse.

The second phase of the attack came after midnight:

As usual there was a steel-helmeted sentry in front of the wall between the two Zeughausstrasse houses (the wall of the former synagogue with the barracks behind it). In passing I asked him whether there was a warning – 'Yes.' – Eva was two steps ahead of me. We came to the entrance hall of no. 3. At that moment a big explosion nearby. I knelt, pressing myself up against the wall, close to the courtyard door. When I looked up, Eva had disappeared. I thought she was in our cellar. It was quiet, I ran across the yard to our Jews' cellar. The door was wide open. A group of people cowered whimpering to the right of the door, I knelt on the left, close to the window. I called out several times to Eva. No reply. Big explosions. Again the window in the wall opposite burst open, again it was bright as day, again water was pumped. Then an explosion at the window close to me. Something hard and glowing hot struck the right side of my face. I put my hand up, it was covered in blood, I felt for my eye, it was still there. A group of Russians – where had they come from? – pushed out of the door. I jumped over to them. I had the rucksack on my back, the grey bag with our manuscripts and Eva's jewellery in my hand, my old hat had fallen off. I stumbled and fell. A Russian lifted me up. To the side there was a vaulting, God knows of what already half-destroyed cellar. We crowded in. It was hot. The Russians ran on in some other direction, I with them. Now we stood in an open passageway, heads down, crowded together. In front of me lay a large unrecognisable open space, in the middle of it an enormous crater. Bangs, as light as day, explosions. I had no thoughts, I was not even afraid, I was simply tremendously exhausted, I think I was expecting the end.

Klemperer found himself surrounded by fires. He could think of nothing but Eva. Had she been able to save herself?

In my hands I held the precious bag and – yes, also the small leather case with Eva's woollen things, how I managed to hold on to it during all the clambering around is a mystery to me. The storm again and again tore at my blanket, hurt my head. It had begun to rain, the ground was soft and wet, I did not want to put anything down, so there was serious physical strain, and that probably stupefied and distracted me . . . I walked past the shell of the still-burning Belvedere and came to the Terrace wall. A number of people were sitting there. After a minute someone called out to me: Eva was sitting unharmed on the suitcase wearing her fur coat. We greeted one another very warmly, and we were completely indifferent to the loss of our belongings, and remain so even now. At the critical moment, someone had literally pulled Eva out of the entrance hall of no. 3 Zeughausstrasse and into the Aryan cellar . . . So now it was Wednesday morning, the 14th of February, and our lives were saved and we were together.[13]

Such is the emotive impact of Dresden, until recently every anniversary of the inferno attracted wide German press coverage with dramatic eye-witness accounts. Understandably, those written years after the event are not always reliable. One of the legends, given credence by David Irving,[14] is of low-level machine-gunning of fleeing civilians by Allied fighters. It didn't happen or, at least, there is no evidence that it happened beyond stories in shock-horror magazines first published in the 1950s. These sources are discounted by modern historians.[15] But this is not to minimise the horror of Dresden which in the immediate aftermath slowly permeated through to the political leadership.

Churchill was still on board the *Franconia* on his way home from Yalta when he was handed a telegram from the War Cabinet Office listing eleven news items from the previous day's military activities. Dresden was tenth. There was no estimate of casualties or damage. A more detailed report later in the day noted 'great material damage' but stopped short of further analysis since the interpretation of photographs was 'rendered difficult . . . by the haze from fires still burning more than 36 hours after the last attack'.[16] There was no immediate reaction from Churchill. In the absence of a detailed report he probably failed to take in the full significance of Dresden. But another raid, one that caused far fewer casualties but was all the more tragic for being misdirected, did catch his attention. On March 3rd, while Churchill was visiting Allied troops on the Dutch-German border, British bombers took off on one of their frequent raids on German V2 rocket sites. The target was the Hague Wood. Instead, it was The Hague itself that was hit.

The death toll was 520 with half as many again badly injured. Some 4,500 houses were destroyed or damaged beyond use. Twelve thousand people were made homeless. The fires started by incendiaries raged unchecked because there were only six poorly equipped fire engines on hand and too few firemen. The others had been sent on forced labour to Germany.

The actual bombing lasted just ten minutes, but the chaos was complete. Many of those who in their terror had sought refuge beneath stairs or in cupboards with pans on their heads perished in the rubble. Survivors fled onto the streets and found themselves in a hell. Many met their ends there.

'The old cabaret artiste Koos Speenhoff came out with his wife. They were later found dead in front of their house,' recalls A.J. Stemerding. Some people went mad. Stemerding: 'Bembergen, the kindly yet always very nervous man, stood in front of his house along the Charlotte de Bourbonstraat and started throwing paper money into the air.' J. Poot cycled along the Schenkkade just after the disaster: 'I saw a woman's leg with the same colour stocking as my wife's. But the leg had a different shoe on. So it wasn't her! Close by lay the head of a man. It had been covered with a jacket but that had been blown aside.'[17]

It was not until Sunday evening, thirty-six hours after the bombing started, that the last of the fires was put out. Twenty-two-year-old Pim de Bruyn Kops took part in the raid. It was his thirteenth mission with the 320 squadron of the Second Tactical Air Force. As the bombs fell he knew there had been a big mistake. What made it worse was that de Bruyn Kops was bringing destruction to his own home. The house in which he had been raised suffered a direct hit and his guardian died under the rubble.

The excuses for a tragic error – stronger winds than anticipated and false reports that the area hit had been evacuated – did nothing to pacify the Dutch government in exile. Churchill was told bluntly that Dutch public opinion had 'become violently anti Ally as a result of this bombardment'. Churchill responded with an acid memo to Sinclair and Portal.

> This complaint reflects upon the Air ministry and Royal Air Force in two ways. First it shows how feeble have been our efforts to interfere with the rockets, and, secondly, the extraordinarily bad aiming which has led to this slaughter of Dutchmen. The matter requires a thorough explanation. We have had numerous accounts of the pin-point bombing of suspected Gestapo houses in Holland and of other specialised points; but good indications are given in this account of the wood where the rockets are stored, and of the railway lines which, if interrupted, would hamper the supply of rockets. All this ought to have been available from Air Intelligence. Instead of attacking these points with precision and regularity, all that has been done is to scatter bombs about this unfortunate city without the slightest effect on their rocket sites, but much on innocent human lives and the sentiments of a friendly people.[18]

Sinclair promised a full investigation which he pre-empted somewhat by observations on the 'difficulty of attack on these rocket objectives' placed deliberately 'in and near built-up areas in Holland'. But any hopes of softening up Churchill were frustrated by detailed reports of what had happened in Dresden. Now seriously worried, the Prime Minister fired off another salvo.

It seems to me that the moment has come when the question of bombing of German cities simply for the sake of increasing the terror, though under other pretexts, should be reviewed. Otherwise we shall come into control of an utterly ruined land. We shall not, for instance, be able to get housing materials out of Germany for our own needs because some temporary provision would have to be made for the Germans themselves. The destruction of Dresden remains a serious query against the conduct of Allied bombing. I am of the opinion that military objectives must henceforward be more strictly studied in our own interests rather than that of the enemy.

The Foreign Secretary has spoken to me on this subject, and I feel the need for more precise concentration upon military objectives, such as oil and communications behind the immediate battle-zone, rather than on mere acts of terror and wanton destruction, however impressive.[19]

Portal persuaded him to tone down his statement but not before it had been seen by Harris who responded in equally robust terms, describing Dresden as 'a mass of munitions works, an intact government centre and a key transportation point to the East' (a gross exaggeration of the city's true importance), dismissing the medieval grandeur of Dresden as a sentimentalist attachment to 'German bands and Dresden shepherdesses' and concluding that as far as he was concerned 'the bones of one British grenadier' were worth more than all the remaining German cities put together.

Churchill let it ride. There was too much else to occupy him, not least the imminence of the next stage of the Allied advance, across the Rhine and towards Berlin. He put in a half-hearted plea on behalf of Potsdam ('What was the point of going and blowing down Potsdam?') but when told that it was now the Luftwaffe operational headquarters, as if that mattered any more, he fell silent.

And so the raids continued. A week after Dresden, Operation Clarion began. Primarily directed against railway yards, tracks, bridges and rolling stock, over 8,000 bombers and fighters brought havoc to towns and villages from Cologne to Chemnitz and from Hamburg to Munich. Seen from the German side, the idea of an effective defence, let alone retaliation, was laughable. Night fighter pilots joked about the low levels they had to fly to live long enough to earn the Knight's Cross. On February 21st, a young Luftwaffe pilot took part in the defence of Würzburg, a city better known for its hospitals than for any military significance.

I had been in readiness with my wing from 1900 hours. We still did not know which German city was to be rotted out within the next few hours. Division merely said that two large formations had started from the London area. I got ready with my crew . . . Half an hour later the fighter-directing officer fired a green flare. Orders to take off . . .

'Achtung, achtung! Bombers are flying in the direction of Nuremberg. Probable objectives, Nuremberg and Würzburg.'

I thought for a moment. Würzburg or Nuremberg. I decided for the former and changed on to a northerly course . . . In the distance we saw the ribbon of the Main. The moon lit up the great river. Grasshoff reported contacts on his radar. Then the storm broke. We were approaching the bombers. Before we had got to the enemy, the Master of Ceremonies had dropped his marker flares over the city. Parachute flares drifted slowly down, making the night look ghostly . . .

'Mosquitoes,' shouted Mahle.

I took avoiding action. The British pilot's tracers went wide below my right wing. The hunt started again. Now we were flying directly over the city among the bomber stream.

Then the appalling destruction began. The four-engined bomber crews opened their bays and rained incendiaries on to the city below. The phosphorous ignited as soon as it hit the air and joined into a huge burning cloud which slowly settled on the city. It was a Dantesque and terrible sight. By the glow of the doomed city the bombers found their direction.

Then a four-engined Lancaster crossed my path. Without a thought I poured a long burst into its fuselage and wings. The crate exploded in the air and spun down with its crew. That was my only kill over Würzburg and incidentally my last kill of the war. It attracted the entire enemy night fighter pack on my heels. We could hardly watch the bomber crash on the ground before they set upon us.

Mahle shouted in terror, 'Mosquito close behind us.'

Even as I banked the burst hit my machine. There was a reek of smoke and fire. Terrifying seconds ahead, but I let my machine dive to be rid of my pursuer. The altimeter fell rapidly – 2,500 . . . 2,000 . . . 1,500 . . . 1,000. Now I had to pull out unless I wanted to go straight into the ground. I pulled with all my might on the joystick and got the machine under control. Luckily the controls answered. There was still an acrid smell of smoke in the cabin. Perhaps a cable was smouldering, but the engines were running smoothly.

We hedge-hopped over Swabia towards our airfield in Leipheim.[20]

The offensive was sustained throughout March and April. On February 26th, Berlin suffered its four-hundredth raid. Other records were noted at this time. On March 12th, Dortmund achieved the dubious distinction of being the city to receive the heaviest bomb load – 4,899 tons – in a single raid. At the end of the first week of April, Harris conceded that Bomber Command had exhausted all worthwhile targets. Three days later, however, the Eighth took one last hit at Berlin. In all, 75,000 tons of bombs had fallen on the capital.

What will be the verdict of history on the bombing of the German cities? As Richard Overy has pointed out, at a critical period in 1942 and '43, when the war was still an open contest, bombing helped to open up a Second Front by 'diverting large quantities of manpower and equipment away from the Russo-German conflict'.[21] It speeded up the re-entry to Europe of western forces, created the conditions for the defeat of the Luftwaffe and prevented the development of a German economic superpower. Mistakes were made and the impact of bombing on the production of military hardware was nowhere near as devastating as the Allied planners liked to believe. (Armament production continued to mount until mid-1944.) Moreover, successes were achieved at the cost of 140,000 American and British airmen, a cruel sacrifice of young lives though one that was generally accepted as a precondition of victory on the ground. It is only for the last stages of the conflict that the doubts set in. This was when the bombing campaign was at its most intense. In the last year of the war 1.18 million tons of bombs fell on Germany. The total for the entire war was 1.42 million.[22] With such a weight of destruction the long-running dispute between the American and British air forces as to the selection of targets became largely academic. The AAF continued to give priority to specific military targets – oil refineries, transport links and industrial complexes – 'pinpoint' or 'pickle barrel' bombing as it was called; while the RAF made for the city centres. But since only about 20 per cent of bombs aimed at precision targets fell within their designated area, the impact on the civilian population was much the same whoever was dropping the bombs.[23] Seventy cities were bombed heavily and of these twenty-three had more than 60 per cent of their built-up areas destroyed. Dresden stands out but in Düsseldorf, Cologne, Hamburg, Berlin, Bremen, Duisburg, Essen, Frankfurt, Hannover, Munich, Nuremberg, Mannheim and Stuttgart the damage to life and property was as bad or worse.

When the defeat of Germany was all but certain, how could destruction on this scale be justified? Early post-war debate was inhibited by a decent sensitivity for the feelings of aircrews who had risked their lives and for families in mourning. Defensive arguments – the need to support the Russians, the minimising of casualties among troops leading the advance into Germany and the natural desire to take revenge for Nazi excesses – were accepted at more than their face value. The witness of German military leaders was frequently quoted – Doenitz who said that Allied air power was decisive in the submarine war, Jodl who said that air superiority was the single biggest factor leading to Allied victory and Speer who argued that bombing could have won the war without a ground invasion. But at this point no one seemed to take account of the natural inclinations of those responsible for the war on land and sea to look for excuses for their own operational deficiencies.

The counter-arguments started in the autumn of 1945 with the US Strategic Bombing Survey based on reports of a team of investigators who had followed the advance of the Allied armies. Conceding that pinpoint bombing had its limitations, the Survey concluded that the German experience emphasised 'the importance of careful selection of targets for air attack'. There was a dig at Harris *et al* who had stressed the impact of intensive bombing on civilian morale:

> The mental reaction of the German people to air attack is significant. Under ruthless Nazi control they showed surprising resistance to the terror and hardships of repeated air attack, to the destruction of their homes and belongings, and to the conditions under which they were reduced to live. Their morale, their belief in ultimate victory or satisfactory compromise, and their confidence in their leaders declined, but they continued to work efficiently as long as the physical means of production remained. The power of a police state over its people cannot be underestimated.[24]

Harris reacted angrily against what he took to be a personal slight. In the wake of Hiroshima, which killed 40,000 people with a single bomb, the implied criticism of Harris's scatter-gun tactics could be confidently dismissed. But just as Hiroshima came to burden the American conscience so too did the destruction meted out by Bomber Command begin to look like an overreaction to military requirements. That Harris was less than concerned by civilian casualties was confirmed by his memoirs, published two years after the war, in which he defended his reputation in typically knockabout style. His first line of argument was to claim that he was merely the implementer of a policy adopted at a higher level, an argument, one might have thought, that was perilously close to the common excuse for German atrocities, 'I was only obeying orders.'

Harris went on to assert that the order to embark on the general disorganisation of German industry 'allowed me to attack pretty well any German industrial city of 100,000 inhabitants and above'.[25] He then admits that the aiming points 'were usually right in the centre of town' and that the 'objective of the campaign was to reduce production . . . at least as much by the indirect effect of

Field Marshal Sir Bernard Montgomery, Commander of 21st Army Group, checks a situation map with Major General Matthew Ridgway, Commander of 18th US Airborne Division.

General Dwight D. Eisenhower, Supreme Allied Commander of the Allied Armies in north west Europe 1944–45.

General Omar Bradley, Commander of 12th Army Group.

Field Marshal Walther Model, Hitler's favourite commander, chose suicide in preference to an honourable surrender.

Field Marshal Karl Gerd von Rundstedt, Commander-in-Chief West.

Lieutenant General Miles Dempsey, commanding officer of the British Second Army, 1944–45, part of 21st Army Group.

General de Lattre de Tassigny signing the German surrender on behalf of France in 1945.

Captain Tom Flanagan of the Fourth King's Own Scottish Borderers, whose diary provides one of the most vivid accounts of the Allied advance into Germany.

82nd Airborne troops bring in a young German SS trooper.

American MPs check the credentials of refugees fleeing from
the German counter-attack near Bastogne, Belgium.

A German
soldier beside
a disabled
American
half-track
signals his
unit to
advance.

Airborne army over the Rhine.

Men of the 15th Scottish Division leave their assault craft after crossing the Rhine.

The attack on the Shell House, Gestapo headquarters in
central Copenhagen.

Alone on the road.
A young German
surrenders to American
troops.

American soldiers admire Nazi loot, including a 15th-century statue of Eve and three Rembrandts.

Russian and American soldiers rest on the banks of the Elbe following the link-up between the US First Army and the Russian First Ukranian Army at Torgau.

Field Marshal Montgomery signing the Instrument of Surrender of German forces in north west Europe at Lüneburg Heath, 4 May 1945.

The symbols of defeat. The white flags fly in Berlin.

damage to services, housing, amenities, as by any direct damage to the factories or railways themselves'.[26]

And what of ordinary people?

All wars have caused casualties among civilians . . . I never forget, as so many do, that in all normal warfare of the past, and of the not distant past, it was the common practice to besiege cities and, if they refused to surrender when called upon with due formality to do so, every living thing in them was in the end put to the sword. Even in the more civilised times of to-day the siege of cities, accompanied by the bombardment of the city as a whole, is still a normal practice; in no circumstances were women and children allowed to pass out of the city, because their presence in it and their consumption of food would inevitably hasten the end of the siege. And as to bombardment, what city in what war has ever failed to receive the maximum bombardment from all enemy artillery within range so long as it has continued resistance?[27]

Having played down the effects on enemy morale ('an imponderable factor') he justified the bombing of Dresden as 'a large centre of war industry', while adding that the fire-typhoon did hit morale 'not only in Dresden but in far distant parts of the country'.[28] All true, but as critics were quick to point out, the Allies professed to aim for rather more civilised behaviour. At the very best it had to be recognised that what was described as terror bombing when carried out by the Luftwaffe over southern England could not be justified as strategic once the Allies had air supremacy.

Sixty years on the issue is still in dispute. It is only recently that the German side of the story has been told. Last year a leading academic, Jörg Friedrich, and one of Germany's greatest modern writers, the late W.G. Sebald, simultaneously dared a full frontal assessment of the bombing devastation and its impact on the German people.[29] Why has it taken so long? Sebald argues that the pain of loss was so great it was simply blocked out of the collective consciousness. The reverse side of this act of denial was 'the declaration of a new beginning, the unquestioning heroism with which people immediately set about the task of clearance and reorganisation'. It is not too fanciful to suggest that the speed of recovery may in part have been the Germans' reaction against the efforts of Harris and others to wipe them from the earth.

The prerequisites of the German economic miracle were not only the enormous sums invested in the country under the Marshall Plan, the outbreak of the Cold War, and the scrapping of outdated industrial complexes – an operation performed with brutal efficiency by the bomber squadrons – but also something less often acknowledged: the unquestioning work ethic learned in a totalitarian society, the logistical capacity for improvisation shown by an economy under constant threat, experience in the use of 'foreign labour forces', and the lifting of the heavy burden of history that went up in flames between 1942 and 1945.[30]

Friedrich intersperses his catalogue of horrors with harrowing eye-witness accounts, particularly of fire bombing. His strongest criticism is reserved for Bomber Command's play on the word military which was stretched to include any target that would burn well. So it was that Pforzheim qualified as a military target for no better reason than that the town was built largely of wood. But neither Friedrich nor Sebald can be said to be partisan. Friedrich may be unsparing in his portrayal of Bomber Command as 'the team ordered to kill en mass' but he stresses that, while the heavy casualty rate suffered by aircrews made their missions 'honourable', the Germans flouted the concept of military honour by launching unmanned V1 and V2 rockets against Britain. This in turn hardened the Allied military planners who no longer felt bound by the convention that civilians must be protected.

Sebald goes further, conceding that 'the question of whether and how it could be strategically or morally justified was never the subject of open debate in Germany after 1945, no doubt mainly because a nation that had murdered and worked to death millions of people in camps could hardly call on the victorious powers to explain the military and political logic that dictated the destruction of the German cities'.

The majority of Germans today know – or so, at least, it is to be hoped – that we actually provoked the annihilation of the cities in which we once lived. Scarcely anyone can now doubt that Göring, with his Luftwaffe, would have wiped out London if his technical resources had allowed him to do so. Albert Speer describes Hitler at dinner in the Reich Chancellery in 1940 imagining the total destruction of the capital of the British Empire: 'Have you ever seen a map of London? It is so densely built that one fire alone would be enough to destroy the whole city, just as it did over two hundred years ago. Göring will start fires all over London, fires everywhere, with countless incendiary bombs of an entirely new type. Thousands of fires. They will unite in one huge blaze over the whole area. Göring has the right idea: high explosives don't work, but we can do it with incendiaries; we can destroy London completely. What will their firemen be able to do once it's really burning!' This intoxicating vision of destruction coincides with the fact that the real pioneering achievements in bomb warfare – Guernica, Warsaw, Belgrade, Rotterdam – were the work of the Germans.

And, as we think of the nights when the fires raged in Cologne and Hamburg and Dresden, we ought also to remember that as early as August, 1942, when the vanguard of the German Sixth Army had reached the Volga and not a few were dreaming of settling down after the war on an estate in the cherry orchards beside the quiet Don, the city of Stalingrad, then swollen (like Dresden later) by an influx of refugees, was under assault from hundreds of bombers, and that during this raid alone, which caused elation among the German troops stationed on the opposite bank, forty thousand people lost their lives.[31]

Given these sentiments it is perhaps surprising that the reaction in Britain (though not in the States) to the publication of both books was to spark off a round of anti-German rhetoric on the lines of 'let us not forget who started the war'.

But the most thoughtful response came from the veteran journalist, W.F. Deedes:

Ever since the day I entered the city of Bremen with leading elements of General Horrocks's 30 Corps, very close to the end of the war, and saw the consequences of our fire-bombing, my mind has been torn by what we did there.

We set the city alight with fire bombs and incinerated much of the population in a single night . . . But the tiny corpses I saw there unburied in Bremen, shrivelled by the tremendous heat that the fire bombs had engendered did enter doubts in my mind. Later, within weeks of the war ending, when I took a long drive south to visit a battalion of our regiment in Klagenfurt and saw valleys of destruction in some of Germany's main cities, my doubts took root. Even though this was the most desperate of wars, we had in most departments sought to uphold certain rules.

We did not shoot prisoners – not even after some of the Hitler *Jugend*, boys of 14 and 15 conscripted late in the war, began to play foul; nor, under orders from the corps commander, did we loot or needlessly defile property.

But it is unnecessary to bring one's personal doubts into this argument. The way in which our establishment came to view the consequences of saturation bombing, after the war had ended, is evidence enough that Jörg Friedrich's case cannot be swept aside. He wants us to face up to what happened on the ground, after the bombs had left the plane, then to make up our minds how far we moved in the closing months of the war from warfare to the indiscriminate massacre of civilians.[32]

And here is the historian Alistair Horne, another first-hand observer of the devastation:

At 17 I dreamed of diving out of the clouds in a Spitfire; in fact, disqualified by my eyesight, I ended in a noisy and smelly tank. But if I had got my wings, 99–1 I would have been sent to Bomber Command, with a fair certainty of being shot down, or to survive with a nagging conscience. Just after the war, as a foreign correspondent, I used to rove the devastated Ruhr with the *Daily Mail*'s Ken Ames, ex-Flight Lieutenant, DFC. He had bombed every city we visited; progressively it haunted him and three decades later he shot himself.[33]

Six hundred thousand Germans were killed in bombing raids, three and a half million homes were destroyed and seven and a half million made homeless. But, says Sebald, 'we do not grasp what it all actually meant.' Maybe the apportionment of blame is a fruitless exercise. More relevant is the inscription on the memorial to Hamburg victims: 'May those generations who come after us be spared this. May this mass grave be a warning and exhortation to humanity.'

8

The Little Guys Fight Back

The German occupation of Denmark and Norway in 1940 had come as a great surprise to everyone, not least the Germans who had no idea it would be so easy. Both countries 'passed their last hours of peace blind to the dangers around them. It was as if the two Scandinavian countries, determined to maintain their neutrality at any cost, unconsciously refused to give credence to the gathering evidence that Germany was preparing a knockout blow.'[1]

Denmark was taken in a single day, the army having put up a token resistance. The invasion of Norway was more of a challenge. Whereas Denmark shared a frontier with Germany there was at least, as Churchill put it, a ditch protecting Norway. A combined airborne and amphibious assault was held off long enough for the royal family and government to escape. In the north, Narvik was held by the Allies until the crisis in France called for the evacuation of the expeditionary force, a retreat that left wide open the supply routes of Swedish iron ore to Germany. The consolation, with hindsight, was the consequent fall of the British government and the rallying of support for Churchill as Prime Minister and war leader.

The Scandinavians took a severely practical view of the occupation. After the fall of France, resistance seemed hopeless. All they could do was to put their liberal ideals into reserve while trying to minimise German interference in internal affairs. Then and subsequently they came in for heavy criticism from those who had to fight on to protect the way of life Scandinavians held most dear. But it is hard to see how a sacrificial gesture would have served the Allied war effort. The accommodation reached with Germany by Denmark and Norway and also by Sweden, which avoided occupation by proclaiming a neutrality that, in reality, gave more comfort in Berlin than in London or Washington, made the best of a desperate situation. What the Scandinavians sold to the Reich from their farms and factories would have been taken anyway. It made sense to try to keep up the appearance of sovereignty until there was a chance of getting back to the real thing. The diplomatic cat and mouse game was played skilfully by the Swedes who managed to keep on good terms with the Germans, chiefly by providing their war machine with iron ore, while offering a helping hand to their Nordic neighbours. Stockholm became a regular meeting place for Norwegian and Danish dissidents who could rely on financial support from public and private sources. Pre-empting a general round-up, Danish Jews escaped across the Sound to find refuge in Sweden. Young Danes and Norwegians who were eager to fight went to Sweden for military training and, as it turned out, for a long, frustrating period of waiting.

In the early days of the occupation, a semblance of free government was kept up in Denmark. Dr Werner Best, the SS general imported to head the Nazi administration, counted himself as a sophisticated man who could win Danish support for the German war effort by reasoned argument. Relations were polite, even cordial, while German victories mounted and the received wisdom was of a Europe destined to be ruled from Berlin.

Resistance, such as it was, attracted those who were directly under threat such as members of the banned Communist Party, many of them veterans of the Spanish Civil War. On the political right were the nationalists who refused to compromise on Danish sovereignty. Those who carried out occasional acts of sabotage were usually from one of the youth movements or students who had got together with the vague notion of 'doing something'. They had their work cut out trying to persuade anyone to take them seriously.

The heavy hand came down faster in Norway. Curt Brauer, the first German to head up the occupation, was a moderate who, like Werner Best, saw himself more as a conciliator than a despotic bureaucrat. For a short while he pinned his hopes for an easy-going compromise on Norway's small but vocal Nazi Party led by a former defence minister, Vidkun Quisling, who was only too keen to be made Prime Minister. He got the job and the trappings, including a waterside mansion and a platform seat at Nazi rallies, but without the skills or the popular backing to act as mediator, he cut a pathetic figure. Impatient with Quisling's inability to create an effective if compliant government, the Germans took over.

Brauer, who despised Quisling, was dismissed to be replaced by the hardline Joseph Terboven, friend of Goering, a tall, humourless man who took the title Reichskommisar. Quisling became the token Minister President. Most Norwegians adapted with well-concealed ill-grace and though a loosely organised resistance movement known as Milorg soon emerged, it was no match for the Gestapo. Of far greater practical benefit to the Allied cause was the speedy resolve of the Norwegian government in exile in retaining command of its merchant fleet, one of the world's biggest. Over 1,000 ships were pressed into Allied service; half of them would be lost by the end of the war.

Militarily, little else made news from Scandinavia until, post-Stalingrad and El Alamein, German supremacy could no longer be taken for granted. It was then that Danish and Norwegian resistance came into its own. In the first four months of 1943, Denmark claimed 173 acts of sabotage, more than the total for the previous three years. Many of these were of irritant value only but for the German authorities they signalled worse to come.

Werner Best kept his job but he now had to defer to a Gestapo force led by a hardliner SS general, Günther Pancke, who reported directly to Berlin. His chief assistant, described by the Swedish newspaper *Expressen* as 'the Gestapo's strongest brain and weakest backbone', was thirty-two-year-old Regierungsrat Hoffmann, a graduate of Cambridge University who came on like an English gentleman in all but his purposeful brutality.[2] A round of strikes led to martial law and the imposition of the death penalty for sabotage. But repression was counterproductive. As air drops of arms and equipment became more frequent so too did the number of resistance fighters. Railway and factory sabotage became a speciality with the best hit scored against the Globus plant in

Copenhagen which made parts for V-2 rockets. By late 1944 most resistance groups, known collectively as the Danish Home Army, had a ready supply of rifles, sten guns and pistols. Even so, the Gestapo remained the superior force, as is now clear from a report on resistance activities prepared at the end of the year by the head of the German security police in Denmark, Otto Bovensiepen. An eighteen-page document detailed the identity of key personnel in the resistance movement, information gained from interrogation of captured saboteurs and agents of the Special Operations Executive (SOE), the guerrilla organisation set up with Churchill's encouragement to cause disruption in occupied Europe. Even the Freedom Council, a seven-man coalition of active resistance groups and, in effect, Denmark's political leadership under the occupation, was known to the Gestapo, though its members were still under cover.[3]

Realising the Gestapo was getting near to closing down the entire resistance movement, the call went out to London for bombing raids on German intelligence operations. The first choice of target was the campus of Aarhus University where the Gestapo had requisitioned a building. The destruction of records held there was calculated to throw counter-insurgence efforts into disarray. It was the tallest of orders. The Allied air forces were not exactly noted for bull's-eye targeting. In May 1943 a squadron of Lancasters had successfully attacked the Mohne and Eder dams in the Ruhr with their bouncing bombs but the achievement of the Dam Busters was at the cost of eight aircraft and fifty-four crew members and there had been no repeat performance.

Eighteen months on, technology had reduced pilot error. With radar, not previously used for low-altitude bombing, navigators were able to close in even on unseen targets. Also, Allied air supremacy made success more likely. But in one particular, the proposed attack on Aarhus was far more challenging than the breaching of the Ruhr dams. The 1943 raid was on enemy territory where civilians could be expected to take their chances. But in Denmark, civilian casualties, even in the best of causes, were liable to be turned into a propaganda victory for the Gestapo. It says much for the importance attached to the operation that it was decided to take the risk.

The job went to RAF 2 Group, commanded by Air Vice Marshal Basil Embry. If precision bombing was in its infancy, Embry was doing his best to help it grow up. A stickler for detail, he had set out to prove that his light Mosquito bombers were capable of finding and destroying any target down to a single building, by day or night, with the margin of error down to 200 yards for medium-altitude bombing.[4]

But with technology dependent on pilot skill rather than the other way round, Embry insisted on lengthy planning and rehearsal. Using plaster models of the prospective target and its surroundings:

> we examined at eye level, obtaining exactly the same oblique view, in miniature, as if we were flying over the town at a height of fifty feet. We then selected a combination of easily recognisable landmarks, such as church spires and factory chimneys, which we adopted as navigational markers to define our approach route to the target. At the start of the approach the landmarks might be as far as two miles apart, but the distance between markers would be gradually narrowed down until eventually it was as if we were flying down a visual beam.[5]

Experience brought further lessons. Returning from a mission across the French coast, Embry's plane was struck by a duck. With such a fragile aircraft, constructed chiefly of wood, this could have been disastrous. Embry called in the naturalist Peter Scott to advise on the flight habits of large birds.

Having carried out sorties against rocket and flying bomb launching sites in northern France (thirty-two were destroyed by 2 Group), Embry proved what more could be done by attacking the prison at Amiens where of the 700 French resistance militants awaiting trial and almost certain execution, 258 prisoners escaped. There followed a daring assault on Gestapo headquarters in The Hague, a five-storey building opposite, of all places, the Peace Palace. The attack went in at fifty feet. Not a single bomb missed its mark. Bombs were seen going clean through the front door between two Gestapo guards. The building was blown apart and all the records destroyed. Not one civilian was killed. On October 31st, 1944, it was the turn of the Gestapo headquarters at Aarhus University.

> The weather was ideal for a low attack, cloud base being twelve hundred feet and in the target area visibility about a mile and a half, making interception by enemy fighters unlikely. We flew the whole way at about fifty feet. As we approached Aarhus I noticed a German transport aeroplane flying on a reciprocal course to ours and about two hundred yards to one side. If the occupants saw us, they must have had quite a shock.[6]

An attack lasting eleven minutes had a devastating impact. By chance, the Gestapo chief for the region had chosen that particular day to hold a briefing session for his colleagues throughout Jutland. Two hundred and forty of them gathered at Aarhus; not one survived. But several resistance fighters did escape. One of these, Pastor Harald Sandbaek, was under violent interrogation as the Mosquitoes flew in over the coast.

> I was taken to an office where Deputy Gestapo Chief Werner told me that this would be my last chance to tell the truth. I declared that I had no more to say, after which they dragged me up to the attic and took off all my clothes. I was thrown on a bed and whipped with a leather dog whip. I was then taken down to the office again for further interrogation. Suddenly we heard a whine of the first bombs, while the planes thundered across the University. Werner ran out of the room. I saw him disappear down a passage to the right and instinctively I went to the left. This saved my life because shortly afterwards the whole building collapsed and Werner was killed.[7]

As a final curious twist to his story, Sandbaek was rescued by his persecutors. German soldiers searching through the ruins found him, barely conscious but sharp enough to speak to them in German. Failing to recognise him, they packed him off to hospital where his resistance friends took over. After six weeks in hiding, he and his wife escaped to London.

The success of the Aarhus operation was a blow to the Gestapo but one from which it was able to recover all too quickly. The resistance was made vulnerable by communication problems, exacerbated by conflicting personalities, the widest division being between former army officers who believed in operating by their rulebook and the civilian volunteers who saw no reason why they should submit to military discipline.[8]

Political differences also contributed to the general confusion as left and right, eagerly anticipating a return to free elections, jockeyed for ascendancy. The job of trying to get the four largest resistance organisations to work together and to prepare for liberation fell to the Freedom Council which brought together the leaders of the main political parties, including the Communists.

The autumn of 1944 became a catalogue of street shoot-outs, deportations to concentration camps and executions, culminating in the arrest of Mogens Fog, an eminent neurologist and a well-known figure in Danish society but, more importantly, a leading member of the Freedom Council whose knowledge, if it could be forced out of him, would bring the whole resistance edifice crashing down. Shortly after Fog was taken, Aage Schoch, who headed the illegal press and was on the Freedom Council, was also arrested. In the Shell House, the handsome art nouveau building in central Copenhagen, used by the Gestapo as its headquarters, the mood of triumphalism started at the top with Dr Karl Heinz Hoffmann. He was convinced that he was only a step away from outright victory over the insurgents. The only comfort for the resistance was a friend within the Gestapo ranks, no less a figure than Hans Hermannsen, Hoffmann's deputy and right-hand man. Thanks to Hermannsen, terrorist suspects pulled in for questioning had a fair chance of being released without charge, an apparent miracle not unconnected with the fact that 'Uncle Hans' had copies of Hoffmann's signature and was himself responsible for keeping the records of arrests. His motives remain a mystery. The good Nazi, who died in Hamburg in 1952, was never asked for his side of the story.[9]

With the resistance in disarray, it was up to the SOE to pull things together. But there were problems here since the Allies' chief representative in Denmark, Flemming Muns, was not only under threat from German intelligence but no longer trusted by his own people who suspected him of purloining resistance money for personal use. The replacement for Muns was Ole Lippmann, a twenty-eight-year-old Danish activist who had worked at SOE's headquarters in London's Baker Street since August 1944. Lippmann arrived in Copenhagen by a circuitous route via Stockholm in early February 1945. His first objective was to restore a semblance of order to resistance activities, a task which called for delicate negotiations between warring factions. But diplomacy was not enough. What was needed was a mighty boost to morale, a display of strength that would unnerve the occupying forces. One option was to activate a plan to attack the Gestapo's central head-quarters in the Shell House. The idea had been fleshed out after the successful Aarhus University raid. If Embry and his RAF 2 Group could pull off a repeat performance, the Gestapo would lose valuable records and, possibly, many of its key staff. But there were serious objections. Taking out an enemy stronghold in the middle of an otherwise friendly city highlighted the question of civilian casualties. Nearby the Shell House was a large hospital and apartment blocks. Moreover, some of the leading figures in the Danish resistance, including Mogens Fog, were held prisoner on the two top floors of the Shell House. When the bombs fell they would be among the first fatalities. Which, of course, is why the Gestapo put them there: as a deterrent. Against this, many of the prisoners were facing execution. Was it not a fair assump-tion that if they had to die they would rather it was in an RAF raid than in front of a firing squad? For Lippmann, the clinching argument was the imminence of another round-up of resistance workers following the capture of a regional leader who was carrying a list of names, contact locations and meeting dates.[10] On March 4th, he signalled London with the code word – Carthage – that was supposed to trigger the attack.

But Embry had yet to be convinced. What he was being asked was 'a crazy way to do things'. Copenhagen's most modern office complex was easy enough to find. The detailed planning model showed a building that could be seen clear across Sankt Jørgens Lake, its heavy camouflage making it more not less prominent since, ironically, the Shell House was the only structure in the neighbourhood to have a protective cover.

The worry for Embry was the inevitability of killing many of those he most wanted to save. He also had the fate of his own men to consider. To succeed with such a daring low-level raid, every bit as hazardous as that undertaken by the Dam Busters, the weather had to be kind. In March, over the North Sea, that was asking a lot. The agony of waiting was almost too much for Ole Lippmann. On March 10th, he repeated his Carthage signal. The next day he followed up with a gloomy assessment of his chances of holding the resistance together as a fighting force.

> We have been living through what has probably been the darkest of all dark periods . . . there is no military leadership, all military leaders down to group level have been lost. In addition, all operational plans . . . have fallen into the hands of our friends (the Gestapo) and there is no doubt that they are aware of the entire resistance organization.

Operation Carthage would not solve all problems. The best that Lippmann was hoping for was 'the little breathing space we desperately need'. But when, after another week, the Shell House was still in place, he accepted what he now felt was inevitable. 'We have given up clamouring for Carthage – there must be some reason or other, which we perfectly understand. It's a pity, but it's part of the game.'[11]

Then, on March 19th the weather turned. With clear skies forecast for the next forty-eight hours, Embry gave the order for the picked crews to assemble at Fersfield airfield in Norfolk. Their briefing did not minimise the difficulties. While easily identifiable, the Shell House was built of steel and reinforced concrete, as near bomb-proof as anything could be. Incendiaries would have enhanced the destructive power of Embry's force but few were carried to minimise the risk to the prisoners on the sixth floor. For the same reason, the bombs were to be aimed at the first floor of the building.[12] Nobody had to be told that the dividing line between success and disaster was so slender as to be almost invisible.

Three waves of Mark VI Mosquito bombers – eighteen in all – with a fighter escort of twenty-eight Mustangs set out from Fersfield in Norfolk at 0855 on March 21st, 1945. Each Mosquito carried forty-four 500-pound bombs. They were fused to allow a delay of nine seconds between impact and explosion. It was just long enough for the last aircraft in the last formation to clear the area before the first bombs exploded. The raid was led by Group Captain Bob 'Pin Point' Bateson with Embry as number three in his formation. It was a rough ride across the North Sea. Flying low above gusty waves, windshields were soon covered by an oily salt spray. When the glycol in the washers ran out, the dry blades of the wipers scraping across the screen were worse than useless. At 250 miles an hour, pilots opened their side windows to clear the view with their gloved hands.

After an hour and forty minutes of 'fighting with your wrists to control the aircraft', as Bateson put it, the coast of Jutland was sighted. Throttling up to 270 miles an hour, the three waves of attackers swept across the Danish countryside at little above tree height. Embry saw that many of the farmhouses were flying the Danish flag. Workers in the fields cheered them on. Copenhagen came into view and as buildings flashed past, Peter Clapham, Embry's navigator, spotted the target.

> We were now tensed for the moment of bomb release. Suddenly a bridge appeared ahead of us and I saw some poles, possibly light standards, sticking up. I eased the aeroplane up a little and then down again a few feet. By this time Peter had the bomb doors open, and the target seemed to be approaching us very fast. I pressed the bomb release and pulled up just over the top of the Shell House, and then down again almost to street level. Glancing up, I could see flak bursting just above the roof-tops. Next instant a Mosquito passed over us, certainly not more than ten feet above. Below us I saw people in the street throwing themselves flat and others dashing for doorways.[13]

Behind Embry, Wing Commander Pete Kleboe, flying his first low-level daylight raid, was no longer in the formation. Just short of the target, he clipped a light standard, probably a searchlight mast, which rose 130 feet above a railway freight depot. From his third-floor apartment, Karl Thane saw what happened. It was his belief that Kleboe left it just too late to clear the standard. With part of his undercarriage torn away, he struggled and failed to regain control. The plane rose suddenly at a steep angle and turned on its side before crashing in Frederiksborggade. Three of Kleboe's bombs fell in Søndermarksvej, killing eight. Now there was a great pall of smoke and flame rising a hundred feet, directly in the line of attack to be followed by the second and third wave of Mosquitoes. Close by was the Jeanne d'Arc School where the children had heard the air raid siren and were filing into the cellar.

Sister Rehne, an English nun, had charge of a class of twenty girls. Among them was twelve-year-old Inge Marete Jensen whose project for the morning was to draw a hexagonal ice-cream carton. Reluctant to see good work go to waste, Inge looked for a safe place for her carton, at last depositing it carefully in a washbasin before running down the stairs. On the first-floor landing she found her friend, Bente, a frail child, swaying on her feet. As Inge reached her, Bente fainted. Then Sister Rehne arrived and told Inge to run while she took care of Bente. Inge never saw either of them again.

Of the second wave, at least two and possibly four Mosquitoes mistook the inferno on Frederiksberg for the target. Four more aircraft in the third wave did the same. Crowded into the school cellar, with its small sandbagged windows high on the outside wall, the children were talking nervously, some were crying, when there was a quick succession of explosions and the walls caved in.

> The air was filled with choking dust and everything was suddenly dark and still. Soon there were sounds of movement as some of the older girls began clearing a hole through one of the windows. One by one they crept out into the daylight. As they came out into the street they saw more bombs falling and ran to find whatever cover they could as walls fell round them and flames rose into the sky.[14]

Eight-year-old Hanne Pedersen and her sister, Kirsten, a year younger, were not so lucky. They had just reached the cellar when there was a terrifying roar and the walls and floor collapsed. Hanne

Pedersen fell into a room below that was used as a food store. She was found an hour later and taken to hospital. Kirsten also fell but down some steps into another cellar, where she was unconscious for about two hours.

> When she opened her eyes everything was dark, but she could feel that the cellar was full of water. Her chin was supported just above the level of the water by a long nail which had pierced her jaw. Her legs were trapped beneath the bodies of other children. A fireman managed to scrape a hole to reach her, and once she even succeeded in grasping his helmet, but each time more of the wall collapsed and the fireman was forced to withdraw.[15]

Only eight bombs hit the Shell House – but they did their work. It was the west wing that took the brunt of the initial damage. As it started to collapse in flames, gusts of wind spread the fire to the rest of the building.

When Mogens Fog heard the roar of aircraft he assumed that they were German fighters. Even the rattle of machine-guns did not convince him that the Shell House was under attack but, curious, he climbed to the top of his double bunk to peer out of a tiny window. The planes were coming straight at it. Leaping down, he scrambled under the bunk, shielding his face with a suitcase as the first bombs struck.

On the floor below, Jens Lund was being threatened by Gestapo heavies. Suddenly there was a crash and the room tilted. As the walls crumbled Lund made a dash for the stairway. When he saw that it was crowded with people pushing and screaming, he slid down the banister. At the second floor the stairway was so packed that he had to get off the banister. Part of the stairs collapsed and just in front of him a man vanished in a dark cloud of smoke and dust. To one side he saw a gaping hope in the wall and the street below, so he jumped on to the pavement.[16]

As the leading Mosquitoes passed overhead, Fog got out from under his bunk and threw himself against the locked cell door. Then he heard the second wave coming in and made another dive for cover. A few cells away, another prisoner, Christen Lyst Hansen of the Danish police, felt the building sway. He grabbed a stool and battered down the wooden door. As he ran into the corridor he looked up to see open sky. The entire roof had been blown off. Now he could hear Fog and other prisoners shouting and hammering on their cell doors. Grabbing the keys from a guard, who seemed to be transfixed with fear, the released prisoners fled down the back stairs, away from the conflagration in the front. Fog followed but then reasoned that the Germans must have gone that way too and would be waiting below. As he made for the front of the building which had taken the brunt of the attack, he came across a fellow prisoner, Dr Brandt Rehberg, who was standing in shock, surrounded by a dozen dead bodies. Fog slapped his shoulder and said, 'Shouldn't we go on?' They made their way through the wreckage to the main door, where there was an injured girl lying on the floor. They were dragging her into the street when the wail of sirens warned of the arrival of the police. They abandoned the girl and hurried away.

Eight prisoners died in the raid. Twenty-seven escaped. The survival of so many was seen as one of the outstanding achievements of the operation. But there is little doubt that had the full load of bombs found their target few, if any, would have lived to tell their stories. Of the nine prisoners held in the west wing of the Shell House, hit by six bombs, only two escaped. However, from the south wing, which escaped bombing, all fourteen prisoners were able to get away. Of the twenty Mosquitoes taking part in the attack, sixteen returned. After the loss of Peter Kleboe, three of his co-fighters were shot down off the northern coast of Zeeland on their way back to Norfolk. One of the Mustangs crashed in flames in the Faelledparken in Østerbro. Ten pilots and crew were killed in the attack.

Eighty-six children of the Jeanne d'Arc School died, along with seventeen teachers and helpers. Some were killed by blast, some burned to death, some were killed as they tried to rescue others. There were miraculous escapes. Just one girl out of an entire class survived because she had been sent to the headmistress's study for misbehaviour. One of Inge's sisters was saved because she disobeyed the nun's order to walk to the cellar in an orderly fashion. She ran all the way. The remainder of her class were killed on the stairs as they collapsed.

As for the Gestapo chiefs, the intended victims, nearly all of them escaped, though the official in charge of records, a central figure in the German intelligence network, went the way of most of his files. His more fortunate colleagues happened to be away from the office that day, attending the funeral of a fellow Gestapo agent who had died of natural causes. As Ole Lippmann commented, 'That damned funeral should have a great deal on its conscience.' Of the eighty Germans killed, most were guards or office workers.

So was it all worthwhile?

The day after the attack, the underground Nordic News Service acknowledged 'with gratitude the pilots who destroyed . . . the Gestapo terror in the heart of Copenhagen'. But for the parents of the children who died, 'there is no consolation; we can only express our deepest compassion.'

The breathing space that Lippmann had asked for proved its worth. German reports naturally emphasised the loss of civilian lives and may indeed have persuaded many ordinary Danes that the attack was a pointless display of Allied air power. But the resistance did get a new lease of life, mounting raids on German organisations and military installations that ranged from destroying a prototype U-boat engine to stripping out the German Chamber of Commerce, thereby collecting evidence on firms that had collaborated with Berlin. The most common form of sabotage was against the rail network. Much was made of this in SOE reports though the effect on Danish morale was almost certainly more significant than the usually minor delays caused to German troop movements.[17]

There was one more RAF assault on the Gestapo in Denmark. On April 17th, their headquarters in Odense on the island of Funen was hit. With Embry again leading from the front, the attackers had problems actually finding the building which was in a thickly populated area and well camouflaged. This turned out to be a blessing. People on the ground knew well enough what the target was likely to be. With the warning roar of fighters overhead they had time to move out before the bombs fell. The Gestapo suffered another reverse but not a single Danish life was lost.

A few weeks after the end of the war Group Captain Johnnie Johnson, a friend of Embry and another flying ace, happened to be in Copenhagen where he was shown what was left of the Shell House.

> As we walked round the empty fabric, the Danes fell silent and I sensed an atmosphere of uneasiness. Some of my hosts had resorted to their native tongue and shrugged their shoulders in expressions of despair. I asked what the trouble was.
>
> For a moment or two they avoided the issue and then one of them blurted out the story of the convent school and the many children who died or were maimed. But, concluded the Dane, these things happen in war.[18]

The full extent of the tragedy of Jeanne d'Arc School had been kept from Embry. When he heard about it from Johnson it was along with an idea for an air display by 2 Group Mosquitoes to raise money for the survivors. A quarter of a million spectators turned out for the show. Today, the Shell House is no longer Shell except for a gas station. The rest of the starkly functional building is a medley of offices. Operation Carthage is commemorated by a small brass plaque on the outside of the building and by a larger stone memorial in an otherwise unadorned foyer.

Opposition to the German occupation of Norway took longer to get going. Small groups operating over mountainous country worked independently and often to mutual disadvantage. Rather more successful than the local resistance were the London-trained Norwegian fighters who worked in cooperation with the SOE. The SOE had hitherto focused on the destruction of the Norsk Hydro stock of heavy water, vital for German ambitions to build the first atomic bomb. The failure of direct attacks on the plant itself spurred one of the most audacious SOE operations of the entire war. It was learned that all reserves of heavy water were to be shipped to Germany. Thanks to Norwegian SOE agents, the route – by rail from Vermork to Rjukan, by ferry across Lake Tinnsjö and by train again to a sea port – was made known to London. Having decided on the ferry as the soft target, Lieutenant Knut Haukelid was left with the tricky assignment of planting on board explosives that would detonate when the boat was over the deepest part of the lake. The charges blew at 10.45 on Sunday morning, February 20th, 1944. Within minutes the freight cars carrying the heavy water had broken free of their deck anchors and were on the way down into 1,300 feet of water.

Until late 1944 other successful acts of sabotage were few and far between. This was in some part a failure of Milorg organisation. SOE agents smuggled into Norway found that training was poor, equipment non-existent and motivation weak. A justified fear of reprisals deterred all but the most dedicated combatants, while the deep distrust that existed between Milorg and the Communist underground put paid to many otherwise well-laid plans. But the weaknesses were not entirely self-inflicted. In the run-up to the D-Day landings, and for the weeks following the liberation of France, the Allies refused to be diverted by what were regarded as peripheral matters. It was enough that Norway was holding down over 400,000 crack German troops (in addition to the 200,000 mostly younger or over military age in Denmark), ready to defend the country against the invasion that Hitler believed, mistakenly, was imminent. The passive strategy was put bluntly to the Milorg leadership in a SHAEF memorandum: 'No Allied military offensive operations are planned for your theatre, therefore no steps must be taken to encourage the Resistance Movement as such to overt action, since no outside support can be forthcoming.' Sabotage on a limited scale was permitted as long as it was undertaken 'in such a way as not to commit the Movement as a whole, whose primary role is protective'.

At the same time, efforts were made to equip the Norwegian resistance as an 'offensive reserve force', ready to act when it was judged appropriate. New supply lines were opened in late 1944. In addition to 171 air drops, arms were brought in by agents based in Sweden and on boats from the Orkney and Shetland Islands operating along the Norwegian coast. The 'Shetland Bus' completed seventy-three missions to deliver 138 tons of arms and equipment. The expectation of more concerted action before too long was encouraged by Russia's recapture of all its northernmost territories. This brought the Soviet army to the Norwegian border and into Finmark, a sub-arctic region, home to the nomadic Lapps. Kirkenes, the only town of significance in the Russian path, was all but destroyed in bitter fighting and the civilian population forced to move south. The Red Army pushed on another sixty miles before a hard winter put supply lines at risk. There was no point in taking chances. The real action for the Russians was on the eastern front. In Norway they were content with stalemate though the Germans were not to know this. The military, and Hitler in particular, was nervous of a surprise northern incursion not only from Russia but also across the border with Finland which by now (October) had declared war on Germany. That nervousness was intensified by resistance activity. Among the more adventurous of Milorg operatives was Gunnar Sonsteby, a former economics student who had signed on in the early days of the occupation. He was now in command of a group of saboteurs known as the Oslo Gang.

> We learned that the Germans had a big store of oil down in the docks. We were told to destroy it. Six of us were to do the job – Tallaksen, Rasmussen, Manus, Gram, Houlder and me. Our plan was this: At 9.45 in the morning we would set off in the Nash with Manus driving, Tallaksen beside him, and me on the flat together with two sixty-gallon drums of gasoline, a pile of incendiaries, and a number of two-and-a-half pound charges of plastic explosive. The other three were to follow on bicycles.
>
> On Thursday, October 12th, we drove out from our garage. There was thick mist over the docks and it was raining steadily. As we reached the part of the docks where the store was, we caught sight of a German truck with about fifteen soldiers sitting nearby . . . After a tedious half-hour wait, we saw them get in and drive off. Tallaksen and I walked into the store office. There was nobody. We

went into the store, where we found four men. Tallaksen told them to put their hands up and keep away from the telephone. Then I took them into the office. Tallaksen signalled to Manus, who drove up. The others followed on their bicycles and went to work.

Charges were fixed to four oil-drums and connected with an exploding fuse. The incendiary bombs were scattered along the line of the fuse but a little away from it; then the gasoline was poured over the whole thing. We also fixed a charge to the fire hydrant at the store, to put that out of action. Then we started a five-minute fuse.

The explosion was quite effective. 50,000 gallons of oil were burned and a considerable quantity of special gear oil.[19]

The Oslo Gang was also credited with disrupting production at the Korsvold aircraft factory, the acid factory at Lysaker and the locomotive works at Kragerø. A destroyer was sunk at the Horten naval yard and the factory making anti-aircraft guns at Kongsberg was blown up, as too was the headquarters of the German-controlled state police in Oslo.

Then in November, a Communist-led group based on the Akers shipyard, where absenteeism ran as high as 33 per cent of the work-force, decided to go for broke. A plan to put the entire yard out of action was ill-received by Milorg, ever at loggerheads with the Communists but on this occasion convinced that ambition had outreached common sense. The saboteurs were not to be deflected. Going ahead without Milorg support, they found their own supply of explosives. The big bang put much of the yard beyond use. Fifty thousand tons of shipping went down while the only crane capable of lifting heavy tanks and artillery was turned into scrap metal.

The action was better timed than even the perpetrators could have imagined. When the Wehrmacht launched its surprise attack through the Ardennes, it would have made sense to bring in reinforcements from Norway where troops were trained for winter fighting. Instead, with the resistance gaining strength, most of them were told to stay put. Meanwhile, a new Allied directive urged the destruction of railway installations. The aim was put a stop to the movement of troops and to make Hitler think twice about a logical redeployment of his

Nordic forces to the western front. In the critical months of December 1944 and January 1945, thirty sabotage attacks were carried out. Most of these caused only minor damage and inter-rupted traffic for days or just hours but north of Trondheim, an SOE action group sent in from England blew up an important railway bridge on the only north-south connection in the area, destroying a Germany military train and blocking traffic for two weeks.

The Gestapo-controlled state police responded with a propa-ganda campaign against 'banditry', threatening death without trial for captured saboteurs. When a general call-up for the civil guard was largely ignored, night raids on private homes became common-place. Those like Tore Gjelsvik, who were active in the resistance, had to be more than usually vigilant. In late January he was hiding out in the west of Oslo. Towards midnight there was a ring on the doorbell. When he failed to answer, the lock was broken and three state police troops burst in. Gjelsvik had every reason to be worried. After four years, he knew the names of far too many people – not only among the civil resistance leaders, but also in Milorg and the intelligence service. He had to get away.

> The police knew that there was something mysterious about me, and I was put through it for half an hour with blows and kicks and repeated demands to tell the truth. When that failed, the leader went off to a telephone. The other two stood in such a way that the one who waved a pistol about could not fire without endangering his colleague. I spotted a chance. I tore open the door and was away on to the staircase. I was three or four yards ahead down the stairs. I felt the whiplash of a bullet on my shoulder and thought 'That was a close one', while I rushed round each turn in the staircase. The next second I was outside in the street.
>
> I now felt my shoulder beginning to smart and the arm stiffening: I had after all been hit, but there was no time to think about that. After a detour to a nearby stream to destroy the scent for police tracker dogs, I ran at a steady trot to a good friend who would put me up.[20]

At about this time, the head of the state police, General Karl Marthinsen, was ambushed and killed on his way to his office in

Oslo. The reprisal left twenty-seven prisoners and five hostages dead against the wall. There was talk of a People's Strike but in the absence of broad-based support for open rebellion (why risk lives when the war is so close to ending?) or approval of the government in exile in London, the Home Front worked out its frustration with a general warning of imminent retribution for war crimes and collaboration. The counter-propaganda familiar to all those living in occupied countries was an appeal for a united front 'to save Europe from the peril in the East'.

The war of words had little effect either way but sabotage against selected targets – the approved method in London of mitigating the German war effort – brought spectacular successes. With the ever increasing supply of weapons (there were 470 air drops in the first four months of 1945 against 200 for the whole of 1944) Milorg kept up the good work of delaying, even halting, the transfer of German troops and equipment to sectors where they could more effectively defend the Reich.

The climax came in March with Operation Cement Mixer, a coordinated campaign of disruption of railways throughout southern Norway. Lines were broken in nearly a thousand places while the headquarters for the German railway administration fell to the Oslo Gang. Gunnar Sonsteby was its leader.

A friend in the fish trade had a warehouse just opposite the railway building. Morland drove down to the warehouse in broad daylight with four suitcases of explosives and two machine pistols with silencers. All this was placed against a wall behind some fish boxes. At nine o'clock that evening we assembled at the warehouse. Nordahl and two others were to place the charges and link them with the cordtex fuse. Pevik and I were to handle the guards.

At the back of the Railway Building was a small two-storey building that housed several offices and the caretaker's flat. A covered passage-way led from this small house to the Railway Building, a distance of about 25 feet. If we used this passage-way we hoped to take the guards by surprise.

At 9.30, Pevik and I left the warehouse. I walked ahead to unscrew the light bulbs at the entrance to the smaller railway building. Morland and one of the others made a quick round of the offices to see if anyone was there and found two or three people working overtime. They were escorted at pistol point to the caretaker's flat. Pevik and I then went on down the passageway to the big building. We let ourselves in quietly and were soon at the glass compartment by the main door. In it sat a German with his pistol on the desk in front of him. Pevik kept him covered with a machine-pistol.

Nordahl and his helpers now got busy with the charges. While they were occupied with this, the German recovered from the shock and got into a fine fury. He went for Pevik, kicking him and shouting as loud as he could to warn his companions on the floors above. I went to see if Nordahl was ready but he wasn't. When I got back to the main door, the German was still bellowing. Pevik called to me that we must make him quiet or people would hear him and give the alarm. We hesitated a moment for we would have preferred not to kill him but he kept on shouting so we had no choice. A burst from the machine-pistol silenced him.

Five minutes later, the charges were all in place and linked with cordtex. While Pevik had been struggling with the German, I had locked the main door, so we now went back the way we had come. In the smaller building, Morland and his assistant joined us and, taking the later workers and the caretaker's wife with us, we walked out and mingled with the evening crowds. Then we made our various ways back home, with the roar as the building collapsed still in our ears. There had been no way of warning the guards without endangering the whole enterprise. They had to be sacrificed.[21]

After West and East met at the Elbe, Montgomery's forces veered north towards Scandinavia to secure the Baltic ports and to pre-empt any ambitions lurking in the Soviet war plan to enforce Communism on Denmark and Norway. German strength in Denmark was around 200,000 but of these few were of fighting calibre. Leaving aside the non-Germans – mostly Hungarians with a few Russian and Polish volunteers – the rest were either too old, too feeble or too green to put up much resistance.

Norway was more of a challenge. By Christmas 1944, there were somewhere between 400,000 and 420,000 German troops in Norway, including the Twentieth Mountain Army lately withdrawn from Finland. All were of top quality, an elite fighting unit which had been spared the ordeals of the rest of the Wehrmacht. While there was talk of mounting support in military command for a peace deal, Terboven was determined to hold out. At a celebration of Hitler's birthday in Oslo on April 20th, the greeting sent to the Führer must have given him some comfort, 'Norway shall be held.'

German hopes and Allied fears of a last stand in Norway were short-lived. News leaked out of talks between Himmler and Count Falke Bernadotte, head of the Swedish Red Cross, on a possible nego-tiated surrender. When Hitler repudiated Himmler and appointed Grand Admiral Doenitz as his successor, there were rumours spread of the German forces in Norway being used as a bargaining counter to soften Allied demands for unconditional surrender. But there was to be no bargaining. On May 3rd the German civil and military leaders in Norway and Denmark were summoned to a meeting with Doenitz. The Danish representatives wanted to settle. Their armistice in Denmark came into force two days later at the same time as German forces capitulated elsewhere in Europe. But Norway had to wait. Terboven, supported by his Gestapo chief Heinz Fehlis, was not ready to quit. Having much else to think about, Doenitz left the Reichskommisar to make his own decisions.

On the evening of the 5th, Home Front leaders were telegrammed by Eisenhower telling them to make available to the German Commander-in-Chief in Norway the wavelengths and call signals for making contact with SHAEF. It took two more days for the final act to be played out. To the last, Terboven waited for an encouraging word from Doenitz. None came. On the afternoon of May 7th, Tore Gjelsvik, now a veteran of Norwegian resistance, was cycling to his cover address in Oslo.

Several of my colleagues arriving at the flat were able to confirm that the BBC had announced that the German forces had surrendered unconditionally on all fronts, the capitulation having been signed by the new Supreme Command in the early hours of the same morning. Yet we did not feel safe until early the next day.

It was still not peace or even an armistice; the latter would only come into force more than 24 hours later, at midnight on the 8th-9th. A victory proclamation had already been composed, which should adorn the front page of the next day's *Oslo Press*.[22]

The unfinished business did not take long to complete. Joseph Terboven followed the example of his Führer, though rather more messily. He blew himself up with a hand grenade. Fehlis chose a bullet. Five months later Vidkun Quisling faced the firing squad.

There is a postscript. At the end of every human ordeal there is for some a feeling of anticlimax, of missing out on the big events. In Norway and Denmark the sensation was most acute among those who had volunteered for Harry Soedermann's armed brigades, young Danes and Norwegians who had spent the war years in Sweden, training and preparing themselves for the day when they would drive the invaders from their homelands. Soedermann was a well-connected Swedish criminologist who acted as a contact man between his own government and the official and unofficial authorities in the neighbouring countries. Somewhere along the line he came up with the idea of creating an armed force of young expatriates who would be ready to take a lead in the liberation of their countries. Neutral Sweden provided the cash, accommodation and military support in the form of camps, uniforms, arms and instructors. By the early spring of 1945, there were some 17,000 highly trained Danes and Norwegians ready to go on the attack. They waited in vain. The Daneforce, as it was known, did get to within striking distance of Copenhagen but was then told by the British military that further movement would merely provoke a German reaction.

The Norwegians were even more frustrated. Two days after the German capitulation, 13,000 eager young soldiers were held at the border while British forces and the Home Front were cheered on the streets of Oslo. War, they had to tell themselves, is not a precise science. While some remember deeds of valour, others have to make do with thoughts of what might have been.

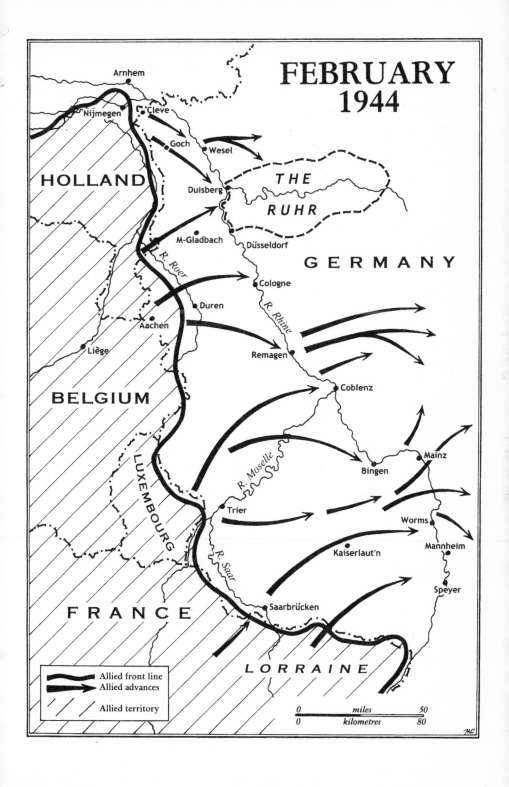

FEBRUARY 1944

Arnhem

Nijmegen
Cleve
Goch
Wesel

HOLLAND

Duisberg

THE

RUHR

M-Gladbach
Düsseldorf

GERMANY

R. Roer

Cologne

Duren

R. Rhine

Aachen

Liège

Remagen

BELGIUM

Coblenz

R. Moselle

LUXEMBOURG

Bingen

Mainz

Trier

Worms

Kaiserlaut'n

Mannheim

R. Saar

Speyer

Saarbrücken

FRANCE

L O R R A I N E

Allied front line
Allied advances

Allied territory

0	miles	50
0	kilometres	80

9
Advance to the Rhine

In the war of words, fought in the newspapers and on radio, both sides exaggerated the strength of the Wehrmacht, the Germans because they had to keep faith with the promise of ultimate victory, the Allies because they feared that if the Third Reich was known to be tottering their own people would weaken their resolve to achieve unconditional surrender. So it was that with some eighty German divisions facing some eighty Allied divisions the length of the western front, the combatants were seen to be evenly matched. The truth was otherwise.

Everywhere the German defences were suffering chronic manpower shortages. The only possible response to the forthcoming Allied attack was to watch for signs of enemy activity and to concentrate in strength at potential trouble spots. But this was made near impossible by mounting supply problems. Allied air forces had brought chaos to the transport network and there was not nearly enough fuel to keep the tanks and munition trucks rolling. By the beginning of February, oil production was down to four synthetic oil plants and reserves were all but exhausted.

The contrast on the Allied side could not have been more stark. American war industries were now at peak production feeding the military machine in the Far East as well as the forces on both European fronts. Moreover, in planning the final push into the German heartland, Eisenhower could count on a steady build-up of manpower. The flood of new recruits was a mixed blessing – their level of training was the despair of veterans – but there was no denying strength in numbers which were now so great that a new American army, the Fifteenth, was created to add to Bradley's Twelfth Army Group.

With so much counting against the Wehrmacht, the question arises, why did it risk all on a contest west of the Rhine? It would surely have been more sensible to make a stand across the river, one of Europe's most formidable natural barriers. Over a mile wide in parts, with a flow powerful enough to sweep away unpractised navigators, the Rhine had long been Germany's strongest protection against invasions. The last army to have crossed the Rhine was led by Napoleon and that was in 1805.

There were two reasons for the defiance of military logic. The first was more emotional than strategic. For the architects of the Third Reich, the Rhine was an exclusively German river with west-bank cities like Krefeld and München-Gladbach as much part of Germany as Berlin itself. Needless to say this was not how the French, Dutch, Belgians and Luxembourgers saw it. What was or was not German territory had long been in dispute. Neighbouring countries had felt safer with the Rhine as their eastern border and the Germans behind it. The post-First World War compromise had tried to reconcile French demands for security with a degree of self-determination for the German-speaking population on the left bank by designating the Rhineland a demilitarised zone, thirty-one miles deep. A multi-national occupying force was supposed to remain for fifteen years but left after twelve with promises from Germany designed to smooth away French fears.

Then in 1936 Hitler ordered his troops into what one of his apologists described as Germany's back garden.[1] After much huffing and puffing from the French and the British, the Führer was told that he could stay, which he had every intention of doing, as long as he behaved himself, which he had no intention of doing. Almost immediately the German military started to build a three-line defence network of concrete pillboxes, anti-tank ditches and minefields. The West Wall or Siegfried Line ran through the Reichswald Forest, itself a formidable barrier. There was also the Hochwald, more forest, with 'layback' defences covering the approach to the Rhine at Xanten. This was the second reason why Hitler chose to fight on the west bank of the Rhine. For him, the Siegfried Line was much more than an impressive piece of military engineering. He saw it as an impenetrable line of concrete fortifications. Behind it the Reich, so he confidently predicted, was secure.

The first and by far the strongest assault on the German-held positions along the Rhine was to be launched at the northern end of the Allied line. Montgomery's Twenty-First Army Group intended a set piece battle that would clear the way to the industrial cities of the Ruhr. This was Operation Veritable. The main thrust of the attack was to come from the Nijmegen area through the forests of the Reichswald. The general charged with the responsibility for bringing it off was a feisty Canadian, Henry Crerar. He was not Montgomery's favourite, probably because he was not inclined to be deferential but he did have a way of making things happen.

Crerar had the Canadian First Army, including the British Thirty Corps under General Brian Horrocks, in all 300,000-strong, to achieve his objective. A second-stage attack, Operation Grenade, fell to General William S. Simpson's US Ninth Army. After crossing the River Roer, Simpson was to drive northeast to crush German resistance in the Düsseldorf, Krefeld, München-Gladbach region before linking up with the Anglo-Canadians at Wesel. An essential preliminary to Grenade was the capture of the seven Roer dams to stop the Germans holding up the Ninth Army simply by opening the floodgates. This task was allocated to General Courtney Hodges' US First Army.

It all looked so good on paper. There was some American criticism of the time it took Montgomery to prepare for battle but there was no denying that he had used his opportunity to build up a formidable array of military hardware. Meeting war correspondents the day before the attack, Crerar reeled off the figures – 1,880 tons of bridging equipment for five bridges across the Meuse into the forward assembly area; 100 miles of road constructed or improved; 35,000 vehicles and 1,300,000 gallons of petrol to carry troops and equipment; 1,000 tanks; 500,000 air reconnaissance photographs; 800,000 maps and 350 types of ammunition.[2] These statistics, undeniably impressive, detracted somewhat from an even more striking achievement – the organisation and sheer physical labour needed to make best use of what was on offer. Lieutenant Colonel Baker, a planning officer with the Second Canadian Corps, worked 'like mad' throughout the last week of January and the first week of February, managing only two to four hours' sleep a night.

3–5 February 1945: We have all reached the state where we are completely pooped and have had to resort to the use of Benzedrine tablets and black coffee to try and stay awake. The Brass around here are apparently quite concerned about our physical condition as they sent a doctor in to administer the Benzedrine tablets from time to time and to keep an eye on us. The pills did a wonderful job, and it was really amazing the way they woke us up and cleared our heads. It was amusing when Tommy O'Hara and I walked into our Mess for a quick bite of dinner. We had been away for about a week and were both pretty well worn out. We apparently showed it because Gus Sesia took one look at us and immediately ordered up a double Scotch for each. It certainly helped.[3]

The build-up went largely undetected by the Wehrmacht. General Alfred Schlemm, whose 12,000-strong First Parachute Army held the critical sector, later asserted that he had known something was up but had been unable to convince Rundstedt who 'felt that the main offensive would come further south opposite Venlo'.[4] The argument was largely academic. The under-manned German defences were so tightly stretched that any movement from one sector to another ahead of a major battle was bound to create dangerous weaknesses.

Before Veritable and Grenade could get underway, there was some mopping up to do in the Roermond triangle where two German divisions held a twelve-mile section at the meeting point of the Roer and the Meuse. This was an operation delayed by the Ardennes offensive but which had now taken on fresh urgency as the US Ninth Army prepared for its Roer offensive. To bypass the Germans, the only enemy forces left on the west side of the Roer, would have been to risk a damaging attack on Simpson's left flank before he had even got to the river. The attack by Thirty Corps was launched in the early morning of January 16th 'in fog, darkness and bitter cold'.

In a series of pincer movements the Seventh Armoured Division (the Desert Rats), including the Eighth Armoured Brigade, crossed three belts of heavily equipped defences before closing in on Heinsberg, a small town flattened by bombing but seen as the last stronghold in the triangle. The hard going through mud and minefields was eased somewhat by the second appearance on a battlefield of the First Rocket Unit of the Royal Canadian Artillery, a daunting battery of twelve rocket projectors each of thirty-two barrels. Firing at ranges up to 7,000 yards, each salvo was capable of delivering over 350 rockets simultaneously into an area 200 yards square. Survivors on the receiving end emerged from cellars so dazed and shocked that 'they walked blindly into walls'.[5] But even with a superiority of firepower, the penalties for underestimating the opposition were liable to be severe. In one local operation, twenty tanks were lost, eleven of them in a single night. It was never made clear what had happened, but rumour said that the tanks had been parked along the main street while the crews disappeared into the houses to do a little quiet looting. Some Tigers – some said only one Tiger – had arrived and brewed-up the lot.

Heinsberg fell to the Royal Scots and the King's Own Scottish Borderers on the morning of January 24th. The Lowland Division, meanwhile, set up its headquarters at Hongen, thus earning the distinction of being the first British unit to put down roots in German soil. Four days later the division commander, his four brigadiers and some twenty other senior officers were heavily and accurately bombed by their own aircraft. The first to rise to his feet was the officer commanding the machine-gun battalion. 'Ah,' he was heard to remark, as he inspected the prone figures around him. 'I now seem to be commanding the division.'[6]

If the Siegfried Line was a boost to German confidence, so too was the lie of the land. Between the Meuse and the Rhine was some of the worst fighting terrain in Europe. The Reichswald was not just thickly wooded; it was also hilly and it was the Germans who held the high ground. Armour had to move along narrow dirt roads which were vulnerable to surprise attack. The weather too brought comfort for the Wehrmacht. In early February the snow had turned to heavy rain. Much of the battle area was ankle-deep in mud. In some places amphibious vehicles had to be used to carry troops from one island of land to another.

A tank officer with the Argyll and Sutherland Highlanders recalls the build-up of forces with forty-mile tailbacks on the only roads that were still passable.

> Two days remained before we were to concentrate for the battle, and they were spent in trying to get our clothes dry and peering at the Reichswald. From the forward edge of the Groesbeek woods the ground sloped gently downhill, across open fields dotted with the crashed gliders of the American airborne troops who landed here on the extreme right flank of the Nijmegen operation of the previous September. In the valley clustered the houses of a few scruffy villages which marked the Dutch-German border, and beyond loomed the solid, forbidding bulk of the Reichswald. It was not a pleasing prospect, and as the rain poured down we could imagine what the mud was going to be like on the low-lying ground before us.[7]

To the rear, officers and troops were listening to or giving final briefings. Captain Moore was among those who gathered at a cinema in Helmond to hear their divisional commander spell out the aims of the offensive.

> As a backcloth to the stage, there was a large map, quite the largest I have ever seen, showing on a large scale the whole area around and beyond the Reichswald Forest. Then, with a display of great confidence, the divisional commander began to describe the expected progress of the oncoming battle. Whenever a place was mentioned, its location on the map would be indicated by an immaculately dressed young staff officer, with the aid of a long pointer, and we were all aware that, within the next few days, while we would be up to our necks in mud and snow, he would still be immaculately dressed. However, the General himself confidently described how, when we and the Canadian Division attacked the Reichswald, the Ninth American Army would strike northwards towards us. All looked plain sailing and we were convinced that nothing could go wrong.[8]

Others were more cynical. Corporal Dai Evans was with the Royal Welsh Fusiliers based near Groesbeek.

We had a meal just before dark, followed by a last briefing from our officer. 'You'll be woken at oh-five-hundred-hours, lads; that's when the barrage starts. After breakfast we will march to the edge of the village [Groesbeek], there we will pick up our tanks and ride on them in order to follow the first waves of infantry who are to start off from a point about two miles away at oh-eight-hundred-hours. When they have reached their objective we will take over from them and advance to form the second wave. Early reports say there is no sign that the enemy is expecting our attack.'

This we took with a huge pinch of salt. Jerry was too good a soldier not to be alert to such a tremendous build-up of opposing forces . . . We found sleep impossible; we were cold, uncomfortable and very nervous of what was to come . . . Sometime after midnight we gave up the struggle, got up, organised ourselves, lit a fire with some broken stair-rails, and waited for five o'clock. The hands of our watches seemed to move in slow motion, but eventually on the very dot the barrage burst out. Being some way behind the front we were in the zone of the medium artillery, the 5.5's. Further to our rear the heavy guns were thudding away, their shells roaring over us. Stunned by all the din our company formed up in the street outside, there to find our cooks ready to dish out breakfast to those who wanted it.[9]

By the evening of February 7th, the Canadian First Army was in position and everything was ready.

The woods and outskirts of Nijmegen were thick with troops, guns, vehicles, workshops, tanks – all the paraphernalia of modern war. It would have been almost impossible to drop a pea into the area without hitting something . . .

Though the difficult and complicated concentration had been achieved secretly, our prospects of a swift success had dwindled since the original plan had been made. The thaw had been a great blow, because in front of us in that low-lying valley the going was certain to be bad. Luckily for my peace of mind I did not realise then just how bad.[10]

Operation Veritable got underway in the early morning of February 8th. During the night heavy bombers blasted Cleve, Goch, Weeze, Udem, Calcar and other communication centres behind the Reichswald. After they had done their work, the artillery was called into play.

The barrage was to commence at 5 a.m. though the tanks were not to fire until 5.30. We were to fire to a timed programme, and after an hour or two the whole thousand guns were to cease fire for a few minutes, so that any Jerry gun that might be firing back could be located.

I was on guard that night . . . Soon after we had begun to patrol around the tanks the night was filled with the roar of heavy bombers passing low overhead towards Jerry. Flares lit up the sky in three different areas over the horizon, and we heard the distant thud of bombs. The raid lasted about half an hour, and then silence fell again.

We woke the squadron up soon after four o'clock, and all the crews had breakfast and moved their kit up to the tanks.

At one minute to five that morning everything was peaceful. It was still dark and there was a slight mist. At five o'clock all hell broke loose! It was as bright as day, and the noise was like nothing on earth . . . At 5.30, as arranged, the tanks began to fire. The hard work fell on the operators, because all the gunners had to do was to sit still, treading on the firing button every time the breach closed on another round.

We fired for set periods, with rest intervals. During the firing periods we had to fire five rounds in each minute. We got ours off as fast as I could load, and then sat back until the minute was up. Le Maitre [tank commander] stood by with a stop watch, and Bert Morsley and McCarthy kept passing rounds up into the turret. After several hours of firing I was pretty well limp. I may have got a bit careless but, about twenty minutes before we finally stopped, a hot case ejecting from the gun split open the top of one of my fingers, so Le Maitre had to load the last few rounds while I took the stop watch.

The squadron had two casualties during the barrage. A round went off in Mr Martin's hands as he was passing it up on to his tank. Only the propellant charge exploded, not the shell, but Martin's hands were badly mangled and he had other injuries. Ron Mole was also injured by the explosion and they were both taken away in an ambulance.

At last the squadron finished its part in the firing, but the barrage still went on. The row was absolutely beyond belief, and long before it had finished I had a splitting headache. It wasn't only the concussion of the bigger guns, but the ceaseless sharp hammering of the Vickers just beside our tank. Every now and then a tremendous explosion from somewhere very near would practically shatter our eardrums. We strolled through the trees behind the tanks and discovered a clearing in which stood a huge 7.2" howitzer. Every time it fired the earth shook, and it ran backwards up wooden blocks on its big rubber-tyred wheels. Three shots would drive the blocks so far out of place that the gun had to be hauled back into position by a massive Scammel lorry.

After a long time – actually in the early afternoon – the guns and the mortars and the rockets were quiet. Silence fell on the Reichswald. The regiment moved to a village not far from Nijmegen, to get ready to take an active part in the big attack.[11]

For those soldiers trying to catch up on their sleep, the barrage was an alarm call that could not be ignored.

The ground shook with the fury of the cannonade and the walls of the sixty-pound tent whipped in and out like sparrows' wings. We sat up in our blankets, and by means of a mixture of shouting and sign language we agreed that we'd never heard such a noise. Sleep was quite out of the question, so we dressed and went outside the tent. Overhead a solid curtain of Bofors tracers indicated that even the 40 mm. anti-aircraft guns were being used to thicken-up the barrage, and the sky behind us was alight with the continual flicker of gunfire.

From the front of our wood it seemed that the edge of the Reichswald was a solid mass of explosions and it appeared impossible that anything could live in that inferno.

'It should be a walk-over by half past ten!' shouted Bob Webster; but we both knew that the Germans had a peculiar aptitude for emerging unscathed from the fiercest bombardment. Still, it was an encouraging thought.[12]

General Horrocks saw it all from his command post, a small platform halfway up a tree.

The noise was appalling, and the sight awe-inspiring. All across the front shells were exploding. We had arranged for a barrage, a curtain of fire, to move forward at a rate of 300 yards every twelve minutes, or 100 yards every four minutes, in front of the troops. To mark the end of the four-minute period when the guns would increase their range by 300 yards they all fired a round of yellow smoke.[13]

In the northern sector, south of the River Wael, the Germans had breached the dykes, flooding the main road from Nijmegen to Cleve and the surrounding area. Now, as the rain poured down, the river itself broke one of the few remaining dykes, flooding as far east as the Siegfried defences.

Every night as soon as it was dusk, the 3rd Canadian Division set out on what were almost maritime operations, each one designed to capture one or more of the villages which, owing to the flooding, looked like small islands jutting out of the sea. Artillery would fire on the village while the Canadians in their buffaloes (amphibious vehicles) sailed off across the intervening lake and carried out their assault.[14]

The consolation of this hazardous enterprise was the freedom to float over anti-tank ditches, wires and mines. Those who were spared the water suffered the mud. On the right of the advance, the leading wave of the Canadian Second, Fifteenth Scottish, Fifty-Third Welsh and Fifty-First Highland divisions was led by the 'funnies', tanks with flails in front to clear passages through the minefields. They were soon bogged down, leaving the infantry to move forward as best they could.

Entering a wooded area where the road was a quagmire, Brigadier Charles Barker of the Gordon Highlanders came across an unnerving sight.

On either side were long lines of trenches full of young German soldiers staring at us in an upright position but quite still. The force of the gunfire must have thrown them against the back of the trench and there they remained. It was one of the most extraordinary sights I witnessed during my five campaigns and one of the most macabre. They were all youngsters with no experience of warfare rushed to the front to save the Nazi regime.[15]

But there was no time for reflection. Such was the exhaustion of concentrated fighting over a long day that, at one point, Brigadier Barker fell asleep while giving orders over his wireless. 'I was laid aside for an hour or two.'

Of all the hazards faced by the infantry as they made their laborious way along dirt tracks and across open country it was the *schu*-mines, planted just below ground surface, that were liable to give most trouble.

There was a loud bang and Danny fell down with a groan.

'Everybody stand still exactly where you are,' I shouted, for it was obviously a *schu*-mine. 'Danny, how bad is it?'

I knew it was either a broken ankle or the whole foot blown off – what the doctors call traumatic amputation. Danny's language and Porter, who at great personal risk stepped two or three paces over to him and applied a first field-dressing, told me that it was not too bad. We shouted at the tops of our voices to the Canadians for pioneers with mine-prodders and stretcher-bearers. I looked around and realized now that we were in a narrow no-man's-land, only fifty yards wide, between the German and Canadian positions. Danny, Porter and I were in the middle of a minefield, but fortunately those behind us were still in the old German diggings, so I told them to go back.

A Canadian company commander came forward to a wire fence in front and said that the stretcher-bearers would not be long. Danny was getting restive lying there on the ground and his language progressively worse.

'Never mind, Danny,' I shouted. 'The moonlight's lovely and I'll get you a bar to your M.C. for this day's work, you mark my words.'

But I, too, was becoming impatient for all this time I was standing on one leg – literally, and for about three-quarters of an hour – not daring to put the other to the ground. I don't think I've ever felt quite so foolish in my life. Then the Canadians came bustling up with two or three officers and four or five stretcher-bearers. I thought there was altogether too much bustle. 'For God's sake –' I shouted, and there was another loud bang and one of them fell down, badly injured. It now took a long time to get out the two wounded men, with every footstep being prodded first. Danny had ceased to be talkative, and I learned that he had received a lot of wood splinters in the back of the head, as Porter had in the face. When the stretcher party had left, the Canadian pioneer sergeant prodded his way up to me and led me safely out of the minefield by my planting my feet precisely in his footsteps.[16]

As the men of the Fifty-Third Welsh spread out along the road, keeping their distance from each other to reduce the chance of casualties should the Germans get lucky with their shelling, a few succeeded in hitching a lift on one of the accompanying Churchill tanks.

We climbed aboard, no mean feat this as they were not designed to carry men on their hulls. Perhaps one or two men could find a comfortable spot, but when a crowd tried it, well, it wasn't an ideal form of transport.

We moved off, passing through the light artillery zone where 25-pounders and Bofors guns were belting out shells as fast as they could load them. There was no formality, no parade-ground method, just highly skilled and experienced gun teams working smoothly together to a set plan designed to smother and annihilate the German front-line troops.[17]

The rain had turned to a miserable drizzle which threatened to get heavier again as the day progressed.

On we rolled – or rather rattled, the tanks bucking and plunging over the rough forest tracks, we hanging on to any protrusion. It sounds dashing and romantic, riding the tanks into action, but it isn't so. For one thing it is most uncomfortable; for another it is damned dangerous. One is so exposed perched up on high, an easy target for enemy machine-gunners and riflemen. There is no cover, the armour plate makes it worse as a bullet or shell splinter that misses someone on the way in has a second chance as it ricochets away. There is also the very real danger of being thrown off the vehicle and being caught by the tracks.[18]

The Fifty-Third were advancing through an area that had been no-man's-land throughout the winter months of stalemate but the dismal relics of past fighting were everywhere to see.

Houses were burned out husks or heaps of rubble. Corpses of farm animals and men lay unburied, sometimes bloated, sometimes half-eaten by foxes or crows . . . A dead German lay on the bank of a ditch, rifle at his shoulder as though to fire; his face and hands were chalk-white. How long his corpse had lain there we couldn't guess, probably a week or so as the cold weather would have preserved it; there was a gaping hole low down his back through which his blood had drained, leaving his skin that ghastly colour.[19]

If riding the tanks was misery for the infantry, it was hardly more tolerable for those inside the vehicles.

The column moved on in fits and starts all the night. It was horribly cold and I was frozen stiff, even in a zoot suit and a jerkin. As a matter of fact I was very sorry for myself, because the trip was made especially unpleasant for me by a bad attack of diarrhoea. You can imagine how awkward it was. Every time we stopped I had to crawl over the two infantrymen on the turret floor, squeeze past Le Maitre and get out of the hatch, and climb down into a field by the roadside. Having got there, I had to divest myself of a leather jerkin, a zoot suit, a suit of denims and a battledress – with the column likely to move on at any moment. It was awful![20]

Nobody in the thick of the fighting really had any idea of how the battle was progressing. Moving through Croesbeek at a slow crawl, Captain Moore's little convoy of jeeps followed the railway line before turning off into a field.

It was here that chaos started. I could see a number of tanks embedded several feet in the boggy ground. Other vehicles were either left abandoned or were milling about in search of firmer ground, not daring to stop lest they might sink. Had it not been for the superlative driving of Pte Nixey we too would be bogged down. As it was, I had to jump out when I saw my two jeeps sunk, axle-deep, in the mire.

I decided to abandon the jeeps: we would proceed on foot. Each man carried a mine-detector and a Bangalore Torpedo as well as his own rifle and equipment. L'Corporal Brain, of great physique, carried two torpedoes. Now on to Heikant and, if the leading companies needed the torpedoes, they would have to wait.

Overnight shelter was in a farm which attracted a heavy fall of mortar bombs.

The outbuildings containing the pig-styes were hit by three or four shells at once: the roof fell in and the place burst into flames, blazing furiously. Although some of the occupants escaped, several were trapped inside. Ten prisoners of war and two of our Intelligence Section were killed or burnt to death.

To our left, where all the Tactical Headquarters were assembled, we could hear the agonised shouts of the seriously wounded and the frequent calls for stretcher-bearers. Some troops of another regiment passing through had been caught by the roadside and suffered casualties. As it grew dark, the intensity of the shelling was maintained, while the flashes grew more startling. A shell landed about three feet from the hole in which we lay with an ear-shattering explosion, sending jagged pieces of red-hot metal into the hole. One piece of shell tore between my outstretched fingers on the side of the hole and embedded itself in the soil, burning my fingers.[21]

The progress report from Montgomery's headquarters later in the day was in the best tradition of military communiqués – laconic, giving little away.

At 10.30 this morning British and Canadian troops of the Canadian First Army renewed their offensive. The maximum scale of air support was provided during the night preceding the operation with Goch and Cleve being heavily bombed. Good progress initially has been made, and forward troops have reached the western outskirts of the Reichswald Forest. Fighting is going on in the outer defences of the Siegfried line. Several hundred prisoners have been taken. Full advantage of flying conditions has been utilized by the R.A.F. and the American Air Forces in strength in support of the ground troops.

The 'good progress' included the decimation of six of the seven German battalions forward of the Reichswald. The bad news was the realisation that Crerar had been set an impossible schedule. Thirty Corps was supposed to be at the Rhine by February 11th. In the event, on that day they were no further on than the outskirts of Cleve. When Horrocks got news that Cleve had been taken by the Fifteenth Scottish (after 1,400 tons of explosive had been dropped on the town) he ordered up his first line of reserve, the Forty-Third Wessex Division, intending that, having passed through Cleve, they would put fresh energy into the attack.

This was one of the worst mistakes I made in the war. The 15th Scottish had not got nearly so far as had been reported, and one of their brigades had not yet been employed at all. There was already too much traffic on this one road, and it was impossible to deploy across country owing to the boggy ground. The arrival of this extra division caused one of the worst traffic jams of the whole war, only equalled, I believe, by the scenes in the Liri valley in Italy after the battle of Cassino. The language heard that night has seldom if ever been equalled.[22]

For those in the thick of battle, a big worry was not knowing where the next meal was coming from. One evening, five carriers with rations for the First Battalion of the Black Watch of Canada got bogged down over a mile away from Tac HQ.

Capt. A.R. Hanna had gone on to Bde Tac HQ to report vehicle casualties for the day and on his way back he commandeered a small bulldozer which, however, proved unable to pull out the carriers. Capt. A.R. Hanna then went beyond Bde and managed to procure the use of a large bulldozer. On the way back to the carriers 'jerry' began shelling, using the sound of the bulldozer as the target. Shortly before this, at 2000 hrs, the enemy lightly shelled and mortared the x rds forcing the drivers to seek cover. The shells and bombs followed the bulldozer all the way causing great discomfort to the T.O. who, being unable to get into the armoured cubby hole of the big veh, was walking along behind it. Every time a shell or bomb began its whistling descent he would sprint around to the opposite side he figured it would hit. Despite the intensive fire two carriers were sent on their way and by 2100 hrs a third was free of the clinging mud. The fifth was discovered to have a split bogie wheel so the T.C. with the help of CQMS Hunter, G.E. proceeded to repair it. At 2350 hours CQMS Oxley, R., who had delivered his rations to A Coy, stopped and offered to help with the work. Shortly after they were shelled again and CQMS Oxley, R. was hit, his leg being nearly severed above the knee. They did what they could for him and put him onto an armoured 15cwt which was going by a CCP. A few mins later the carrier was repaired, towed out, and proceeded on its way to its coy.[23]

After two days of Veritable the first of the three Siegfried zones was pierced and 1,800 prisoners taken. But Montgomery's battle timetable was already in the bin. The entire operation had not been expected to last more than four days. Instead – on an advance of just twenty miles the only worthwhile objective in sight was the capture of Cleve. With all its handicaps, the Wehrmacht was still proving to be an indomitable enemy. The overwhelming force that Montgomery had amassed found itself up against four parachute, four infantry and three Panzer divisions. Of these, the most daunting were the troops of the First Parachute Army who enjoyed the title only as a courtesy; neither the aircraft nor the time had been available to teach them how to jump. But these young men, 'fresh from a Luftwaffe that had ceased to exist', were among the best at the Wehrmacht's disposal, ready to fight to the last man for a cause which still held their undiminished loyalty. Up against their stubborn refusal to accept the inevitable, it was not until mid-February that the Allies were able to lay undisputed claim to the Reichswald.

Cleve was a mess and so too were the roads leading in and out of it.

1 March 1945: I have been pretty busy the past couple of days trying to sort out a jumble of poor roads. We have so much traffic to move and so few roads on which to move it that we have to get the maximum use out of every one of our Corps roads. I made a complete road recce yesterday and at one point inadvertently got too far forward between Calcar and Udem. I came back damned quickly as soon as I saw the Hun positions and received some very broad smiles from a bunch of English troops who had taken shelter behind some battered buildings.[24]

While the Fifteenth Scottish and the Forty-Third Wessex forced their way into the ruins of what had once been the home of Anne, the fourth of Henry VIII's wives, the Fifty-Third Welsh pushed on into the Reichswald.

From now on the battle developed into a slogging match as we inched our way forward through the mud and rain. It became a soldier's battle fought most gallantly by the regimental officers and men under the most ghastly conditions imaginable. It was a slog in which only two things mattered, training and guts, with the key men as always the battalion commanders. The Germans rushed up more guns and more divisions. Eventually we were opposed by more than 1,000 guns, 700 mortars and some ten divisions; they were certainly fighting desperately to prevent our getting to their famous Rhine.[25]

On February 13th, an advance force was in sight of the Rhine opposite Emmerich. But this was small comfort for the failure of Operation Grenade to get off the ground – assuming, of course, that the Ninth Army could have found any. The original plan had been for the Ninth Army to begin its pincer movement twenty-four hours after the commencement of Veritable. But this rapid follow-on was dependent on the capture of the Schmidt dams at the head of the Roer, south of Düren, by General Hodges' First

Army. In retrospect it was an impossible assignment for the allotted time. The Germans may have been short on manpower but they had the great advantage of a last line of defence, the dynamiting of the flood barriers at the moment when they were forced to evacuate a dam. There was some hope that they would resist such a desperate act. The two largest dams supplied hydro-electric power for much of the Rhineland and many Germans and their property would be swept away if the dams were blown. The defenders did indeed recognise the awful logic of their predicament and fought hard to put off the moment of decision. Attacking by way of the Hürtgen Forest, the First Army encountered furious resistance. The village of Hürtgen changed hands fourteen times, the forest itself eighteen times and, as something of a record, the village of Vossenach twenty-eight times. But eventually the German forces bowed to the inevitable. The sluices on the Roer dams were opened and the river embankments blown up to put a large part of the west bank of the Rhine ahead of the American forces under three feet of water. 'An extreme disappointment,' commented Montgomery euphemistically.

With the unseasonal thaw extending south to the snows of the Eifel, Simpson's troops had to traverse 'a score of rushing streams' which ruled out boating or bridging operations. There was little to do except wait for the flow to exhaust itself. When the Ninth Army offensive at last went forward, on February 23rd, thirteen days after the last dam had been captured, the Roer was still eighty yards wide with a current running at five to eight miles an hour. Simpson, 'a paternal figure', said Horrocks, distinguished by a completely bald shaved head, came in for criticism for failing to keep up with Montgomery's timetable but it is hard to imagine what more he could have done. He was favoured in one respect. Confident that Simpson was all but land-locked, German command sent some of its best troops north to frustrate the Anglo-Canadian advance. These included the Eighth Parachute Division and the Panzer Lehr Division, the latter a veteran force from the Normandy battles. Only four divisions were left to patrol the Roer front. Simpson decided to take them at a rush.

As I began to move out, I heard Christopher hollering. Wall, one of the new men, had fallen in the water and, as it was almost chest deep, Chris couldn't locate him. I waded in and managed to locate him. We cut his equipment off; and since he couldn't walk, I carried him back to the road which was several hundred yards away. Lt. Cox came running back crying, 'If these men can't keep up, leave them.' Well, I wasn't going to leave anybody because I sure wouldn't want to be left. Chris had some very unkind things to say to the lieutenant and he emphasized them with a loaded MI. The lieutenant was finding out things weren't exactly like OCS. At the road I put Wall down and he said he thought he could walk. Several hours in the water in February is kinda hard on the circulation.

As we were withdrawing, our artillery fired smoke into the German positions to cover us. As we came back into our lines Capt. Chappell was there to count us all in. He said to me, 'Graff, go on back to the weapons platoon as they have breakfast and a fire; and by the way, how was it out there?'

I answered, 'Mighty damn wet.'[26]

The first objective was to cross the Roer north of Aachen, a task that required an armada of Ducks and Alligators and Weasel carriers. Preceded by a day-long air attack on German positions along the Roer and on supply lines between Düren and Cologne, the warm-up climaxed with a concentrated artillery bombardment beginning at 2.45 a.m. along a twenty-five-mile stretch of river from south of Düren to the north of Linnich. The first crossings started at 3.30 a.m. under moonlight so bright that a smokescreen had to be put down, probably the first occasion of its use at night. Some boats capsized, others were swept downstream by a current made more powerful by swollen waters and yet others fell victim to floating mines or underwater stakes that could pierce a hull. But most of the assault craft got to the east bank and by noon the first pontoon bridge was in position. Twenty-four hours later, four divisions were across the river. Düren and Jülich had been flattened and Simpson's troops were in command of an eight-mile stretch of the road north. Captain Howard Sweet was with 908th Field Artillery Regiment.

Our objective was a small town a mile or so to the northeast [of Neuss], the spires of which were plainly visible up the main highway. A company of doughboys took off in that direction. They deployed and worked in on the town from different angles. Just then a messenger from the 908th came up and handed me my mail, which I stuffed in a pocket. I decided it was time for Freeman, Hetrick and me to head for the village. Our infantry company was now there, and a few tanks were heading in. Freeman stepped on the gas and we tore straight up the highway – it's hard to hit a moving target. Before we went over a ridge into town, we stopped on the road ahead of us, and we all piled out of the jeep and jumped into some foxholes beside the road. Sitting there in the foxhole while an occasional mortar round landed up the road, I pulled out the mail and read a letter from Mother. As soon as things had quieted down, we hopped into our jeep and made a dash for it.

Their purpose was to find their command post which turned out to be a beer parlour sans beer. By now the advance troops were sending back prisoners, mostly older men who had been recruited to defend Cologne.

Sixty or seventy Germans were lined up in three or four files in the road. Their captors made the prisoners empty their pockets and throw the contents on the ground. Then the guards pawed about in the debris, appropriating anything that looked desirable. Just at this moment German artillery began to shell the area. For a few minutes the fire was fast and furious, gouging out great holes in the field 100 yards away. The prisoners looked nervous but they kept in ranks and after the shelling let up, they were marched to the rear . . . A middle-aged German woman watched the first group of prisoners come marching in, arms in the air, and she turned away and wept quietly.[27]

The strength of the resistance varied hugely from one town or village to another and could never be predicted with any accuracy. One war reporter found himself at the centre of some of the fiercest close fighting of the war.

Several hundred yards away I noticed Jerries running out of a gun position waving a white flag. A black puff of smoke a few hundred yards to my right caught my attention, then another closer. I saw some men fall on the right flank. The black puffs crept in. There were whistles and cracks in the air and a barrage of 88s burst around us, spaced like the black squares of a checkerboard surrounding the reds. I heard the zing of shrapnel as I hugged the earth. We slithered into the enemy 88 position from which I had seen the prisoners run. Somebody threw a grenade into the dugout.

We moved on. Some prisoners and a couple of old women ran out onto the field from a house, Objective One. There was the zoom and crack of 88s again. A rabbit raced wildly away to the left. We went down. I saw a burst land on the running Jerries. One old woman went down on her knees in death, in an attitude as though she were picking flowers.

. . . I looked to the right flank and saw a man floating in the air amidst the black smoke of an exploding mine. A piece of flesh sloshed by Sgt. Fred Wilson's face. Some men didn't get up. We went on. A couple of men vomited. A piece of shrapnel cut a dough's throat as neatly as Jack the Ripper might have done it.[28]

Approaching Geldern, James Graaf also found the going tough.

As the lead tank approached a bridge over a canal at the edge of town, the bridge was blown up. A bazooka round hit the lead tank and knocked it out and the road was now effectively blocked. The tanks were roadbound because of mines along the shoulder of the road. Capt. Chappel escaped injury when a bazooka round hit the tank he was on. A piece of shrapnel cut his pistol holster and lodged in two plugs of tobacco in his hip pocket. Several other men were wounded and we all dismounted and got down in a ditch along the road. The colored tankers were really laying down a barrage. The muzzle blast of the tanks firing over us was terrific. The colored boys hollered out of the tanks, 'Hey, white boy, pick them out and we will shoot them.' The combination of the mine explosion and these muzzle blasts of that day has continued to affect my hearing to this day.[29]

The flow of German prisoners was building up, though there were occasions when it took some persuading for the white flag to be raised.

We settled down to the 50% stand-to situation, which mean that each man took turn and turn about with his trench-mate to relax, the other keeping watch the while. Our lieutenant crawled over to our trench, calling softly to me, 'Corporal, have you any grenades?'

'Yessir, of course, why?'

'One of the tank officers has found a deep dug-out. He thinks there are some Jerries in it.'

I climbed out of my trench and went with him. We found the tank officer, some distance away from our position, crouching by a square hole in the ground.

'What's the matter sir?' I asked him.

'I'm bloody sure that I heard voices down there.'

The hole was some ten feet deep, with a ladder leading down into it. One of the 'tankies' had gone to bring a torch from his vehicle. Shining it down the hole revealed what appeared to be a steel door at one side. As far as we could make out the thing seemed to be a typical underground bunker, roofed with logs then covered with earth and finally grassed over.

I fired a burst from my Sten at the door, it made a hell of a row in the quiet that had now fallen but brought no result. I threw a '36 grenade into the pit and we stood back until it had exploded, then went to peer into the depths once more. The door was intact, so it was obviously very strong. I climbed down the ladder with the officer's torch lighting the way. I banged on the door which was a solid sheet of metal with large hinges and fittings protruding from it. 'Komm, raus,' I shouted, mouth close to the door. There was no reply so, feeling rather foolish, I repeated the command. To my surprise, a voice came feebly through the door, 'Bitte, schiessen Sie uns nicht.'

'Naturlich nicht,' I called.

'Wir kommen raus,' replied the voice from inside, stronger now.

'What the hell's going on down there?' called my officer.

'There's some Jerries in there who want to surrender,' said I.

'Well, what the hell are you blathering to them about?'

'I'm just saying that we won't shoot them.'

'Oh.'

The door creaked open, letting through a faint light from the inside. A man came out, holding a white handkerchief in front of his body. Behind him a cloud of thick fug was escaping through the doorway and in the dim glow of an oil lamp I could see a number of Germans. I called up this information to the officer and he came down the ladder to me, we then both went into the bunker to see what was going on.

There were several soldiers there, but we didn't recognise the uniforms which were different to those of the enemy soldiers we had seen up to then. It turned out they were an anti-aircraft unit who had taken shelter from the bombardment. They were all frightened out of their wits, scared of being shot by us and only too willing to be taken prisoner. The unusual uniform was due to the fact that they belonged to the Luftwaffe, which they told us all German anti-aircraft gunners wore. Two of them had pistols, of a type which I had not seen before. We were told they were Czechoslovakian and very common amongst such rear-line units; the two tankmen took them. By now a few more of our lads had come down to see the affair and were busily searching the prisoners, taking anything of value that they had. Wrist-watches we took as a matter of course, with no pangs of conscience: they were issued by the Wehrmacht to all officers and most NCOs, therefore could legitimately be looked upon as 'spoils of war'.

After disarming them, our officer sent his runner to report the incident; meanwhile he told Colin to put a couple of men from our section to dig a trench near the bunker, from which they could both look to the front *and* guard the prisoners. I told this to the Germans, explaining they were safer in the bunker than anywhere else; they agreed.[30]

10
Hanging Out the Washing

By February 15th, the Canadian First Army held ten miles of the west bank of the Rhine facing Emmerich. Having captured Kessel on the southern edge of the Reichswald, the next objective for Thirty Corps was Goch. The only good road to the town was strongly defended and though armoured vehicles were able to make use of half-tracks, movement over uncharted territory put them at the mercy of any obstacle, contrived or natural. Trooper Baker's tank, otherwise known as Shaggy Dog, was the last in line of its squadron.

We hadn't gone more than a few hundred yards into the forest when the path crumbled under one of 'Shaggy Dog's' tracks and we slid sideways into the ditch, to lie there hopelessly bogged. I called up Bob Gibbens in the tank in front and he was just backing to give us a tow when Bill Riley told him to carry on and leave us to be pulled out later – a pretty silly decision, as it turned out.

The squadron disappeared up the path and we were left there. It was already nearly dark and it had started to pour with rain. But the fact that we were left behind was not by any means the worst aspect of the situation. The trouble was that the path was so narrow that the tank completely blocked it, and all the huge column of vehicles which was following behind us was held up. The forest on either side was too thick for them to make a detour. It was rather a tricky situation.

Tracking back along the column, Trooper Baker came across another tank capable of pulling Shaggy Dog out of the mud but that wasn't much use since there was no way it could move to the front of the queue.

Hour after hour went by. We tried everything, but nothing was any good – not even the logs we carried were any help. Various people from down the column came up to see what was the matter. Tempers got a bit ragged and Le Maitre had a flaming row with an officer and a staff-sergeant from some other unit. All the time the rain teemed down.

Then from the opposite direction an ambulance came bumping down the tracks. It was carrying two casualties from a knocked-out tank. One of them was able to walk but the other had lost a leg and an arm as well.

Of course the ambulance couldn't get past, but somehow these two chaps had to be got back down the line. Luckily there turned out to be another ambulance a few hundred yards along the column, and in a position where it could be turned around. Four of us carried the wounded man to it on a stretcher. We kept him as steady as we could, but it wasn't too easy to squeeze past some of the trucks. He was only semi-conscious but he complained that the bandages on his leg were too tight – the missing leg, that is.

The log-jam was finally broken when a bulldozer managed to clear a path round Shaggy Dog.

All the trucks and carriers passed us, and the B squadron tank was at last able to reach us and tow us backwards out of the ditch. Just to round off the night, Bert Morsley carried on in reverse after he was clear of the ditch, backing into the towing tank and pushing its gun back into the turret, amid a chorus of shouts and curses from the B squadron crew. I hope no serious damage was done.[1]

After the Forty-Third Wessex division had driven the enemy out of the Forest of Cleve, capturing the high ground above Goch, the Fifteenth passed through to attack the town from the northeast while the Fifty-First came in from the west. Both forces had to overcome the strongest fortifications yet encountered in the campaign: pillboxes mounted in concrete two feet thick with embrasures of four-inch steel. Mines and tripwires covered the approach to each post. But for some reason, there were few anti-tank guns in the area which meant that the pillboxes were vulnerable to heavy shelling. When the entrances were blasted open, flame-throwers finished the job.

The German commander at Goch acknowledged the inescapable and surrendered on the second day of the attack. But many of his men chose to fight on and it took two more days of house-to-house fighting before the town was secure.

Shaggy Dog, the tank we met earlier in the reminiscences of Trooper Baker, stayed in Goch for two days. There was nothing much to do 'except explore the ruins and watch Typhoon attacks going in at intervals a couple of miles away'. But a memorial service was held for a tank crew that had suffered a direct hit. 'This seemed a little odd to me, because not very long before chaps had been getting killed right and left without their passing being commemorated in any way. But fatal casualties had been much rarer during the last few months and deaths seemed more of an event.'

Accommodation was found in an abandoned farm, overlooking a stretch of open ground.

> This was a reserve position and there was no danger of an attack without warning, but it was a lonely spot.
>
> It was a smallish farmhouse with a cowshed full of cows. I walked through the shed twice before I realised that all the cows were dead. Luckily they hadn't begun to smell.
>
> Unfortunately, the only room that seemed suitable for us to live in had a very messy dead Jerry lying in the middle of the floor, but we scraped him up and put down some clean straw and made the place habitable . . . A small party set about burying some of the mangled Jerry corpses which lay about the nearby fields.[2]

Having secured Goch, the Canadians and British were across two of the three main defensive belts of the Siegfried Line. The next step was Calcar and then Xanten where the third fall-back of the Siegfried Line ran through the densely forested Hochwald. Making best use of this awesome defence system was the elite Panzer Lehr Division with an infantry division in support. Crerar decided to take them head-on in a daring attack called, appropriately, Blockbuster. Once again Thirty Corps, with Horrocks in command, was in the thick of desperate fighting.

We attacked every day and every night for five long weeks, and our casualties began to mount . . . Every day I was visited by General Crerar, the army commander. He was always very well-informed because, in spite of the bad weather, he made constant flights over the battlefield in a small observation aircraft . . . After the first week the front widened sufficiently for the 2nd Canadian Corps, commanded by General Simonds, to come in on my left, or northern flank. Simonds was a first-class commander with a most original brain and full of initiative. It was his corps which now bore the brunt of the assault on the strongly-held Hochwald position.

They were faced by determined resistance from German paratroopers and it developed into a dour struggle. The Royal Winnipeg Rifles said it was 'the heaviest shelling the battalion had ever experienced'. The Regina Rifles reported 'Just as bad as anything encountered in Normandy'.[3]

Blockbuster was launched on February 26th. At 0430 hours, after a forty-five-minute artillery barrage, Canadian forces attacked under artificial moonlight. It turned out to be an inauspicious beginning as crews struggled in icy rain to free their vehicles from glutinous mud. It was a particularly unhappy time for one Canadian private.

The area was a sodden field alright; it was mud. It was late winter and it was, I'll swear . . . a ploughed field. They had unloaded all kinds of supplies in that particular area; it was a staging area. They had fields full of crates of hard tack, bully beef, canned food, things of that sort . . . They loaded us onto troop carriers that were sort of tanks . . . and most of us . . . were suffering from diarrhoea. That was basically because we had found some canned apricots and had gotten into them and it was disastrous, let me tell you. They loaded us onto these things and they took us on and dropped us off someplace in the dark in a barn and told us to sleep there for the night and we just dropped wherever we could. The next morning I woke up and I had dropped in a cow stall and I was covered in crap . . . You were dead tired, you didn't know where the hell you were.[4]

As the German artillery opened up (Montgomery said later that it was the heaviest 'volume of fire from enemy weapons . . . met so far in the campaign') the forward troops were pinned down for hours on end, some 'up to their necks in icy water'.

We were in the middle of it, standing, trying to push forward. Well, we didn't stand long. We went to ground damn fast. You just lose everything. You can't do anything about that . . . You really hunker down and pray to God that you come out of it all right, because you can't do anything for anyone, really. You look around and see if anybody is wounded and help them, but I didn't see anybody. They were all pretty well experienced and had found rat holes or something like that . . . I think at that point, I was buried a couple of times and got out of it. [The area was] mud, just mud . . . I remember hearing the shelling and then after a while I didn't hear anything, but I saw it . . . I remember the huge explosions all over the damn place. At that time I crawled under a tank to get away from some fire and I could sense the tank settling down in the mud, so I got the hell out of there . . . [There was] no cover. Trees are no cover, especially in shelling because you get limbs and you get shrapnel coming down on you . . . We didn't get any further than that.[5]

It took two days for the Canadians to reach the outer fringe of the Hochwald. Unfortunately, this was precisely where the German forces were concentrated. Counter-attacks were beaten off but only after heavy losses.

I remember stopping and asking this new lieutenant who had no battle experience where the hell the rest of the companies were. We were losing Shermans: they were running over mines; blowing tracks; getting stuck. I said, 'We'd better stop until we've got communications.' He had the radio . . . He says, 'I lost radio contact, but we've got to take the crossroads.' 'Well,' I said, 'if that's your wish, we'll push on.' . . . So we head up to the crossroads, and by the time we get there, we've got one lousy Sherman left and the Rams [armoured vehicles] we were in, the heaviest armour we had on them was a .50 calibre [machine gun] . . . There was a hedge. So we dug part of the platoon along the hedge. We kept the Rams in the back and the

Sherman started moving around and they knocked it out. So there we were, sitting ducks, with no heavy armour . . . Then they started counterattacking. I had the driver from one of the Rams who had never had battle experience in one of the next slit trenches. When they started machine gunning, he stands up to see what's going on, which is only reasonable, and he got a burst across his chest.[6]

It was not until March 4th that the Canadian Second and Third Divisions were able to clear the Hochwald. Xanten fell on the 8th but fighting in the surrounding area continued for two more days. In the course of a battle in which 'grenades and bayonets were freely used',[7] two Canadians, Sergeant Aubrey Cosens, who led a platoon reduced to four men in an attack against enemy positions, and Major F.A. Tilson, who with a serious head wound led an attack, 'shouting orders and encouragement and using his Sten gun with great effect' until he was barely conscious, were awarded VCs. Tilson lived to receive his medal. Cosens, in the moment of triumph, was shot dead by a sniper.

With the battle almost won or at least, in Alan Brooke's diary entry, 'going wonderfully well', Churchill decided on a visit to the front. He was on good form. Departing Simpson's headquarters he turned down the suggestion of using the lavatory, instead waiting until his convoy of vehicles reached the Siegfried Line where, Alan Brooke recorded, 'we processed solemnly out and lined up along the line . . . I shall never forget the childish grin of intense satisfaction that spread all over his face when he looked down at the critical moment.'[8] It was also with the Ninth Army that Churchill lost his false teeth.

But in spite of this inconvenience he started on his programme imme-diately he arrived. In the middle of the proceedings an interruption took place. Some despatch riders appeared in a cloud of dust, and they were followed by a jeep. Someone jumped out, rushed forward and handed over a sealed packet for the Prime Minister. The onlookers thought that here was a signal of great importance, some critical decision referred to him by the Cabinet. Churchill, however, took the packet and slipped it into his pocket – unread. A ghost of a smile crossed his face. Here were, of course, the missing dentures![9]

Having captured Xanten, Thirty Corps turned east towards Wesel where the enemy west of the Rhine was confined to a fast-shrinking bridgehead. Meanwhile, the US Ninth and First Armies had joined bridgeheads across the Roer, creating a front thirty miles long and seven miles deep. They now began the push towards the Rhine across the Cologne plain.

The Roer towns like Jülich and Düren had been obliterated by battle. But moving up to the front a few days after the first Allied troops had taken command of the streets of rubble, Saul Padover, an American intelligence officer, found survivors living in the cellars of shattered houses. Most were slave workers who had escaped the SS and at least two of them, young Belgians from Antwerp, could be said to have thrived in adversity.

They had worked in Cologne until last November, they told us, when they heard that Belgium was at last fully liberated, and so they decided to escape home. This they did by the astoundingly simple process of hitch-hiking. Germany was then already in such a state of confusion that the two blue-eyed Flemings had little trouble with the authorities. A Wehrmacht vehicle, thinking them German labourers on the way to work, gave them a ride without further questions, and took them as far as Julich. Unable to cross the Roer River, they went underground and patiently bided their time.

Julich was empty of civilians and the two Flemings selected for themselves the most comfortable cellar, and one stocked with the good things of life, and settled down to a luxurious existence. During the day they stayed in the cellar, and at night they went out and scrounged a few extra luxuries, such as chickens and cognac.

They lived as they had never lived before and never expected to live again. They slept on soft mattresses, ate the choicest foods, drank the finest liquors. There was an oven in the cellar and plenty of briquettes. They also had four petroleum lamps and a stock of candles. In the two months of their subterranean existence, they consumed a total of twenty-two large cans of meat, one hundred and fifty-one eggs, numerous cans of conserves, and two hundred bottles of cognac and champagne. Each of them drank at least one bottle of cognac and champagne every day. In their drowsy leisure hours they read romantic novels and travel books, and, since they found cameras and film, they snapped pictures of each other.[10]

München-Gladbach and Krefeld, important industrial centres, fell in the first week of March. Both had suffered heavy air attacks and in the population at large there was almost a sense of relief at the rumours of an imminent arrival of the Americans. Marie Therese Fuegling, an art student who had been put to work on a farm before returning to her parents in Krefeld in late 1944, recalled life in the city in its last days under Nazi rule.

People prayed a lot, even those who hadn't done so for a long time. We lived our lives in the cellars, with makeshift beds and cooking facilities. For days we had no electricity, water or gas. The German airforce was busy elsewhere, so we were subject to constant air threats with no aerial protection. Sleep deprivation led to constant over exhaustion. But it numbed us to the terror and panic. We wished for the end of the war simply so that we could get a good night's sleep . . . Men over 60 and boys were called up to the Volkssturm and armed with Panzerfausten. Women and the foreign forced labourers had to dig trenches. On the radio there was no end of motivating slogans – telling us to hold on and goading us into werewolf action, meaning that the enemy had to be vanquished with claws, teeth and any method possible. Cowards and traitors were threatened with the death penalty. There was talk of a wonder weapon which would annihilate the enemy at the last minute.

In Krefeld the frightening question was raised of whether we should be declared a fortress – anyone in their right mind knew what this would mean and wanted as quick an end as possible. Our anger wasn't even directed at the Allies, but at our own leaders who had brought this disaster upon us. But of course one could not say that out loud. Any criticism was seen as 'subversion of the fighting forces' and was met with death. Yet while the leadership appealed for our courage and stamina with serious threats, many men from the upper echelons had already made off over the other side of the Rhine.

The first Americans were sighted on the afternoon of March 2nd. To Marie Therese Fuegling it came as a huge relief.

That night in the cellar I remember a lively discussion on what we could expect of the Americans. The views were divided between those who had the worst fears and those who had longed for the American liberators. It became clear who had been listening to the propaganda of the German radio and who had listened to the BBC . . . Once home, we were shocked by loud banging on the door. Three heavily armed American soldiers wanted to search our house for weapons. As the only English speaker in the family I showed them around . . . In the kitchen our fox terrier jumped up at one of them and sunk its teeth into the machine gun. Miraculously, he got away with it and wasn't shot to pieces. The three were visibly pleased to find a bottle of French cognac in the cellar, which they made off with along with a camera, inviting me to visit America as they left.[11]

The day after the Americans entered Krefeld, the citizens began to emerge from hiding. As life came back to the streets, the mood was almost buoyant, revealing the sense of relief at not any longer having to live under the threat of annihilation. Reporting on civilian attitudes, an intelligence officer noted that 'everybody was anxious to be helpful'. An American uniform was an immediate invitation for an excited crowd to gather. 'A man on a bicycle wore a white handkerchief around his sleeve and we asked him why. "It means," he burst out, "that I am free, free – I am liberated."' Then came the most extraordinary encounter of all.

A tall woman, carrying ashes in a street piled with rubble and ashes, came over to our halted car and addressed us in flawless English, English that was not American. She was, she said, an Englishwoman from Yorkshire and had been married to a German for twenty-five years. We asked what she considered herself to be. 'I regard myself as almost German,' she said with dignity. 'The people here are good people. And now everyone is happy.' We wanted to know why she was carrying ashes, and she explained that she was looking for an ashcan. 'The street is full of debris,' we pointed out, 'so why don't you just dump it anywhere?' And her answer revealed that she had not lived in Germany for a quarter of a century in vain. 'Oh, no,' she exclaimed. 'We are still *ordentlich* [orderly], you know.'[12]

As two major cities straddling the Rhine, Düsseldorf and Cologne were destined for a period of divided rule. As their western suburbs were penetrated by American forces, the bridges to the east bank heaved under the force of tons of dynamite, sending smoke and debris high into the air. The Düsseldorf-Oberkassel bridge was one of the first to go. All that was left was a few iron girders sticking out of the river. Soon afterwards water, electricity and gas supplies to the west were cut off.

For those German soldiers remaining on the wrong side of the river, it was a desperate race to get to one of the remaining bridges before the Americans and before the charges were blown. In a letter to his mother, a young officer described the fighting around Düsseldorf's Northern Bridge.

Dear Mother,

Were I to write to you in any more detail than I am about to, you would have a heavy heart, for the last days and weeks, but especially the last few hours have been the hardest I have ever lived. Some of the chaps there had been at the battle of Stalingrad, but even they said that the butchery that went on back then wasn't this bad. Out of 420 men just four officers, four sergeants and thirteen men emerged alive just moments before the Düsseldorf Northern Bridge was blown up – by the skin of our teeth we squeezed our way through the vanguard of American tanks, those engaged in blowing up the bridge and the remote controlled Goliaths already making their way over the Rhine.

You can well imagine that the vanguard of American tanks had no interest in taking prisoners – instead they used everything in their power to mow down hundreds with their tank and machine guns . . .

The gruesome act began as we approached the banks of the Rhine at dawn – there were around 200 soldiers – Volksturmers and members of school brigades (15–16-year-olds).

Hordes of American tanks ploughed into us from the land and

on the other side of the Rhine the German artillery, assuming we were American artillery, shot at us. About 12–15 of us survived as far as the bridge, but then the fun really started. Everyone had to manage on his own, however possible. They almost got me at Ekne Str just before the bridge. I jumped out of a building where two American infantrymen had just got off their tank and were standing at the side door. As my left hand was already wounded I had my carbine on my back, and my last bazooka with the safety catch off, was in my right, good hand on my hip. A fraction of a second later and the gentlemen would have pulled at their machine guns. The highly sensitive bazooka (which actually it is illegal to carry with the safety catch off) did its job with fine precision, extending my life while sending the other chaps off to the happy hunting grounds forever. But at times like these you just put yourself first.

So I'm the longest serving man here now. Of course I will be deployed in the infantry again. Yesterday I slept for the first time in eight days and eight nights. I really was about to collapse physically. I slept through for 16 hours – apparently I talked like a madman the whole time.

Believe me, mother, I will never forget these hours.

Corpses, murders, burning, heads, screaming injured without their arms, legs, eyes, piles of them. And then so many other terrible details I can't tell you. Now I've ended up as the infantry leader in the Volkssturm – I have 55–61-year-old men in my group who are now buried in civilian dress without having even been home. But luckily the people are satisfied with me and trust me. And I'm doing everything I can think of to ease the terrible fate of these old men.

I hope we will all return home safely to you,

Love, Uwe.[13]

The Wilhelm family watched the arrival of the American troops, noting the soft rubber soles of their shoes trampling on the carefully laid-out white flags.

The first measure they imposed was a curfew – we were only allowed out between 9–12. This was certainly for our own protection, as the towns of Heerdt, Oberkassel, Niederkassel and Loerick were situated on the immediate front, being defended to the hilt by their own frenzied countrymen who shot at anything that moved, determined to blow it out of the sky. Unfortunately, the victims of their shooting were mostly their own people from Düsseldorf.[14]

Of all the divisions that took part in the advance of the First and Ninth Armies, it was the Eighty-Third that was first to Düsseldorf and could thus also claim to be first to the Rhine.

War correspondents rushed to our area, and we received more publicity than we had known since the surrender of 20,000 troops to us in the Loire Valley the previous summer. Now we were at the last major barrier to the heart of Hitler's Reich.

We took up defensive positions in and about Neuss [the western suburb of Düsseldorf] and maintained the 'Watch on the Rhine' . . . We were no longer in contact with the enemy, but we kept a close watch on the far side of the river. The third battalion's OP was on the sixth floor of a high-class apartment house. Never did artillery observers have it so good. Below us the glassy Rhine flowed in a lazy curve, separating Neuss from Düsseldorf. Seldom did we see any signs of life across the river.[15]

While civilians were generally helpful, for some old habits died hard. In Vohwinkel, an elderly man opened his door to the loud knocking of a search party.

Upon seeing the uniforms, the white-bearded, doddering character snapped up to attention, clicked his heels and shooting his arm forward and upward in the Nazi salute, shouted 'Heil Hitler!' The NCO, who spoke German, remarked laconically, 'Wrong army, bud.' To this the old fellow replied, 'You'll have to excuse me, gentlemen. It was just a force of habit.'[16]

Others were not quite so submissive.

Joseph Strack, a German civilian reported to be a block leader of the Nazi Party, was picked up by Company C of the 302nd infantry. This man who freely confessed his Party connections was placed in a jeep under guard; the group then departed for CIC headquarters. The prisoner and his guard were in the rear of the vehicle while the driver rode alone in the front of the jeep. Suddenly, the prisoner attempted to hook his left arm around the driver's neck, at the same time reaching for the .45 that the driver was wearing. Unable to bring his carbine to bear, the guard drew his own pistol and shot the civilian in the neck. It is believed that Strack died immediately.[17]

Two days before the Americans entered Cologne, Otto Greve, a police captain, was told he was now under military discipline with immediate orders to form a company to defend the city. He remembered that something of the same had happened to him in the First World War but:

In those days the men were young, trained lads with a bright enthusiasm for the war and a knowledge of weapons. Today? I in my mid-50s seem to be of the younger men, and these chaps, until recently proven to be physically unfit and psychologically destroyed after long nights of bombing, were almost apathetic. As we look at the guns more closely, we recognise that they are faulty war booty from the earlier years and our German ammunition doesn't even fit them. Such things for men who don't even know how to handle weapons! Nobody has a clue how to handle the bazookas or hand grenades. What's the point?! Then someone says I know what they mean now by wonder weapons . . . it's a wonder we can work out how the things work! . . . My men, the hour of action is upon us – time for deployment! We all look at each other, rather confused.[18]

Germany's third largest city and the biggest prize so far in the Allied list of gains, Cologne was entirely bombed out. Two hundred and sixty-two air raids had killed 20,000. The last raid was on March 2nd, four days before the First Army captured the left bank of the city. (The right bank remained in German hands until April 21st.) Military and civilians joined the rush across the river before the five bridges were destroyed. One badly damaged bridge fell without the help of explosives. 'It was just after 5.00 a.m. and the bridge was full of traffic – men, horses, carts, refugees and tanks – the weight plunged the whole lot into the river.'

After the last artillery bombardment hit Cologne's medieval old town, Karl Juesgen, a clergyman who had been trapped in an air raid shelter for ten days, mourned the destruction of St George's on the Waidmarkt, the last church to have been left standing in this part of Cologne. 'I saw craters 30 metres wide and six to eight metres deep among the ruins. The police station was also badly hit – two of the cellars caved in, burying all the SS people and leaders who were having a meeting about the evacuation of the city.'[19]

Orders given with no bearing on reality were obeyed with the same disregard for the inevitable. A seventeen-year-old schoolboy, one of a group of teenagers who were warned they were about to make the ultimate sacrifice, recorded his impressions of events just hours before the Americans took possession.

> On the morning of Monday March 5th the PVT was alarmed early. It was said that the Americans had crossed the military ring road in the north west and north of the city. The boys appeared at the bunker and were issued with weapons from a depot. Provisions for a day were handed out, and Oberbannfuehrer Wallrabe held a short speech, along the lines that it would get serious now in the battle against the American intruders. During his appeal a small van approached the bunker . . . and the local doctor, Dr H., got out and exchanged a few words with W. which those of us standing around him couldn't hear. It later materialised that that Dr H. was delivering an order by the Febietsfuehrer to send the boys back into east-Rhine Cologne and not to deploy them against the Americans.[20]

There were other youngsters who stayed to shoot it out. Josefine Heinrichs remembered:

> The next day the Americans arrived in well ordered convoys; each was brandishing a live weapon. I took out my white handkerchief and crossed their convoy. Nobody did or said anything. I hurried to get to Bensburg, where I saw the sorry-looking German army of 15-year-old boys marching home. Then the shooting started again and we had to retreat to the air raid shelters because a Hitler Youth had opened fire at the Americans . . . On the doorposts of houses were the names of

the survivors who had lost their homes – things like 'Maria, where are you? I am at so-and-so's.' . . . This chalked writing could be read everywhere.[21]

And when it was nearly over there were still heartbreaks to be suffered by ordinary people like Gertrud Geimer's family.

As we came home I heard mother saying 'So, children – the war is over and I'm going to make us a nice cup of coffee from our last coffee beans.' She had barely got upstairs as the very last bomb fell. A fragment of it hit her. She managed to drag herself downstairs, her hands pressed together on her stomach, she looked at us imploringly. Father leaned over her and saw what had happened. I had never seen him cry before, but now he couldn't hold back his tears. We had to fetch a doctor as quickly as possible – I yelled to my sister to stay with mother while I fetched one. I jumped on my bike, stammering 'Mother, Mother'. No German doctor would dare go outside in this chaos, so I went to the Americans. Now I could use my English for the first time, but under what circumstances! An ambulance went with me to have a look at her – she was so seriously injured that they had to take her with them. A soldier told me where they'd be taking her so I could take some of her things there. We packed her things at breakneck speed, with two bottles of wine we still had for the American doctor . . . I was hoping I could go with her but it wasn't possible. I just gave our address as she lay in a Red Cross vehicle and was given a blood transfusion.

What with the curfews and the absence of any sort of transport, it took Gertrud several days to find out where her mother had been taken. She and her father walked from one casualty centre to another, hoping for news. It was Gertrud who succeeded; she was only just in time.

She was dying, but she was so pleased I had found her. She wanted desperately to see father, and I promised to fetch him . . . The worst thing was, that because of the curfew we couldn't set off very early in the morning, and lost a lot of valuable time . . . It was a very hot day as we set off to Waldbroel. There were no buses, trains or any type of transport. Our throats were dry as we reached the hospital, and there was nowhere we could go in for a drink. We were afraid for mother. When we reached her room, she was no longer there. We both feared the worse, and then heard that she had died. In his despair, Father cried 'These damned Nazis have really ruined my life now!' We found out that she was in the morgue. In spite of all her suffering we saw a peaceful, pretty face and I just couldn't believe that she was dead. Father dealt with all the formalities . . . He explained that we'd have to bury mother in a sack if we didn't go to fetch a coffin 14km away. It was clear what we had to do and we set off on the way. It was a beautiful, very warm spring day, which made the situation even worse. I let my tears run free. Everything was blossoming and showing us that the world around us was alive – only our mother wasn't able to experience the end of the war.[22]

Bonn was next to fall. After Cologne it was a relatively easy occupation. Thirteen-year-old Ingrid Schampel was among those who busied themselves preparing for the Americans.

We were given the order to put out a white flag . . . Some of our neighbours had hung white bedsheets out. We were afraid that the Americans might get violent if we didn't show enough flags, or if they found something in the house that pointed to the Nazi past. We had children's books with pictures of Adolf Hitler inside – we cut the pictures out. We had toys wearing the uniforms of the powers that be and buried them all in the garden, even my fallen uncle's officer's sabre. This turned out to be a rather good idea, for in houses where such a sabre was found, they slashed the furniture and paintings. We stood so fearfully behind the curtains when the first American soldiers turned up on March 8th. They were such a contrast to our German soldiers that we were almost giddy with excitement. They were affluent soldiers – they looked very strange to us compared with our skinny and gaunt troops – we couldn't believe what wide behinds and stomachs they had. They also had bad posture and were clearly afraid themselves, keeping their machine guns trained on our house all the time. They crept around on their crepe soles . . . There was no violence that first day, although we heard from patients of my father, who was a doctor, that there had been some isolated rapes – plundering, looting and destroying houses was rife. Barter flourished – American cigarettes and Nescafe were especially popular, in exchange for Rhine wine or other souvenirs. The soldiers were keen on cameras and especially Agfa film.[23]

Another youngster, eleven-year-old Peter Schoeneseiffen, had been waiting for this moment with all the excitement of anticipating a birthday treat.

For us, the end of the war began on March 6th 1945. 'They are in Uechesdorf and they'll be here tomorrow,' we heard on the radio. The next day someone suddenly shouted 'They're coming!' We children ran out from our street to the old church . . . White flags were hanging out of windows – some on flagpoles and beanpoles.

There they were! On the main street from a southerly direction came the first. With his machine gun cocked, he was checking the houses on his left and right, especially the cellar windows. He was around 200 metres away from us and behind him a second soldier was walking carefully. A third one appeared with his machine gun at the ready. It was strange to watch the teetering steps of these people, as if they expected a landmine to go off under their feet at any moment. A fourth man followed about 20 metres behind, and more followed at short distances. We stood and waved at them. Suddenly the first soldier, who had come very close to us, turned and pointed his gun at us. Later we discovered that he was joking . . . We were free of the damp smell of life in the cellar! For the first time in years that night we'd be able to sleep peacefully in our beds . . . The Americans had assembled a dozen citizens in the main street – top Nazis, teachers, our neighbour, the vicar. But what were they doing with their hands? Not as we knew it – Hands Up!, but their hands were interlaced together on their heads . . . The second day of occupation was rather less euphoric. Our aunt and uncle next door were turfed out of their house and the Americans confiscated it . . . One day a soldier handed me a little packet down from his vehicle. Quickly, so no-one would notice, I ran into the shed with it, but my brother, who was a year younger, had noticed the transaction and followed me. Disappointed, we brought the package back

– it contained 3 cigarettes. The soldier took it to my mother and discovered that the two of us – 10 and 11 years old we were – really didn't smoke. He said his son the same age as us already did. Our mother got the cigarettes instead – at the time we weren't aware of their value . . . We had lots of time now and didn't have to go to school. It started again in the autumn of 1945.[24]

For the older citizens of Bonn, handing over their city to the invader and doing so willingly, in some cases enthusiastically, was a strange sensation.

Mother stood in the kitchen and said to me with a strange faraway look – 'When World War I was over I was 18. The Germans still had a love of their Fatherland in those days – they weren't happy to see foreign soldiers turning up. But us today – we're glad to see them finally arrive. They may be our victors, but they are also our liberators from Hitler's terror regime.' A memorable day – then we had to think about it – what day was it exactly? 'The 9th of March? Well it's your birthday!' – we'd almost forgotten – 'Happy Birthday.' We carried on with the cleaning up. It was my 14th birthday.[25]

After the capture of Bonn the First and Third Armies joined up between Remagen and Koblenz. Montgomery having achieved his objective in the north, there remained the cleaning-up operation west of the Rhine from Koblenz southwards. This was carried out by a converging attack by the US Third and Seventh Armies, the latter supported by the French First Army. But it was Patton who grabbed the headlines. With his new Pershings he had at last tanks that could outpace and outgun the German opposition. It is not hard to imagine Patton's delight in finding that the power traverse of the Pershing turret enabled the gunner to continue firing even while the tank was on the move. This was attack as he understood it, men crashing through the enemy positions with all guns blazing – the US Cavalry riding on chargers of steel.

Patton had launched his offensive against the Siegfried defences along the border with Luxembourg. This had called for an advance over the wooded hills of the Eifel. An early objective was Prüm, a road junction southeast of the Eifel.

From the high ground just east of Sellerich, it was possible to look down into Niedermehlen and up to the hills surrounding Prüm. All roads running into this area could be observed by the enemy for miles and as a result vehicle travel was greatly restricted. A vehicle driver in this type of terrain had to be a calm, collected individual. Oftentimes drivers were expected to travel alone to secure ammunition or rations and to return to the front lines. When sitting in a vehicle with the motor running, it is impossible to hear the deathly whistle of incoming artillery; mortar barrages creep down like a swarm of bees; direct fire weapons find no better target; and snipers easily pick off the occupants. There are no safe jobs in the infantry, only varying degrees of comparative safety.[26]

Prüm was taken on February 11th but not before the first Americans into the town had suffered the damaging attentions of snipers holed up in the surrounding hills.

These hills were found to contain trenches five feet deep with built-up firing positions. Observation from these trenches was so clear that it was possible to see men moving about inside of the houses in Prüm. This was obviously the reason the units in Prüm suffered so heavily in casualties from sniper fire. Communication wires extended throughout the trenches and to listening posts on the Prüm River.[27]

The woods and hills also gave the advantage to German artillery and mortar fire.

While the Second Battalion was in Prüm, it maintained its CP in the rear of a four-storey former department store which was subjected to constant enemy shelling from higher ground.

One shell had come particularly close to the front of the building when someone was heard running toward the CP at full speed. It was Captain Stephen J. Sanders. He skidded to a stop before Major James Burnside and said: 'Hey, Major, did you hear that last shell?'

'Sure did,' replied Burnside.

'Well, sir,' said Sanders, 'you can now see all the way through to the ladies-ready-to-wear!'[28]

While chalking up successes, Patton was beside himself with frustration. Dismissive of Montgomery's achievements, he wanted more than anything else to be given a free hand in his own sector, to show what a 'real' commander could do when the advantage was clearly with the Allies. Instead he was on orders from Eisenhower, via Bradley, to limit himself to 'probing attacks' until the campaign west of the Rhine had reached a decisive stage. In other words, hold in reserve until Montgomery was home and dry. Patton was not having that. Assuming a liberal interpretation of his probing role, he felt free to probe with maximum strength. Having fought his way through the outer belt of the Siegfried, he embarked on a punishing drive towards Trier, one of the oldest cities in northern Europe, now flattened by months of Allied bombing when the Americans stormed the town. The only construction still in place was Porta Niegra, a huge stone remnant of a wall built by the Romans.

Patton made light of the Siegfried defences, arguing that, like the walls of Hadrian and the Great Wall of China, they were hopelessly over-elaborate for their purpose and, giving false comfort, were vulnerable to a 'resolute and ingenious opponent'.

There were quite a number of pillboxes on the far side of the river. One, I remember, was camouflaged like a barn, and a wooden barn at that. When you opened the door through which the hay was supposed to be put, you came to a concrete wall nine feet thick with an 88mm. gun sticking out. Another was completely built inside an old house, the outer walls of which were knocked down when it became necessary for the pillbox to go into action. The amazing thing about all these defences is that they produced no results.

. . . From one point on the road along which 76 Division had successfully advanced, 15 pillboxes were visible in addition to dragons' teeth and anti-tank ditches. Yet this relatively green division went through them. We visited the command pillbox for the sector. It consisted of a three-storey submerged barracks with toilets, shower baths, a hospital, laundry, kitchen, storerooms and every conceivable convenience plus an enormous telephone installation. Electricity and heat were produced by a pair of identical diesel engines with generators. Yet the whole offensive capacity of this installation consisted of two machine-guns and a 60mm. mortar operating from steel cupolas which worked up and down by means of hydraulic lifts. The 60mm. mortar was peculiar in that it was operated by remote control. As in all cases, this particular pillbox was taken by a dynamite charge against the back door. We found marks on the cupolas, which were ten inches thick, where our 90mm. shells, fired at a range of two hundred yards, had simply bounced.[29]

It was then on to Koblenz which fell on March 7th, although sporadic street fighting continued for at least a week afterwards. The city was in fair chaos with looted alcohol fuelling an 'end of the world carnival' atmosphere.

In a living-room up the street, a group of American soldiers were fast getting drunk. Going tipsily out into the dark hall to look for the bathroom, they found themselves, in confusion, bumping into German soldiers who had been holding wassail on the second floor and had come downstairs on the same mission. 'Scuse me. Beg your pardon. Wanna get through here,' one American found himself saying to an equally drunken German in a polite, Alphonse-and-Gaston act.

Don Stoddard dashed in off the street to escape a heavy artillery barrage, and running into a dining-room, looking for the way to the cellar, he came upon one of his litter squad having sexual intercourse with the woman of the house.

At intervals between the shelling, the cobbled streets just outside the hospital rang with the heavy clatter of German boots as long streams of prisoners came past. There were as many as 40 or 50 at a time, hands up, being chivvied along by two small infantrymen, one of whom invariably was unsteady on his feet. Many of the prisoners themselves were drunk; their canteens were filled with cognac.[30]

The Seventh Army had no big cities to take but it did have its share of drama. From the memories of that time what stands out are the small scenes within the wider picture, the way the flow of battle was often determined by the individual soldier reacting instinctively, perhaps recklessly, to events. This is what happened when a company of the 274th Infantry Regiment approached a small town. The officer commanding was Lieutenant Wilson:

There was no glamour, no dash about it when Lt Wilson gave an order. He spoke with a quiet voice which encouraged rather than demanded.

We pulled back away from the wire and followed Wilson around toward the right flank.

'We went through woods to the right until Wilson was satisfied that we had gone far enough,' said Pfc. Corrigan. 'Then he said, "Okay, out of the woods and into the clearing, boys, just keep walking until fired upon."'

We formed another skirmish line and headed toward the edge of the woods. As soon as we got into the clearing, machine guns opened up on us and everyone hit the ground. The only one left on his feet was Wilson. He just said, 'That's all right men, we'll just keep going. We'll cross this in short rushes. Come on now, let's go!'

One by one the men leaped up and dashed across the open ground in short bounds. Wilson remained on his feet among them urging them on. 'That's it,' he would say when a man made a good rush. 'About ten steps and hit the dirt!' Then he saw another that didn't quite satisfy him. 'You there, soldier. That wasn't a rush . . . that was just a flop. Let's see you get up and give a good rush.'

It was one of the most amazing things I've ever seen.

Later:

Sgt. McNeely came running over from across the street to enter the house. As he was climbing through the window two shots rang out from outside and hit him in the head. He dropped to the floor, his feet still on the sill. Then he started gasping and coughing and rolled back his half open eyes. Blood was coming from his nose and mouth. Corrigan and Doyle dragged him away from the sill.

'Don't worry, Sergeant,' said Wilson. 'We'll fix you up.' The three men took care of him as best they could until medical help arrived. In the meantime Wilson and Corrigan went down into the basement of the house to see if any more snipers were concealed there.

'I asked Wilson if I should toss a couple of grenades down before us,' said Corrigan. 'He said not to, though, because he didn't want to mess it up. So he went down first and walked right into the basement.

If there had been anyone down there he would have made a perfect target. Luckily the place was deserted. When we made certain that everything was all clear we went upstairs. Just as we did so, one of the engineers who had accompanied us was shot in the hips and back as he was coming through the window. Of the twelve engineers who started out with us at the top of the hill, only three got down to the bottom . . . and now one of them was wounded.'

The sniper in the pillbox apparently was using some sort of a machine gun pistol because his shots always came in twos. He had the window of the house zeroed in perfectly and was picking off every man who tried to get in or out. Finally Wilson took two men, Brancieri and Donovan, and went up to the second floor to see if they couldn't knock the sniper out. Upstairs, Wilson walked over to the window to see if he could find the sniper when he saw several of his men outside who were starting to dig in near the railroad tracks. He leaned near the window and shouted for them to come over to the house in five minute intervals when suddenly he jerked and stepped back pale-faced from the window.

'My God, I'm hit!' he cried.

Before anyone could realize what had happened he was standing in the middle of the room with his feet spread wide apart trying to brace himself. 'That's all right, I'm . . .' he tried to reassure them. Then he must have felt himself starting to fade.

'Slap my face! Slap my face!' He knew he was going but couldn't make himself accept the fact.

Brancieri struck him across the cheeks but his life had already drained from him. He fell to the floor and doubled up his legs and kicked a heavy oak table across the room. That was all. He was dead.

'When I went upstairs it was all over,' recalls Corrigan. 'I opened his shirt and found two small bullet holes just above his heart. There was not a trace of blood on the outside. He must have bled internally. I realized sooner or later he would have been killed but now that it had happened none of us could quite believe it. I took the codes and overlays out of his pockets and looked at his AGO card. He was only 21 and as he lay there he didn't look anywhere near that. His hair was cropped close and he had no beard at all. He was just a kid, yet he proved himself to be the driving factor of the whole company. He was everything that could be expected of an officer and soldier. When he died, the spirit of the company died with him.'[31]

As units of the Seventh Army approached Saarbrücken they encountered what was first thought to be the forward column of a German counter-attack. But these were not fighters but men dying on their feet.

'They were straggling for miles all up and down the Metz Highway,' said T/Sgt. James Wilson. 'They seemed to wobble over the road like they were drunk. Some of them would fall to the ground and then drag themselves up again with a great effort. Then we found out that they were Russians who had escaped from a large prison camp on the edge of town. Most of them were in a pitiful condition. They had not had anything to eat for days and were so weak and emaciated they could hardly stand up. When the Germans saw them getting away they turned machine guns on them and killed a lot of them. Others wandered into the minefields along the road and were blown to eternity. Still they kept coming towards us. Those who were too weak to walk just fell along the side of the hill and lay still. The rest of them came plodding on. They were so hungry they would scrape the empty cans our K rations were in, even when they were infested with ants and flies.'

'We got the German prisoners to help them back,' continued Pfc. Hershey. 'It was nothing to see half a dozen of them sprawled on the road half dead from hunger and exhaustion. We gave them all the rations we could spare but they didn't half go around. We put some of them in trucks and sent them back to the rear where they set up special camps for them.'[32]

Civilians caught up in the fighting were so used to the hammer of guns they seemed almost oblivious to the danger. Seeking out a billet in an otherwise pulverised village, a gun crew found a cottage where an elderly French woman and her two granddaughters were still in residence. She had refused to go, putting her trust, as she said, in the Lord, a faith well rewarded when a shell landed within yards of the house blowing in the windows but leaving the structure intact.

Children were a particular problem. Moving continuously through streets likely to harbour snipers or be booby-trapped, GIs would find themselves surrounded by excited kids begging for chocolate and cigarettes. 'By the time we had gotten a hundred yards into a place,' bemoaned one sergeant, 'our approach had become as tactical as a Frank Sinatra appearance at an old maids' club.'[33]

Barricaded cellars were an invitation to tragedy. It was impossible to tell who was behind the doors – women, children and old men frightened of coming out or armed fanatics ready to sacrifice their lives for the opportunity to blaze away one last time with automatic pistols.

> 'We came to one house where we could hear them moving around down in the basement, but when we shouted down for them to come up we received no answer,' recalls Sgt. Desmond. 'So I threw a grenade down to give them a little inducement. When it exploded we heard some awful screaming including several women's voices. Pretty soon one of them hollered up that there were no soldiers . . . only civilians there. We went down with fingers against triggers and found a deep underground room well fortified by heavy logs. Inside of it were about twenty people, young and old, men and women. They seemed pretty glad to see us. I gave them a few cigarettes and told them we threw the grenades only because we thought they were Krauts. It seemed as if all of them were sleeping in one bed. They had little to eat so I gave them some chocolate and they fell all over me.'[34]

Along the entire left bank of the Rhine, the third week of March was largely spent mopping up remnants of German forces hanging on to isolated positions. Their withdrawal across the river was badly managed, not for any fault of military planning but because Hitler was demanding a fight to the last while refusing to believe that anything more than a revival of the fighting spirit was needed to roll back the Allied advance. The result was not so much conflicting orders as no orders at all. So it was that German units in the last line of defence were ill-informed and thus ill-prepared for action. Often it came as a traumatic shock to discover that the enemy was in their midst.

It was pretty funny seeing the Krauts walking down the streets into the muzzles of our guns. Most of them didn't think we were within five miles of them. We took a good number of prisoners and got a few laughs to boot. The expressions on their faces when they saw us were quite comical. Some of them froze. Others started to bring their weapons against us but that was the last thing they ever did. Eagen, a slow Oklahoma farm boy, gave one Kraut the scare of his life. He caught one light hearted Heinie dancing around the street without a care in the world. Eagen just stood quietly staring at him burning his guts out with his eyes. Then he said in a slow deadly drawl: 'Put your gawd damned hands on your head.' The Kraut turned about ten years older in a matter of seconds. He was brought into a house and then he broke into tears.[35]

It was beginning to get easy. The growing mood of confidence showed itself in the scramble for souvenirs ('We came out of that battle loaded down with prizes.') and in stories of encounters with the enemy that were seen as acts of bravery at the time but were liable to engender uncomfortable memories.

A little while later we reached the town of Krughutte. At last we were in Germany. We halted at the crossroads while the men went to clear some houses. Lt. Gustly and Sgt. Smith caught two Krauts walking down the streets at sling arms as if they were a thousand miles from the scene of action.

'We caught them just as they came around a corner,' said Sgt. Smith. 'After we halted them, one made a break for it. Both Lt. Gustly and I opened up on him. He was hit several times but kept on stumbling through yards and over fences until he finally got away. A few minutes later Tec. 4 Van Holdt, one of the most even tempered and calmest men I've ever known saw a Kraut Captain strolling down the road like a character in the Easter Parade. When he was ordered to halt the Kraut went for his "burp" gun instead. Van Holdt, seeing he was going to be nasty about the thing, let go with his M-1 and hit the Kraut in the leg. He lay there, in the front yard for about two hours before he finally died. After that the rest of the men ribbed Van Holdt by calling him killer for a long time afterwards.'[36]

By March 25th every part of the west bank of the Rhine was in Allied hands. Nearly ten years after Hitler had reclaimed his back garden, the Allies were once again in possession. It had been a long and costly fight. Against some 16,000 dead on the Allied side, the Germans had lost some 90,000 of the best soldiers remaining to the Wehrmacht. Moreover, in March alone, over 340,000 German soldiers were taken prisoner.

It was, said Horrocks, 'unquestionably the grimmest battle in which I took part' and Eisenhower told Crerar, 'Probably no assault in this war has been conducted in more appalling conditions', adding that these last weeks had been among 'the most anxious of the entire campaign'. Among the troops who led the way into Germany there was a sense of wonderment that the promised day had at last arrived.

'What's this striped pole across the road, sir?' said Pickford.

'The frontier!' I said, pointing to the deserted hut which had housed the frontier police and customs men.

I stared curiously at my first German civilian. He was an old man, dressed in shabby serge and an engine-driver's sort of cap. His grizzled face regarded us from above a bushy white moustache as we clattered over the broken frontier barrier. And then I heard *Angler's* driver's hatch being thrown open, and when I looked over my shoulder I saw Smith 161 leaning out and staring questioningly at the old German.

'We on the right road for Berlin, mate?' asked Smith 161, with a perfectly straight face.

I swear the old blue eyes winked, as the man tugged at his grizzled moustache and said: '*Berlin? Ja, ja! Gerade aus!!*'

'I thought the Germans had no sense of humour,' said Pickford, when we got moving again.

'I know,' I said. 'But he can remember Germany before Hitler, and probably before the Kaiser, too.'[37]

There was some surprise at the rarity of any civilian hostility. Having been warned so often that all Germans were mad fanatics bent on destruction, the appearance of white flags hanging from windows with recognisably ordinary women and children peeping out from behind the curtains took some getting used to. Nonetheless, these were not liberated people but citizens of an enemy country who were now subject to military discipline – or indiscipline. Looting was commonplace and generally excused as a permissible wish to acquire souvenirs. The search for weapons and men prepared to use them was a fine excuse for breaking into cellars where wines and spirits were more likely to be hidden.

With his facility for languages, Corporal Dai Evans found himself in demand as an intermediary. In one instance, the consequences were bizarre and disturbing.

'Corporal, we need you in the house.'

'What for, Sir?'

'The farmer is trying to tell us something about his mother.'

'But she's dead.'

'So I gather, but the farmer keeps mentioning "Mutter", so we want to ask him what it's all about.'

I went with Jack into the house . . . 'Ask him what he wants,' said Jack.

'Was ist los?' I asked the man.

He explained that the family were grateful for the way in which they had been treated, fed and given first-aid. He and his family wished to bury the old lady, his mother, in the front garden. First they wished to make a coffin for her and, of course, dig a grave. Would the '*Herr Offizier*' allow it?

Jack went to find the major, who readily granted permission but told Jack to supervise the business discreetly . . . Having made the coffin (which was necessarily a crude affair, of course) they carried it into the house, then went into the front garden to dig a fairly deep grave. Returning, we found the womenfolk had been busy lining the coffin with hay: a very appropriate material for a farming person. For a pillow they had made a thicker pad of the same material . . . Carrying in the old lady's body the menfolk laid it in the coffin, the women weeping the while. They gathered round, then the farmer said a few words about the dead person, followed by all intoning a '*Vater Unser*' (Our Father). We held our heads down respectfully while this was going on.

What happened next was almost farce. The men put the top on the coffin but it wouldn't go down as the whole thing was too shallow and the old lady's body stopped the lid from fitting. The men lifted her out, removed some of the hay, replaced the body then tried the cover again. Still it would not fit. Taking the body out again they removed all the hay and put her back once more, only to find the old lady's stomach was holding the two halves apart by a matter of a quarter of an inch or so. At a word the two men knelt on the lid, forcing it down while the coffin was nailed together. We burst out laughing. It was wrong, totally wrong and most irreverent and I have never ceased to regret it; but at that time and under those circumstances the death of a very old lady hardly mattered when, every day, hundreds of fit, healthy young men of both sides were being killed or wounded.[38]

German propaganda kept up the pressure but by now there were few on the Allied side who were prepared to take seriously the Forces Programmes put out by German Radio.

They are supposed to contain the right mixture for the Allied troops, 'something old, something new, something gay and something blue'. Phooey! It stinks. It is largely a faked American-type programme thickly coated with a lot of sob-stuff to try and play on our sympathies. The Hun propagandists are now doing their best to try and tell us that Jerry is not such a bad fellow after all, and that he was just doing his duty the same as we are. Everything about these programmes is so forced that you can almost see their blasted announcers standing stiffly to attention at the microphones between announcements.[39]

Allied triumphalism was best illustrated by the lines of washing strung up along the Siegfried Line. Not surprisingly the mood on the other side of the Rhine was less euphoric. In the post mortem, which sent Hitler into paroxysms of rage, the future of Field Marshal Karl Gerd von Rundstedt, Commander-in-Chief West, was hardly at issue. Dismissed without ceremony, he was replaced by

Field Marshal Albert Kesselring. A former Luftwaffe Chief of Staff and subsequently commander of German forces in the Mediterranean, Kesselring had secured his reputation with a masterly defensive campaign in Italy. Now, in March 1945, he was called upon to apply the same skills in defending the Reich. Appearing for the first time at his new headquarters, Kesselring knew that he was the last hope. It was not altogether without a sense of irony that he addressed his fellow officers, 'Well, gentlemen, I am your new V-3.'

I I
The Hunger Winter

They called it 'Mad Tuesday'. September 5th, 1944. This was when the Dutch started to celebrate the imminence of liberation. All around were signs of an occupying power on the edge of collapse. The rail stations were crowded with Germans and Dutch Nazi sympathisers on the way out. Resistance fighters emerged from hiding. Everywhere there was excited talk about how the country was to be run until democracy was restored. People waited on the streets hoping to catch the first glimpse of the Allied advance forces. Tomorrow all would be well.

But tomorrow did not come; at least not in the way that was expected. Allied troops had crossed the border south of the rivers Maas (Meuse) and Waal but had then stayed put. This left the most heavily populated sector of the Netherlands, including Amsterdam, Rotterdam, Utrecht and The Hague, in German hands. The reason was not immediately apparent to the civilian population but was obvious enough to the military command. Though Antwerp had fallen to the British, the other Channel ports were still in German hands. And not even Antwerp was secure since the Schildt estuary controlling entry to the port had yet to be captured. So where were the supplies to come from to keep the Allied troops on the move?

The realisation everywhere that the war would not be over by Christmas was disappointing enough. But the Dutch had their own particular concern. Reporting from the liberated sector of Holland on September 27th, United Press correspondent Walter Cronkite warned, 'There is not enough food in the Netherlands.' He went on, 'People are living almost wholly on cabbages, turnips and backyard vegetables.' It was to get worse.

As the Allies fought to clear the way into Antwerp – the first convoy did not enter the harbour until November 28th – any remaining hopes that German defenders would recognise a lost cause disappeared with the tragic fiasco at Arnhem. Such a humiliating setback for the Allies had the reverse effect on the occupying forces. Regaining confidence and under pressure from Berlin to restore order in the Netherlands, Reichskommisar Dr Arthur Seyss Inquart reacted to a nationwide railway strike by confiscating canal barges and alternative transport including bicycles and by holding back on food supplies. By the end of the year the daily ration in the cities was a third below subsistence diet.

Reporting in London on the turn of events in his country, L. de Jong, Editor of Radio Orange, spoke of the provinces of North Holland and Utrecht, now occupied by German paratroopers.

> Street control has been tightened in towns and villages. Every man who leaves his home risks being sent to an unknown destination. Even old men and boys of 15 years have been picked up in the last few days. Official rations have again been halved. Even for the Germans there will be no more electric current available in a few days and the regular water supply will be stopped within a fortnight. Stocks of coal and fuel are totally exhausted.[1]

In Amsterdam, pre-war judged to be one of the cleanest cities in the world, there was a fear of epidemic as doctors and hospitals ran out of basic medicines. In one church there were 1,500 corpses which could not be buried for lack of transport.

Writing to her daughter and family in London, Mrs J.D. Van Den Bergh Schmitz, an elderly widow who had taken refuge in the St Barnado's convent in Amsterdam, reflected on a country always so rich in food now having gone to the other extreme.

> this week we are only getting 600 gms of bread, that is one and a quarter small loaves, and we have to make do with that for the whole week. The following weeks we will get 1000 gms, that is one large loaf and a quarter of a small loaf. It will be like this as long as the stocks last, that is two slices per day. I am keeping my sauce or juice, whatever you like to call it, to smear on my bread. I have bought some Taai-Taai (Ginger Bread) to make up, one can at least eat that without fat. Sugar is unobtainable and there is no milk at all. If it

continues like this then there will be a lot of people who will not live to see the spring. You can see hunger in people's faces. The bread vans have to be accompanied by police to prevent plundering. In The Hague it has already come to that, and the people who took to plundering were immediately shot dead and left lying in the bread shop window for all to see as an example to others.[2]

The Dutch government in exile piled on the diplomatic pressure without getting anywhere. The first objective, it was told, was to strike at the German heartland; anything else had to be an unwelcome diversion. A campaign to free the Netherlands was seen as just that, a risky and unnecessary enterprise that would weaken the main offensive. It was not put quite so brutally to the Dutch politicians fretting away in London. They were reminded that whatever suffering their countrymen were about to endure, it could be worse if the Germans carried out their threat to destroy the flood barriers. Nearly all the occupied territory was under sea level. If the dykes were breached much of western Holland would vanish under several feet of water. The prospect was enough to give pause to the fiercest patriot.

There was no consensus on how long the Dutch people could hold out. There were those, like General de Guingand, Montgomery's Chief of Staff, who thought that the Dutch were 'rather inclined to exaggerate the conditions of starvation'.[3] More realistic observers at SHAEF worked on the assumption that the urban areas could last out until February or March. The Dutch government in London and the International Red Cross reckoned that food stocks would run out at least a month earlier. But predictions of hardship to come were of scant interest to those who already had hardship enough. On top of food shortages there was the winter to contend with. It turned out to be the hardest in fifty years. Since there was no coal, gas or electricity the only means of cooking and heating was to raid the streets for anything that would serve as fuel. Amsterdam gave every impression of a city literally falling apart. Empty houses were stripped of floorboards, balustrades, staircases and beams; trees disappeared from the roadsides and parks; even the sleepers between the tram lines were torn up.

A few days after Christmas, Mrs Van Den Bergh Schmitz reported that her central heating had been turned off 'for good', so she thought.

It is freezing. The temperature is 8°C. The canals are frozen over. It is bitterly cold and we are all wrapped up in overcoats, rugs and footwarmers, but that doesn't seem to help. I feel cold right down to my bone marrow, inside and out, and right into my soul. I have never known what it was like to be cold and hungry. Most people here spend the whole day in bed and only get up for their meal. I shall keep going as long as I can.[4]

Many queued for the soup kitchens which opened at irregular intervals in the main towns. But how could people survive, it was asked rhetorically, when the only meal of the day was a half litre of cabbage and pea flour soup?

Hunger brought dishonesty. It was hard to blame the culprits. As one said, 'If you don't have any food and you don't see any, then it is not too bad because there's no other option, but if it's right there in front of you, then you can't keep your hands off it.' For a twenty-nine-year-old engineer living in The Hague, temptation grew when he discovered that his boss kept supplies in a loft.

If you haven't had any milk for a month, then the want of protein is so great that you really crave a bowl of gruel with milk, so it simply had to come from the big pile. The door opened quite easily with the help of a screwdriver; although there turned out to be no milk powder, there were at least 50 kg of different kinds of peas, along with lots of maize and chickenfeed, to guarantee the boss's fresh eggs. Such a sight is simply too much, especially since the boss's primary needs were not being compromised, and so I filled a tin with maize and another with beans for myself.

The beans went to a friend who had nothing left for his wife and children but there was still some work to be done on the Puritan conscience before it settled.

So I don't call this stealing, but taking away. Stealing is something completely different: it is the enrichment of yourself at someone else's expense, which is what I would have been doing had I sold or exchanged those beans. And if someone took a kilogram of potatoes from my crate in order to still his hunger, then I wouldn't hold it against him, though I would take more care hiding them. One mustn't create the opportunity.[5]

With little food coming into the towns, the towns had to go to the food. What became known as 'hunger trips' to the country-side to buy or beg food off the farmers became a weekly, even daily, routine for most city families. The next best thing to having a square meal was owning a bicycle, the essential means of transport in a small, flat country at a time when nearly all motor vehicles had been commandeered by the occupying forces. When the snow was heavy, in early January, a sledge came in handy. This is what a student from Haarlem used to visit a friendly farmer.

Thursday, the first day of the storm, I went into *de Meer* with a small cart to get 50 kg of wheat in exchange for the fur rug. I arrived home more dead than alive. The snow is still on the ground and it has become hard due to the light frost that set in afterwards. Yesterday, I went back into *de Meer* with a sledge. I gave 'Drip-eye' (a curious farmer who always has watery eyes and a dripping nose) two nice pairs of fur gloves (one for his wife and one for his daughter). When he asked me what I wanted for them, I gave him the same answer he always gives us when he gives us something: 'Well . . . don't worry about it . . . it's all right.' And after that: 'If you could let us have some potatoes every now and then . . .' He didn't have any spuds and I got a quarter of a hectolitre of swede. When I was just about to leave, he said: 'Do you want some peas?' I got at least 25 pounds of peas. So I hadn't gambled unwisely! It's impossible to get hold of vegetables. Today, we ate (evening meal) 1 plate of bean soup, only swede with sugar beet, and three sugar beet and wheat Scotch pancakes. My stomach is rumbling with hunger tonight, it's making me feel a bit sick.[6]

The Hunger Winter destroyed what was left of sympathy for the occupying forces. When the Germans had first crossed the border there was an element in Dutch society, not to be underestimated, that welcomed the 'bringers of new order'. Certainly, on the German side there was hope that the two countries, so close in language and culture, would be able to work out an arrangement that precluded active resistance. And for a time, so it proved. Deeply imbued with a respect for authority, Dutch society adapted to the needs of the new imperialists. The resistance movement, such as it was, had support from London but the bungling of SOE in not realising that the Germans had all the information they needed to capture one agent after another all but destroyed its credibility.[7]

Now, however, with widespread malnutrition and the threat of worse to come, resentment against the German occupation gathered strength. Resentment too from the Dutch who had to live off scraps against those who still seemed to be doing quite nicely.

Bernadina de Vries went as supervisor for a group of children from Amsterdam families who had been sent to stay with relatives in Friesland. 'When we went into a restaurant we just couldn't believe that people would leave food on plates and walk away. Our poor kids from the city were on the verge of starvation and it was all we could do to make them sit quietly. They wanted to devour the leftovers and who could blame them?'[8] Bernadina exchanged silver cutlery and other of her engagement presents for food to take back to her family. The problem was getting transport. Since the only way out of Friesland was across the dyke causeway, she had to wait until she found a driver who was prepared to chance a random search. Bartering black-market tobacco, she was given a lift in a truck carrying a delivery of cheese for the occupying force in Amsterdam. She arrived in the early hours with food treasures intact: bacon, cheese, suet, skim milk and potatoes. 'All more valuable than silver or gold.'

Occasionally, a Red Cross relief ship got through from Sweden or Portugal. But hopes of substantial relief foundered on the German tendency to divert supplies. The best news came from liberated Holland where, after the opening of Antwerp in early December, 500 tons of food and other essentials arrived daily by train. Meanwhile, emergency reserves were building up on the other side of the Channel and, with longer-term prospects in mind, on the other side of the Atlantic. But all plans for early relief were thrown into disarray by the German offensive across the Ardennes. Food stocks held in Britain were all but exhausted by the Belgian population who once again found themselves in the front line.

The reversal of Allied fortunes was seen by the Nazi leadership as an opportunity to put pressure on the able-bodied to come to the aid of the German war effort. Extravagant promises were made to tempt volunteers. On February 2nd, Seyss Inquart pledged a sound basic diet for those willing to go to Germany, with the added incentive that they could leave behind their ration cards for their families to use. The 50,000 who signed up fell a long way short of the half million target. A counter-campaign by the resistance had its effect but so too did reports of conditions in the work camps and, probably the strongest disincentive of all, the growing conviction as the Ardennes offensive faded that the Third Reich was in its death throes, protracted but nonetheless assured. The German response was a general call-up of able-bodied men irrespective of age. Teenagers who had so far avoided forced labour were urged to go into hiding. But this left their families at the mercy of an increasingly edgy Gestapo.

> One particularly well known and respected family arrived home last week after attending church and were surprised to see a vehicle standing outside their house. They have three sons and two more in hiding, thus five boys. I don't know what the Germans asked them, but the man had hardly begun to reply when the stinking Bosche shot him straight through the mouth. His brains were literally shattered to pieces. His wife had to watch it all and could say nothing otherwise she would have gone the same way. Are they not beasts?[9]

In Texel, a young accountant witnessed the hanging of a Russian caught trying to escape from forced labour.

> Melle Zegel and his wife were taken away because they had hidden the Russian. According to the Germans, both will be shot. In the evening posters were put up everywhere with a warning to civilians. Anyone who provides food or shelter to a Russian will be punished

by death. They will be shot on the spot and their house will be burned down.[10]

The writer fumed at the 'nasty, foul, filthy *Mof*' (the Dutch slang for German soldiers dating back to the muffs they wore in the 1914–18 war) who had put Texel under a reign of terror.

Ron Groeneveld hid out in the cowshed of his family farm where a room was created from bales of hay. Ron, who post-war emigrated to Canada, shared his retreat with resistance workers one of whom, Wim Byl, was on the run after he had been caught collecting intelligence from Rotterdam airport. He spent all of two and a half years alongside the cattle, enough to put him off farming for the rest of his life.

The regime had its weak spots, however, with German administrators often ready to bend the rules to make life a bit easier for their unwilling subjects. A photographer in Amsterdam recalls a story about his father who was active in the resistance. Needing a travel permit for his ordinary and illicit work, he had to renew his papers at frequent intervals. The German official who dealt with his case and who was no fool, took to breaking off an interview halfway, leaving his desk unattended for a few minutes. On each occasion, in clear view, was a pile of signed but undated travel permits. Fearing a trap, the Dutchman passed up the first opportunity but when it happened again, he took his chance. He eventually lost count of the number of work exemptions, bicycle permits and other useful documents he collected in this way.

The depths of the Hunger Winter were reached in late January and early February. While Eisenhower asserted that relief for nearly five million civilians was dependent on 'the rapid completion of our main operations', those same civilians were forced to sustain themselves through the waiting days by munching on sugar beet and tulip bulbs. Normally used for cattle feed, sugar beet was eaten in a number of none too subtle guises.

> If you had enough fuel you could clean them, cut them into chunks, boil them, and when they were a little softer, grate the chunks and boil the gratings. Then you put the pulp in a clean cloth and wrung

out the juice. If you had still more fuel, you could boil the juice down to syrup or eventually sugar.

Later on, when we had sugar beets, we just cut them up and cooked them and ate them whole. They were hard to eat though because they were very hot in the throat. 'If we only had some potatoes to go with them,' father would say.

'Yes, or some nice, cool cucumbers with oil and vinegar!' I would help him wish. With the aid of some more wishes, the sugar beets would get eaten. They did fill the stomach.

Tulip bulbs were more of a challenge. Tulip bulb soup was 'completely tasteless and horribly thick'.

> Mother was quite surprised to see me come home with something and we were anxious to try the bulbs. Mother had a bit of oil of uncertain origin in a bottle and we got out the frying pan, cleaned the bulbs as if they were onions and fried them. What a beautiful smell! Our mouths watered while we waited for mother to spoon them out onto our plates, and we could hardly wait until they were cold enough to eat. They tasted as good as they smelled, and we were just about to congratulate ourselves on this windfall when I suddenly felt my throat. It was sore! I took another bite: it got sorer. Father and mother and Cobie were eating more slowly too, and soon Cobie stopped altogether. They made your throat feel raw, even worse than the sugar beets. Mother gathered up what we could not eat and said: 'Perhaps we can eat them with the peas.' It was a good idea, and it was too bad we only had so few of them. The man with the tulip bulbs did not come again.[11]

For those who got ill, malnutrition set back any hope of recovery and made the agony of waiting for long promised relief all the greater. A tram conductor in Rotterdam, off work suffering from oedema, was told he had to go to hospital as soon as a bed was available. That same day his only meal was what he described as 'a wholesome mash' made from three kilos of potato peelings.

> Things are looking disconsolate. Not only is the weather foul (it's raining and it's awfully cold), but there's no bread available.

Apparently, the baker doesn't even have flour in stock for next week's half loaf. I give up and don't understand what will become of all this.

Later:

22 March, Sunday – Hungry. Hungry. It's getting worse and worse. Now that we're not even getting that one slice of bread per day, we're at our wits' end. We stare at each other's hollow eyes all day long and every look, every word, every movement betrays it: Hungry! Rien partially understands, but Willem doesn't. He just yawns, whines and cries. The odd bite of a beet and some raw lettuce, without vinegar or herbs (we've run out of those, too) is the only thing that helps for a few moments now. This morning Dien van Zanten came by. She looks just like everybody else, scrawny and bedraggled. One of her sister's legs has been affected by open TB. Another one of those conditions caused by the hunger . . . We decided to go to bed early again. How long will we be able to keep this up?[12]

The Allied crossing of the Rhine and the start of the big push into Germany induced fears among the Dutch that once again they were being left behind, a reasonable deduction since, as a priority, liberation for the Netherlands seemed to fall well below the race to meet up with the Russian forces pressing into Germany from the east. However, on April 5th, a directive from Twenty-First Army Group headquarters ordered General Crerar to begin a 'methodical clearing of western Holland'. On April 11th, an attack was launched on Deventer, to the east of Amsterdam. A country housewife, living five miles from the town, kept a diary.

Early this morning at six o'clock we were woken up by German men on the terrace. I thought, 'Oh God, they've come for Tom.' An officer and four soldiers. 'Aufmachen.' Here we go. 'Wo is der Schlüssel von da drüben?' 'Die habe ik niet,' I said. 'Aufmachen,' he roared. They put canons in the garden and needed somewhere to accommodate 30 men and 10 horses. 'If we start firing you must leave,' he said. 'Where are the English then?' 'Die Tommies stehen vor Deventer,' he roared back.

Good heavens – liberation is near. Finally – the last emotion. I can't cry, can't laugh, I simply stare into space. Very matter-of-factly, Tom said, 'Wife, we must go to the cellar. Cook the last of the corn and beans, a pan-full, and drag the mattresses downstairs. Lock the children in the cellar and give the girls a sip of the bromide mixture. Keep the escape suitcases handy, boil the morphine needle, woollen blankets and coats and roll down the shutters. I'll pile some stones up against the outside wall and see if I can see the battery approaching. To work!'

As the attack closed in, the diary became the hold on sanity:

Aeroplanes are screaming overhead – anti-aircraft fire, it's an absolute hell. Sometimes the whole house shakes. Jetty sobs every now and then. Tom and I are calm. With this diary on my knees, a glass of water beside me and the morphine needle on the shelf. Buckets of water and bags of sand are standing ready in the hallway. The most frightening thing about it is the whistling of the shells because after each German volley, a volley comes back.

The next-door neighbour calls through the trapdoor to tell us that Deventer is on fire. They're in the cellar, too. We can see each other through a crack. Every now and then tanks thunder past – the paving will be ruined – a tree comes crashing down onto our lawn. Then, suddenly, there's a bang against the wall and everything rattles and shakes. Tom smells smoke and wants to leave the cellar – but it must have been powder-smoke, nothing happened. Going to the toilet is a bold venture. We're afraid of going through the hallway and this crazy situation makes you need to go more often.

Wednesday, 11 April – 7.00 am: *The Tommies are in the garden with their tanks*. We're free!!!![13]

The Tommies were, in fact, Canadians. In Delden, six of the newcomers found lodgings with Mrs Hilsum-Beuckens who later wrote a book called *Thank You, Canada*.

Where was I going to find room for them all? We still had four people with us who had been hiding from the Germans. 'Put a couple of beds side by side,' the Canadian lieutenant advised us. 'They're not hard to please.'

A few minutes later our house was unrecognisable. Machine guns, rifles, shovels, grenades, kit bags lay everywhere and the soldiers were stretched out in our chairs.

One, Lesage, was of Belgian descent. He spoke a little Flemish, and at 21, had a wife and two children. He proudly showed us a snapshot of them. There was a boy who looked like Mickey Rooney. His name was Hearst and he was 19. Kelly and Garnett were the names of the two others. When they saw what we had to eat they immediately gave us food. Both had just had a birthday. Kelly was 29 and beginning to grow bald, Garnett was 19. The corporal, Podolski, was a friendly good-looking boy.

Lesage discovered our violin and scraped away happily on it. They took our children off to their unit's cookhouse, and brought back a large jug of tea, sugar and milk and thick slices of dazzlingly white bread. They sat and talked about 'back home' and what they were going to do when the war was over. They'd been on the go for 40 hours without a break.

The following evening the lodgers were told to be ready to leave on five minutes' notice.

Two went to bed fully dressed, four sat up with us. We told them about our resistance movement, they told us about their homes. I had to promise to write to their families.

We sat in the dark, our glowing cigarettes signalling our positions like tiny beacons. Now and then we heard guns in the distance. My heart ached as I listened to their stories, plans and fears. All of them were afraid. Afraid that even now, at the eleventh hour of the war, something might happen to them.

Next morning the dreaded message came: they had to leave. Without a word they picked up their gear and put on their camouflaged tin hats. 'Keep your fingers crossed,' one of them said, and they left.[14]

Regimental records show that a private soldier by the name of Lesage was killed in action on April 10th, 1945.

For reasons that were never clear, Dutch citizens living close to the German border were often told to pack a suitcase and move east.

Elise Boombergen, a forty-nine-year-old artist, was among those who, with her family, was forced to evacuate from Roermond. Crossing the border, they found refuge in Lütterbracht.

At first, Frau Strutges had some objections, but when she realised who we were, refugees, her good heart opened to us. Leny and the girls stayed with the Strutges and we were boarded out to a kind old lady, Frau Geurts, who took care of us as a mother would her children. These were Germans, the enemy, but we forgot all about that. We attacked the warm meal like hungry beasts, sauerkraut and greasy *wurst*. Coffee and milk from our own stolen cows that were being kept in the area! We slept in a small room next to the stables. The stables were empty. Their animals stolen by their own troops.

There was another married couple with children lodging there, too. They were evacuees like us, and in the evening we talked around a warm stove in a small room with the old lady, who, although she never said so explicitly, let it be known that she did not like the Hitler regime. Strutges was an anti-party man, too. When we sat with them in their kitchen, he would tune the wireless to England. He was one of the few non-party members in that once wealthy farming village.[15]

As the Canadians pushed on, the sequence of battle for the ordinary soldier defied all logic.

After about ten minutes I found a couple of Germans hiding under a bush, ordered them to come out and when they did my buddy and I searched them for hidden weapons, finding none we went through their papers and was surprised to find one was a boy of 15 who had only been in the army for 30 days while the other lad was 16 years old, and was only two months in the army.

We returned to the town Otterlo where our new officer a Lt. Hare told us to take it easy as we were in reserve for a day or two. So my section settled in an empty house next door to a building that had been destroyed by shellfire. It was the first time in about a month that I took my boots off, or any of my clothes for that matter.

We settled in for the night, then along about eleven o'clock we were awakened by mortar fire, and here we were in our longjohns half naked, we managed to get dressed in about 30 seconds flat. I climbed out the window and started to dig a slit trench as fast as I could. A German patrol passed by and 'Red' Senior our Bren gunner opened up and all hell broke loose. I could hear the lieutenant shouting 'surrender you are surrounded' to the Germans but all they did was shoot him.

Then a scout car was on the road putting up artificial moonlight and one of the men was yelling 'over here, Harry', directing him what to do while shells and bullets were flying everywhere.

What a comedy of errors. Then a Churchill tank parked on the side of the road started to fire his Howitzer at us and Nix who was digging with me ran to the tank, climbed upon it opened the hatch and with a hand grenade in his hand yelled at them and told them if they didn't stop firing at us he would drop the bloody hand grenade inside and close the lid.[16]

There was still some mopping up to be done.

A car came speeding round a bend in the road and slithered to an abrupt halt. It contained a Lieut. in the German Artillery and his driver. He was acting as FOO and had been sent out to find the enemy. (N.B. He found them.) In interrogation of this officer we found that he had followed much the same route as ourselves having been in the Reichwald, Calcar, Xanten and Wesel. It would appear that he may reach Canada before many of us.[17]

The entry into Arnhem was an emotive occasion.

Last September the world stopped breathing to watch this town. If the British Army had been able to link hands with the British First Airborne Division, which had landed round Arnhem, the Rhine would have been turned while the German armies were disorganised, and the armoured divisions would have poured into the plains of Hanover and Westphalia. But the effort was a bit too much for us, the weather was against us, and in fact we didn't have enough strength at the decisive place.

Now the town, once among the most beautiful in Holland, was a wreck, 'a smoking shell'. 'A lone Dutchman, the first civilian we had encountered, came slowly down a long street. He shook hands.

"You have come back," he said quietly. Just that. The British had come back, as they always do.'[18]

By the first week of April the German occupation was concentrated on the major cities – Rotterdam, Amsterdam, Utrecht and The Hague – where the death toll from starvation became an emotive point of issue between the Allies. Churchill argued that there was barely enough in the British larder to feed his own people; it was up to America to make up the shortfall. Roosevelt, however, was wary of an open-ended commitment to keep Europe stocked up with food. It was not until April 9th that Churchill was persuaded to open negotiations with Seyss Inquart and the Dutch Nazi government to give relief under the auspices of the International Red Cross, a move endorsed by Roosevelt.

In the event, Seyss Inquart already had in mind to let the Allies bring in supplies on condition that they held their advance into western Holland at the Grebbe Line: a system of blockhouses, trenches and defensive waterfalls east of Utrecht. On April 1st, his deputy, Ernst Schwebel, had been told to fix a meeting with Dr Koest Hirschfeld, a representative of the Free Dutch government and the top food official in the Netherlands. Seyss Inquart arrived hot foot from Oldenburg where Albert Speer had revealed his opposition to Hitler's 'scorched earth' orders for those countries that had failed him. Encouraged by Speer, Seyss Inquart was eager for a settlement with the Allies that stopped short of capitulation. The Dutch coast would be defended but if the Allies acted reasonably there would be no further destruction.

It was an offer calculated to lengthen the odds on Seyss Inquart's own survival. As the rest of the Reich crumbled away, he saw himself as the undisputed king of Fortress Holland, maybe even the essential mediator who could reconcile the Allies to Germany's survival. Seyss Inquart's offer of a truce started a lengthy exchange of cables between London, Washington and SHAEF. It was the first indication that reality was bearing in on the Nazi leaders. From the Allied point of view there were no military obstacles to a deal. To halt at the Grebbe Line had positive advantages for Eisenhower. For one thing it would release troops to join Montgomery on the final push through northern Germany. For another, it removed the risk of German forces releasing the sea water to flood occupied Holland and cause a massive evacuation. The Russians had to approve what might have seemed like a step back from the demand for unconditional surrender. This they did on April 24th. While BBC radio gave notice of an imminent air drop of food, a negotiating team led by General de Guingand flew to Nijmegen. From there they were driven to a village school, the selected rendezvous just across from the German lines.

> There was an atmosphere of subdued excitement around us, for it was obvious to everyone that something of great moment was taking place. It had been arranged that the enemy delegates should be blindfolded when leaving the German lines and that they should be driven in jeeps by a very roundabout way to the meeting place. Eventually the convoy arrived with white flags flying on each car and a rather miserable and cold-looking collection of Germans got out who were then led into the school.[19]

On the German side it was Schwebel who led the negotiations. He listened without interruption while de Guingand made the offer of help on condition of assurances that the food would reach the Dutch and not be taken by the Germans. Schwebel, 'a plump, sweating German who possessed the largest red nose I have ever seen, the end of which was like several ripe strawberries sewn together', agreed in principle but would make no definite commitment until he had reported back to Seyss Inquart. But de Guingand had something else on his mind. The second part of his brief was to sound out the prospects for an early surrender of German forces in Holland. When the meeting broke up he took Schwebel aside. Guessing what the conversation was to be about, Schwebel insisted on having the representative of his army staff alongside. De Guingand spoke of reports from the Dutch resistance that suggested the German high command in Holland was well aware of the hopelessness of its position, isolated as it was from any possible outside assistance.

> I pointed out how difficult the feeding of the Dutch would be if hostilities continued. For our part we were prepared to hold fast on

the line of the Grebbe and Eem Rivers. As I expected, I got very little result, and Schwebel looking rather uncomfortable and glancing repeatedly at the soldier next to him, said he was not empowered to discuss such matters. He agreed, however, to convey my remarks to his chief.[20]

Operation Manna began on April 28th. Two hundred and fifty-three American and British Lancaster heavy bombers, braving a freak blizzard above the English Channel, swooped low over the Dutch countryside to deliver thousands of 'mercy bombs'. The targets were marked by circles of green flares with red lights in the centre. On the perimeters were crowds of people 'madly waving flags, bed sheets and other white articles'. Major Tinley of the G-5 SHEAF Mission to the Netherlands talked of a civilian population going 'mad with joy to see manna from heaven'. In that first run, 600 tons of food reached the hungry citizens of Holland. In the next ten days American and British aircraft dropped 14.5 million ration pack-ages.[21] A day or two later lorries began to pass through the German lines, bringing more food into Holland.

At a reunion of Manna veterans in 1990, Squadron Leader Ken Butler recalled: 'The operations were all flown in daylight at low level and over half in very bad weather. We were flying so low we could see the Germans at their anti-aircraft guns, the barrels pointing at the sky over the River Schelde. The Dutch people had written Thank You on the ground near the drop zones in big white letters.' Seventeen-year-old Arie de Jong was on the receiving end. She wrote in her diary: 'One could see the gunners waving in their turrets. A marvellous sight. Everywhere we looked, bombers could be seen. No one remained inside and everybody dared to wave cloths and flags. What a feast! Everyone is excited with joy. The war must be over soon now.'

The next Allied-German meeting took place on April 30th. This time General Walter Bedell Smith, Eisenhower's Chief of Staff, and Prince Bernhard, Commander-in-Chief of the Dutch military, joined the Allied team, while the Germans were led by Seyss Inquart with General Blaskowitz's Chief of Staff in tow. Prince Bernhard arrived in a Mercedes with the licence plate RK-1. It was the car that Seyss Inquart had used until it had been captured by the resistance. After detailed talks about the relief plan, Bedell Smith turned the discussion to that of a general truce, arguing that it was only weeks, possibly days, before Germany capitulated, so why not give up now and so avoid unnecessary bloodshed and suffering. To the amazement of the Allied negotiators, Seyss Inquart accepted the inevitability of defeat but added that he had no orders which would allow him to surrender and in any case it was for the Commander-in-Chief, General Blaskowitz, to make the decision.

To this, Bedell Smith said, 'But surely, Reich Kommisar, it is the politician who dictates the policy to the soldier, and in any case our information points to the fact that no real Supreme Headquarters exists any longer in Germany today.' The German rather avoided answering the question and merely said, 'But what would future generations of Germans say about me if I complied with your suggestion – what would history say about my conduct?' It was then that Bedell Smith got really tough. 'Now, look here, General Eisenhower has instructed me to say that he will hold you directly responsible for any further useless bloodshed. You have lost the war and you know it. And if, through pigheadedness, you cause more loss of life to Allied troops or Dutch civilians, you will have to pay the penalty. And,' continued the Chief of Staff, 'you know what that will mean – the wall and the firing square!' Seyss Inquart slowly turned his watery eyes towards us and said rather quietly and slowly, 'I am not afraid – I am a German.' That ended the meeting.[22]

Five days later, May 5th, 1945, General Blaskowitz surrendered all German forces in the Netherlands.

Eleven years old, I was still too small to be noticed, but I listened eagerly to the grown-ups, emaciated and sallow, but so relieved, happy as I had never seen them before. Montgomery had done it, and the Canadians would come tomorrow. Here and there in spite of the radio's warning – 'the Germans are still around' – flags appeared. In the middle of a little group I discovered a Jewish girl I had known years ago but whose existence I and all the others had forgotten. She had spent three years in an attic room of our neighbour's and nobody had known it. She was deathly pale but her eyes glittered and she just could not stop talking. A little farther on a group of young men were looking around them as if dazed. Years of 'diving' indoors had given them the same paleness and the same stiffness of movement as the girl.

Suddenly a radio in a window blared the Wilhelmus, our national anthem. A silence fell and some began with trembling voices to sing; others followed. In the lane around the corner the sound of a gramophone: 'When the Saints Go Marching In'. Some people began to dance. Someone had found a bottle of Genever, saved for this occasion, and did the rounds; someone else gave cigars away, and everybody laughed and cried and shouted and danced. Five frightful years of oppression, eight terrible months of hunger, were over. A new world was about to begin.[23]

A resistance worker in Amsterdam joined the 'great crowd of people all congratulating each other', before witnessing a less appealing, if inevitable, reaction to the liberation.

Years of suppressed anger is being vented by young men who are taking girls who associated with the *Moffen* and gave themselves and cutting all their hair off. I witnessed this people's court in session four times. And nobody did anything about it. They got their punishment. They'd grab one of those girls and using pocket scissors, even knives, you could see them cutting off all the hair. Like plucked chickens you could see them fleeing through the crowd of thousands. They lifted one of the girls from her bed. She stood among the crowd in just her pyjama trousers and a vest. She ran off towards Amsterdam on bare feet. It was no elevating sight, but they had been warned for years and now they had to feel it, too. Many of the girls had hidden themselves. Doors were bashed down, and if they couldn't get in through the front, then you'd see the guys enter the house through the back. And they went from one to the next. They'd made lists of who qualified for the treatment. That's how this eventful day ended.[24]

And what was it like on the other side of the ideological divide? For those Dutch youngsters who had allowed themselves to be misguided by the promise of a Nazi-led new world order, the future as an SS volunteer looked far from rosy.

As soon as we heard the reports about the Führer's death we all felt that the war had entered a crisis out of which it could no longer be saved. Admiral Doenitz directed a proclamation to the German people, in which he declared that the war against the Soviets was the only important one . . .

Shortly thereafter we heard the news that arms had been lain down along the entire western front. The civilian population appeared on the streets everywhere, in many places there were great celebrations and, unfortunately, shooting incidents, too. Our regiment's quarters in Leersum were attacked by a group of armed men. As a consequence, a razzia against these partisans was immediately organised, resulting in nine people being shot in Leersum alone. There were a number of shooting incidents in Amersfoort, too.

The civilian population told us that the Fortress Holland had capitulated unconditionally, and in the English lines this was celebrated by lighting up the sky with flares. This, incidentally, appears to be a mistake. We don't know anything for certain, unfortunately. The flood of rumours has not yet subsided. Yesterday, we were given to understand the following by the battalion: there were to be negotiations about ending the occupation of Fortress Holland for the fight in the East. We would be secretly transported there. From this, one could conclude that the Allies want to give us a free hand in the fight against the Bolshevists.

But we hear other stories, too. The adjutant is supposed to have said that all SS-officers are to be shot and that the rest will be treated as criminals. It appears that he's already given a number of men leave so that they can try to get home, at their own risk, of course, because there's a great danger that anyone wearing a German uniform will be shot at.[25]

It was not only the defeated who feared for the future. Those returning from enforced labour or who emerged from months or years of hiding found a hardened society. 'There was no one to meet us . . . People shrugged their shoulders in response to our story. Then they told us of their own hardships; everything had been rationed, their bicycles stolen . . .' And from another witness: 'When I came back I was in rags. There was no kind of shelter. I expected something from the Reformed Church but they didn't do anything.'[26]

Sixteen thousand died as a result of the Hunger Winter. In all there were 200,000 Dutch war fatalities, half of whom were Jews sent to concentration camps.

12

The Bridge at Remagen

Those German generals not entirely besotted by Hitler, Rundstedt among them, had urged an early withdrawal across the Rhine. Instead there was a desperate fight for every last inch of ground. But in the end even Hitler came to realise that in a choice of evils retreat was better than defeat. When, after intense negotiations with commanders in the field, the word was reluctantly given for a pull-back of this or that unit, preparations were put in hand for the follow-up destruction of their route of escape. One after another, the twenty-two road and twenty-five railway bridges of the Rhine were blasted in the wake of the German withdrawal to the east bank. Setting off the fuses was a matter of close timing. Hitler's preference was for keeping the bridges intact for what he imagined as the glorious return of his armies. On the other hand, if any bridge was captured the officer responsible would answer with his life. General Alfred Schlemm of the First Parachute Army, who had faced the Anglo-Canadian onslaught, had nine bridges in his sector. As he told his post-war interrogators, 'I could see my hopes for a long life rapidly dwindling.'[1] His task was made all the harder by officers who were reluctant to accept his authority. When he gave the order for the bridge at Hamburg to be blown, the colonel in charge wanted endorsement from Field Marshal Model, Head of Army Group B. Schlemm's response was to threaten to do the job himself before shooting the colonel and anyone else who stood in his way.

On March 9th, Schlemm was visited by one of Hitler's staff intent on discovering if the general really had no choice but to pull back the rest of his forces. 'To the great detriment of his fresh and crinkly uniform', his visitor was sent forward to experience the Anglo-Canadian bombardment at first hand. The next night, what was left of the First Parachute Army withdrew in good order before the bridges at Wesel were reduced to a partly submerged heap of concrete and girders.

Having long since given up any hope of securing a Rhine bridge, Montgomery was concentrating on the next phase of Eisenhower's grand plan, a full frontal assault across the river scheduled for March 23rd–24th. To his south, there was greater optimism. Simpson's Ninth Army made several attempts to 'bounce' Rhine crossings. One of these was at Ürdingen near Düsseldorf.

Edwin Kolodziej was with the 379th Infantry Regimental Combat Scouts, a forward unit feeding back information for intelligence. Ürdingen was on their list of priorities.

> The lieutenant decided that Curran and I, being the two most experienced guys that were left, should investigate . . . When we moved up, they had already assembled several battalions of infantry: there were tanks and anti-tank guns lined up all along the roads, quietly, with no lights at all, because they were going to try and spring this bridge. They brought us up, I think twenty-some of us, and put us in front, and we started across. We started walking, and the further we got, we started crawling. Jumbo and I were crawling along the bridge and, of course, we were talking by radio back to our commanding officers who were following us. The big sweat there was that if the bridge was mined you had to be careful because if you touched the mines you'd blow yourself to bits. All of a sudden we reached a point where, as we were crawling along, there was no concrete under hand, and so he and I were hanging over the edge and we said, 'Damn bridge has been blown already.' So whatever intelligence that said the bridge was there was wrong.[2]

Intelligence was better informed about the bridge at Obercassel, a suburb of Düsseldorf. On March 2nd it was still in German hands but vulnerable to a surprise attack. A task force of German-speaking Americans was sent forward on tanks disguised as German armour. They managed to get through enemy lines but just short of the bridge they were caught out by a suspicious motorcyclist who asked one too many questions. The shots that followed him when he made his escape were sufficient warning to the defenders. The bridge exploded 'in a shower of planks, beams and German horsecarts'.

The run of bad luck for the Americans ended at Remagen, an ancient town on the edge of the Rhine midway between Koblenz and Bonn. There was no great confidence that the bridge could be secured. In fact, the assumption was that it had already been destroyed by Allied bombing. Then, on the morning of March 7th, advance units of the Ninth Armoured Division met a surprising sight. The Ludendorff railway bridge at Remagen was damaged but in use. The first reaction was to bring down mortar fire on the mass of men and vehicles moving across the bridge, their progress impeded by having to take it slowly over planks slung across the rail track. But Lieutenant Karl Timmermann, reckoning more firepower was needed, held back on the order. By now news of the sighting had filtered back to higher command along with intelligence from local citizens that the Germans were intending to blow the bridge within the hour. The timing was later disputed but preparations for demolition were well in hand and it could be assumed that any effort to capture the bridge was likely to end in failure. The buck stopped with Brigadier General William Hoge who decided that the chance was worth taking. It was Karl Timmermann's company that was given the dubious privilege of carrying out the order.

As the American tanks moved along the narrow roads of the west town, bringing up the infantry who were about to embark on what some of them were convinced was a suicide mission, the defenders, knowing full well what was about to happen, worked frantically to prepare the bridge for its demise. Timmermann and his men had little time to think through what had to be done. But as an explosion on the approach road brought the tanks to a halt before a thirty-foot crater, they knew that whatever happened they were on their own. On the hillside Hoge took in the scene through his binoculars. He could see German engineers on the bridge. It was a fair chance that they would set off their charges when the attackers were midway or, a marginally better prospect, once they were over and cut off from their support.

Why did the Germans allow the Ludendorff bridge to remain standing for so long? The decision sprang from a miscalculation at the highest level. Remagen held no attraction to the Americans, it was argued. They would know that on the east bank of the river was the Erpeler Ley, a 600-foot escarpment with only the rail track to give easy access to the ground beyond the natural barrier. Getting troops across in sufficient numbers to create a bridgehead of any size looked to be a challenge beyond ordinary military aptitude. But this was to forget that after so much destruction along the Rhine any bridge was a prize worth having. Hoge, who had been told to push south with all speed to link up with Patton's Fourth Armoured Division, was technically disobeying orders by attempting to gain the Remagen bridge. But he was well aware that success would excuse everything. On the other hand, if he failed . . .

Had he known of the confusion on the German side, he would have taken comfort. Now it was clear to the defenders that the Americans were seriously intent on capturing the bridge, the question of what to do and when rested with three officers. Captain Willi Bratge led a motley force of Volkssturm (a variation on *Dad's Army*), schoolboys of the Hitler Jugend, some hundred Russian slave labourers and an assortment of infantry who, knowing what they were up against, were disappearing at an alarming rate. The engineers who were making the bridge ready for destruction were the responsibility of Captain Karl Friesenhahn, while overseeing all was Major Hans Scheller who, though senior to the other two, was dependent on them for any decisions that might later have to be justified before a military tribunal.

If the bridge was blown too soon, all three would surely face the firing squad. If too late, their fate was not to be thought about. All decisions were made with future recriminations in mind; hence the frequent request for written confirmation of orders when instant reaction was called for. Bratge wanted to set off the charges, Scheller wanted to wait, Friesenhahn was caught in the middle. In the rail tunnel huddled the women, children and old men seeking refuge from the barrage of American artillery and machine-gun fire. Here too was where the German officers held their frequent but inconclusive confrontations. It was only when American tanks were lined up on the west bank, firing directly across the river, that Scheller gave the order to blow the bridge. But there was yet another delay.

Karl Hechler was one of a four-man team of combat historians who was to follow events at Remagen and, in the aftermath, interviewed many of the participants.

> Both Bratge and Friesenhahn felt that, the command situation being as confused as it was, it was important to clarify responsibility for the destruction of the bridge. So Bratge carefully directed Lieutenant Siegel [Scheller's executive officer] to write down the exact time and wording of the demolition order. It therefore became a matter of record that the demolition order was given by Major Scheller at twenty minutes past three. Bratge then rushed back toward the tunnel. As soon as he came within shouting distance of Friesenhahn, he cupped his hands and gave the order: 'Blow the bridge!'
>
> Now it was Friesenhahn's turn to become slightly bureaucratic. Knowing that Hitler had ordered all bridge demolitions to be approved beforehand by higher headquarters or in writing, Friesenhahn said to Bratge: 'I must have that order in writing.' Even to a correct old veteran like Friesenhahn, the words just about stuck in his mouth. They sounded to Friesenhahn just as absurd as they were; so he didn't wait for a reply from Bratge but immediately turned around and prepared to set off the main charges to blow the bridge.[3]

Those in the tunnel were told to lie down, cover their ears with their hands and keep their mouths open to protect their eardrums. They waited.

> Friesenhahn had mixed feelings when he ran up to turn the key that was to destroy the bridge. He knew that the circuit had just been tested, and he had been told a few minutes before that the circuit test was positive. He did not worry about the possibility that an American shell would break the circuit, because the wiring was enclosed in a thick pipe on the bridge. But he was concerned lest the rumbling vibrations from American tank fire upset some sensitive feature of the firing mechanism. Nevertheless, he was pleased that

he would have ample time to set off the charge before American infantry ventured onto the bridge.

Taking his place just inside the tunnel, Friesenhahn gave the key a turn. The mechanism operated like a watchspring. When the key was wound tight, it was supposed to set off the demolition. He wound it once – nothing happened. Frantically, he wound it again – still with no success.[4]

Something, probably an American shell, had broken the circuit. Friesenhahn's reaction was to send a repair team but the intensity of fire ruled out that option. Instead, a single volunteer went out on to the bridge to light the primer cord of a demolition charge placed where the smallest amount of explosive would cause the maximum damage.

There was a sudden roar as timbers shot into the air, and the bridge seemed to rise from its foundations. All the Germans on the east side of the Rhine breathed a tremendous sigh of relief.

But they reacted too soon. A moment later, their relief turned to horror as they watched the bridge slowly settle back on its foundations.

It was still standing![5]

Heard from the west bank, the explosion had the same immediate effect on the Americans – a feeling of relief, though in their case it was relief that they would not now have to attempt a dangerous crossing. As with their opponents, the euphoria was short-lived.

Timmermann stared into the thick haze and yelled 'Look – she's still standing!' As the dust and smoke cleared away, they could see Germans working frantically – it looked like they were going to try and blow up the bridge again. Timmermann saw that the bridge was damaged but passable. He called the platoon leaders together and gave the plan for crossing the bridge. The men hesitated – they were tired and it looked like certain death. Timmermann stood up to rally them to follow him, but had to duck as a machine gun from one of the two towers opened up. He ducked down, but a tank shell opened a big crack in the tower and the firing ceased. Timmermann moved out to the bridge urging his men to 'git going'. They followed. The engineers joined them and began cutting demolition wires.[6]

But less than halfway across they were pinned down by ferocious fire. A machine-gun in one of the towers at the far end of the bridge was spraying the approaches, there was more fire from the tunnel and trouble too from snipers on a partly submerged barge. A well-aimed shell put paid to the barge but it was sheer manpower, in the shape of a platoon sergeant, Joseph DeLisio, who took care of the machine-gun. Having made it to the tower, he pushed aside the bales of hay blocking the door and ran up the spiral staircase.

There were three floors in the tower, and he couldn't take anything for granted. He heard machine-gun fire above him, and then it suddenly stopped. Had the Germans heard him coming, and was he heading into a trap?

He slapped open a steel door with the heel of his hand and burst in on three German soldiers. They were bending over a machine gun, as though it were jammed. There was an agonizing second as the three men jerked their heads around. DeLisio pumped out a couple of shots with his carbine, firing from the hip.

'Hände hoch!' he yelled.

The three Germans wheeled around with their hands in the air. DeLisio motioned them to one side with his carbine, and seizing the gun they had been using he hurled it out of the window. Men starting across the bridge saw the gun plummet from the tower and began to move with more confidence.[7]

There was growing confusion on both sides. While the anti-tank crater at the approach to the bridge was being filled, it was the American infantry alone that had to take the brunt of the counter-attack. Some of those who made it over the bridge were soon driven back only to meet foot soldiers coming the other way. At least half of those in the three companies that crossed the Rhine on March 7th ended up back in Remagen by nightfall. Only a handful managed to scramble to the top of the Erpeler Ley where, sensibly, they decided to keep their heads down until reinforcements arrived. Fortunately, the defence command was equally chaotic. It was several hours before Field Marshal Model realised that events at Remagen were more than a local skirmish.

The Americans were sharper on the uptake, not least Bradley who had yet to be persuaded that Eisenhower's plans for an assault river crossing under Montgomery's command was the best way to break into Germany. Providentially, Bradley was meeting one of Eisenhower's principal staff officers, Major General Bull, when the Remagen news came through. He had just heard the unwelcome news, a 'larcenous proposal' he called it, that four of his twenty-six divisions were to be transferred to the US Seventh and French First Armies for General Jacob Devers to make the breakthrough into the Saar.

Suddenly my phone rang. It was Hodges calling from Spa. 'Brad,' Courtney called, with more composure than the good news warranted, 'Brad, we've gotten a bridge.'

'A bridge? You mean you've got one intact on the Rhine?'

'Yep,' Hodges replied, 'Leonard nabbed the one at Remagen before they blew it up –'

'Hot dog, Courtney,' I said, 'this will bust him wide open. Are you getting your stuff across?'

'Just as fast as we can push it over,' he said. 'Tubby's got the navy moving in now with a ferry service and I'm having the engineers throw a couple of spare pontoon bridges across to the bridgehead.'

I pulled the long lead wire from my phone over toward the mapboard. 'Shove everything you can across it, Courtney,' I said, 'and button the bridgehead up tightly. It'll probably take the other fellow a couple of days to pull enough stuff together to hit you.'

I hung up on Hodges, turned on Bull, and thumped him on the shoulder. 'There goes your ball game, Pink,' I grinned. 'Courtney's gotten across the Rhine on a bridge.'

Bull blinked back through his rimless glasses. He sat down before the map and shrugged his shoulders. 'Sure, you've got a bridge, Brad, but what good is it going to do you. You're not going anywhere down there at Remagen. It just doesn't fit into *the* plan.'

'Plan – hell,' I retorted. 'A bridge is a bridge and mighty damned good anywhere across the Rhine.'[8]

Bull had a point, of course. As Bradley readily conceded, the steep woodlands beyond Remagen posed a formidable barrier to any rapid advance east. But whatever the handicaps, it would be madness to throw up the chance of striking at the enemy where he least expected it. Moreover, seven miles east of Remagen was the Cologne–Bonn–Limburg autobahn which opened the way to Frankfurt and to Giessen. There was then the prospect of moving up into the Ruhr to meet with Montgomery's forces in a pincer movement, assuming that Montgomery succeeded, or if he failed or stalled, taking over from him in the race to Berlin.

Bradley was not about to say all this to Eisenhower but he knew that the Supreme Commander could hardly put the dampers on an American achievement that would soon be filling the front pages back home. When Bradley telephoned Eisenhower with his news the reaction was, as he had anticipated, enthusiastic. It was, Eisenhower recorded in his memoirs, 'one of my happy moments of the war'. Bradley remembered him saying, 'Hold on to it, Brad. Get across whatever you need – but make certain you hold that bridgehead.' But, as soon became clear, this was not to give Bradley carte blanche. The following day he was told that only four divisions could be spared for Remagen. Meanwhile, Montgomery, who might have been expected to oppose any diversion of resources from his own mission, responded phlegmatically: 'It will be an unpleasant threat to the enemy and will undoubtedly draw enemy strength onto it and away from the business in the north.'

Belatedly, the German high command recognised that it faced a serious threat. By March 9th, the front platoon of Pershing tanks was across the bridge, having moved nose to tail in pitch darkness with only a white marker line to guide them. The rail tunnel had been evacuated and a number of prisoners taken, including Captain Bratge. Twenty-four hours after the capture of the bridge, the US First Army had nearly 8,000 men over the Rhine. The man chosen to restore German fortunes was General Fritz Bayerlein, commander of the Panzer Lehr Division which had taken a prominent role in the Ardennes offensive. But his own force was reduced to 300 men and fifteen tanks. Three other Panzer units were at his disposal but all were undermanned and under-equipped. Bayerlein was shocked at the fitness of the men in his command and their reluctance to fight. Rolf Pauls, who was to become West Germany's first ambassador to Israel, had a first-hand demonstration of the odds stacked against them.

I had lost my left arm in Russia, but continued to serve as a staff officer. During the final stages of the war, we were ordered to bring tanks and artillery to the right bank of the Rhine, near Cologne. The next morning, we were ordered to go down to the vicinity of Remagen and meet the Americans for a last stand – it all ended in the vicinity of Düsseldorf. Herr Grohé, the *Gauleiter* of Cologne, enthusiastically told the division commander that he would send three of four battalions from the *Volkssturm* consisting of approximately 3,500 men. He maintained that the *Volkssturm* could hardly wait for the opportunity to defend their own hometown.

Hearing that, my boss blew up, slamming his fist down on the table so hard that the hats flew up into the air. He yelled back, 'I'll tell you what the *Volkssturm* can hardly wait to do – they can hardly wait to get out of here! The last 24 hours have proven that – they are taking off in all directions. And to tell you the truth, I can't blame them.' Herr Grohé was rather shocked by this outburst and left.[9]

Bayerlein came up with a plan – to attack through the middle of the bridgehead and then roll it up to the north or south. This put the onus on Model to provide the necessary combat troops, something he was unable to do. Reluctant to confess his impotence, he ordered Bayerlein to deal first with an immediate threat from American tanks. Model's problems were not limited to manpower shortages. With the removal of Rundstedt as Commander-in-Chief of the western front (the capture of the Remagen bridge was given by Hitler as the cause of his downfall) a gap in the command structure opened up until the arrival from Italy of Field Marshal Kesselring. Meeting Hitler in Berlin on March 9th, Kesselring, known to his troops as Smiling Albert because he was always breaking out into a cheerful grin, found the acid test of his sense of humour. Remagen was his first priority. The enemy had to be held back, he was told, until 'new fighters and other novel weapons could be employed in overwhelming numbers'.

> Hitler largely blamed the Luftwaffe for previous defeats; but he had now personally taken over its technical direction and guaranteed success.
>
> The Commander-in-Chief of the navy, Admiral Doenitz, would soon make his new U boats felt and would substantially relieve the situation. He was full of praise for the superhuman efforts and endurance of the people at home.
>
> Arms production was co-ordinated in the hands of Saur of the Armament Ministry, in whom he had implicit confidence that he would satisfy the essential requirements of our armies in the field. There would, however, have to be some diversion of production to new units being formed, which would be the best the German Wehrmacht had seen during the war. He himself would be responsible for their getting first rate leadership. So it was once again a battle for time!
>
> Hitler's exposition, which lasted hours, was remarkably lucid and showed an astounding grasp of detail. My mission was clear: Hang on![10]

If Kesselring was inspired by this diatribe, it did not take long for him to come back to earth. It was now March 11th. Conferring for the first time with Model and Bayerlein, he was shocked to hear that Bayerlein's plan had not progressed further than the wall map. Model made the inevitable excuses – an insufficiency of men, fuel and military hardware. Bayerlein added that every time he prepared for an attack greater than a local skirmish, the Americans captured his jumping-off ground. Kesselring revealed his back-up plan. Before leaving Berlin, he had persuaded the commander of Luftwaffe West to put all his efforts into destroying the Remagen bridge before the Americans could take a decisive hold on the high ground of the Erpeler Ley.

The holding of the Rhine line hinged on Remagen. If the bridge-head was enlarged at the previous pace and to the previous extent, there could be no hope of preventing a break-through. If the enemy succeeded in breaching the German switch-line in front of the bridge-head he would throw in his mobile forces to open the gap, and in whichever direction he drove would unhinge the defence of the river at least between the Ruhr and the Hahn, and possibly as far as the Main. Thus we simply had to prevent an eruption from the bridge-head. In spite of the immense difficulties I thought it might be at least delayed.[11]

But, as Kesselring later conceded, he had not reckoned on the rapid success of the American armoured forces, the war weariness of the German troops and the inability of the Luftwaffe to deliver the promised knockout blow. On March 15th, the Luftwaffe sent in their strongest force so far – twenty-one bombers including several jets, but American anti-aircraft defences brought down sixteen. Bombs falling near the bridge shook its foundations but the structure held – just. Heavy weapons, including a 17-centimetre railroad gun, were unable to get the bridge in range. The shells, fired from the far side of Erpeler Ley, all landed beyond the target in Remagen itself. It was the same with the V2s, eleven of which were aimed at the bridge. All missed.

Armed Duplantier of the 272nd Field Artillery had two reasons for never forgetting Remagen. One was the sight of the air battle over the bridge with German jets coming in every five minutes, each making a death dive in the face of intensive anti-aircraft fire.

This morning we stood atop a hill near C Battery and watched the area of the bridge for several hours. There's a guard of P.38's (about 7 or 8 planes) on constant patrol to try to scare off the suicide jets but without success. On one occasion as two P.38's chased a jet, they made miscalculations and crashed wing-tips. Both planes caught on fire immediately, but not before the pilots had a chance to bail out. Seemed to us like one made it on this side, and one on the other, but in either case we could see the tracer bullets going up after the pilot, and each one pulling at the drawstrings of his parachute trying to dodge the bullets . . . The din caused by the anti-aircraft fire when one of these jets comes in defies description. The sky being literally covered with tracers makes one wonder how in the hell anything can survive such a saturation.[12]

The other reason Duplantier had for remembering Remagen was the birth of his son. The news was relayed to him the day before he crossed the bridge.

By now, the Americans were pouring in all the troops they had within marching distance. Roger J. Moore, a radio operator with the Ninety-Ninth Infantry Division, slogged most of the way from Cologne without knowing the purpose of the exercise until he and his buddies arrived in Remagen.

We ducked along streets by dead bodies and shattered houses. After half-an-hour in a cellar, we walked some more to the bridge, which was a big surprise to us. Every couple of minutes a heavy gun fired a shell at it. Sometimes it hit and sometimes it missed, and engineers were at work repairing the damage. We were very tired from that long walk, but we had to go on. We climbed up the stairs in the stone tower at the end of the bridge and stepped on the bridge itself. Then we *ran*, breathlessly, all the way to the other side. I don't think my heart beat once all the way. Shells were flying over us and crashing into Remagen, and regularly, every couple of minutes, a large shell screamed down, over the top of the hill across the Rhine, down to the bridge. Oh, but that was a long bridge! I have never been so scared.[13]

The action was no less terrifying seen from the air. Among those fighter pilots sent in to foil the German bombers was Ray Wetmore who at the war's end would be acknowledged as the highest scoring American ace still on active service in Europe. Though promised that the anti-aircraft guns would be stood down when his fighters arrived on the scene, Wetmore and his group were hidden from clear ground observation by heavy cloud. The result:

The gunners heard our ships descending and pumped everything they had into the clouds at the 'Germans' attacking the bridge. While we

258

were still in the overcast, I was startled to see flames erupt from the underside of Wetmore's ship. Still engrossed with his instruments, Wetmore did not know he was afire. The thumping of the hits in the clouds with no visual evidence of flak could be indistinguishable from turbulence.

Knowing that it would be suicide to bail out in thick flak, Wetmore put his still burning plane into a steep climb back into the clouds. At a safe altitude, he made ready to escape but when he pulled the jettison handle, his canopy jammed.

Trapped in a plane set afire by our own anti-aircraft, Wetmore called for a homing to a field, any friendly field where he could put down.
He was vectored to a field – no good – bulldozers were still making it. No room to land. Minutes went like hours until a second field further away seemed OK. He was going in and then went off the air . . . Back at the pilot's quarters, I learned the score. No Germans racked up, but three of our ships and two pilots lost. Wetmore was safe. The fire had burned out before he reached the second field, and with his hydraulic system shot out he bellied in safely without wheels or flaps. They said it took about 20 minutes to pry the canopy off after he was down.[14]

Wetmore's skill and luck held out until 1951 when he was killed in a jet crash at the Otis Air Force Base in Massachusetts.

By March 16th, nine days after the Americans had entered Remagen, three corps of the First Army were over the high ground and within striking distance of the Frankfurt autobahn. Their bridgehead was twenty-five miles across. But the frequent vibrations from near misses, plus wear and tear from the constant stream of heavy traffic, took its toll on the bridge. The end came at mid-afternoon on March 17th.

There was no warning noise, such as popping of rivets, and no apparent cause for its falling at that particular time. No enemy action had been recorded in the preceding two hours, although German as well as our own shelling had been severe for 24 hr. prior to that. No work was taking place that would influence the structure toward failure. In falling, the main span suddenly rotated upstream, then crashed vertically. The approach spans were lifted and dropped onto the dry flood plain, resting in an upright position. In conclusion the bridge was standing with a very small margin of safety and it appears that the vibration of our artillery coupled with that of the enemy's artillery caused the final failure.[15]

Of the 200 engineers working round the clock to hold the bridge together, more than twenty were crushed by falling girders, while others were flung into the icy water. For the Germans, it was all too late. Interrogated by his captors after the war's end, Reichsmarschall Goering claimed that events at Remagen 'upset our entire defence scheme along the river'. Moving reserves to the Remagen bridgehead weakened the defence of the Rhine to the south between Mainz and Mannheim where Patton was to make his breakthrough. 'All this was very hard on Hitler,' added Goering.

As with everything that went hard with the Führer, he had to have his revenge. Major Scheller paid with his life, as did three other officers including an engineer major who, after the Americans had taken the bridge, led a daring attack to blow it up.[16]

Remagen was indeed a terrible blow to German morale. If the enemy could not be held back on one of the more impenetrable sectors of the Rhine, what chance was there for the depleted Wehrmacht to check the massive assault planned in the north? To make matters more problematic, Patton now decided to get in on the act. Angered that it had been the First Army with the painstaking and cautious Hodges in command that had won all the plaudits for Remagen and made doubly furious by the prospect of Montgomery taking credit for the northern crossing, Patton embarked on his own adventure to show that 'I can outfight that little fart any time'. In the early hours of March 23rd, a day before Montgomery was to embark on Operation Plunder, a division of the Eleventh Infantry Regiment of the US Third Army took to the assault boats at Oppenheim and simply paddled across the Rhine without meeting any real opposition. Patton was ecstatic but was cautious on parading his achievement, urging Bradley to keep the news to himself 'until we see how it goes'.

Bradley could hardly wait to put the knife into Montgomery. Two months of mounting resentment at the way Montgomery had treated him over the Battle of the Bulge found its release in a stinging communiqué with its none too subtle reference to Monty's elaborate preparations. 'Without benefit of aerial bombing, ground smoke, artillery preparation and airborne assistance, the Third Army at 2200 hrs, Thursday evening, March 22nd, crossed the Rhine River.'[17] By the following evening, Patton could no longer contain himself. Again, he telephoned Bradley. '"Brad," he shouted and his treble voice trembled, "for God's sake tell the world we're across. We knocked down 33 Krauts today when they came after our pontoon bridges. I want the world to know Third Army made it before Monty starts across."'[18]

It took some time for Patton to calm down. Halfway across one of the pontoon bridges, he stopped abruptly.

He whipped out his pecker and proceeded to piss into the Rhine River, saying, 'I've waited a long time to do that. I didn't even piss this morning when I got up so I would have a really full load. Yes, sir, the pause that refreshes.' When he reached the eastern bank of the river he faked a fall, rose with two hands of German soil and remarked, 'Thus William the Conqueror', in emulation of the victor of the Battle of Hastings in 1066.[19]

It wasn't all as easy as the official communiqués made out. Hopes pinned on the use of amphibious tanks, the latest wonder weapon to emerge from the armaments factories, were largely disappointed. Russell Cloer had the job of guiding four amphibious tanks to the water's edge.

So we got down right to the riverbank. I looked over the edge and it was about a four-foot drop to the water. It was flowing very fast. The current was eight miles an hour, and the river was about 400 yards wide. And these amphibious tanks would be dropped in there. Oh, my God, a four foot drop into eight mph water, 35 tons, crazy! And it was so quiet! There was no firing, there was no artillery, there was nothing. It was unnatural! It was eerie! I could hear the water swishing against the bank of the river, the only sound other than the soft idle of the jeep's engine. So we turned around, came back to the CP, and here were the four amphibious tanks lined up. The tank platoon leader proudly showed me the features of the tank. It had a metal framework, with rubberized canvas on it, that would raise hydraulically and give the tanks sufficient buoyancy to float. They had two small propellers in the back, so they could steer and propel it, and there were four of them, each with a 75-mm gun up front. I said, 'Okay, then, follow me,' and we got in front with the jeep and we went forward in a single column. The clanking of the steel tracks and the roar of their engines sounded deafening, and I thought to myself, 'My God, when we get down to that river bank, with all that noise, they're going to alert every German within five miles.' The four tanks followed us back up to the river . . . We got down within, oh, I guess, it was ten yards of the river bank, and we slowed down and stopped and I told them, 'This is as far as I go.' . . . And with that, a shell came across the river from underneath the bridge ramp, hit the tank behind me, no more than 40 to 50 feet away, exploded and the tank started burning. When it started to burn, it lit up the whole area, and then they started firing at the other three tanks . . . Then artillery air bursts began right over our heads. I mean, it was like the 4th of July. You could see the things exploding, but it was shell fragments coming down, not fireworks. They all seemed to be bursting at the same height, and that puzzled me, because the Germans didn't have the proximity fuse then, but we did, so I figured it's got to be our own artillery firing short . . . But it didn't much matter whose it was. We couldn't stay there. So Steele and I took off running. In the meantime, this overhead shellfire was still going on. So far as the tanks were concerned, one was totally destroyed, two more were damaged to the point where they couldn't use their inflatable gear, and the fourth one was missing, which means he turned around and ran.[20]

Even when they did make it into the water, amphibious tanks were seldom a match for the current. Swept down river, they were liable to capsize before they reached the opposite shore. But more conventional efforts to span the Rhine were hugely successful. Eighteen hours after the first assault craft of the Fifth Infantry Division had landed on the east bank, a treadway bridge was carrying traffic. A second bridge was in place the following day. By March 27th, five divisions with supporting troops had crossed these bridges. The entire Sixth Command Division crossed in less than seventeen hours. Patton was on his way. His tanks entered Darmstadt on March 25th. The following day they reached Frankfurt.

Bradley and Patton can be forgiven their triumphalism. Remagen and Oppenheim were extraordinary achievements, though it has to be said that without Hodges, described by Bradley as a 'quiet and methodical commander', neither would have happened. Then again, Hodges would never have jumped in with advice to Montgomery as Bradley had done to 'crash the river on the run'. This was to overlook the contrast between the Twenty-First and the Twelfth Army Group sectors. As Montgomery's biographer points out:

> The British and Canadian troops had been fighting hard since 8 February, a whole month, in the most appalling conditions. If they were to cross the Rhine, encircle the Ruhr and finish the war in northern Germany it was imperative that as many divisions as possible be withdrawn from battle rested, re-equipped, reinforced and trained for the next battle.[21]

It was undeniable that German defences had been weakened by the transfer of tanks and infantry to plug the Remagen gap but the best of what was left of the Wehrmacht – the Fifteenth and Fifth Panzer Armies and the First Parachute Army – was concentrated on the vulnerable stretch of the Rhine between Wesel and Arnhem. Everybody knew that this was where the main Allied attack was to come. To 'crash the river' was a risk too far. It was unwise to underestimate the strength of German opposition, as Montgomery and Bradley both knew to their cost. Montgomery was not about to repeat that mistake. At the same time, there was justification in the American complaint that Montgomery took so long in preparation as to lose every element of surprise. A dense smoke screen along the river may have hidden the precise disposition of nearly a million troops but the Germans had a fair idea of what was going on and had plenty of time to dig in. Their orders were to hold on until, in Kesselring's words, 'our new fighters and other novel weapons could be employed in overwhelming numbers'.[22] It was, as he knew very well, a forlorn prospect against 'the enemy's extraordinary superiority in men and material on the ground and his absolute ascendancy in the air'.[23] Over the entire front, Kesselring could count on no more than one hundred combatants to every kilometre.

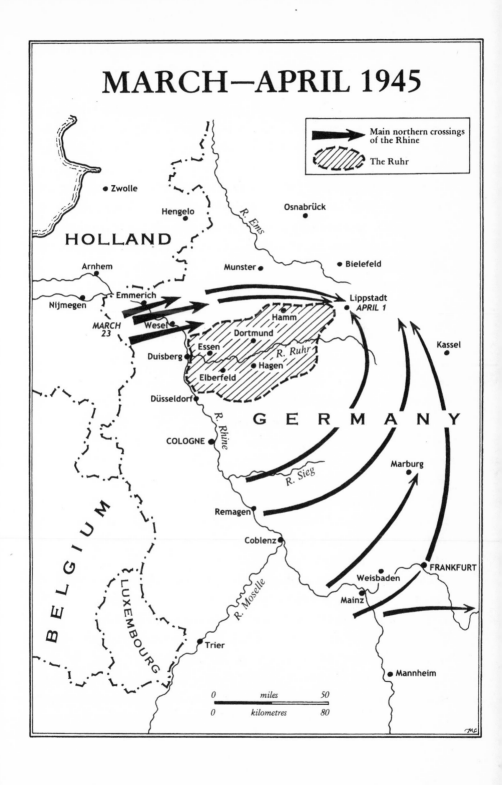

MARCH–APRIL 1945

Main northern crossings
of the Rhine

The Ruhr

Zwolle

Hengelo

Osnabrück

R. Ems

HOLLAND

Arnhem

Munster

Bielefeld

Nijmegen

Emmerich

Lippstadt
APRIL 1

MARCH
23

Wesel

Hamm

Dortmund

Kassel

Duisberg

Essen

R. Ruhr

Elberfeld

Hagen

Düsseldorf

R. Rhine

GERMANY

COLOGNE

Marburg

R. Sieg

Remagen

B E L G I U M

Coblenz

FRANKFURT

Weisbaden

R. Moselle

Mainz

L U X E M B O U R G

Trier

Mannheim

0	miles	50
0	kilometres	80

13
A Set Piece Battle

Operation Plunder was finalised at Montgomery's headquarters on March 9th. The start date was the night of March 23rd–24th. After a massive air and artillery bombardment intended to shatter enemy morale and open up gaps in their defences, the British Second Army, commanded by Lieutenant General Sir Miles Dempsey ('an exact and energetic technician – not so much a popular leader as a remarkable coordinator and planner'[1]), was to cross the Rhine on the left of the Allied advance, aiming to seize Rees and Wesel. Simultaneously, Simpson's US Ninth Army would attack on the right between Wesel and Duisburg. Both crossings having been made by troops in amphibious vehicles and landing craft, the engineers would move up with ferries and Bailey bridges. It was then up to the tanks to carry forward the attack on the east bank. They were to be helped by a daylight air drop by General Ridgway's US Eighteenth Airborne Corps consisting of the US Seventeenth and the British Sixth Airborne Divisions. This was a departure from conventional strategy which put airborne troops ahead of ground forces. For Operation Plunder, Montgomery argued that they would be less vulnerable to a punishing counter-attack like that of Arnhem. The codename for the air drop was Operation Varsity.

The combined attack of infantry, armoured and airborne forces aimed at creating a bridgehead forty miles long and ten miles deep within twenty-four hours. Thereafter, the objective was to encircle the industrial cities of the Ruhr before breaking out on to the north German plain and, as Montgomery fervently hoped, making straight for Berlin. While all this was going on, Canadian forces would cross the Rhine at Emmerich on the far left of the advance to liberate that part of Holland still under German occupation.

In the month leading up to Plunder, Allied air forces struck at communication links essential to the movement of German troops. Starting February 21st, targets included bridges, viaducts, airfields and railyards from Bremen down to Frankfurt. The Ruhr cities suffered the heaviest attacks. On March 11th, Bomber Command set a record by dropping 5,000 tons of bombs on Essen. The record lasted until the following night when 5,487 tons fell on Dortmund. In all these operations only five bombers were lost.

But even more critical to the success of Plunder was the expertise of the American and British navies. With a width of 1,500 feet, the Rhine in Montgomery's sector flowed at a rate that would take ordinary boats way downstream. Montgomery needed a ferry service capable of carrying tanks, bulldozers and guns and men to secure the east bank before even temporary bridges could be thrown across the river. After dummy runs over the Thames and Severn rivers, the vessel chosen was the LCM (landing craft mechanised), better known as the Buffalo, which in its earliest form had seen service on the Normandy beaches. Shaped like a barge with a bow at the front over which sat the driver, the half dozen or so types of LCM could let down a ramp for quick loading and unloading. The LCM-3, the most common example, could carry thirty tons of cargo – anything from sixty men to the largest tank. To manoeuvre a Buffalo across a fast-flowing river and to land at the appointed place called for navigational skills of a high order. The naval attachments who did the job, 200 miles away from the sea, dubbed themselves the Rhine Navy.

Landing craft had to be brought in by roads built to order by army engineers who were also responsible for preparing bridging sites. By March 19th, over 25,000 tons of bridging equipment had been brought up. From his assembly point on a T-junction on the Xanten road where a narrow lane wound down towards the Rhine, Tom Flanagan, a lieutenant with the Fourth King's Own Scottish Borderers, had a front-row view of the battle preparations. 'Enormous articulated lorries lumbered slowly by pulling trailers loaded with huge segments of bailey bridges like pieces of Meccano . . . 15cwt trucks went up and down loaded to their canvas roofs with ammunition boxes . . . and large guns with sacks over their muzzles were pulled along by tractors.'

But most impressive of all was:

a boat being towed along on a massive many wheeled low loader. Outriding MPs cleared the way ahead for the journey as behind them, moving at a speed slower than walking pace, came the boat, towering above buildings and of a great length. It seemed odd to see sailors driving the towing rig and others walking alongside keeping an eye on the lashings holding the boat to the raft of the low loader. The vastness of the task became clear – '. . . waiting to cross the Rhine . . .' was a simple statement in the newspapers but it hid the intense preparations for it of which these great loads were just a part.[2]

Flanagan's platoon relaxed in the spring sunshine, none too worried by the long wait before the action started. Fresh bread to go with the packed rations arrived each day along with day-old newspapers but meat that was not out of a tin had to be 'liberated' from nearby farms. This could turn out to be awkward for the liberators.

One morning Tom Flanagan was sitting outside reading the *News Chronicle* and listening to music on Dufflebag, the American forces radio station, when four plump geese came waddling along the road.

Shouts of 'Come and have a look!' rang out from behind me and several hands opened the yard gate encouraging the geese to enter the yard. Others crowded round the quartet and waved their arms about and shouted what they obviously intended to be herding calls but which only panicked the geese who proceeded to dash about all over the farmyard. Eventually, after much chasing, laughter and swearing, the creatures were herded into the barn.

'Fetch Tony!' someone cried, 'he's a butcher by trade, he'll know what to do.' The corpulent figure of Tony was soon to be seen hurrying over to see what all the fuss was about, and on being told, asked the crowd to move away and let him alone in the barn so that he could make a start. I had moved away, trying not to hear the squawks and mutterings which accompanied whatever was taking place in the barn, when I saw a soldier dashing down the road, hat in hand, his head bathed in sweat. Seeing me, he stopped, put his hat on and giving me the hastiest of salutes, he puffed and blew through his words, 'Excuse me, Sir, puff, puff, have you seen . . . puff puff . . . have you seen four white geese . . . puff puff . . . come by at all?' I could hear the unabated noise from the barn as I struggled for a responsible answer. 'You see . . . puff puff . . . Sir,' he continued, 'I . . .', and he stopped speaking.

His mouth agape, I watched as he raised his arm, pointing beyond me to the group of Jocks I could hear. I turned and saw three geese scattering over the yard honking and squawking as a group of Jocks, led by Tony with a broad smile on his face, approached. 'I got 'im, Sir,' he yelled, swinging the dead goose by the neck. He was about to say more but before he could draw breath the frantic soldier beside me leapt forward and grabbed the goose from Tony's grasp and began to berate Tony.

'Bloody Hell! . . . B . . . l . . . oody Hell!' he cried. 'I don't know what my C.O. will say . . . B . . . l . . . oody Hell! I don't!' He was beside himself with anguish and his eyes had a transfixed glaze on them as he continued his ravings. 'We've had these geese at the Battery for four years! They're the C.O.'s pets, they is! He wouldn't let us 'ave 'em at Christmas when we was 'ungry . . . now look what you've gone and done! I won't half cop it when I gets back . . . there's no telling what he'll do!' So saying, he rounded up the survivors and stalked off across the yard towards the artillery battery behind our farm, still muttering as the dead goose swung from his hand. Silence descended on the yard as he went and the Jocks dispersed, soothing Tony in his disappointment. I was glad to hide once more behind my paper.[3]

Briefings and last-minute preparations reminded veterans of D-Day, though there were critical differences. For one thing there was more confidence. 'Is this the last battle?' war reporter Alan Moorehead asked General Dempsey. 'Yes,' came back the immediate reply. The British Second Army was to attack on a three-way split: on the left zeroing in on Rees before taking Emmerich, on the right towards Wesel and in the centre towards Xanten. The drop of the Eighteenth US Airborne Corps was to be near the River

Issel where there were vital bridges to be captured. On the right flank of the Second Army, the US Ninth Army, having crossed to the east bank, was to make for the Ruhr. It was all meticulously planned and no one doubted that it would succeed.

Straining a sporting metaphor, as was his inclination, Montgomery talked of 'going into the ring for the final and last round'. In a personal message from the Commander-in-Chief to be read out to all troops he promised to 'continue fighting until our opponent is knocked out'. The last round, he said, 'is going very well on both sides of the ring' (a reference to Soviet successes) 'and overhead'. He prophesied 'the complete and decisive defeat of the Germans' as a certainty. He went on:

> The enemy possibly thinks he is safe behind this great river obstacle. We all agree that it is a great obstacle; but we will show the enemy that he is far from safe behind it. This great Allied fighting machine, composed of integrated land and air forces, will deal with the problem in no uncertain manner.
>
> And having crossed the RHINE, we will crack about in the plains of Northern Germany, chasing the enemy from pillar to post. The swifter and the more energetic our action the sooner the war will be over, and that is what we all desire: to get on with the job and finish off the German war as soon as possible.
>
> Over the RHINE, then, let us go. And good hunting to you all on the other side.

For a week before Plunder got underway, a smokescreen was put up along twenty miles of the west bank. It rose 200–300 feet, 'a tall white cloud', as one observer called it, 'curling at its top like a wave crest caught in slow motion'. For those who had to work within its reach, the smoke seemed to be more trouble than it was worth. Patrols were likely to lose their bearings while drivers and others involved in moving up equipment suffered 'when the wind blew the smoke towards us and made everyone feel sick'.[4] But there was a lot to be said for masking the precise crossing points and for hiding last-minute preparations such as, on the day before the crossing, the movement of field guns close to the riverbank. The idea was that as soon as the action started fire would be directed over the advancing troops to break the Germans' second line of defence.

As the critical hour approached, the sappers worked under cover of smoke to fill in the anti-tank ditches dug by the Germans to cover their withdrawal. Since they were operating close to the river they needed patrols to guide them from and to their own lines. One of these patrols was led by Tom Flanagan.

I left two sections guarding the sappers and took my HQ section and No.3 section and patrolled the riverbank either side of the working party, going several hundred yards in each direction. As the smoke from the cylinders behind us started once more to pour out the foul stuff, our task was made much more difficult as we kept losing contact with each other, and I was forced to stand and wait a lot before the others caught my group which was leading this part of the patrol.

We came across a large barn in the field close by where the sappers were busy which we entered to search. Suddenly I was aware that someone was there! My heart flew straight into my gullet and I was aware I had begun to breathe very deeply if quietly as I flashed my torch to the accompaniment of the rattle of slings on rifles as the lads brought themselves rapidly from the 'trail' to the 'guard' position. There in the bright circle of light crouched a khaki clad figure. I could feel the tension drain from us all as we gazed at 'one of ours'. He was a member of another sapper group, he explained, and was taking his turn in the barn for a smoke when he had been taken short . . . that was why he was crouching when we found him! That one of the men did not open fire in that sudden moment of tension was, on reflection, astonishing. Some time afterwards there were ribald recollections of how 'one of ours' was all but killed with his trousers down! Less cause for merriment was the fact that we lost our way on leaving the barn, the whole area now enveloped in thick smoke. Physical features had disappeared and I had to bring all my experience of fieldcraft to get us out of the smog. I ended up walking in a crouched position as near to the ground as possible trying to keep below the smoke and by this method I eventually located the fence and the track and the sappers just ready to leave.[5]

The artillery, over 5,000 guns, opened up at 5.00 p.m. on the evening of March 23rd. 'Came the hour,' wrote a staff captain with the Tenth City of Glasgow Field Regiment, 'and the world exploded. The noise was ear-splitting and got worse as the German guns hit our side of the river.'[6] Miles to the rear, the ground shook so violently, farm animals broke loose from their stalls, causing more damage than enemy shells. The bombardment was intended to destroy the enemy emplacements ranged along the critical sector of the front. This, in large measure, it succeeded in doing, though the outstanding, if unintended, achievement was to remove General Schlemm who was seriously wounded in a direct hit on his headquarters.

The first crossings began just before 9.00 p.m. First over was the Fifty-First Highland Division, making for Rees. Part of Horrocks' command, he watched them anxiously from high ground over-looking the Rhine, as they faced a barrage of tracer bullets and artillery shelling. The problem with the Buffaloes was that while they were capacious carriers, they were slow movers, four knots at most, which made them easy targets. Fortunately, supporting fire-power inhibited the opposition who were inclined to keep their heads down. The chief threat came from strategically placed snipers. An RASC officer who thanked his guardian angel for getting him across unharmed noted that the poor chap behind was less fortunate. He was 'shot to bits by a round from a 25-pounder fired by a sniper high up in the bucket of a crane'.

A few minutes after 9.00 p.m., Horrocks heard the welcome news that the first British troops, the Black Watch, were safely on the far bank. But there was hard fighting ahead. The bridgehead was established but widening it, as Horrocks conceded, 'was a particularly hard nut to crack'. In Rees there were fierce clashes with German paratroopers who got their revenge for the removal of General Schlemm by killing the divisional commander of the Fifty-First, Major General Thomas Rennie.

As the night wore on enemy resistance stiffened and when the

Fifteenth Panzer Grenadier Division hit back with a vicious counter-attack, it soon became hard to tell where everybody was.

As one platoon could not be located, 19-years-old Lieutenant J.R. Henderson volunteered to take out a patrol to try and find how far the Germans had penetrated. After going a few hundred yards he came under intense fire, so ordering the rest of the men to take cover he went forward accompanied by only one man carrying a bren gun. Almost immediately an enemy machine-gun opened fire at very close range. The bren gunner was killed and Henderson's revolver was knocked out of his hand. Undaunted he charged the machine-gun position alone and killed the gunner with his shovel.[7]

Horrocks reflected:

It says a lot for the morale of those German parachute and panzer troops that with chaos, disorganisation and disillusionment all round them they should still be resisting so stubbornly. Their casualties during the last nine months had been very heavy, and the reinforcements arriving from Germany had not been of the old calibre at all, yet somehow the tough, experienced officers and N.C.O.s who were such a feature of these parachute and panzer formations managed to turn the callow youths into good soldiers.[8]

While the Fifty-First was making its painful way into Rees, the First British Commando Brigade took to their boats to secure a second bridgehead at Wesel. They were preceded by an air strike that all but wiped out what was left of the town. But here again there was strong resistance so that every yard had to be fought for. With both flanks secure, the third British assault force, the Fifteenth Scottish Division, was able to cross the river without too much trouble. BBC reporter Wynford Vaughan Thomas was in one of the Buffaloes.

The driver feels for the edge of the water – we're guided up right to the very edge by a long line of small green lights that have been laid to take us to the jumping-off ground: we've reached the water's edge and we see the Rhine – not running, as we thought it would, bright under the moon, but running red; because right on the opposite side of the village every single house and haystack you can see is burning, beaten down by the fury of our barrage. We can't tell whether there's anything coming at our boys: we hope all the stuff that we hear is going into Germany.

Having got underway, the battle was with the current.

The Buffalo springs and points its nose upstream now – we're tussling – fighting the current to get over. We're over midstream now. The driver's still fighting the current. It's running at millrace speed, it seems to us, carrying us down all the time off our landing-point on the other bank. Now the tracer is quiet, drowned by the revving of our engines; but all the time that bank which we've been thinking about so much during the last few weeks is coming nearer and nearer. A signal flashes from the shore – the first Buffaloes are off. We've reached the other side, climbing up into the skirl of bagpipes – the men of Scotland who've piped their men into battle across the Rhine.

In all the relief and excitement, there was just one problem:

The Commanding Officer gave the signal, the piper lifted his pipes to his lips, and he blew, and only an agonised wailing came from his instrument. Again he tried, and again the wail. If ever a man was near to tears, it was our piper. His great moment, and now, as he cried in despair: 'Ma pipes, man, they'll no play.'9

To the south, the US Ninth Army had enjoyed equal success. Starting at 1.00 a.m. on the 24th, an artillery bombardment delivered close on 70,000 shells while 1,500 bombers targeted German communications. An hour later, at around the same time as the Fifteenth Scottish Division was on the water, the Thirteenth US Infantry Division, with the US navy in charge, was ferried over in their grey-painted landing craft to Büderich, Wallach and Rheinburg. The Seventy-Ninth Infantry Division followed, landing at Walsum and Orsay. This was achieved with few casualties. As usual, the greatest hazard was the Rhine itself which was running here so strongly as to turn about one Buffalo whose occupants proceeded to mount an assault on their own launch site.

It was now the turn of the airborne forces. The objective of

Operation Varsity was to deliver the knockout punch. But was it needed? The river crossing had all but annihilated German defences and, though Kesselring brought up the 116th Panzer and Fifteenth Panzer Grenadier divisions, he had few other reserves to call upon. Any fighting still to do was well within the capacity of the infantry already in place either on one of the numerous beachheads fanning out on the east bank or at the assembly points waiting for the reopening of the Rhine bridges, a task which the engineers were discharging at commendable speed.

Yet Operation Varsity, an assault that dwarfed the D-Day landings in Normandy, went ahead without second thoughts. The need to take out artillery positions that were still in range of the river crossings and the worry that Kesselring, never a general to be underestimated, had a few more tricks to play, must have entered the calculations. But human nature in its military and political incarnation being what it is, the attraction of producing the greatest show on earth overrode doubts of those such as General Ridgway.

The first light of March 24th promised a cloudless blue sky for the rest of the day. For the aircrews and the parachutists at air bases in England and France, the tension was lightened by the commotion of final preparations. As the common complaint had it, there was too much to carry. Apart from hand weapons, cartridges, belts and grenades there were such items as entrenching tools, trench knives, reserve parachutes, even in some cases a bazooka which, heavy and cumbersome, made jumping all the more hazardous.

'The day before the jump,' recalls Thomas Hashway, who was with the US 513 Parachute Infantry Regiment, 'we spent studying maps and sandbox images of our drop zone. Some of the boys were shaving their hair and giving each other Mohawk haircuts using scissors and safety razors; painting their faces using charcoal. We were fed steak dinners that evening.'[10]

And apple pie.

The next meal promised to be less tasty. K rations for three days were supplanted by two D rations or chocolate bars for emergency.

The infantry converging on the crossing sectors of the Rhine first knew of the airborne invasion the day before when they were warned not to fire on paratroops – 'they will be ours.' They were also told to stay under cover for the morning when 'heavy objects may fall from the sky'. It did not take a military genius to guess that the reference was to glider tow ropes.

'Everyone was very cheerful,' Major Gerald Ritchie wrote later when he was able to reassure his wife. 'It was not quite the gay hilarity there was before D-Day but a more confident cheerfulness. For many of us it was our second party and practically all had been in action of some kind and that does make a difference.'[11] Major Ritchie was speaking for the parachutists. There was less good humour among those who were to take flight in frail but over-loaded gliders.

> When we were taken out onto the airfield, I noted that the WACO we had loaded the jeep in the previous day was positioned behind a C-47, with another glider off to one side. Dual lines stretched back from the single plane to the two gliders. We were going to be pulled in tandem! The thought of that two-engine, propeller-driven aircraft pulling two heavily loaded gliders at the same time made my blood freeze. I was going from bad to worse and began to think that I would never get out of this affair alive. How in the world were those pilots ever going to keep the gliders apart? An explanation that one tow-rope was longer than the other, so that the gliders' wings would not collide, did little to assure us. What was to keep the wing from being ripped off by the other tow-rope? Evidently, gliders had been towed in tandem before, I told myself, or they would not be doing this; but I had not encountered the procedure in the numerous flights I had taken back in training in the States. We later learned that the severe shortage of transport planes had demanded either tandem pulls or aborting the entire operation.[12]

Starting at 9.00 a.m., some 1,500 bombers and transporters with 1,300 gliders in tow took to the air. When they all met up over Brussels, the US Seventeenth Airborne Division and the British Sixth Airborne Division formed two unbroken aerial convoys stretching 150 miles. They carried twelve parachute battalions (six US, one Canadian and five British) along with 800 vehicles and artillery pieces with back-up equipment. A swarm of American and British fighters, over 1,000 in all, manoeuvred round the heavy aircraft to give protection against the feeble attentions of the Luftwaffe, while over the drop areas, countering a more serious threat, the bombs fell on German flak batteries in and around the drop area to the north and west of Wesel.

For John Kormann, the take-off was the most terrifying part of the journey.

There were six of us in the WACO, plus the jeep fully-gassed and loaded with equipment. While we waited apprehensively, the C-47 in front of us gunned its engines, taxied slowly, taking up the slack in the tow-ropes, and then started sluggishly down the long runway, with us bouncing along behind. 'How is that puny, old plane ever going to get this double load into the air?' I thought, 'I can't believe this!' If I had qualms, those poor glider pilots must have been beside themselves!

It took us forever to get into the air and, for a while, I thought our pilot was going to release the tow-rope while we were still only 75–100 feet off the ground. We lumbered along slowly, anxiously keeping our eyes on the other glider. Our air speed could not have been more than 100 miles an hour. Everything shook and rattled and seemed to be coming apart. In the midst of this travail, I must have sensed that this was one of life's unforgettable moments. I looked out at the sky to see clouds still tinged pink with the dawn. Down below us were green meadows. Off to the side, I saw a French farmer and his horse plowing the fields. Just then, a few hundred feet below, we passed right over the top of Chartres Cathedral in all its magnificence. It was so close that I felt I could almost touch the tips of the spires with my hand.[13]

'The sky was black with planes and gliders, moving over in a continuous stream for two or three hours,' recalls A.E. Baker, a wireless operator with the Eighth Armoured Brigade. 'While the Armada was passing overhead I sat on top of a tank, listening to the American forces radio. One of the tunes they played was String of Pearls. Every time I hear it now I picture the Airborne going over.'[14]

With half an hour or so to go before the gliders were released and the parachutes opened, nerves tightened.

I glanced round my plane & watched each person's expression, & it was very interesting. Portens opposite me, looking much the same as usual, one signaller fast asleep, further down the plane a couple being quietly sick. I caught my sergeant-major's eye & I think he saw that I was looking at everyone & he smiled quite cheerfully. He is quite imperturbable at any time.[15]

As a good American paratrooper, John Kormann chewed on an unlighted cigar. It didn't help.

By the time we came near the drop zone, most of us were sick or very queasy from the stench of vomit. The general paratrooper airsickness procedure was to separate one's steel helmet (pot) from the plastic liner (inner helmet) and use the former as a receptacle. That might have been fine in training, but in combat one had better have a full helmet on, when the shooting starts. Consequently, the moment we came under fire, those who were ill jammed the liner into the steel pot and put their helmet on, vomit dripping down around the edges. It was enough to turn a grown man ashen![16]

For some, tension was relieved by heart-rendering of the hit parade including 'MacNamara's Rag Time Band' and, in one plane, 'The Call of the Canyon'. James Bramwell exchanged a sickly grin with his colonel. 'I thought they won't be singing that for long.'

Troops waiting to cross from the west bank of the Rhine were treated to a massive spectacle of air power. 'The Lancasters, Halifaxes, Stirlings, Fortresses and Dakotas flew in majestically,' wrote a tank officer, 'slow, at eight hundred feet – a steady solid phalanx, like the pattern of a carpet in the sky.'[17]

Lieutenant Tom Flanagan recalls:

At nine o'clock we could hear an approaching roar in the sky, and from behind the farm and stretching back to the pine-tree studded horizon beyond, came wave upon wave of aeroplanes flying in such close formation that it was almost impossible to see the blue of the sky! Over came the Dakotas loaded with paratroops, no doubt with tensions rising, as they neared the dropping zone. This gigantic formation was right overhead and the noise was deafening as the Dakotas were joined by Stirlings, towing Horsa gliders. These flew much lower and we scattered as one man to the side of the buildings as the gliders' noses dipped as they released their tow. The release appeared to be simultaneous for the aircraft zoomed upwards as the Horsa's nose drooped and the great wire tow rope fell at lightning speed hissing as it dropped almost horizontally with barely a suggestion of a kink at either end.

As each glider was released the aircraft banked westwards out of the path of the glider which continued to descend and sped off into the distance to be hidden from our sight by the trees beyond the river. The flight path was the same for them all, each aircraft, once freed, banked steeply to the west and flew away. Some Dakotas returning from their drop appeared to me at this point in the display to fly under the gliders, low though they were, as they weaved their way out of the battle zone, flying almost at rooftop height over the farm. The noise was incredible![18]

An audience of Allied VIPs was led by Winston Churchill who had repulsed every attempt to persuade him that he would be one less problem to bother about if he stayed at home. His mind had been made up on his visit to Montgomery's headquarters at Geldrop on March 2nd. General de Guingand was there when the coming battle for the Rhine was discussed.

Churchill said he wished to see the operations and expected me to help him. He made it crystal clear that this did not mean that he should be located in a safe place far from the crossing places, but that he must have a close-up view, and even pay a visit to the eastern bank. He would like to be allotted a tank and be hitched on to the early waves of the assault. I did not feel too sure of my grounds, for I knew Montgomery's views about visitors during battles. I said I would do what I could, and would talk to the Field-Marshal about it, and that I thought something could be arranged. As the evening wore on I realised that the Prime Minister was absolutely determined on this project. He talked about the battles he had been in during the last war, and that he insisted upon being in the thick of it once more. I even began to wonder whether this great man had decided that he would like to end his days in battle, at a time when he knew victory was upon us![19]

How times have changed. The idea of one of our current political leaders attending on war in quite so blatant a fashion is anathema to our refined sensibilities. Yet it was little more than half a century ago that a prime minister's appearance at the front, along with full entourage, was seen as to his credit. The only hostile comment came from troops who witnessed the elaborate picnics set out on white tablecloths and even then it was not the incongruous luxury that nettled them but the neglect of the simple rules of camouflage. Churchill 'enjoyed every minute of it' according to Ismay.[20] De Guingand agreed. 'Churchill enjoyed himself a great deal. He stayed at Montgomery's Tactical Headquarters and saw the opening stages of the battle from a small aircraft and a tank or some other armoured vehicle.'[21]

The war reporter, Alan Moorehead, stayed close to Churchill. Standing on a hilltop together at Xanten:

[they] looked down across the morning battle mist to where the troops were crossing on boats and rafts. 'I should have liked,' Churchill said, 'to have deployed my men in red coats on the plain down there and ordered them to charge – but now my armies are too vast.'

Suddenly the prime minister sprang to his feet and went coursing wildly for a few steps down the hill. 'They're coming,' he shouted, 'they're coming.'[22]

The mood of gleeful anticipation did not extend to the young men who were about to risk their lives. 'There's a difference between being nervous and scared shitless,' recalled one paratrooper, 'and I was scared shitless.'

Matters were not improved when, to pass the time, radio operators tuned into Radio Berlin to hear Axis Sally, otherwise known as The Bitch, warn of a hot reception. 'Men of the Seventeenth Airborne Division. We know you are coming. We are waiting and ready for you on the Rhine. You won't need your parachute; the flak will be so thick you can walk down.'[23]

When the moment came, Major Ritchie lost all sense of fear; it was as if in spirit he was somewhere else as his body went through the automatic motions.

As we crossed over the Rhine the ground below became a bit hazy with smoke, no one was visible at first, but a lot of cracks & bangs became apparent. I remember thinking 'There must be quite a battle going on down there,' but then it suddenly occurred to me that it was the Boche shooting at us!! I was standing at the door by this time watching the ground, although the warning light was not on as it should have been; as we passed over another dropping zone I could see all the 'chutes on the ground & people running about. The haze & smoke came on very thick there & one could hardly see the ground at all. The pops & bangs still went on but nothing hit us, all of a sudden the green light went on, but as no red warning light had come on I hesitated a moment, glanced at Portens & then seeing other parachutes beneath went out. Floating down the pops & bangs became even more apparent, in fact much more so, & one could make out gunfire & machine gun fire, but even so, as it was in Normandy, so in Germany I felt no great fear & it didn't seem that the bangs were anything to do with me, also my attention was taken up with the fact that I was coming down right over someone else, who it was, I don't know to this day, & my feet were touching his parachute, however we floated apart & I landed OK. While I was disentangling myself a burst of German machine gun fire whizzed over my head, which brought me into a proper frame of mind quite quickly.[24]

More green lights flashed and to jumpmasters' shouts of 'Go', thousands of canopies opened over the Wesel drop zones. In fruitless attempts to avoid the flak, troopers tried to direct their parachutes; some even climbed their suspension lines, hitting the ground 'with their heads in the silks'.[25]

With all the flak hitting the plane, the men on First Sergeant Donovan's C-46 knew they were close to the DZ. The intense groundfire was too much for the jumpmaster – one of the replacement lieutenants – to endure. He 'chickened-out,' said Donovan, and went to the front of the plane leaving the job to the first sergeant. PFC Sarrell and Donovan, still standing on the door bundle, watched helplessly as black smoke started to pour out of Number 11's left engine. Then, a flak shell burst close and the ship bucked. Sergeant Harvey, who was standing in the right door, was knocked back onto the floor, killed by shrapnel. Donovan lifted Harvey's body and pushed it out of the plane – there was nothing else he could do. Then the buzzer sounded and the green light came on. Donovan and Sarrell 'got off the bundle, gave it a little push, Donovan followed and [Sarrell] was right behind. With the engine on fire everyone was pushing to get out,' remembered Sarrell. PFC Ken Olson went out with the static line under his arm and was whipped around when the chute deployed. He landed in a field in about five inches of water.[26]

On the ground, many had problems getting out of their parachute harnesses, making them easy targets for German infantry. Other victims of ground fire were those who landed in trees or who caught up in high-tension wires. There was not a lot of faith in the new quick-release parachute. Lieutenant Calhoun had only been released from the hospital six days before and had missed the practice jumps. But he was given a brief explanation of the quick-release parachute.

'Upon leaving the aircraft,' he was told, 'pull the safety fork and give the quick-release a half turn. When you're ten feet off the ground, press the quick-release and you'll hit the ground running!' Remembering these instructions, he pulled the safety fork and gave the quick-release a half turn. It was then he saw an empty parachute harness float past – its former occupant lay four hundred feet below, dead where he fell. Concluding that the dead man had either released the harness by accident, or that the quick-release device had been hit by shrapnel after the man removed the safety fork, Calhoun quickly replaced his own safety fork and rode the chute all the way to the ground.[27]

Sergeant Derek Glaister, with the Seventh Battalion, came down near a German-occupied farmhouse.

Just before my feet touched the ground, a bullet smashed through my left elbow, so I lay on my stomach and pretended to be dead. I saw nine of the others come down, some into trees. The Germans shot them as they hung there helpless – it was a sickening sight.

I tried to give myself some cover by throwing a smoke bomb, but just as I was making for the nearest ditch, a German SS officer came up and shot me in the back from ten yards away with a Luger pistol. I shall never forget him – he was about six foot four and covered in boils. I spun round and fell down, and this officer grabbed my left arm and shoved it through the straps of my webbing. Then he took my water bottle, flung it in a ditch and looted whatever he could. I was worried that he'd finish me off with my knife, but I had the presence of mind to lie on it, and when he had gone, I got hold of it and threw it into the ditch.[28]

Gerald Ritchie was equally fortunate. Landing well short of the designated rendezvous a mile and a half behind the Rhine, he had to cross open ground which was under heavy shell fire.

The shells kept whizzing over our heads with a most unpleasant crack, so we made a bit of a detour towards the gun which was actually the safest spot, but had we but known it, took us to within 300 yards of the gun, which was an AA gun, there were four of them but the crew of 3 ran away fortunately . . . Eventually we arrived at our rightful spot & we soon had the company sorted out & attacked & rounded up the few Boche in the neighbouring farms who hadn't very much fight left in them. The gun had ceased firing & we rounded up its crew. All my officers & nearly all my men turned up eventually & considering the noise & carry-on in the first hour or two we had very few casualties in the company.[29]

By now the landing looked rather like 'a fairground in the process of closing down, the discarded parachutes resembling struck tents, and all the litter of war lying around. Only the still figures of the dead gave a grim reality to the scene.'[30]

Luck did not favour Thomas Hashway who, along with comrades of the 513th Parachute Infantry Regiment, was crowded into one of the seventy-two Curtis Commandos (C-46s), the heaviest aircraft on duty that day. Loaded with paratroopers, artillery and supporting engineers and pulling two gliders, the C-46 was as near to a sitting target as a flying object could be.

> As we approached the Rhine, the flak was thick enough to walk on. 'Stand up', 'hook up', 'check your gear'. I must have done that three times. You could hear some praying aloud. 'Stand in the door,' the jumpmaster yelled. This is, 'Red Light go!' We shoved each other out the door because everybody feared being hit by flak and going down in flames. I had a quick descent with a low branch landing. While releasing the harness, I looked up around and saw flaming planes and crashing gliders, wondering if those troops got out alive. Gunfire brought me back to reality. I crawled towards a few troopers, saw Co. Coutts, and joined him in the move to the assembly area. We had missed the drop zone by a few miles; firefights and skirmishes continued through the day. Some troopers were killed during descent, others in tree landings, some on rooftops, and a few with chutes wrapped around high wires.[31]

Twenty-two C-46s were lost and of those fourteen caught fire in the air as soon as they were hit. This happened when a wing tank was punctured and the fuel ran along the fuselage. All it then needed was a well-aimed incendiary shell to set the whole aircraft aflame. The older C-47s, fitted with self-sealing fuel tanks, emerged with a far better safety record.

> This was the greatest single aircraft loss we had in any operation during the war. Most of the paratroopers got out, thank God, for in every parachute aircraft there is an abandon-ship bell. When it rings, the sticks go out regardless of where they are and they stand not on the order of their going. They pile out the door in a pell-mell rush, and so far as I know, not a single paratrooper went down with the falling planes. We did lose a number of combat crews, though, for those brave youngsters stayed with the flaming ships until the paratroopers had cleared, and in many cases they stayed too late to save themselves.[32]

There were problems too with the B-24s, big four-engined Liberators, and B-17 Flying Fortresses which had to come in so low to deposit their cargo that they were liable to be hit by rifle or small arms fire.

One Fortress I shall never forget; it came lower and lower over our heads, glistening silver in the morning sunlight, the flames which streamed from one wing a deep orange against the azure blue. As it passed us parachutes blossomed from the side and we counted them anxiously, and watched with horror as one failed to open and plunged straight to the ground in a white streak, the man kicking desperately up to the last moment, until we know that remaining in the blazing plane alone, whether alive or dead, was no one but the pilot.[33]

James Byrom, a tank officer of the Argyll and Sutherland Highlanders, did what he could to help the wounded which was not much more than putting them in the shade and giving first aid.

Till a nearby village had been captured there was no question of beginning surgery. There was certainly nothing we could do for Geordie, the rough little Tynesider, who had slept opposite me in the Bulford barrack room. 'Follow the crowd' had been his theme whenever discussion turned on the forthcoming operation. 'I've always followed the fuggin' crowd, and I've always been all reet.' And one felt he had – as an urchin playing in the street, as an adolescent hanging about outside the cinemas, and as a volunteer for parachuting. His other phrase was 'Whose side are ye on?' – and that was the real key to his character. He had always been 'one of the gang' in a world of rival gangs and football teams. Now it was his only articulate remark as he lay on the stretcher, mortally wounded, listening to our hollow reassurances. He could already feel himself sinking into the anonymity of death, and wished to be sure that we knew who he was.[34]

In one of the Flying Fortresses which never made it back to base was a reporter from *Colliers* magazine, Richard C. Hottelet.

Smoke began to pour down through the plane, and in the left waist window. A tongue of flame licked back as far as the window, and the silver inner skin of the ship reflected in its orange glow. The crew chief told Lieutenant Albert Richey that gasoline was sloshing around the bomb bay . . .

This Fortress carried two thousand gallons of aviation fuel, which can almost ignite in a hot wind. One engine was burning; the one next to it was catching fire. The ship was still under control. But there was no telling for how long.

As we staggered out, we watched the C-46s come in and apparently walk into a wall of flak. I could not see the flak, but one plane after another went down. All our attention was concentrated on our own ship. It could blow up in mid-air any moment. We moved closer to the windows. From the pilot's compartment came streams of stinging smoke. The intercom went out.

Up in the cockpit, Colonel Baldwin was keeping the ship under control, watching the fire eat a larger and larger hole in the left wing like a smouldering cigarette in a tablecloth. Looking down on the wing from above, he could not see a large fire. The flame was mainly below the wing.

Suddenly we went into a sharp dip. Back aft we did not know what was happening. All we had was the smoke and the deafening noise, and the tiny fragments of molten metal which the wing was throwing back and which twinkled in the sun as they raced past the waist window.

We pulled on our flak suits and helmets. I reached down and buckled on my chest chute. It was obvious we would have to jump.[35]

Hottelet had his just reward. Landing in pasture he found himself in the British Second Army area where 'true to the old Battle of Britain tradition' he was revived with tea and whisky.

From Churchill's vantage point, his private secretary John Colville saw the casualties mount as 'this apparently endless armada flew over the Rhine'.

A host of Dakotas appeared flying low and in close formation, the doors in each fuselage wide open and a parachutist standing ready in the aperture. A solitary Flying Fortress accompanied them. To our left came another great fleet and behind yet a third. They vanished in the haze across the Rhine, but not before we had seen hundreds of parachutes open. Fleet after fleet of Dakotas followed while the first contingent streamed back empty over our heads. The Fortress reappeared, on fire, and the occupants baled out one by one as the aircraft flew steadily on, the flames spreading towards its tail. Soon there were fleets of gliders too. As each was released over the river, its tug-aircraft turned steeply away for home. Several of the returning Dakotas were in trouble and three or four crashed before our eyes, bursting into flames as they struck the ground. One, struggling low over Xanten, lost height irrecoverably and there was a great explosive flash as it crashed at the bottom of our hill, right on top of one of our heavy gun positions.[36]

The main casualties were the gliders, which began their approach to their landing zones at 10.30 a.m., their sirens wailing.

A fearful dryness filled one's mouth, as if one had eaten dry sand. The door in the front and rear was flung open, we jumped onto the ground and threw ourselves flat. The crackle of machine-gun fire opened up. It was difficult to tell from which direction. The earth began to fly up in pellets where it was struck. The line of bullets drew away from us. I gulped instinctively and popped some gums into my mouth. Someone shouted, 'Dig in'. A glider landed in front of us, about 30 yards away, and almost at once blew up in a yellow flash. The wreckage burst into red flames. Only a few fellows ran clear of her. Then the wreckage hid them. Another glider came in lazily low down just behind ours, but just two seconds after she had touched down, she too was hit by something and went up in smoke. I think all her crew must have managed to get out. They ran off like hell in the opposite direction. The sound of motor engines came from behind the farmhouse. Tanks? Hadn't we better run like the others, and not lie in the middle of an open field doing nothing? We couldn't see anything to fire at. At least not till then, when two S.P. guns rolled out from behind the farm. The earth in front suddenly fountained up, again and again. They were aiming at our glider now. It was queer that they should miss. Their other shots had been only too dead accurate.[37]

Lieutenant Colonel J.C. Watts of the RAMC was in Deerforstenswald wood evacuating casualties to the area held by the Fifth Parachute Regiment.

Several gliders were burning briskly, having been caught in a burst of machine-gun fire on landing, which had ignited the petrol in the jeep inside. The British glider was a better proposition than the American Waco, which was of fabric over a steel framework. If it crashed the occupants were trapped in a cage, whereas the British Horsa, being of wood, could be quickly chopped through, although this was usually unnecessary, as it tended to fall apart.

I saw one burnt-out Waco with the charred bodies of the occupants, the whole looking for all the world as if some monster had set a bird-cage on a bonfire.[38]

The Horsa proved its worth to another observer:

A glider landed not far away and went straight into the side of a house. Fearing that there would be several casualties, I sent Stevenson over with a first-aid haversack, whilst I unloaded the jeep to get at the rest of my equipment. By the time I had the jeep out I saw Stevenson running back across the field. With a sinking feeling that they were all killed I asked him why he had come back. 'Nobody hurt, sir,' he said.

The statement seemed incredible, but was quite true. The Horsa glider, being made of three-ply wood, had smashed to pieces, but in doing so had absorbed the shock and all the occupants had escaped.[39]

Lost in heavy mist and smoke, many gliders came to earth miles away from their landing zone, exposing them to German heavy guns.

One glider containing a much-loved battery commander of the Light Regiment came down almost on top of an 88, which, in the few seconds which must elapse before the occupants can get out, put a round of high explosive through the nose, killing them all. A battery commander of the Anti-Tank Regiment who had won a splendid M.C. in the Normandy landing was identified several days later by half his identity disc.[40]

Unable to judge their height with any accuracy, gliders crashed into farmhouses and farms. Others broke up in the air, spilling out men and machines. John Kormann's glider came down at the edge of a wood, one wing hitting a downed glider while it was travelling at speed.

We smashed into the earth in a belly-landing, bounced and careened and scraped along until the nose struck the trunk of a tree with full force. In the landing, we were all thrown about wildly. I was momentarily knocked unconscious. When I came to, I heard moaning and cursing. The realization that we were being shot at prompted us to push out the door and tumble frantically out of the glider. Once on the ground, I could hardly move. My left pants leg was ripped, exposing a very bloody and swelling knee. It seemed I had cuts, scrapes and bruises everywhere. Actually, I may have been in better shape than some of the others, particularly the pilots, who took the brunt of the nose collision. There were no medics around and for minutes we all lay hugging the ground. In the collision, the jeep had flown forward, partially lifting open the nose of the glider and wedging it upward against the tree.[41]

Watching the gliders land near the Issel canal, Major Edwards saw a glider heading straight for one of the narrow steel bridges.

That sonofabitch [the British glider pilot] lined himself up – and he hit the entrance to the bridge and sheared both wings. The fuselage then rattled right on across the bridge coming to rest on the far [eastern] side with all the British personnel inside happy and well. In less than two minutes they had their machine-guns out and ready to go.[42]

One of the gliders had a BBC correspondent on board. As it came in to land, he heard the 'wicked snap' of machine-guns a second before they 'started picking out their trade mark in the thin skin of the glider'. Then everything happened at once:

There was a doom-like lurch and a great rending as smoke, dust and daylight came from nowhere. I saw the Bren carrier go inexorably out of the nose of the glider, carrying the whole works ahead of it, and wiping two signallers off the top of it like flies. Even then the bullets kept crashing through the wreckage. It didn't seem fair; but then there is no 'fair' or 'unfair' in airborne fighting. At the moment of impact a jeep trailer that was chained just behind me came forward about six inches and caught me in the small of the back. Mercifully, the chains held on. Somehow Captain Peter Cattle and I hurled ourselves out of the mess into a shallow ditch by a hedge. Looking up, and clearing my eyes with the back of my hand, I saw a man pinned across the chest by wreckage. One of the glider pilots was getting him out. How those glider pilots and the two signallers on top of the carrier escaped the mass of that hurtling iron carrier I'll never know, but they did.[43]

Paddy Devlin of the Sixth Airborne Division was one of the lucky few who landed in an undamaged glider. But after jumping to the ground he had little time to consider his good fortune.

As I ran I suddenly noticed two Germans working on a Spandau (MG34) machine gun, they were at the edge of the wood on the far side of the road, the gun I expect was jammed. I knew I had to get to the ditch before they repaired it. Whilst still about 20 yards from the ditch and possibly 80 yards from the Germans they got behind the gun and started to feed a belt magazine into it. As I was the only one in view, up and running directly towards them, I was their target. It flashed through my mind to zig-zag, I didn't have time, but I must have turned to zig when I was hit. Instead of getting a burst in the stomach I had turned out of the line of fire and was hit in the right fore arm below my elbow breaking the bone, along my right side and across the small of my back, right side only. I was thrown forward in a kind of jump, letting a shout of 'OH' and fell flat on my face with my arms in front of me to protect my head as I fell. It all happened automatically and I lay there for some seconds before I knew I was hit and did not move. They did not fire again as they thought they had killed me. I found I could not move which was just as well for me as I might have attracted more fire from them and I had a small anti-tank mine tied on the strap of my small pack on my back. If they hit it I'd be blown to pieces, so I kept still. It was as though somebody had hit me a severe blow across the small of my back with a big stick. The pain wasn't too bad, like a nagging toothache, but I could feel what I thought was my blood pouring along my right thigh and I thought I would bleed to death. I discovered later it was the two tins of Carnation evaporated milk I had in my side pack which had been ripped open by the burst.[44]

Tom Flanagan watched aircraft returning from their mission. It was no time to relax.

Out of this noisy sky came a roar transcending the uproar above and with yells and shouts from all sides to take cover, we dashed into the shelter of the farmhouse as above us, descending with both engines' propellers spinning, we could see a Dakota about three hundred yards away! It was dropping lower and lower as we watched in terror as it swept over the roof barely missing it and catching the end wall of the barn to crash in the meadow! A huge flash of flame erupted from the wreck and sped for yards over the grass. We watched in stupefied horror, our minds sluggish, reluctantly trying to locate thoughts which would prompt an act of rescue. Before anyone had made a move, a gigantic explosion scattered wreckage around the meadow . . . A stream of bright green liquid flowed into the yard making puddles with surfaces like liquid marbling on the inside covers of office ledgers. Marvelling at our luck, we could see in the distance, white parachutes bringing the crew slowly and safely to earth. We now felt more confident about what we would find in the crashed Dakota so I took my HQ section out to the wreck but no sooner had we satisfied ourselves that none of the crew were left in the wreckage than we scattered again as two more Dakotas came crashing down into the four or so acres of fields behind the barns. Once again our eyes searched the skies to be relieved to see parachutes dropping on our side of the river but some distance away . . . On the way back I picked up a packet of cream cracker biscuits which had been thrown from the Dakota on impact with the ground: there was not a crumb out of place in its cellophane wrapping![45]

By one o'clock it was all over. Richard Hough, a fighter pilot whose job it was to identify and destroy the flak batteries that were giving so much trouble, was convinced that the battle had turned out badly for the Allies. 'The kaleidoscope of falling planes and men, gliders landing seemingly without plan if they were not shot out of the sky first, of smoke of every shade and hue, and sometimes the sharp blaze of flame from building or machine, all seen from the solitariness of a fighter's cockpit, left me stunned and anguished.'[46]

Hough believed he had witnessed 'a terrible Allied defeat'. Eisenhower's report to the Combined Chiefs of Staff told a happier story. 'Some losses were sustained from A.A. fire over the target, but the total of 46 planes destroyed (3.98% of those employed) was remarkably low considering the fact that, to insure accuracy of dropping and landing, no evasive action was taken. I witnessed as much of this operation as could be seen from observation posts west of the river and was struck by the courage of transport pilots flying relatively slow aircraft steadily along their allotted routes in spite of heavy flak barrage.' But no mention was made of the number of gliders lost or of total casualties.

Estimates of losses of men and machines vary wildly. Those who give the lowest casualties also tend to understate the numbers involved. At least a hundred aircraft and gliders were destroyed and up to 350 damaged beyond immediate repair, 1,078 men of the Sixth Airborne Division were killed or wounded. An entire battalion of the 507th Parachute Infantry Regiment fell on a German artillery nest and was shot to pieces as it hit the ground. Among the American airborne troops 675 were killed and 834 wounded. Most of the equipment carried by the gliders was lost.

In part an ego trip for Montgomery – intended perhaps to wipe out the memory of Arnhem – Varsity has been justified as the final undeniable demonstration of an inevitable Allied victory. But it was Ridgway who got closest to an objective judgement on the last big airborne assault of the war. 'We learned a lot,' he concluded, 'but the knowledge cost us dearly.'[47]

14
Into Germany

There could be no doubt in anyone's mind that the Rhine had been well and truly breached. Even German newspapers recognised what was coming. 'It is very difficult to be an openly declared, courageous Nazi today, and to express one's faith freely,' conceded a leading article in the *Völkischer Beobachter*, adding, 'We have no illusions now.' The Swedish newspaper *Expressen*, which had a correspondent in Berlin, reported that 'panic has struck military circles'.

By the early hours of March 25th, while the troop-carrying ferries were lumbering back and forth, the first two Bailey bridges were almost in position. Bulldozers were carving out approaches to the riverbank and a little way back in the meadows assembly areas were marked out with white tape for the lines of guns, lorries and troop-carriers to edge their way down to the crossing. By nightfall the two floating bridges were in constant use and others were under construction. On the far bank the Americans and British had linked up near Wesel to create a bridgehead thirty miles long and seven miles deep.

Louis Albrecht, a US army engineer, found the going surprisingly easy.

We left Krefeld Easter Sunday and in two or three days we had ridden all the way to the Weser River almost unopposed. There we had to make a river crossing. You cannot imagine the feeling of paddling around in an insubstantial boat in the middle of a river – wide and deep – the first forces across, expecting all hell to break loose. We got across and into town. We walked through the first town meeting little resistance. The whole operation from there on was magnificent. You must realise our opposition came from untrained troops – band, home guard, even women and cripples – but our outfit worked

293

wonderfully. We got about halfway to the next town when they finally organised resistance. We took 50 prisoners there after fighting for an hour. We worked on into town fighting house to house . . . So thoroughly did we surprise them that we caught several high officers – one leaving a building on a motorcycle and running straight into us. We got him, and a lot of others.[1]

In many units there was a lightheartedness that worried officers.

Was the Army losing control, since here and there officers and men appeared to be indulging quite indiscriminately whatever wanton fancies entered their heads? In the Kehrum-Appeldorn area, I saw soldiers pulling furniture out of houses to fuel bonfires; just as energetically Royal Engineers, using their Polish mine detectors, were searching gardens beside what had been well appointed private houses in the hope of locating buried treasure. Some sights bordered on the bizarre, such as a soldier driving horse and cart, using telephone wire for reins and another leading a pig to its obvious fate by a rope hitched to a foreleg. Then I came across two soldiers, sitting on the tailboard of a grocer's van with a rug over their knees. For their profit or more likely to amuse their pals, lettering on the van read, 'You loot, we buy, all the best prices'. Such jests raised smiles, but not a dispatch rider who, feeling he was being chased by a dog, stopped and fired a burst from his sten at it.[2]

But elsewhere on the front there had been some hard fighting along the way, particularly on the northern flank where the First Parachute Army and the Fifteenth Panzer Grenadiers fought stubbornly to protect the gateway to Holland and the approaches to Emden and Bremen.

Rees, Bienen, Millengen, Megchelen, Isselburg all represented a stiff tussle before they became ours. We were still battering our heads against the paratroops, and they fought with a grim hopeless bravery that no man could fail to admire. To defeat them was to kill the majority, and then a few might surrender; in Megchelen they even continued to fight from houses that we had set on fire with the 'Crocodiles'. Fanatical and misguided, yes; but brave and well-disciplined, also yes.[3]

One of the hardest jobs had been to get the first tanks over the river while bridges were still being built. With such a weight on board, there could be no guarantee that a motorised craft was capable of holding out against the current. The only alternative was to use wire ropes to winch the tank-carriers across. Major Roland Ward was one of the engineers who developed the system. 'The raft was composed of five large pontoons, about 25 feet long and five feet wide, connected up with steel panels, with ramps at each end.'

There were the inevitable teething problems, including one raft that broke free from its moorings. It was up to Major Ward to save the day – and some valuable equipment. He commandeered a motorboat to take him out to the raft.

I jumped on board and I found the crew were petrified. Their motors wouldn't hold, they were drifting down the lines and the next stop was the German lines, you see. The officer, I think, had lost his head a bit. The anchor didn't seem to hold and the motors didn't work, but by a bit of luck someone had brought out a rope from the far side and he joined it up to a bulldozer. I thought, if he pulls too hard he'll break it. So I said, 'You can direct the motors by signalling with a whistle and your arms.' There was no radio or anything like that. They engaged the motors so that the rope pulled slowly. When we were halfway across, the Warrant Officer, who had kept his head, said to me, 'There is the end of the anchor cable. What shall I do?' I could see what he meant. I said, 'Let it go.' And that was it, because the raft swung round and we came in perfectly.[4]

Others were not so lucky. Having watched a misguided attempt to load two tanks at the same time, with the result that one of them slipped off the raft and sank, waiting crews were justifiably nervous at taking to the water.

The Rhine is a big river, and we seemed to be afloat for hours. When we were right out in mid-stream, a Jerry plane started to drone around in the darkness, and we saw streams of tracers from its guns as it shot up some target a mile or two along the river. Then it came over us – so low that when the Bofors gun opened up at it, their shells only just cleared the opposite bank. I couldn't make up my mind whether it would be better to get inside the tank in case we got shot up, or to stay outside in case we sank. I compromised by sitting on top of the turret, ready to dive off or in as the occasion might arise.[5]

Tom Flanagan's Fifty-Second Division crossed the Rhine at night over 'Sussex Bridge', as it was called.

Our trucks were driven without lights except for the glowlight which shone on the white painted rear axle to enable following trucks to keep in touch in convoy. The narrowness of the Bailey bridge was made plain for the drivers by small lamps fixed to the sides of the girders placed every few yards along the way.

As we drove up the ramp and onto the bridge I could barely make out the swift flowing black depths of the river below nor could I hear anything but the noise from the engine of my Bedford Troop Carrier on which I rested my right arm, it being an over-head drive vehicle, as it ground its way along in low gear. Seated in the back, my HQ section, silent now as we slowly made our way, rocking up and down as the pontoons holding the structure moved with the weight of the lorry, into the cleared area of the west bank of the Rhine. Our packs strapped to our backs thrust us into a uncomfortable position in our seats and our steel helmets created an unaccustomed weight on our heads.[6]

Travelling the Bailey bridges was like 'a wild scenic railway as we rose and fell with each pontoon sinking slightly as we drove over it'. The worry of losing men overboard inspired some rudi-mentary precautions against a watery exit.

Each of us was given a number of rubberised linen bags, shaped rather like long sausages with tapes fastened to their ends. These were lifebelts. Inflated by mouth, then tied around our bodies, they were supposed to give us a chance if we were dumped into the river. There were no instructions as to how to wear them but someone had worked out that if tied around the waist they would very likely turn us over in the water due to the weight of our equipment. It was decided it would be better to fasten them under the armpits, tying the tapes to our epaulettes to prevent them slipping down. We were given enough for each of our men to wear and instructed to tell them that if by any chance they were pitched into the river they were not to struggle but to get rid of all the equipment they could, letting the lifebelt support them. As the Rhine was a very fast-flowing river they were on no account to fight it but to let it carry them downstream while they swam towards the bank. Rescue teams with boats were stationed further down to pick up anyone in the water.[7]

And there were field dressing stations along the river to cope with the injured or half-drowned. Working ahead of the main force, the worry for the medics was finding a base that was free of mines. One doctor had a novel if not altogether a safe way of reconnoitring an area.

While I was across the river I met a doctor in a jeep. The bottom of the jeep was lined with sandbags. He was driving up and down and around and around in a field to make sure it was clear of mines before he set up a field dressing station. The sandbags should have protected him if he had hit a mine, but it was still quite a hazardous thing to do. Fortunately the field was clear so all was well.[8]

Field Marshal Kesselring had hoped to be able to hold Wesel and other strongholds long enough for reserves to be brought up but the impetus of Montgomery's advance was too fast for him. Four days after the first assault troops had set foot on the left bank of the Rhine, German defences had pulled back fifteen miles to a line between Bocholt and Dorsten. By now American, British and Canadian forces were consolidating in massive strength with Montgomery able to count on up to twenty divisions and over a thousand tanks. For once, the pace of relocation had exceeded all expectations, with all credit to the engineers. At Emmerich, Canadian sappers had a bridge up and in use in less than thirty-two hours.

Two days of fighting broke the new German positions. With the capture of Dorsten and Bocholt the whole front collapsed. German losses in prisoners alone averaged 10,000 a day. With the end of March, Simpson's Ninth Army, on the right of the

Twenty-First Army Group, was spearheading towards Magdeburg on the River Elbe, which happened to be not much more than seventy-seven miles from Berlin. Another part of the Ninth Army had sheered off to begin an encirclement of the Ruhr industrial region, an objective achieved when it met up at Lippstadt with the US First Army, closing up from the south. The Second British Army made for Hamburg at the mouth of the Elbe, while Crerar's First Canadian Army was 'to open the supply route to the north through Arnhem, and then to clear North East Holland and the coastal belt eastwards', towards Hamburg. This turned out to be one of the happier assignments, gaining an enthusiastic welcome from the Dutch, though soldiers with a hazy notion of European geography had to be reminded by hastily erected signs along the roads that the natives were friendly.

Once over the Rhine, the way into Germany was through a belt of wrecked towns and villages, victims of artillery and aerial bombing and now 'only gaunt and blackened walls and heaps of rubble'.[9] At Bocholt, Corporal Dai Evans found a platoon of the Volkssturm, 'mostly middle aged . . . pale and grey, with strained looks upon their faces'. They were in a cellar with a collection of weapons that would have done credit to a war museum.

> As I returned to the main room of the cellar with him I saw another of our captives sneaking, or so I thought, up the stairway. I almost shot him, but resisted the inclination as he didn't appear to have any aggression left. I followed him up the steps then into the back garden where he merely stood and gazed upon the devastation around him, tears coursing down his cheeks. 'Alles is kaput,' he said.
>
> 'Sie sind selbst schuldig,' (you are yourselves the guilty ones) was my reply.
>
> 'Ich bin Architekt, kein Soldat,' said he. 'Ich wollte keinen Krieg.' (I am an architect, not a soldier. I didn't want war.) He pointed out his house nearby, or rather the remains of it as the entire roof and top floor had collapsed into a heap of rubble. It had obviously been a fine house, with a large garden. 'Ich habe es selbst gebaut,' (I built it myself) he said.

I asked him where his family was and he told me they had gone to stay with some friends in the far north of Germany, near the Danish border. I took him back down below.[10]

After the wreckage came open countryside where the war had so far intruded only marginally on ordinary life. The contrast was surreal. Among the war reporters who went with the tanks as they moved away from the Rhine was Chester Wilmot, soon to be even better known as the author of *The Struggle for Europe*, one of the war's aftermath bestsellers.

30 March 1945. To-day I've been with our armour east of the Rhine; roaming over the rolling farmlands of Germany's great north-western plain. The leading armour is now far beyond the area which was slashed and torn by our shell-fire. We've left behind that belt of Germany where every village was in ruins, every house had its scars of shell or bullet, every field was pitted with craters or scored with tank tracks. To-day we drove for mile after mile, past farms where the peasants were still working in the fields, through villages where women were doing their washing or tending their gardens; they hadn't felt the shock of battle. And the almost peaceful way our tanks had arrived was a surprise relief.

When they heard our tanks approaching most of them had gone to their shelters and left their white flags fluttering outside. But when they heard little or no firing, they soon came out to watch. We saw them standing by the roadside with their white flags in their hands, and soon, as the traffic streamed by, the Germans began waving and smiling. They didn't get any encouragement from the passing troops, but they continued to stand there and wave . . . not really in welcome but as an expression of their relief that the war for them was over and that the battle had swept past them so quickly and so painlessly. But even so, it was strange to drive past and see the Germans waving.[11]

There was time for a bit of relaxation, even, that rarity, a bath or a shower.

The shower machine was in a tractor trailer. There were some 16 shower heads in the trailer which also housed the heater and water tank. I have no idea whether there was some outside water supply or they hooked up to a well. The water was clean and hot. The soap was provided and we received an issue of clean underwear as well. Boy, did that ever feel good. It is hard to imagine going for three weeks without a bath or shower. I have no idea how we managed staying dainty which we most likely didn't.[12]

Captain Maurice Jupp had come in by glider with the Sixth Airborne Division. Writing home he commented on a housing shortage (many urban dwellers having moved to the relative safety of the countryside), and of a shortage of bread, sugar and butter.

Against that, every house seems to have a remarkably fine stock of preserved vegetables and fruits, and some have home-canned pork. Many families keep, as well as the usual six or seven chickens, a few goats, pigs, sheep, or perhaps, a cow. The allotments are, on the average, much better kept than ours. I get the impression that the cultivation and preservation of vegetables and fruits has been fostered very successfully, on a very wide scale over here: it isn't just the good housekeeper who preserves her produce, everybody does.[13]

Much of this local produce was acquired, one way or another, by the troops on the move but it was noticeable that meals dished up by the army improved markedly. In the American sector there were more A rations, 'about the same as you would have back in the States' or, if on the move, K rations in a waterproofed, six-inch cardboard box. Each box was labelled as breakfast, dinner or supper. Breakfast consisted of a fruit bar, Nescafé, sugar, crackers and a small can of ham and eggs. Dinner and supper contained either a can of cheese or potted meat, crackers, a bouillon cube, orange or lemon powder, sugar, chocolate (or other candy) and Wrigley's chewing gum. And as a bonus, a Red Cross truck would appear 'with good American girls passing out doughnuts and chewing gum'.[14]

One of those Red Cross girls, Sally Peters, was in Cologne. 'Oh, what a shambles the city is, almost every building gutted or crumbling. Only the beautiful cathedral with its tall, slender spires is there and that's pretty well destroyed inside.' There were compensations, even if they were transitory.

Today I heard the most wonderful concert. It was held in a huge auditorium in a building that was partially destroyed – great cracks and holes in the ceiling – with the dull thud of artillery fire in the distance. I sat entranced listening to Lily Pons sing with Andre Kastelanetz directing the First U.S. Band. In the room with a couple of thousand G.I.s a pin could be heard while Lily sang – she was magnificent and as one boy behind me said, 'Yeah, she's a real artist and has a good shape too!'

. . . If only my powers of description were equal to the sights I see – in your wildest stretch of imagination you couldn't visualize the destruction of a huge city like Cologne – as you ride thru the rubble cleared streets, it's exactly like participating in a horrible nightmare – oh, to see a sweet pretty little clean village again where all the houses have roofs and are not gutted by fire and blast.

I'll be glad to get back even to Belgium – this Germany is a morbid, gruesome place that has a sort of death pallor hung over it.[15]

Civilians were mostly passive, barely acknowledging the strangers passing their ruined homes, but there were those, invariably with Anglo-American connections, who were only too demonstrative.

Here we saw an elderly German civilian, who was dressed in derby hat, tails and carried an umbrella. He wanted to visit and he spoke English with a British accent, the result of having lived 30 years in England. All through our travels in Germany we were to encounter German civilians and soldiers, who at great danger to themselves, were anxious to converse with us because at some time or other they had lived in the US or England. One was an old ex-German sailor who had been an embassy guard in 1909–10 at New Orleans. Another ran a gauntlet of German machine-gun fire, which resulted in his being wounded in the leg, just to talk about his captivity in German East Africa during the First World War. He was a German sailor who had been captured by the British.[16]

Others, fed on propaganda, were fearful of what the conquerors might do to them.

My friend Laddie Thomas went into a German house and found all the odd 20–30 men, women & children convulsed with grief. The men were sobbing, the women & children howling with grief. One woman pulled herself together sufficiently to ask: 'Where do you want the children put?' 'What do you mean! Where do we want the children put?' asked Laddie, thru' his interpreter. She explained: 'Where do you want us to put the children, to be shot?' When Laddie explained that he didn't do that sort of thing, the children accepted it and brightened up at once; it took 5–10 mins, however, to convince the grown-ups.[17]

In the south, the US Third Army was surging forward to outflank Frankfurt. The city fell on March 29th, by which time the Third had linked up with the eastward-thrusting First around Giessen. This brought within easy reach the Kassel–Würzburg autobahn, a prize much savoured by Patton whose tanks, two abreast, could then roar on to Hannover. Not that Patton depended on clear roads for his purposes.

Opposition was so light he was able to send out armoured columns as if on training exercises. A few road blocks were lightly defended and there was the occasional sniper to contend with but more often the surprises were pleasant ones – an important bridge thought to have been destroyed but captured intact, a supply dump with arms and ammunition waiting to be purloined, whole companies of German troops in search of someone to accept their surrender. In one week the First and Third Armies handed in 70,000 prisoners. Others were kept waiting.

We had one of our trucks go out one day to do some repair work and they were told to take a particular route. And it was a big heavy wrecker truck. And they went along this road, there was a bunch of soldiers along the side of the road, and they suddenly realized these were German soldiers. And there were two guys in the truck, the driver and the assistant driver, and they had a 50 calibre machine-gun and a ring mount in the truck, you know. So you could stand up and shoot at things. And the assistant said, 'What do I do? Do I shoot at them?' The driver said, 'God no!' They just went right ahead and went right through town.[18]

First and Third Army casualties were minimal. On the worst single day of March, the dead and injured totalled 150. The one big effort by the Germans to stem the advance was at Aschaffensburg where the students of an officer cadet school mounted a reckless counter-attack. Five hundred were taken prisoner; 200 killed.

Even war reporters found it hard to keep track of Patton.

I've just returned from an unsuccessful attempt to try and catch up with some of General Patton's tanks now thrusting deep into the heart of Germany, but after jeeping for five hours without catching even a glimpse of them I gave up the chase. Jeeps cannot compete with Third Army tank columns on the loose.

This is surely the fastest advance in the history of war – an advance where divisional command posts make big jumps forward two or three times a day which is some indication of the way things are going out there. And if the burden of the fighting is thrown on the shoulders of the tankmen and the doughboys who are racing behind them in trucks to take over the towns they've overrun, the bigger burden of keeping the army commanders behind in touch with every move in this swift game is falling on the shoulders of the tireless signal corps men – the wire-stringers who are performing incredible feats of sheer endurance in keeping open the lines of communication. All day long, out on those roads on the east bank of the Rhine, I've watched fleets of small trucks spewing out cable behind them – cable which runs through the leather-gloved hands of the wire-stringers, mile after mile of wire which in short time will be carrying vital orders. Signal corps sections are working in leap-frogging movements along these roads, dozens of teams wiring up long stretches of road all at the same time then quickly linking up each section. German facilities are commandeered and used wherever possible. These wire-stringers are giving everything they've got to get the job done. An eighteen-hour day is commonplace. Some of them have worked right round the clock, spurred on by the excitement and the knowledge that theirs is a vital job. And here and there along those roads I came across wire-stringers who'd just finished, dead to the world, sprawling fast asleep, undisturbed by the thunder of passing trucks and clouds of dust.[19]

Though reporters made much of the challenge of keeping up with Patton, he was never far away from the press. Like Montgomery, he was in love with headlines though rather better than his bête noire at coming up with quick quotes to support his image as a war leader. Presiding at a ceremony to open the Roosevelt Railroad Bridge near Mainz, he was invited to cut the ribbon with a large pair of scissors. He gave them back demanding 'a goddamned bayonet' adding he wasn't 'a goddamned tailor'[20] as if anyone in their wildest imagination supposed he might be.

Further south again the French First Army was evoking the days of Napoleon with a Rhine crossing aimed at Karlsruhe with Stuttgart as the ultimate prize. Acutely conscious of the supporting and thus secondary role Eisenhower had in mind for General de Lattre de Tassigny, his political master in Paris had feared a last-minute change of plan that would deprive France of sharing in the Rhine offensive. So that there could be no misunderstanding de Gaulle sent his own unambiguous directive to de Lattre. 'You must cross the Rhine even if the Americans are not agreeable and even if you have to cross it in boats. It is a matter of the greatest national interest.'[21] This was all very well but where were the boats to come from? Putting out the call for anything that would float and carry men and equipment, de Lattre put together a motley fleet ranging from stormboats, propelled by outboard motors and each capable of taking just six men, to rubber dinghies that had to be paddled across. Given the firepower that the enemy brought to bear on the French sector, it was a miracle that any of the assault force survived. Of ninety vessels, fifty-four were hit and over forty were sunk. But two narrow bridgeheads were secured and, by March 31st, French troops were fanning out to capture more than twenty towns and villages. It was the day, said de Lattre, when France 'succeeded in raising the stone under which Germany had sought to entomb her'.[22]

Young German soldiers, barely out of training or not trained at all, wandered listlessly, not knowing what to do.

Our infantry battalion had dissolved. Our officers had disappeared, which one could hardly hold against them as our battalion virtually consisted of just 15–18-year-old children and old men . . . The situation in the forest looked desolate: burned out guns, smashed machine guns, countless ammunition, gas masks, tin helmets and cartridges were piled up all over the place. The five of us, all upper school boys from Stuttgart, stood around and wondered what to do. Should we make our way to our own troops over the Danube or should we make our way home to Stuttgart? Our mood was low.

They decided on Stuttgart.

That wasn't so easy though. We only had a map of a 1:500 000 scale and a little pocket compass. It was also obvious that we could only march at night, and had to hide in the woods during the day so that we wouldn't be taken prisoner. We didn't want to part with our weapons, partly because we wanted to take them home with us, partly because we thought we might keep an enemy post covered (maybe we had played too many war games as boys) . . . Half of Germany seemed to be on the march in the woodland between the Neckar and Danube rivers. The former soldiers were heading as far afield as Hamburg, Berlin and Vienna. 'We've got plenty of time,' they'd say, which said it all in those days as the end of the war approached. We'd heard that safe conduct passes were being issued in Endersbach . . . In exchange for our service book we could get a safe conduct pass, which said, 'Please let Mr . . . pass. He wants to return to his parents in Stuttgart.'[23]

Nuremberg (Nürnberg), known as the 'Reich's treasure chest' for the cultural heritage that had since disappeared in the bomb craters, woke up on the morning of April 16th to a tank alarm. This was something new. Citizens were used to the calming radio voice of Uncle Baldrian warning them of approaching enemy aircraft. But tanks? It could only mean that the Americans were at the gates.

Wednesday 18 April: Today is the heaviest day so far. Morning was quieter, but artillery fire heavier towards midday. We had to eat lunch in the cellar. In the afternoon the shooting was so dangerous we had to stay in the cellar most of the time. Even heavier fire in the evening. The area surrounding Fuerth is ablaze. Nuremberg-Fuerth is in a fog of gunpowder smoke and a glow of fire.

As the day wore on the artillery attack intensified. It reached its pitch in the two hours before midnight.

Soldiers have been absconding from the Hoefener flak station, they come to us in the cellar, exhausted, with sweat on their brows and their eyes inflamed from the gunpowder smoke. They tell us of comrades lying dead by the guns, and one flak gun after another is shot to smithereens . . . after midnight it is better, everything outside is bathed in a bloody red light . . . the great granaries, food stores and barns are burning.[24]

One of the more dramatic incidents in the battle for Nuremberg actually took place some way north of the city. For a month past the village of Zapfendorf had been the resting place for an ammunition freight train. At last, but inevitably, it attracted the attention of American fighter planes. On a Sunday evening, the fires started and the call went out for everyone to leave their homes and to take refuge in the forest. Few took any notice. At around 8.30 there was a massive explosion. 'The destruction of the ammunition train loaded with explosives creates a colossal air pressure which rips off roofs. The streets are knee-deep in rubble. The walls of the houses crack from top to bottom.'[25] Most of the villagers who had stayed at home were killed in the blast.

Nuremberg was the scene of yet another of those battle excesses that the victors would prefer to forget.

The US soldiers came with tanks and jeeps and surrounded the bunker . . . A doctor came out with a white flag and surrendered the bunker which was full of civilians. The US soldiers went into the bunker, blocked off the exits and fetched out the 200 or so German soldiers, all unarmed, many holding up white handkerchiefs. From what I could see from my hiding place around 500m away they were old Volkssturm men, police, landeschutzen, flak helpers, Hitler youth, air shelter and SHD people, and a few medics.

306

The prisoners had to line up in three rows behind each other. One of them said something and was beaten by an American soldier until he was lying on the floor, two men who wanted to help him were shot. Suddenly the Americans began shooting with machine guns and pistols and soon all prisoners lay lifeless on the ground. Some had tried to run away but were shot . . . Before darkness fell a convoy of three large trucks came along and all the dead were thrown on the lorries like dead animals and the trucks drove off in the direction of Moegeldorf. Only then were the civilians allowed to leave the bunker.[26]

On the wider front, resistance was more or less dangerous according to chance. German units that were ready to fight were liable to find themselves wandering the countryside looking for opposition, the Allied armour having long since passed on.

I borrowed the observer's binoculars and managed to see some krauts in the vicinity of an underpass directly to our front. As the mortar crews could not bring their weapons to bear on them, I went downstairs to ask the assistance of the tank crew. They informed me that an officer would have to order them to fire, but I suspected they were afraid of exposing their position or didn't want to have to clean their gun. Lt. Neel (our executive officer) happened to come along and I told him of my observation. He ordered them to open fire which they did with three well-placed shots.

Next morning James Graff and two of his comrades ventured forward to investigate the underpass. They found a heavy water-cooled machine-gun with the bolt jammed by a piece of shrapnel and signs in the dirt where a wounded man had been dragged away – two parallel marks as if a man had been dragged out by his arms.

A pair of boots had been cut down the sides to take off someone's feet and I found a shoe with a sock sticking up out of it. Upon closer examination I found the boot still contained a foot and ankle. His leg had been severed just above the sock. As Bob Landrum was always sending home souvenirs, I threw it to him and said to send that home. We took the damaged machine gun back to show the tankers the results of their marksmanship.[27]

Moving cautiously through the village of Sinderen, a forward tank of the Eighth Armoured Brigade was knocked out by a bazooka. Slowing to a walking pace, A.E. Baker, in his tank Shaggy Dog, worked the periscope, trying to spot where the German gunners were holed up. Suddenly, he was thrown sideways by a tremendous crash.

My first thought was that we had been hit by a mortar bomb, but looking across at Johnny I saw him in agitated movement. He was tearing off his headset and pushing open the turret flap.

He yelled: 'Bale out!' through the microphone and vanished upwards through the hole.

I didn't need any more telling to make me realise what had happened – we had been hit by hard shot. I dived under the gun and was pulled up sharply by my headset lead. I ripped the thing off and my hat came off with it. McCarthy and I rose out of the hatchway almost simultaneously, getting in each other's way rather.

Mac actually got clear first and then, for a horrid moment, I found myself with one leg over the side of the turret, perched up high – a perfect target for anybody interested. I thought I saw a tracer flash past, but I may have imagined it, and then I had rolled across the engine covers and dropped off the back of the tank. A puff of white smoke and a shower of glowing fragments mush-roomed out in front of 'Shaggy Dog' as I took a header over a low hedge on the right and scrambled on all fours across the garden to the side of a house downroad from Jerry, where Mac and Johnny were already crouching.

Entering the house by a side door they found their entire leading platoon taking cover. 'They had Bren gunners and riflemen in position in all the downstairs windows and they were getting a small mortar into action in the back garden. We sat on the floor of one of the front rooms.' There were more explosions outside as the Germans put a few more rounds into Shaggy Dog. Then they attacked the house. 'For a few minutes there was a great deal of noise – the hammering of Brens, the crack of rifles and the barking of the mortar in the back garden. We sat tight on the floor, leaving it to the infantry and hoping for the best. McCarthy made himself useful filling Bren magazines.'

A lull in the fighting allowed both sides to take stock.

I got up and went into the hall. Through the window of the right-hand front room I could see . . . two Jerries lying motionless about 15 yards away. As I watched two more appeared, bearing a white flag with a red cross on it, and carried the others away.

I went back into the first room . . . After a bit Bert Morsley made the most ridiculous suggestion I had ever heard. He said that he thought a cup of tea would do everybody good, and he proposed to crawl out to the tank for the cooker and compo. tea powder, which were in one of the boxes welded above the exhausts. This seemed to be carrying coolness a bit too far.[28]

Corporal Dai Evans was caught up in a fight for a tiny village between Wesel and Bocholt. It started as a textbook assault over open farmland while support artillery 'softened up' the target.

Reaching the road we spread along its length, sheltering in the ditches which ran at each side. Suddenly, with a maniacal screeching and whooping, a storm of shells dropped around us, explosions rent the air, splinters whined and droned about and a number of men were hit. We dug frantically into the bottom of the ditch to gain better shelter. In the middle of all this Lieutenant Chambers hastened along the line shouting 'It's all right men . . . they're our shells.'

Dave grabbed him and pulled him down. 'I don't give a fuck whose shells they are, Sir,' he said, 'but they'll kill you just as surely as Jerry ones will.'

When the barrage moved forward, Dai Evans and his friends followed into the now burning village to be met by concentrated machine-gun fire.

One nest in particular was a source of trouble to us. It was in the basement of a house and well supported by riflemen who picked off anyone trying to get round the flanks. There was too much debris for a Crocodile tank to get near, so we were forced to mount a company-scale attack upon it, each platoon firing at all possible points so as to keep the heads of the enemy down while we spread out in turn, leapfrogging nearer and nearer.

At last, one section managed to get round the back of the house. Sending a burst of machine-gun fire through the door they broke it down and charged in.

Unfortunately for one of our men, a German soldier rushed up the cellar steps in time to fire a magazineful of Schmeisser bullets into him at point-blank range, killing him instantly. His death was followed a split-second later by that of the German as our lads cut him down. Going through the house they threw grenades into each room and the cellar. No prisoners were taken and several Germans were bayoneted as they attempted to surrender.[29]

In the early days after the Rhine crossing the big worry was of booby traps – a length of wire stretched across a road at the height of a motorcyclist's head, food stocks that had been poisoned or mines dug in where they were least expected. Of the latter, the most dangerous was when a vehicle hitting a mine set off a chain reaction with bombs dug into the side of the road knocking out an entire convoy.

We were forbidden to enter deserted houses. Some of the infantry did, and some were blown up when they stepped on the doormat. Others would get killed or severely wounded when they flushed the toilet which would set off a mine. If they lifted a nice clock off the shelf it would be enough to detonate a mine. They even left mines under the dead so that when we moved them our English troops could be blown up. In my job of burying those bodies we took the precaution of attaching a long rope to them and would get a fair distance away and move the corpse to be sure it wasn't booby trapped.[30]

But confidence increased as resistance diminished. Injuries caused by accident or sheer carelessness were almost as common as those inflicted by the enemy.

One of our guys climbed up on a M-8 armored vehicle. He was supposed to have his lock on his rifle engaged, so he couldn't pull the trigger. He didn't, and he climbed up. The trigger was pulled, and the guy standing above him was shot and killed. Another guy, probably didn't want to stay in combat, he put his hand around the outside of a pill box and let a grenade go off and blew his hand off. Another guy was cleaning his pistol, and he shot himself in the leg. Another guy was searching a house in Witzenhausen with another fellow and the guy had a B.A.R., and a B.A.R. was a very sensitive gun. You could look at the damn thing and it would go off, and a lot of rounds, 20 rounds before you knew it. He was searching a house ahead of this guy with a B.A.R., not a good gun to use searching a house and his gun went off and shot the guy in the legs.[31]

As the Allied advance accelerated, Field Marshal Kesselring, Commander-in-Chief of German forces in the west, found his immediate prospects 'anything but pleasing'.[32] On paper, he had three army groups at his disposal: in the north Army Group H, led by General Johannes Blaskowitz, comprised the First Parachute Army and Twenty-Fifth Army; in the centre defending the Ruhr, Field Marshal Walter Model's Army Group B had the Fifth Panzer Army, Seventh Army and Fifteenth Army; while to the south Army Group G, commanded by General Paul Hausser, consisted of the First and Nineteenth Armies.

Just a few months earlier any one of these Wehrmacht units would have been a match for the toughest Allied assault but now they were in disarray, undermanned and with little armour, at risk of degenerating into a demoralised rabble. The rate of desertion was so high that Kesselring resorted to using some of his best men to round up the fainthearts who flooded to the rear whenever a battle started.

The enormously costly battle of the last half-year and constant retreat and defeat had reduced officers and men to a dangerous state of exhaustion. Many officers were nervous wrecks, others affected in health, others simply incompetent, while there was a dangerous shortage of junior officers. In the ranks strengths were unsatisfactory, replacements arriving at the front insufficiently trained, with no combat experience, in driblets, and, anyway, too late. They were accordingly no asset in action. Only where an intelligent commander had a full complement of experienced subalterns and a fair nucleus of elder men did units hold together.[33]

Kesselring's position was made more problematic by the refusal of Hitler and his arrogant but incompetent emissaries to recognise that the defence of the Ruhr was a lost cause. A plan for Model to break out of the Allied encirclement, which would have saved a third of Kesselring's total fighting force, was rejected out of hand. Hitler wanted a Ruhr fortress; what he got was a closing in by the US Ninth and First Armies leading, on April 18th, to the capitulation of the last of the 300,000 men of Army Group B.

For Model it was the end of the line. One of the few who was prepared to stand up to Hitler and even occasionally to ignore orders that he judged impossible to carry out, Model's great talent was for improvisation. At the peak of his career, facing up to the advance of the Red Army, he had been dubbed 'the Führer's fireman', the one who was first to be sent to whatever part of the front needing urgent bolstering. But in the Ruhr, there was nothing Model could do to stave off defeat. In mid-April when American troops were less than two miles from his headquarters, Model received, under flag of truce, an appeal from General Matthew Ridgway which the sender hoped would save further bloodshed.

Neither history nor the military profession records any nobler character, any more brilliant master of warfare, any more dutiful subordinate of the state, than the American General, Robert E. Lee. Eighty years ago this month, his loyal command reduced in numbers, stripped of its means of effective fighting and completely surrounded by overwhelming forces, he chose an honorable capitulation.

This same choice is now yours. In the light of a soldier's honor, for the reputation of the German Officer Corps, for the sake of your nation's future, lay down your arms at once. The German lives you will save are sorely needed to restore your people to their proper

place in society. The German cities you will preserve are irreplace-
able necessities for your people's welfare.[34]

It was Model's Chief of Staff who brought back the reply. The
fighting would continue. Ridgway now gave the messenger a choice.
'He could go back under a flag of truce and take his chances . . .
or he could remain in our custody as a prisoner of war.'

He chose to stay.

Model was more fatalistic. On the afternoon of April 21st, after
a farewell handshake for each of his staff, he walked into the forest
and killed himself with a single shot from his Walther pistol. In
taking this way out he may have provided one last service to his
Führer. When he heard the news, Hitler's reaction was that if Model
could find the courage to take his own life, so could he.

It seemed now there could be no substantial military obstacle
between the Allies and Berlin. Well, that was not quite true. The
foil to the ambitions of Allied generals, and of Montgomery and
Patton in particular, to be first in Berlin was as military as you
could get. It just happened to be their own Supreme Commander.
Having once described Berlin as 'the main prize', Eisenhower had
decided to concede the German capital to the Red Army, shifting
the centre of the advance away from Montgomery's Twenty-First
Army Group in favour of a central thrust by Bradley's Twelfth
Army Group towards the River Elbe, there to meet up with the
Russians.

The decision came as a huge shock to Montgomery who had
already given orders that made Berlin the ultimate goal of his
advance. Indeed it was probably this characteristically high-handed
action by his British subordinate that brought Eisenhower to the
point of resolution. Often accused by his confederates of being
over-sensitive to British interests ('Ike is the best Goddamn general
the British have got,' sneered Patton), Eisenhower had become
increasingly exasperated with Montgomery whose undoubted qualities of leadership did not include political sensitivities. If he had
been so blessed he would have known that Eisenhower, at this late
stage in the war, could not be seen to be paying deference to

Montgomery at the cost of falling out with Bradley, not to mention the establishment in Washington. The worst possible scenario, and one that Eisenhower had every reason to fear, given the antipathy between Bradley and Montgomery, was a race between the Twelfth and Twenty-First Army Groups to be the first to fly the flag over the Brandenburg Gate. The likely consequences for Anglo-American relations, and for Eisenhower personally, were too catastrophic to think about. But if Berlin was taken out of the equation and Montgomery and Bradley were each given a task that matched pride with capability there was a good chance that the Atlantic alliance would emerge intact.

There were also sound strategic reasons for leaving Berlin to the Russians. For one thing they were closer, less than forty miles from the city, with a million-strong force ready for the culminating attack across flat, open countryside. The nearest Anglo-American forces were still 250 miles off target. The rate of their advance was impressive but not so great as to guarantee coming in first. Even assuming that the 200 miles to the Elbe could be covered at Patton-like speed, the other fifty miles beyond was difficult terrain with lakes and rivers to hold up movement. Then there was the nightmare prospect of street fighting in Berlin with no means of distinguishing Russian friend from German foe. What would that do for relations with the Soviets?

Two other factors weighed against Berlin falling to forces under Eisenhower's command. The first was the cost in young lives of trying to outpace the Russians. Bradley, who was content to forego a triumphant entry into Berlin as long as Montgomery did not thereby steal an advantage, calculated that a breakthrough from the Elbe would incur 100,000 casualties, 'a pretty stiff price to pay for a prestige objective'. The warning was not lost on Eisenhower who was under pressure to conserve manpower against the then probability of the war with Japan outlasting the war in Europe by a year or more. Seasoned troops could expect their services to be in demand in the Pacific war zone. The waste of lives would have been made yet more conspicuous if, having reached Berlin, the Anglo-Americans had simply withdrawn all but a token

force. This they were required to do under the agreement on occu-
pational zones which left Berlin in the Russian sector, albeit under
shared control.

The second factor that influenced Eisenhower's strategy for the
closing phase of the German war was the worry, backed by much
hearsay if next to no hard evidence, that the Nazi hierarchy was
creating strongholds in the Black Forest and Bavarian Alps where
it could fight a prolonged and bloody last battle. Eisenhower took
the threat seriously, as did Bradley, basing their fears on intelligence reports of 'considerable numbers of SS and specially chosen
units being systematically withdrawn to Austria . . . and of . . .
important ministries and personalities of the Nazi regime already
established in the Redoubt area'. General Patch confidently
predicted 200,000 SS troops defending 20,000 square miles of
Bavaria, Austria and northern Italy. It was all fantasy, as Patton
was the first to suggest, though it was Patton who was given the
job of proving his own argument by sweeping south to clear out
the non-existent Alpine Redoubt before meeting up with the
Russians at the Danube.

But it was politics rather than strategy that made the running.
At the very least Eisenhower was intent on holding the balance
between American and British interests. Also in the back of his
mind was the knowledge that his President was keen to foster good
relations with the Russians. However naïve this may have appeared
once Stalin emerged in his true colours, it remains a fact that all
those with a first loyalty to Roosevelt were strongly motivated to
treat the Russians as friends and most definitely not as prospective enemies. Roosevelt had his warning voices but they were not
loud enough to reach Eisenhower. What he did hear was the opinion
of his mentor and Army Chief of Staff, George Marshall, who
backed the Berlin decision as part of the American conciliation
policy. For Marshall this had the added virtue of doing down the
detested Montgomery.

Eisenhower knew very well that whatever means he chose to
implement his policy, he had trouble ahead. There were too many
contradictions to be reconciled, too many egos to be massaged,

too many career considerations, not least his own, to be taken into account. To avoid a long and damaging debate he opted for a pre-emptive strike. Passing up the opportunity to discuss Berlin at a meeting with Churchill and Montgomery on March 25th, Eisenhower communicated directly with Stalin, proposing that his forces, once they had secured the Ruhr 'in late April or even earlier', should focus their efforts on a centre thrust to the Leipzig-Dresden area, led by Bradley's Twelfth Army Group.

The logic of this was to allow Montgomery to concentrate on the Ruhr ('if the industrial heart stopped, the political heart would also die'[35]) before moving north to take Hamburg and the other North Sea ports. This would cut off the occupation forces in Norway, Germany's last major source of reserves, and frustrate any Russian designs on Denmark. Meanwhile, having reached the Elbe, Bradley would also turn north, leaving the Russians to sweep up east of the river and, by clear inference, take Berlin. Assuming a favourable response from Stalin (it was hard to imagine anything less than full assent), Eisenhower set his plan in motion by shifting the US Ninth Army from Montgomery's command back to Bradley.

The reaction from London was immediate and hostile. Eisenhower's initiative in going direct to Stalin instead of first consulting the Joint Chiefs of Staff smacked of a plot against Montgomery and a ruse to disappoint British expectations of being in at the kill. Churchill, who had his own election prospects in mind, weighed in with a vigorous protest.

> It seems to me that the chief criticism of the new Eisenhower plan is that it shifts the axis of the main advance upon Berlin to the direction through Leipzig to Dresden, and thus raises the question of whether the Twenty-one Army Group will not be so stretched as to lose its offensive power, especially after it has been deprived of the Ninth United States Army. Thus we might be condemned to an almost static role in the north and virtually prevented from crossing the Elbe until an altogether later stage in the operations has been reached. All prospect of the British entering Berlin with the Americans is ruled out.[36]

But simultaneously Churchill warned his advisers that the Americans would 'riposte heavily', as indeed they did. Eisenhower was riding high as a commander whose judgement could be trusted. When Roosevelt joined with his generals to deny that Eisenhower's plans involved any far-reaching changes from the strategy agreed in Malta, Churchill backed off, denying any attempt to disparage the Supreme Commander or to foster 'misunderstandings between the truest friends and comrades that ever fought side by side'. Eisenhower grasped the olive branch, reassuring Churchill that far from leaving British forces 'in a static condition along the Elbe', it was likelier that 'US forces would be shifted to Field Marshal Montgomery who would then be sent across the river in the north and to a line reaching at least to Luebeck on the Baltic coast.' The destiny of Berlin was left open, though the odds were heavily in favour of the Red Army achieving its dearest wish.

It is just possible that pitted against an ailing President, Churchill could have made more of his chances to influence Washington opinion. His suspicions of Soviet intentions were well known and were rejected by Washington. But after his initial protest at the relegation of Berlin to the list of secondary war aims, he went soft on the issue until well after the war when hindsight enlivened his memoirs. Churchill was a realist. He knew above all else that he had to keep in with the Americans who held the whip hand. That made him the loser in more arguments than he cared to admit. As Chief of Air Staff, Sir Charles Portal, observed of his boss, 'Churchill will fight to the last ditch, but not in it.'

The final decision over Berlin was not taken until mid-April. By then the Ninth Army was at the Elbe while Soviet forces were still battling their way through the Berlin suburbs. As Simpson saw it nothing stood between his troops and Berlin except a wide-open autobahn. His request to Eisenhower to let him go the last few miles was denied. Instead, he was told to keep to the line of the Elbe, while turning north towards Luebeck and south to crack the still to be discovered Nazi Redoubt.

Even if Eisenhower was tempted to give Simpson his head, the risks must have seemed too high. In the critical sector the Ninth

Army was restricted to 50,000 troops. Far ahead of their supply lines they had a single bridgehead over the Elbe to bring up essential artillery and gasoline. The contrast with the Soviet build-up – 1.25 million men backed by 22,000 artillery pieces – could not have been more stark. If ever there was a purely military decision, letting the Soviets get on with their chosen task was it. But in any case, whatever interest Eisenhower had once had in taking Berlin was now lost. On the very day that Simpson reached the Elbe (April 11th) Eisenhower dined with Patton who took the opportunity to urge an American incursion into Berlin. Eisenhower was not persuaded. The city had 'no tactical or strategic value', he argued. If, as Patton claimed, Simpson could take the city in forty-eight hours, this, in Eisenhower's view, 'would place upon the American forces the burden of caring for thousands and thousands of German displaced persons and Allied prisoners of war'.[37]

The decision to sacrifice Berlin was to dog Eisenhower's postwar career. When he stood for the presidency in 1952 it was as a Republican who, in contrast to his soft-centred Democrat opponent, would be tough on the Russians. Time and again he felt the need to 'explain' his actions by highlighting the strategic arguments. But after the wilder assertions of Eisenhower's critics – that, for example, he was duty bound to enforce a secret deal between Roosevelt and Stalin – are summarily rejected, there is every reason to respect his political acumen. For Eisenhower, a battle was part of a wider pattern in which military decisions had political consequences. He may not have been the most imaginative general but no one was better qualified to achieve a political consensus. It was this that kept him at the top.

15
Meeting the Enemy

The Rhine, it was often said, was as much a psychological as a physical barrier, meaning that, after it was breached, German morale sagged and resistance was limited to the ever decreasing band of Hitler's faithful. Less commonplace was the equally valid assertion that for the Allies, too, the Rhine crossing had its psychological impact. Hitherto, the easily understood objective had been to bring death and destruction to the enemy. Now, great swathes of Germany, spreading like a flood tide, were under Allied control. This called for a transition from the prosecution of war to the management of peace.

To say that the military was ill-equipped for the challenge was to put it mildly. In fairness, some problems of administration were beyond rational solution. With the falling apart of the Reich, much of central Europe seemed to be on the move – refugees fleeing the Russians, liberated POWs looking for the quickest way home, slave labourers of a dozen nationalities out for retribution, German soldiers who had retired themselves from service and other German soldiers wandering towards captivity. Even so, restoring a semblance of order took longer than might have been expected.

The faults started with the generally poor quality of military governors. What often happened was that after a town was captured, an officer of the occupying force, usually a captain or major, was given the job of restoring essential services while putting in place a trusted, i.e. non-Nazi, administration. In the early days of occupation these officers were invariably second-raters whose superiors were only too pleased to lose them along the way, leaving the best of the military to get on with the real job of winning the war. With minimum back-up (maybe ten to twenty officers and other ranks), little or no understanding of the German language and a not unnatural fear of reprisals, the strain was too much for some of those who had civil leadership thrust upon them. This was soon made clear to Saul Padover, an American psychologist, when he visited Roetgen, a small town southeast of Aachen. Padover had the job of inquiring into the collective state of mind of a Germany heading for defeat and to do this he needed permission from the military governor to talk to some of his leading citizens. This he was given but not for long. He was in mid-conversation with a former town official when his erstwhile host burst in.

'WHAT THE GODDAM HELL IS GOING ON HERE?'
The interruption came like a sudden explosion and it made us leap out of our chairs. In the doorway, drawn to his full height, his eyes bloodshot, his fists clenched, stood Major 'Windy'. He shrieked, 'WHAT THE GODDAM HELL IS GOING ON HERE BEHIND MY BACK? WHAT THE GOOD HELL ARE YOU DOING SNOOPING BEHIND MY BACK? THIS IS MY TOWN, I WANT YOU TO KNOW. THIS IS *MY* MAYOR. THIS IS *MY* PRESTIGE. *MY* TOWN . . . *MY* TOWN . . . MINE, MINE, MINE . . . !' He pounded his chest with both fists as if he were determined to cave it in. For a moment I was bereft of speech. Then I noticed the smile on Doctor Kerten's face, a smile of undiluted malice. He understood English and he savoured the unseemly scene. This made me so mad that I jumped at the demented Major: 'If you have any accusations to make, make them in private, not in the presence of Germans.' He stepped back in surprise, still flailing his hapless chest, muttering, '*my* town, mine, mine, mine . . .' Then he strode out.

We went to his office. The storm in his breast had subsided, but his eyes were still shot with distended blood vessels. He glared at us epileptically. We asked whether he had forgotten that he had given us permission to work in town. He said he did not mean that we should work behind his back. 'You may work here, but you must talk to people only in my presence.' 'But Major, you don't understand German?' 'That doesn't mean a thing. I want to see what you are doing; I want to know everything that goes on in *my* town.'[1]

Wanting to know what was going on was a familiar wish of military governors but few achieved this happy state. Holding absolute power, they had not the means of exercising it except by delegating authority to German officials who had worked for the Hitler regime. But an association with the Nazi Party was supposed to be a bar to civil employment. Compromises were made, not always successfully. In Aachen, one of the first German cities to experience military government, the job of regenerating a society was handed over to a group of middle-class professionals who had used their connections with the Church as a way of keeping their distance from the Nazi Party. At the same time they all had connections with vital war industries, all had prospered under Hitler and all held political views that were at sharp variance with the familiar concepts of western democracy. Their plan, 'about which the military governor knew little and cared less', according to Saul Padover, 'aimed at setting up an authoritarian corporate state with a paternalistic . . . unfree labour system'.²

The leading advocate, Oberbürgermeister Oppenhoff, spoke openly of a 'tightly knit community of owners and managers . . . supported by a labour aristocracy of foremen and artisans'. Oppenhoff was aggressively opposed to popular elections, political parties and trade unions. When this affinity to Nazi philosophy was pointed out to the military governor by an independent observer who added that several members of the administration elite were known to be former Nazis and one a notorious Gestapo informer, the response was that they were all 'indispensable'.

In one sense the problem solved itself. A month later, Oppenhoff was shot dead by two unknown assailants. The murder may have been the work of left-wing opponents or of rivals within the Oppenhoff camp who thought he was too liberal. No arrests followed but military control was tightened.

All ranks of Allied forces were subject to the non-fraternisation rule, one of the barmier restrictions imposed by SHAEF, ranking for bureaucratic mindset with the ban on political activity of whatever orientation. Both orders were imposed ahead of the entry into Germany when a long-drawn-out struggle was still in prospect. In that event, consorting with enemy civilians, however friendly, risked giving away information, while political activity, though ostensibly anti-Fascist, might have disguised underground pro-Nazi movements. But the determining factor was the fear of repeating the mistakes of 1918 when, it was said, the Germans had worked hard at being amiable, the better to argue later that they had been misjudged as the aggressors. As a veteran of the first German war, Montgomery was a leading advocate of the hard line, arguing that this time there must be no smokescreen put up by 'appeals for fair play and friendship'.

> It is too soon for you to distinguish between 'good' and 'bad' Germans. In streets, houses, cafés, cinemas, you must keep clear of Germans, man, woman and child, unless you meet them in the course of duty. You must not walk out with them; shake hands with them; visit their homes; make them gifts; take gifts from them; play games with them or share any social event with them . . . Remember that those are the same Germans . . . whose brothers, sons and fathers were carrying out a system of mass murder and torture of defenceless civilians . . . A guilty nation must not only be convicted, it must realize its guilt.

It was soon obvious that, even if justified, which was dubious, the non-fraternisation rule was unworkable. But it stayed in place, causing needless confusion, embarrassment and irritation all round. The Americans were more flexible than the British. For one thing, the GIs could not resist the importuning by small children who draped themselves over jeeps begging for chewing gum, chocolate and peanuts. From meeting children it was a short step to meeting their older sisters or widowed or lonely mothers. Non-fraternisation was wrecked on sex, admitted one senior officer who went on to say that to a young man 'bored and fed up with the company of other men, almost anything in skirts is a stimulant and relief'.[3] And German women were not just skirts. They had all the attractions of the northern European physique and they were not overtly prudish.

> We noticed that as the girls from the neighbouring houses came past on their way to and from the food-stores, the soldiers shouted times

at them for meetings, and got quick nods of the head in return. A Lieutenant, listening to one of these rendezvous being arranged, broke in with: 'Listen, Schultz, don't let me catch you, or else it'll cost you sixty-five dollars.' Schultz grinned and flicked a glance at the girl and then back to the Lieutenant: 'Only sixty-five dollars, Mr Miller. It's cheap at the price.'[4]

Sixty-five dollars was the standard fine for breaking the non-fraternisation rule. Propositioning German girls became known as 'the 65 dollar question'. British officers, true to their inhibitions, were liable to take such infringements more seriously.

The Major was shocked to witness the friendly way in which our troops treated the German civilians who were nearly all women, children and old men. He was even more shocked when he heard a bit of impromptu 'screwing' that was taking place when one or two of the girls gave in to the appeals of some of the lads.

'I'll court-martial any man I find co-habiting with a German woman,' he declared. It didn't have much effect. It was an impossible situation, as on the one hand there were sex-starved young men; on the other were women and girls who were happy to be treated civilly and welcomed the cigarettes, chocolate and so on which they hadn't seen for months. Relief was in the air on both sides.

Lieutenant Chambers was missing for a time. I ran him to earth in the front room of a house; the tall blonde woman there didn't appear as innocent as he was trying to look.

'The Major wants you, Sir,' I told him.

The Major wanted all the officers and NCOs to gather for a lecture about the treatment of civilians. We were ordered to keep the men apart from the Germans at all times; to this end we were to turn the inhabitants out of certain houses, making them stay with neighbours while we settled down in their homes. He also set a pattern of standing-to which was designed to keep the men fully occupied for that night.[5]

It was surely no coincidence that attempts to repress ordinary relationships coincided with an increase in real crimes against women. In the last weeks of the war court-martials for rape by

British soldiers against German girls were around eighty a week in the Second Army area alone. Anecdotage suggests that many of the most tragic abuses never came to trial.

The Burgomaster's house was full of weeping women; the only one who was not weeping was a pretty, white-faced young German girl; she seemed too bewildered to do anything, and just stood there while everyone around her talked or sobbed. She had been coming home with her friend, she said, from a visit to the village up the road. They had just passed in front of a wooden defence wall, about a hundred yards away from the first house in Oeyle, when they saw a British army lorry. It was a main road, along which many convoys passed, so neither the girl nor her companion remarked on it; they were not even alarmed, near as they were to the village, when two men in British uniforms jumped out and came towards them, and they just laughed and refused when the men tried by signs to persuade them to come into the woods. Then one of the soldiers grasped hold of the other girl and began to drag her towards the woods. 'She fell on her knees and pleaded with them to let her go. I joined in and pleaded, too, but they just dragged her on her knees along the road. The suddenly she began to scream, and one of the soldiers got his gun and put it to her throat. I don't know whether he meant to fire or whether he was trying to frighten her, but the gun went off. Her throat and chest were all shot away, and the soldiers let her go and ran for their lorry. I ran too, towards the houses to get help.'

That was all. A British corporal ran out of the house at the sound of the scream and the noise of the gun, and saw two British soldiers scrambling into the lorry and driving away. He calmed the hysterical young girl, and then he and his companions helped to move the other girl's body from the road. The military police came around to take depositions, and a search began for the culprits; I don't suppose they were caught, for units were on the move at that time and things difficult to check. In the Burgomaster's house, though there was weeping, there was no resentment at what had occurred; all of them seemed to accept it.

'These things happen in war,' the Burgomaster said. 'We don't blame the British. A German might have done the same thing. There are good and bad everywhere.'[6]

Even when the culprits were known and identified, it was not easy to persuade senior officers to go to the trouble of a lengthy and uncertain prosecution.

One afternoon two German women reported that they had been raped in their home by two British soldiers who then rode off on the women's bicycles. Sgt. Smith took me with the two German women, a mother and daughter, to their home and they pointed out the way the two soldiers had gone. We all went in the jeep about a mile when we saw the bicycles outside a field. There were a lot of soldiers in the field and the women picked out the two soldiers who had raped them and stolen their bicycles. The two soldiers were taken to the Colonel. He said would I tell the women that he had seen the two soldiers all the afternoon and it couldn't have been the ones. The women insisted they were the ones. The Colonel told me to tell the women that they were mistaken. He said the two soldiers were going on leave in the morning and that he had signed their passes, and as far as he was concerned they would be going on leave. I told them there was nothing they could do, and of course the Colonel knew it was them. They were very upset. I advised them to take their bikes and go home. They went away in tears. Sgt. Smith didn't think much of the outcome. He was disgusted.[7]

Some good advice was handed out to occupying forces – beware prostitutes who were likely to hand on a dose of VD, for example, and go easy on the schnapps. But for the most part the efforts to mould attitudes and behaviour were at best muddled and at worse counterproductive. What can we now make of an Anglo-propagandist who, devoted to sweeping generalisations, notes perceived German qualities ('very hard working and thorough; obedient with a great love of tidiness and order') while warning against 'a streak of hysteria', a tendency to 'fly into a passion if some little thing goes wrong' and a character cocktail of sentimentality and cruelty that 'does not show a well balanced mind'? Orders to civilians were to be given in a firm military manner; 'they are used to it and expect it.' Part of the British soldier's job in Germany was 'to teach the German that he can't start a war like the last one and just get away with it', though how the British soldier was expected to teach the Germans anything when he was forbidden to socialise remained a mystery. The only formal relaxation of the fraternisation rule for British soldiers was to allow greetings to children but to offer a 'good morning' to an adult remained a serious offence.

It was not simply the soldiers with raging hormones who were prepared to risk punishment. There were those with families at home but not seen for many months who sought to be reminded of some of the familiar fireside comforts.

It was not long before we made the acquaintance of an English soldier. It was strictly forbidden for civilians and soldiers to mix, but this chap came up as if nothing had happened and asked my mother to boil some eggs for him. He held out the eggs which he got from inside his jacket. Mother declined. 'It is not right,' she told him, 'that you can get eggs and other foodstuffs, just because you have cigarettes and chocolate and can barter. We can get nothing.' Tiffy explained that he missed his family and that he would like to sit occasionally in an ordinary house, pretending to be an ordinary man. In exchange he would bring us food. A bargain was struck and from then on Tiffy was a regular guest at our house. We thought nothing of it, not so my stepfather who returned one evening from being a POW. Most soldiers were released fairly quickly because running vast camps was a logistical nightmare. He arrived in the evening having walked from I don't know where. There was no public transport of any kind. He peered through a window and the first thing he noticed was a soldier in 'enemy uniform' sitting at our table. The misunderstanding could be sorted out and Tiffy continued to be a visitor.[8]

When the Americans came into the village where young Elke Eisenmenger lived she was terrified of what they might do. Bursting into the kitchen:

they didn't look at us at all but were more interested in the black coal oven . . . One soldier put his machine gun down on the kitchen table and leaned over the oven, trying to start a fire. An American soldier may have excellent knowledge of machine guns and other weapons but he had no idea how to operate a tricky Swabian oven. It soon started smoking out of every crack and seam, and the soldiers coughed and cursed. Suddenly an American picked up his weapon and aimed it at my grandmother. She got up, trembling and pale and put up her hands. The soldier pushed her toward the stove. With relief we realised that the tall fellow didn't want to shoot the little woman, but he urgently needed her help. Grandmother sprang into action and began to make 'spaetzele' (a Swabian dish). One soldier got the big frying pan out and fried some corned beef in it. A wonderful aroma of roast meat filled the kitchen and the tension disappeared.[9]

There were frequent cases where good common sense prevailed over a literal reading of the rule book.

I had been put in charge of a number of German prisoners who had been given the job of burying several dead stinking cattle in the farm-yard we occupied at a place named Udem near Goch, over the Rhine near Wesel Bridge. The prisoners had worked all afternoon and everyone was very glad to get rid of the stench of the dead cattle. I went to see the Sgt. Major and suggested the prisoners should be given a hot meal before being returned to the Military Police, which the Major agreed to. I was chatting amiably to the prisoners when one of our officers reported me for fraternising. I was immediately arrested and put under field arrest which meant I was under guard until the next morning when I was tried by a senior officer. Everyone in the unit was disgusted that I had been treated in this manner. Three quarters of the HQ visited me in little groups all through the evening, giving me their sympathy and support. Sgt. Burch came down and said it was a very serious business for me but I must put up a terrible burst of indignation when being tried in the morning, indignation that I was being accused of fraternising with Germans. In the morning at the trial I went mad, even swearing at the officer in indignation. After a while he told me to calm down, and told the Sgt. Major that the charge should never have been brought and the case against me was dismissed. Of course all my rage and indignation was all acting on my part. I was as guilty as it was possible to be. I have often wondered if the officer trying me was on my side. I never had any more trouble and I just continued as I had always.[10]

While the military police had full casebooks of minor offences, crimes against property, as long as it was German property, were ignored or even condoned. It was ironic that Montgomery's last great battle should have been dubbed Operation Plunder. A simple appreciation of the social chaos likely to be encountered on the far side of the Rhine might have inspired a more sensitive codename. In the event Operation Plunder was interpreted rather too literally by young soldiers high on the anticipation of victory.

> German cars by the hundreds were dragged out of garages and hiding places under the straw in barns, painted khaki and driven away. Cameras and watches and revolvers were taken automatically from prisoners and frequently from civilians. Wine was fair booty for everybody. In nearly every town the shops were broached, the distilleries emptied. Even pictures were stripped from their frames.[11]

Stripping farms of their stores and livestock became something of a military sport. The first live action experienced by Noel Ryan of the Canadian Black Watch was a chicken shoot.

> We could hear the roosters crowing and even I could fathom that there were hens to be found as well. I decided to get me a big bird for the pot. I borrowed a rifle and went hunting. Unfortunately, I was not the only one to hear the call of the wild. When I got to the farm, there seemed to be half of several regiments already attacking the barnyard before me, everyone running around trying to catch or shoot a chicken. Bullets were flying everywhere from an assortment of weapons. Everywhere you were caught in a crossfire. I finally got a bead on my intended and shot its head off. A body shot with a .303 would not leave much chicken. Then I hot-footed it away from what I think might have been the heaviest and most dangerous mission of my wartime experience.[12]

Such was Noel Ryan's innocence that in making his way back to camp he crossed a field where there was a sign 'Achtung Minen' prominently displayed, thinking that this was probably the shortest way home.

Raiding farms was one thing but soon there were those who took to looting as a highly profitable part-time occupation. 'I remember one sergeant, he had a jeep full of stuff . . . silverware, china, watches, jewellery of every kind . . . I think he mailed some of it back home, don't ask me how . . .'[13] Werner Sturm, whose memory this is, was disturbed to find that American soldiers could behave in such a way ('I told them I hadn't really planned on going overseas with a band of common thieves.') but those who protested were seldom able to change the popular mood. At Bremerrarde, A.E. Baker stood by while his friends looted a draper's shop. 'The family stood by wringing their hands. I didn't like that very much.'[14]

More disturbing was an incident on the Dutch border witnessed by Tom Flanagan. A family of refugees had set up temporary home in a barn which was needed by the military. It was decided to send the family back down the line.

At first only a group of middle-aged to elderly men appeared and assembled together talking and gesticulating among themselves. The language was certainly not German, yet they looked well in spite of their shabby clothes. Our Intelligence Officer began speaking to them in German, the gist of which they understood as he explained the plans to have them evacuated. It was obvious they were very unhappy about this and began to plead to be left alone . . . They were petrified at the idea of being sent back as they feared they would be treated as deserters and shot! In passing as he walked away, the IO said to John and I that he thought they were either Yugoslavs or Ukrainians.

They were crying and waving to the family who were standing at the doors of the barn as the truck turned in the space and drove away. I had been occupied with this scene to the extent that I had not noticed that the platoon had lined up at the barn doors. There was some good natured scuffling at the front as everyone pressed forward anxious to get to the best spot to make a bed space, and then through the doors came a small group of people led by an old woman. They were bulging from the number of garments they had squeezed into and each carried a case in one hand and blankets or eiderdowns over their other arm.

As I watched at some distance, the men split down the centre and formed an avenue through which the old lady led the remainder of her family; two or three old men, a young woman of about thirty or so and a child, followed by a middle-aged woman.

'You'll not be wanting that, Missus . . . !' The unmistakable voice of a Scotsman and I was rooted to the spot as I saw him snatch the blanket from the old woman's grasp. 'I'm in need of that this night . . . !'

Others followed suit. Blankets, eiderdowns and watches on chains which the old men wore on their waistcoats were snatched by the soldiers nearest to these people as they walked through this gauntlet. Above the noise of banter, I heard my own voice shouting . . .

'Right . . . you men . . . !'

There was a tug at my elbow.

'Leave this to me, Sir, you'll be wanting to go down to Company HQ, the RSM said all platoon commanders were needed. Off you go Mr Flanagan, I'll deal with this . . .'

I left to join the others at HQ trying hard not to believe what I had just witnessed. Those men were behaving as I had always imagined German soldiers to behave, not like the image I held of 'Tommy Atkins', who was kind, tolerant, easily put upon, yet considerate to old folk and especially good with children. This conflict of fact and imagery confused me; why were these lads behaving like this? My innocence had taken another blow.[15]

If the military needed houses, they were simply requisitioned. The bürgermeister was told, 'We want that home, that home and that home and it was his job to clear them out and ten minutes later we would move in.'[16] The results could be tragic.

One pathetic thing [in Frankfurt] when they were clearing an area for SHAEF headquarters, they gave the Germans about 24 hours to evacuate their buildings and it was sad to see them bringing out what little they could save. One woman had a wagon that she was piling her most precious possessions in and she asked me to watch the wagon while she went into the house to get some more stuff. And then they called an ambulance down the block. It seems there was an invalid in one of the apartments and they were told that they had to leave, and the husband couldn't move his wife because she was bedridden, and so he shot her, and then they didn't need the house, after all.[17]

The black market thrived on German cameras, binoculars, watches and pistols. The watches were standard Wehrmacht issue and were of higher quality than any that could be found in the Allied ranks. Many were sent home to friends and relatives; others sold or bartered. But it was the pistols that brought in the real money.

Whenever we went back on 'rest', wherever we finished up, we would soon be located by some Americans. They would roar up in their jeeps, their pockets loaded with English pound notes with which to bargain for any pistols we had. The going rate was £10 for a P.38, and £12 for a Luger; other makes would be the subject of a sale at lesser terms. It may not sound all that much today but as a British soldier received about £1-05 a week, a single Luger represented a couple of months' pay. We would send the money home in the private 'green' envelopes, free from censorship. The money was a welcome addition, especially to the wives and families of those who were living on the basic Army pay. It was freely bandied about that the Americans concerned were deserters, living on the black market. Whatever they were, they did an honest deal by us – though I sometimes wonder how many American citizens have been shot by the weapons we sold.[18]

By late March the non-fraternisation rule, though still formally in place, was widely seen as unworkable. Boy meets girls was one factor (as a national serviceman in the late 1950s I was told the then old joke that every maternity hospital in Germany had a monument to the unknown soldier) but equally hard to resist were the signs of welcome and relief along the way. Many who were genuinely opposed to Nazism now, at last, felt free to speak out;

others were simply gratified that a long-lost cause had finally been put out of its agony. There were notable exceptions, of course, and we will come to those in a moment, but for the most part the demonstrations of amity were spontaneous and convincing. For the invaders, the biggest surprise was their reception in the once mighty industrial cities of the Ruhr. Vital for the war effort, the workforce had been well treated under Nazism.

> Great sectors of the Krupp works and other big industrial under-takings had been sent underground, and when bombs were falling the workers could work, eat or sleep, all below ground, in almost certain safety. They had been privileged, too. There were special rations served in the great underground canteens; there was less of a drink shortage in the Ruhr than anywhere else; and the shops had silk stockings and underclothes, lipsticks and powder for sale in plenty. Even by Paris and Brussels standards, it was a revelation; and compared with the austerities of wartime Britain, it was paradise.[19]

But despite the close attention of the Gestapo and the takeover of the labour unions by Nazi stooges, many on the democratic left had remained true to their principles while others, who may once have been attracted to the regulated and, for a time, highly successful economy created by the Nazis, were disillusioned by Hitler's imperialist ambitions and the inevitable retributions. The irony was that the ban on political activity, imposed as stringently by the Allies as it had been by Berlin, put a temporary brake on social democracy. A more relaxed policy and an awareness that not all those who had lived under Nazism were devoted to the cause, would have brought positive results that went beyond the display of white flags and cheering in the streets.

Long deprived of family life, soldiers who were billeted in German households responded to acts of kindness. They responded also to parents, much like their own except for language, who had lost their sons in war. Tom Flanagan lodged in a house where several campaign medals including an Iron Cross were on display. But what really caught his eye was the medal awarded to the mother. '"For rendering six sons to the Wehrmacht. Heil Hitler." This silenced our talk.

One family to lose six sons in the war, even Germans, was awful, yet it seemed odd that an award to a mother should be made.'[20]

Grudging sympathy became real with Flanagan's next billet. This was at Neinburg, one of the many towns that had surrendered almost eagerly. The roads were undamaged and most houses and shops still intact.

> The luxury of being able to live in a normal house was a contrast which took time to appreciate. I was offered a bed upstairs and we were shown the kitchen and the dining room where we could prepare and eat our food. The men bedded down in the front room. It was like being received at a hotel.
>
> Ludwig, the Frau's husband, remained silent as all this was going on leaving his nervous chatty wife to deal with us. She was able to speak to us in English and seemed to delight in doing anything to make us more comfortable. Yet I could sense that beneath this bubbly exterior there was a terrifying fear. This was understandable. Men of the invading British Army were in her house: she and Ludwig were hostages in the town where they had lived for years. Each move and gesture was of self protection – nothing should offend us, whatever she did was done in order to please us. Ludwig, seemingly immobile in his armchair by the window in the dining room, to whom she would refer for his nod of confirmation during her rapid and continuous conversation with the nearest of us, was ill at ease. At his side, a table littered with the commonplace of home – his pipe and ashtray, his spectacle case, a candlestick and an ornament in the form of a small bowl of flowers, behind which, in a silver frame was the photograph of a young man in the uniform of the German army. An Iron Cross medal hung from the black, white and red ribbon which was positioned over the frame.
>
> By evening the Jocks in my section with their boisterous cheerfulness innocently put at ease this woman who behaved and looked much like anyone's aunt or fussy mother, for she became less frenetic and Ludwig began to lose his grey haunted look. Presently she asked if we would like eggs for tea. Someone replied much to her amusement, 'Ya Frau . . . danke . . . Alles Eieir for "Tommy", ya?'

We spent 36 hours in the pleasant billet with Mr and Mrs Ludwig as the pair came to be known. She would sometimes look at some of the younger Jocks, and she would shake her head in a gesture of both sadness and despair for them. Pity and fear was contained in that gesture as she would look from them to the silver framed photograph.

By this time we had asked who the young man was, expecting the answer that was given. It was Frederich, their only son. He had been killed in action on the 2nd September, 1939, during the invasion of Poland. This was an event in their lives from which neither had recovered. The youngsters who crowded into her front room and who, now that they were becoming familiar to her, would jest and tease her, brought back to them both memories of their soldier son who had been the age of these boys when he died. It was difficult to connect this couple with the hated Nazis.

This motherly lady brought out the good manners of the Jocks. She was given bread whenever they ate. White bread was a revelation to the couple, not having seen any for years. The gift of half a loaf of white bread brought tearful thanks much to the embarrassment of us all.[21]

Meeting up with the enemy could be a confusing experience, leading men on both sides to wonder how they had got to this point.

Guy le Grand was a battalion sergeant major with the 290th Combat Engineer Battalion. Attached to an armoured division which led the way into Bavaria, by April 30th he was in Bernau, twenty-eight miles west of Berchtesgaden. What had been a doctor's house, a sturdy three-storey building, was chosen as a billet. Having assigned sleeping quarters, le Grand chose for himself a bedroom in the servants' wing of the house which had its own entrance. He was writing letters when there was a knock on the door.

I yelled 'Come in'. No one entered and the knock was repeated. I walked to the door and opened it. In the dim light that shone from the bedroom I saw before me a fully armed German soldier, his Mauser dimly silhouetted against the grey-green uniform. I stood cold! What had happened? Where was the guard?

With nowhere to go, thousands of Germans were made homeless by the Allied
bombing campaign in the last months of the war.

Before and after. The Brandenburg Gate at the end of Berlin's Unter Den Linden in 1938 (*above*) and 1945 (*below*).

Berlin residents emerge from an air raid shelter.

Feeding the children. Many went hungry.

Meagre rations. With near-starvation in the cities, a dead horse could not go to waste.

Basic food in the shops always attracted long queues.

Every bombsite had
the potential for a
vegetable patch.

With winter
coming on, Berlin
was stripped of its
remaining trees.

In the ruins of a city there was a semblance of normal life.

Black marketeers are rounded up for questioning.

On the way home. German soldiers straggle across the Dutch border.

The lucky one? A former German soldier contemplates a bleak future.

In the aftermath of war, life goes on.

He was a young man, not more than 22, standing a little under average height and stockily built. He had removed his light wool cap, revealing a dishevelled mass of blonde hair. His blue eyes were tired and sunken, he was badly in need of a shave, and his clothing was so mud-covered that it was hardly possible to determine what gear was attached to his belt.

He spoke first, saying 'I am very hungry and very tired.' He hoped to get something to eat before being taken into a prisoner stockade.

Guy le Grand gave his visitor food, showed him where he could wash and then the two men talked. Their conversation set le Grand thinking. He was giving comfort to one of the Wehrmacht, a soldier who might well have killed Americans. Yet, 'he looked like one of us – like any one of the privates in my own company. With what blame could I fairly charge him? In justice to himself and to the doctrine which had been taught him could he have done otherwise but fight for what he either accepted or gave pretense of accepting? Was he different from me except that he was on the losing side? What hope did the future hold for him?'

There were no easy answers. Le Grand turned over his prisoner to the duty sergeant. 'The Sergeant relieved the soldier of his rifle and took him over to the stockade in the town. As they left, they passed near me. The boy turned his head and in the same quiet tone as when I first saw him, said: "Thank you". I never learned his name.'[22]

It was not all peace and light by any means. There were those on both sides who could not get to grips with what was happening. No one could be quite sure how an area of population, large or small, would react when the first tanks approached the suburbs.

Mannheim surrendered by telephone ('I am one of the city officials. Please don't shoot any more. There are now no soldiers left in Mannheim.')

At Hoxter:

As our infantrymen moved in, a substantial number of German troops retreated across the river and then blew up the bridge. With Hoxter now undefended, the burgermeister, the chief of police and an interpreter appeared under a white flag. I went along with Major Sellars and a few other officers to the town hall where – in a beautifully furnished room – in flickering candlelight the mayor signed an unconditional surrender. But the incident I remember most occurred just after the signing. The German interpreter, who spoke flawless English, turned to us Americans and smiled amiably. 'Is anyone here from Jersey?' he asked. 'I was born there.'[23]

Another town that gave up without a shot was Weimar, birthplace of the post-World War One republic. Representatives of the Third Army gave the surrender ultimatum to the bürgermeister of Troistedt, a village three miles out of Weimar. He promptly cycled off to deliver the message to his grander counterpart who then came himself by official car to deliver up the city of Goethe, Schiller and Liszt. He brought with him the Fischers, husband and wife psychologists who spoke perfect English. Dr Erica Fischer had an American mother who had lived in Germany throughout the war. The curiosities were endless though the greatest of all had still to be revealed, that this city of cultural and political sophistication had by its side the Konzentrationslager, also known as Buchenwald.

The places difficult to handle were those where a Nazi administration – a Gauleiter – still held power. In Hannover, the reigning thug threatened death to anyone who put out a white flag. But deserted by all but a small circle of nervous functionaries, he had to stand by while American infantrymen marched in and then to suffer, for him, the ultimate humiliation as a Jewish captain was appointed military governor.

Düsseldorf was more of a challenge, both to those citizens who were ready to face reality and to the American troops who were installed on the west bank of the Rhine. From March 2nd through to April 17th, those in the main part of the city over on the east side were subject to constant bombardment, at first from across the river and later from encircling forces of the First and Ninth Armies. Gauleiter Karl Friedrich Florian was one of the last of Hitler's old guard. Stubborn beyond fanaticism, his orders were inconsistent and bizarre. While he had faith that 'the Führer will turn the tide of fate this year and that victory will ultimately be ours', he was reconciled to the destruction of Düsseldorf, urging families with children to evacuate their homes so that they could live to fight on in the more secure areas of the Reich. Few believed in his protestations of 'trust in the Volk and the community which will take you in', or indeed in his 'undying support for the Führer with whom we will battle for a victorious peace'.[24] The popular hope was for a quick American incursion that would settle the matter once and for all. Florian's only support came from remnants of the SS and the Hitler Youth who craved martyrdom without knowing what that really meant.

Werner Tabel was a sixteen-year-old Volksstuermer whose first experience of death was witnessing the execution of a deserter.

As the Americans ate their lunch on the other side of the Rhine, it was our turn too to go and eat. Taking our plates down to the cellar, excitement suddenly broke out. A couple of chaps were standing at the cellar window shouting 'The deserter! – he's going to be shot! Why are they carrying the swine? (Let me see too!)'

I deliver him his last wish – a piece of bread and butter and a cup of coffee but he hardly notices . . . I too manage to get a good place by the window, seeing a crowd of grey uniforms. I wonder whether I really wanted to watch – I'd only ever seen executions in films. A sergeant spots us and tells us to clear off and eat our dinner, but our sensationalism is too great.

. . . The delinquent is standing in front of a tall tree, still bare of leaves. He is wearing just a pair of civilian trousers and a light, dirty shirt. Next to the condemned man is another man in a black robe – I could barely believe my eyes – it seemed so out of place in the atmosphere we'd lived in over the past weeks. The clergyman steps back and army doctor P takes the man and ties him to the tree, the vicar making a sign of blessing. The doctor then blindfolds the man with a Hitler Youth scarf. Involuntarily I take a step aside so the wall blocks my view as a voice yells the order to fire. I hear the salvo and then one last shot.

We return to our plates in silence, but before long a cacophony of voices breaks out – everyone feels the need to talk about what he has just witnessed, as we shove huge pieces of food in our mouths. Our appetite gains the upper hand and the executed deserter is almost forgotten. Then our sergeant comes in – 'You two first tables! Grab a strip of canvas and come with me – you can eat your grub afterwards!' Surely we don't have to . . . isn't that for the really hardened blokes who've been at the front? A yellowing, bloody body lies at the foot of the birch tree. 'Have you got the canvas? Put him in it and then chuck him in the pigsty!' Fancy disturbing our lunch for that! We try to move him – his shirt is open and we can see bloody holes on his hairy chest – he's also been shot in the temple. He doesn't have any shoes on! Oh, he was wearing a great pair of jackboots – we should see if we can get hold of them! We all try to heave him in but no one wants to touch the bloody corpse.

We leave him in the pigsty, no one thinks to cover him up. Then we go back to the smell of roast meat in the cellar – better wash our hands first, someone says. I notice that mine are clean – I didn't touch the corpse. I also notice that we're pretty damn hard-boiled ourselves.[25]

Opposition to Florian came from Düsseldorf's business and professional community who knew that they had nothing to gain and everything to lose by prolonging the war. One group, including an architect, a baker, a decorator and a lawyer, hatched a plan for a citizens' surrender of the city. Making contact with Police Chief Franz Juergens who was known to have opposed Florian's evacuation order as the preliminary to total destruction, they were given an encouraging welcome. 'He fetched his last bottle of wine from the cupboard and fished around for four last cigarettes and a cigar. The men drank and smoked together before their decisive act as if they had something to celebrate . . . Juergens distributed passes and even made available a police car – a six-seater Mercedes and driver.'[26]

Confident of their mission, the coup leaders made directly for the man most likely to put up serious opposition, SS Brigadeführer August Korreng. But if they hoped that the arrest of Korreng would bring about the collapse of Nazi authority, they were disappointed.

The SS staged a counter-coup. Five of the peace party, including Franz Juergens, were brought before a military tribunal and summarily executed. Gauleiter Florian made one last appeal to follow Hitler's scorched-earth edict.

The enemy, mercilessly fighting us under Jewish leadership, is telling lies as he always has. His demands to wait and trust him are the cheese in the mousetrap. It is the English and American enemy's intention to starve us to death, just as they have been starving Indians in India, Boers in Africa and native Indians in America for centuries. In the occupied areas they are already ruthlessly carrying out these intentions with German people. The Germans are to die a wretched death as slaves. This Anglo-American starvation is as atrocious as the red Bolshevik starvation. Anyone who believes the enemy's word is a coward and traitor to his own people and to himself. He has forfeited his life for good. Evacuation procedures undertaken out of military necessity must therefore be followed conscientiously. Anyone who refuses is a traitor and will be treated as such. There is a clear reason for this decision and its consequences. The Führer is waiting for the right moment to deploy the entire force of our German will and resistance for us to achieve the expected turn against our misfortune. It is up to him to decide when this will happen. Dear citizens! Absolutely nothing which could be used to destroy our Volk, be it human or material, may fall into enemy hands. It is the duty of everyone to ensure that the necessary measures are strictly carried out. In spite of everything, we believe in German's immortality!

Long live the Führer!

Long live our German citizens!

Long live our sacred homeland![27]

The last act was witnessed by Willi Kallbach.

As fire rained upon us from the other side of the Rhine, we erected a road block of tree trunks, and German soldiers dug trenches to shoot from.

On the morning of 15.4.45 three American tanks were sighted. A sniper hit the first one with a Panzerfaust and it burned up just in front of the pub 'Zur Deller'. The second was also shot head on, and burned down in the little wood just before Vennhauser Allee. The third one shot at the snipers with machine gun fire.

At this time fighting was taking place at the Toennesberg and a German lieutenant who saw that the Sonnenhof farm had raised the white flag shot their barn into flames. After the Americans had taken the Toennesberg they went for the anti-aircraft with tanks and artillery.

They sent a further three tanks to Unterbach in the afternoon – this time they had tied German soldiers they'd taken prisoner at Toennesberg onto the first two tanks. Those tanks came back unharmed.[28]

Florian survived to be put on trial but escaped punishment. Korreng died by his own hand. On that day eleven-year-old Hildegard Kleinfeld had a more pressing matter to think about than the future of her city.

It was my mother's birthday. I was 11, my father was at war, and even with my little pocketmoney I didn't know how to find a present for her. One of my playmates had an idea though, and secretly we crept out of the cellar where we'd been living for weeks on end. We ran quickly to Corneliusplatz, where a beautiful magnolia tree was in blossom. I quickly picked a bunch of flowers and my friend cut off a whole branch with his pocket knife. We felt rather guilty. We wanted to get home quickly before anyone noticed, but then heavy shelling set in. We couldn't find a cellar to hide in, so we pressed ourselves against the walls of dilapidated houses, ran a few steps, heard once more the whistle of the bomb, laid flat on the ground, stumbled forth and then hid in a pile of rubble. We waited for a while, then set off. A large group of people had gathered around a little girl who was lying in a pool of blood screaming. Suddenly it went quiet – she was dead. We held hands and walked home in silence, where my mum waited for us in tears – she had been looking for me all over. My flowers fell to the ground unnoticed as she hugged me hard.[29]

16

On the Way to the Elbe

The discovery and opening of the concentration camps put the brake on expressions of good nature towards Germans in and out of uniform. That the camps were there was common knowledge to occupiers and occupied. As early as January, the Russians had released gruesome accounts of what they had found at Auschwitz in Poland where, it was said, hundreds of thousands of prisoners had been systematically slaughtered. But horrors imagined are more bearable than horrors seen. Those who witnessed the relics of humanity locked in their cages could never cleanse their minds of the terrible imagery.

Ed Murrow, the best known radio reporter of the war, followed the US Third Army into Buchenwald on April 12th.

There surged around me an evil-smelling horde, men and boys reached out to touch me. They were in rags and the remnants of uniform. Death had already marked many of them, but they were smiling with their eyes. I looked out over that mass of men to the green fields beyond where well-fed Germans were ploughing. A German, Fritz Kersheimer, came up and said: 'May I show you round the camp? I've been here ten years.' An Englishman stood to attention saying: 'May I introduce myself? Delighted to see you, and can you tell me when some of our blokes will be along?' I told him 'soon', and asked to see one of the barracks. It happened to be occupied by the Czechoslovakians. When I entered men crowded round; tried to lift me to their shoulders. They were too weak; many of them could not get out of bed. I was told that this building had once stabled 80 horses; there were twelve hundred men in it, five to a bunk. The stink was beyond all description.

In another part of the camp, Ed Murrow discovered where they kept the children, some as young as six.

One rolled up his sleeve and showed me his number: it was tattooed on his arm. B.6030 it was. The others showed me their numbers; they will carry them till they die. An elderly man standing beside me said: 'The children – enemies – of the State.' I could see their ribs through their thin shirts. The old man said: 'I am Professor Charles Richer of the Sorbonne.' The children clung to my hands and stared. We crossed to the courtyard. Men kept coming up to speak to me and to touch me: professors from Poland, doctors from Vienna; men from all over Europe.[1]

Every one of the 21,000 inmates of Buchenwald was in urgent need of medical help. Even after the Americans moved in to destroy 'those stinking, infamous huts' the death rate was forty a day. The desperately sick were moved into the SS hospital outside the compound. For the rest the cleaning-up operation began around them as they were deloused, given fresh clothing and fed a controlled diet of meat and vegetable soup to build them up to strength for a square meal.

Four days after the first reports from Buchenwald, tanks of the Eleventh Armoured Division of the British Second Army, working their way through the pinewoods south of Hamburg, crashed through a high barbed wire fence. They had arrived at Bergen-Belsen where 37,000 prisoners had died from starvation, disease and slave labour. The first soldier into the camp was a young Intelligence Officer, Derrick Sington. Passing through the main gates, barrack blocks and huts, he found an inner compound.

It reminded me of the entrance to a zoo. We came into a smell of ordure – like the smell of a monkey-house. A sad, blue smoke floated like ground mist between the low buildings. I had tried to imagine the interior of a concentration camp but I had not imagined it like this. Nor had I imagined the strange, simian throng, who crowded the barbed wire fences surrounding their compounds, with their shaven heads and their obscene striped penitentiary suits . . .

We had been welcomed before but the half-credulous cheers of these almost lost men, of these clowns in their terrible motley, who had once been Polish officers, land-workers in the Ukraine, Budapest doctors and students in France, impelled a stronger emotion and I had to fight back my tears.[2]

Built to hold 8,000 prisoners, Belsen now had over 40,000 crammed into eighty single-storey huts where they lay on wooden shelves, dead and dying huddled together.

Richard Dimbleby relived the nightmare for BBC listeners. His broadcast went out on April 19th.

> I picked my way over corpse after corpse in the gloom, until I heard one voice raised above the gentle undulating moaning. I found a girl, she was a living skeleton, impossible to gauge her age for she had practically no hair left, and her face was only a yellow parchment sheet with two holes in it for eyes. She was stretching out her stick of an arm and gasping something, it was 'English, English, medicine, medicine', and she was trying to cry but she hadn't enough strength. And beyond her down the passage and in the hut there were the convulsive movements of dying people too weak to raise themselves from the floor.

Dimbleby watched as a woman, 'distraught to the point of madness', flung herself at a British soldier begging for milk for her baby.

> She laid the mite on the ground and threw herself at the sentry's feet and kissed his boots. And when, in his distress, he asked her to get up, she put the baby in his arms and ran off crying that she would find milk for it because there was no milk in her breast. And when the soldier opened the bundle of rags to look at the child, he found that it had been dead for days.[3]

Of the most notorious of Nazi concentration camps, Dachau, outside Munich, had been the first to be inaugurated by Himmler's SS, in 1933, and the last to be closed. US troops of the Seventh Army opened the gates on April 29th.

> Now it is revealed for all to see. I looked upon 400 dead inmates stacked in piles of six before the doors of six large ovens, awaiting cremation. They say it takes one and a half hours to reduce the

bodies to ashes, so if the fires are tended properly, a large number of bodies can be handled in 24 hours. The record daily run for all the furnaces was 2,500. Great piles of clothing remain as mute testimony to those who have departed this world. All the bodies I saw had been subjected to long-term starvation and disease; only skin covering the bones of their naked bodies. The filth and stench was unbelievable and we were unable to partake of food for many hours afterward. Forty freight cars were counted nearby, piled high with dead awaiting their turn at the crematories, while over 30,000 live skeletons or 'political' prisoners were jammed in cages fenced in with charged electric wire. I mention all these gruesome details because the world will never see this place as it is today and will never want to believe that such evil acts took place.[4]

Dachau had been in the grip of the 'angel of death', otherwise known as typhus, since November 1944. Shortly before his own death from typhus, Johann Maria Lenz, a prisoner in Dachau, wrote of his experiences trying to nurse the victims.

Conscientious specialist such as the Czech doctor Blaha, one of our co-prisoners, had dared to report [the outbreak of typhus] to the SS head doctor Hintermaier so that he could take action. The answer was a strict order of secrecy, with the threatened punishment of sabotage. It was only after Christmas that the official order came from Berlin to partially quarantine the camp. Typhus fever had already taken hold of the SS too . . . From the night of February 28th to March 1st Block 21 was to be deloused and disinfected. The poor inmates had to bathe. Their clothes were taken off them to the very last item and they were brought for disinfection. This was a cruel matter, these poor people feared it like death, for it meant for them, staying in the bath from 10–20 hours. Naked – in winter. How many of them broke down and died. How I would have liked to be with them in their last hour. But it was too late – I was no longer able to.[5]

If anything good can be said to have come out of the concentration camps, it has to be the selfless devotion of the medical teams who found life where others had seen only death. Three weeks after Belsen was liberated, war reporter Mea Allan, who wrote for the *Daily Herald* in London, described the camp as 'one vast hospital'.

> the majority of internees are still not human beings, they are still lost in the coma of starvation and horror which has sucked them of their senses, their responsiveness to the world about them, their social responsibility to others. But they no longer scream and wail piteously when food is shown them for they have learned they will get their rations – their food will not be stolen from them.

Each day, a thousand or more former prisoners were dusted, bathed and reclothed. These were the healthy ones, by Belsen standards, 'those fit enough to stand up and drag one foot after another'.

> In a large open-fronted shed, lines of perforated piping beamed the ceiling. Each internee got a piece of anti-louse soap, a flannel and a towel, and the water was turned on the lines of naked bodies standing below. It was such a shock – the removal of clothes, the water, the disinfectant and the heat of the day – that many fainted, some dropped dead. The other section was for the non-fit cases who were too weak to stand. They were lifted from the truck, stripped and laid on the sloping lead-covered tables, to be scrubbed clean of the filth that caked them. Then, wrapped in an Army blanket, the likely survivors were taken to the hospital.[6]

Thousands more were in urgent need of medical attention. Among the volunteers rushed in to help were a hundred students from London hospitals. One of them was David Bradford, who kept a diary of his time at Belsen.

> We continued feeding the patients as well as we could, dosing them with aspirins, etc., and noting any new cases of Typhus. Medical treatment is pretty well impossible under such conditions, and it is awful to have to refuse patients asking for treatment and asking to be taken away to hospital. They are still evacuating people at the rate of 500 per day to the hospital in Camp II and a group of students are clearing huts and turning them into hospital huts by taking the

worst cases from some of the worst huts. At the moment, the hospital at Camp II has over 5,000 patients and has been built up from scratch in 13 days. In this hospital more reasonable conditions prevail, and it is staffed by German nurses and 60 German doctors who have been released from a P.O.W. camp.[7]

For those able to absorb basic food the day started with Bengal Famine soup, so called because it was first used in the Bengal famine of 1943. It consisted of powdered milk, flour, salt and sugar. Most complained it was too sweet. At 2.00 p.m. there was a different soup and jacket potatoes and patients were given two vitamin pills a day. Within a week Bradford was able to give his patients a slice of bread with butter and treacle.

The horrors did not stop with the discovery of those camps with names to remember. Soldiers' reminiscences of this time frequently refer to chance encounters with martyrs of the Reich. The stories continue right up to the surrender and even beyond. Entering Ohrdruf, south of Muhlberg, men of the Fourth Armoured Division of the US Third Army captured an elaborate communications centre with radio equipment and telephone switchboards powerful enough to serve an entire city set deep in concrete bunkers. But there was more. On the outskirts of the village was North Stalag III. A handful of skeletal survivors told how SS guards had murdered and burned 4,000 prisoners.

The grisly evidence was there. Thirty-one bodies sprawled in an open place in the camp. Too weak from hunger and sickness to march, they had been shot. In the throat or head of each corpse was a hole left by a pistol bullet. The wasted bodies could not have had much blood, but the ground was soaked.

In a shed, stacked on each other like cordwood, were 30 more bodies, all naked. Lime sprinkled on the dead did not conceal massive sores and scabs left by disease and brutality. There had not been time to burn these bodies.

The disposal pits were back in the woods, where spruce branches and pine logs could be cut easily for the pyres. Charred scraps of human bodies and grey ashes of bone littered the pits where the dead had been burned and dumped. The method was simple. The cadavers were stacked on a grill of logs and rails and a detail of firemen kept the flames hot enough.

Combat veterans, who had seen death many times, stared silently at the Nazi slaughterhouse. Now and then they cursed softly. They could understand the death of the battlefield, but this deliberate, bestial murder was beyond their understanding.[8]

Another sort of tragedy was related by Dr Arnold Horwell, an interpreter with the Second Army. When, a few days after the German capitulation, troops entered Neungamme, a concentration camp southeast of Hamburg, they found it empty. They soon discovered what had happened to the inmates. 'The Nazis had packed them on some out-dated naval vessels, when the British approached, and anchored the ships outside Kiel harbour, where they were bombed to bits by the RAF. One ship "escaped" – we found it floating in the Baltic, with 2,000 corpses aboard; starved to death.'[9]

Atrocities were not limited to the camps. Approaching the town of Ohligs, the Ninety-Fourth Infantry Division heard rumours of a recent mass burial.

Investigations were started and the grave located in a sandpit off a lonely road . . . As an object lesson, the task of exhuming the bodies was assigned to a detail of 40 known local Nazi Party members, largely professional and business men. Many reported in their best dress clothing and high hats. Numbered among the group was a banker, reportedly one of the wealthiest in the Ruhr. A goodly number of the group were of the opinion that they were being taken out to be executed. Before setting to work the Nazi digging party was admonished that if a careless shovel struck a single one of the corpses the job would be finished by hand. Then the work began. Sixty-four of the 71 bodies found were identified. All were political prisoners. Prior to the fall of the Ruhr Pocket, these people had been brought to the sandpit by truck, tied together in twos and shot through the back of the head. Investigation later revealed the date of the mass murder as April 13th, 1945.[10]

By now public outrage engendered by graphic coverage of Nazi crimes in the world press and radio had turned to calls for retribution. Allied commanders made no attempt to exercise restraint. Quite the opposite, in fact. By rounding up local citizens and forcing them to observe at first hand the horrors perpetuated in their name, they gave credence to the reflex conviction that the Germans were a barbaric people, alone capable of such excesses. No matter that many of the occupants of the camps were themselves German or that many ordinary Germans found it hard to live with such terrible revelations.

One day in early April I went for a walk with my baby. We headed for the railway station, not because I wanted to see the trains again, but because it was such a nice walk. I had a frightful shock as a procession of people, sad figures, came along the street behind the station. I simply froze with my pram and didn't know whether to go on and let these people pass or to stand and stare at them. Soldiers, mostly SS men with fixed bayonets, were walking alongside them and I realised: they are prisoners! My God, they are prisoners! They had all been shorn, they had no hair, you couldn't tell the men apart from the women, they were wearing striped clothing and looked like the living dead. I was so shocked that I didn't know what was happening. Where had these people come from? Where were they going? My God, what was happening?

They were led around the outskirts of the village so as to avoid the centre and it was a huge crowd, there were so many people! Most of them were holding each other up and dragging their feet. They looked undernourished and dirty, just as we had done a few weeks previously. I stayed still and tears of pity flowed down my cheeks. I don't know how long I stood there. I was so emotional, I started to tremble, and my heart ached with agitation and woe . . . Much later I found out that they were prisoners from a concentration camp, I had no idea about that. Prisoners from a nearby concentration camp which this Hitler thug had dissolved as the Americans approached so fast. They thought they could lead these people away so that the Americans wouldn't find them and see what they had done to their own citizens. I went back home with a heavy heart and was beside myself the whole day. I told no one; I simply couldn't talk about it. I was distraught for several days, and kept telling myself that it was bound to come to no good. It would be a miracle if we weren't all killed in the last days of the war, if we weren't to be punished for everything the others had done.[11]

A growing chorus in the popular press in Britain and America called for the extermination of the entire German race, few bothering to point out the parallels between such sadistic outbursts and the Nazi philosophy that had brought the camps into being. Calmer voices went largely unheard.

The British soldiers who took over Belsen had no time to inquire into the background of the SS men and women who had remained behind. They had no time to inquire how Belsen itself had come about. They looked around, and what they saw made them mad with rage. They beat the SS Guards and set them to collecting the bodies of the dead, keeping them always at the double; back and forth they went all day long, always running, men and women alike, from the death pile to the death pit, with the stringy remains of their victims over their shoulders. When one of them dropped to the ground with exhaustion, he was beaten with a rifle-butt. When another stopped for a break, she was kicked until she ran again, or prodded with a bayonet to the accompaniment of lewd shouts and laughs. When one tried to escape, or disobeyed an order, he was shot. Under the circumstances, it was impossible to have any sympathy for these guards. The cruelties they had practised, or the neglect they had condoned, were appalling. The punishment they got was in the best Nazi tradition, and few of them survived it; but it made one pensive to see British soldiers beating and kicking men and women, even under such provocation. These SS guards were a brutalised and inhuman lot, and yet when you talked to their victims it seemed that they were, in many cases, by far the best of the lot; the worst had decamped while they still had time, and would probably never be caught.[12]

Writing in the *Nation*, the movie critic James Agee warned that the atrocity newsreels shown throughout the States encouraged 'us to confuse the German people with the few criminals who perpetrated the crimes', adding 'there can be no bestiality so discouraging to contemplate as that of the man of good will when he is misusing his heart and mind'. In Britain, the left-wing journal *Tribune* made the point, largely ignored by other papers, that the camps were for 'the martyrs of anti-Fascism'.

'Is our Press so gagged as that of Hitler's Germany that no one dares to mention these facts? Has it become so pervaded with that spirit of despicable Jingoist hypocrisy that even the fearful discovery of Buchenwald serves but as yet another peg for the monotonous reiteration of the tale that all Germans are equally guilty?'[13]

So it would have seemed.

The SS could expect no mercy. A detachment cornered a few miles from Dachau was persuaded to surrender, then lined up and shot. The first SS officer to come forward was cut down with an entrenching tool. All told, forty-one men and two officers were executed. No inquiry was ordered or disciplinary action taken.[14] As Tom Pocock noted, 'the liberators, the victors and indeed, all who had been involved with the opening of the concentration camps had, to some degree, been infected by them and it was not with typhus.'[15]

The infection spread. With no direct knowledge of the camps beyond what they read in the newspapers there were those who felt empowered by what they thought they knew, to impose lynch law.

I went back down the lines to see the HLI company who were taking over from us later in the day. I arrived as a very young German prisoner, a member of the Hitler Jugend, was being interrogated by the CO of the company. He called the smaller of the two sentries over and instructed him to take the prisoner back to battalion HQ to hand him over to the Intelligence Officer. The Jock from the HLI prodded the German with the muzzle of his Lee Enfield, indicating to him to move. The German led off down the road with the Jock close behind, his rifle pointing at the small of the back of the German.

Shortly after this we were interrupted in our discussions by the sound of shots outside and we all ducked for cover.

'What's going on?' shouted a voice, 'Can you see anything?' This latter question was addressed to the guard on duty. Before he could answer the prisoner's escort turned the corner.

'It was me, Sir. He kept on saying "I die for my Führer . . . I die for my Führer" . . . well . . . the bugger's dead . . .! Aye . . . he is . . . !'

'For . . . !' exploded the Company Commander, but he got no further and waved his arms irritably, shooing the escort away. 'Get back to where you should be, you . . . you . . .' and he dried up.[16]

It is one of the not so little ironies of these tales of inhumanity that in all the coverage given to the concentration camps, there were few references to the fate of the Jews. Yet they accounted for over half the population of the camps. Even the Soviet reports on Auschwitz, where more than a million Jews perished, made no mention of the one thing that most of the victims had in common. While it is just possible that, despite all the warnings, the public imagination had failed to grasp the enormity of Hitler's final solution, it is inconceivable that the political establishment in Washington and London was ignorant of the Nazi ambition to wipe out European Jewry. A more likely explanation for the tardy response to the particular nature of Jewish suffering was the realisation that making much of it at this stage would have invited criticism of those American and British politicians, now in the forefront of the war effort, who had held back on, even obstructed, efforts to save Jewish lives when there had still been time. Neither America nor Britain had reasons to be proud of their pre-war response to cries for help. Anti-Semitism, in varying degrees of violence, was by no means restricted to Germany and Austria. But to have conceded as much would have detracted from what, almost subconsciously, had become a major Allied war aim – to saddle the Germans with a collective guilt.

To argue that right-minded Germans should have risen up en masse against an undisputed evil was hypocrisy on two counts. Moral and physical cowardice is part of the human condition. Few are able to plead not guilty to one or other or both. It is hard to believe that other nationalities, held by a barbarous regime, would have acted more bravely than the Germans, yet that is precisely what was suggested by the concept of collective guilt. But also studiously ignored by the Allies was the extent to which they themselves had helped to frustrate a civil uprising by failing to support anti-Hitler groups and by bombing out of existence the centres where resistance was likely to emerge. 'What they did by their destruction,' said a witness from the US Strategic Bombing Survey, 'was to disperse the population all over the country and so prevent anti-Nazi men and women meeting and forming an effective opposition.'[17]

Whatever the strength of this argument, it is beyond question that the demonising of the Germans by the Allies was a useful cover to their own war crimes. The ruse did not last for long. Ironically it was the Russians, with most to hide, who gave the lie to collective guilt by creating the east-west divide. In the Cold War, the Soviet Union took over the villain's role. The Germans or, at least the West Germans, were the friends of democracy and so were given a more sympathetic hearing in the west than might have been expected in the early months of 1945 when the victors' self-righteousness was at its peak.

Those survivors of the concentration camps who were made fit enough took to the roads. Sometimes they were helped to find their way home; more often not. They were joined by, and not always distinguishable from, hundreds of thousands of workers who had been brought in from occupied countries to bolster the Nazi war machine. This was a chequered community for whom the collective term – displaced persons – did not even begin to reflect a range of humanity that went all the way from Russian prisoners who had been put on forced labour to French nationals who had been persuaded to sign up in return for spurious promises of special treatment for their families. Czechs, Rumanians, Italians and Dutch, all were strongly represented. How they reacted, as German defeat became ever more certain, invariably depended on how they had been treated by their masters.

We've seen them in bands of several hundreds at a time. They're not always emaciated, starving, ragged. Sometimes you wouldn't know they were slaves, except for their language, and the fact that they're laughing and chattering away, and waving and singing. But I've seen others, hungry, and even barefooted, mad with hate of the Germans, looting shops for food and clothes.[18]

The common aim was to cross the German border into friendly or home territory. Any form of transport was vulnerable if left unguarded. As a child in a family entirely of women, Uschi Lacey had special responsibility for looking after their only bicycle, an especially valued item since they lived some way from the nearest town.

I remember one occasion when two Poles were after my bike. They had to walk past our house and for the last 1.5 km it was a game of cat and mouse. I got off and waited each time they stopped, keeping a good 200 metres between us. They walked on, I rode on at walking speed of course. Our Behelfsheim (emergency housing) was at the edge of a small wood but because of a sharp bend in the road, the front of the house was clearly visible. I waited and waited, the two Poles obviously hiding in the wood. Eventually they got tired and walked on. Only when they had gone past the house did I get on my bike and rode furiously. As soon as they saw me they turned round ready to get me but I just managed to get home before they could get hold of my bike. They then started to abuse me verbally and I retaliated by threatening them with my father, who had not even returned from the war. But it worked, especially when the noise brought out my aunt and sister.[19]

Adding to the ant-like activity across Germany were the young men of the Wehrmacht who had long since given up the battle and were now looking to restore some sense of order to their lives, even if this had to come from their erstwhile enemies. 'We passed hundreds of them just marching down the road towards us,' wrote Major Gerald Ritchie. 'We just let them go on marching, neither side took much notice of the others.'[20]

When, eventually, they did end up in a POW camp, the treatment meted out depended on what was known or what was thought

353

to be known about each prisoner. Gert Hartwig Preis was unlucky. Someone told his British captors that he was in the SS.

A former member of the Waffen SS and four British soldiers with guns at the ready came and took me to an interrogation camp. I don't know if the British called it an interrogation camp but to us it seemed like that. I don't know if there were only Waffen SS prisoners there as it was a very large camp. I was there from May 1945 and was held until Christmas 1945. The camp was under a built up road with beds three and four on top of each other. There was no bedding, blankets or underwear to change into, and only very little food was given to us. We were interrogated occasionally. It was always the same British sergeant who interrogated us. He spoke perfect German and wrote down every answer that I gave him. I think he was trying to find out if I was lying to him. He told me the first time he interrogated me that if I lie to him he would put me away for 25 years. I told him that I do not tell lies. He asked me what I did in the army and I told him that I was a dispatch rider, his answer was 'Bloody Hell! You are the first German I've met that hasn't said he was a cook!'[21]

Another case of mistaken identity was that of Hugo Stehkämper who, two months before his sixteenth birthday, was drafted into the Volkssturm. He was decked out in an ill-fitting and much worn SS uniform. The image of invincibility was further tarnished by him having to wear a captured French helmet. Hugo was captured before he fired a shot but the giveaway uniform landed him in front of an American interrogator.

A soldier sat behind me, a big, strong man with a thick, black beard. Whether it was part of the interrogation, or he just got excited, I don't know, but this man jumped up, put his pistol to my head, and screamed 'You Werewolf!' Up to then he hadn't said a word and as you can imagine, I believed it was all over for me.

Then I was put through a second interrogation that ended with a similar result. Apparently I answered questions too poorly or too clumsily. I can't exactly praise myself for holding up very well.

Eventually, Hugo was thrown in with a group of prisoners on their way to France, where he was put in a special camp for youngsters under eighteen. The journey was memorable for all the wrong reasons.

I only had a sweater to protect me from the pouring rain and the cold. There just wasn't any shelter to be had. You stood there, wet through and through, in fields that couldn't be called fields anymore – they were ruined. You had to make an effort when you walked to even pull your shoes out of the mud.

Today it's incomprehensible to me how we could stand for many, many days without sitting, without lying down, just standing there, totally soaked. During the day we marched around, huddled together to try to warm each other a bit. At night we stood because we couldn't walk and tried to keep awake by singing or humming songs. Again and again someone got so tired his knees got weak and he collapsed. Then the whole group would fall over, and everybody bitched because they'd fallen in the mud.[22]

For the victors, encounters with prisoners were liable to be more dramatic when a high-ranking officer was involved. Reporting for CBS, Bill Downs was with a British unit when they came across a German army car, with a white flag as a pennant, parked in a farmyard.

We went to find out what it was all about and to our surprise up stepped one of the most magnificent German officers I've ever seen, complete with Iron Cross and a number of other decorations. My first-year college German was still intact enough to understand that he wanted to surrender – he had his belongings all packed including a pair of ski shoes – what he wanted with ski shoes I was never able to find out. He turned over his pistol and said that we could drive him back to captivity in his own car. Then the German colonel said that he'd like very much if we would take his entire battery prisoner. He was the commander of a battery of 88-mm. combination anti-tank and anti-aircraft guns. We decided against capturing the gun battery for we were not sure that a battery of 88s would appreciate being captured by just one Sten gun, no matter what the colonel said, but we took the colonel up on his offer to use his car. Sergeant Arthur drove the car – Sergeant Tinker reappeared with a cap full of eggs. The colonel climbed in and we made up a convoy – my jeep in front – the colonel's car in the middle with two sergeants, and the BBC truck with the two unarmed engineers bringing up the rear.[23]

Not so easy to handle was a German naval officer who resented an interrogation by Corporal Dai Evans.

He was about 24-years-old; tall, beautifully uniformed and full of courage. He seemed the personification of the *Herrenvolk* ideals of Hitler and the Nazis. He obviously loathed the idea of surrender, wished to deal only with an officer above the rank of Major and, at first, refused to give any details about himself. Under the circumstances this was ridiculous and I told him so. He made no effort to assist us so I said, 'Smudger, look in his breast pockets, see if there's any identification papers, paybook, passes or suchlike there.'

Smudger put his hand to open the officer's breast pocket. This wasn't to the officer's liking and he thrust the hand away with a fierce gesture. He'd picked the wrong man as Smudger simply backed off a pace, then clouted him on the jaw. The German reacted immediately by backing away and adopting a fighting posture, ready to defend himself.

'This won't do,' I thought, so, cocking my Sten with an ostentatious gesture, I pointed it at his chest. He had enough presence of mind to realise the odds stacked against him and, with an ill grace, put down his hands and submitted to being searched.[24]

The prisoner turned out to be a U-boat officer, one who incurred British odium for attacks on unarmed merchant vessels. But the experience softened Dai Evans who found that he could only admire the man. 'There, surrounded by six of us, he maintained defiance even in the face of a possible beating-up. He was the type any country loves to have on their side. His medals proved his valour, won in a desperate and claustrophobic calling.'

Captain C.T. Cross ran one of the many reception camps set up to receive German prisoners and, as it turned out, anyone else who happened along.

Here the soldiers searched for arms, organised into bodies of 200 approx. and marched off. Many are wounded, many have marched so far that they can go no further. Their own medical services have to be organised to cope with these, transport arranged for them and so on. We are miles ahead of supporting troops so we have no facilities for feeding the blighters. Furthermore we have civilians to cope with. So at all costs we have to keep them moving back. Yesterday I had something like 10,000 through my place. By the end of the evening I had no voice left at all, having been shouting orders in German at them all day. This I did mainly from the back of a horse!

But far worse were the logistical problems of coping with German refugees who had been keeping just ahead of the Russians all the way from east Russia.

I've read of the Great Trek, and I've seen films about covered-wagon trains. But never did I conceive anything like this. Nose to tail all day there has been an unending stream of wagons, each pulled by two or three horses. We cannot let them go further because they would clog completely the lines of supply. So we have to arrange camps for them in the woods. We have appointed little fuhrers to see that latrines are dug and so on. We have to provide water carts for them. They have no food apart from the potato they have bought with them, and there are too many thousands for us to feed. German Red Cross and WAAFs, etc. have been organised to set up some sort of medical facilities. But disease is there, and the people are in poor condition to withstand it. Thank God they are out of doors anyway! Better that a few old ones should die of pneumonia, than a lot of others from typhus, etc. Mixed up with them are batches of Polish and other liberated workers, who have begun to commit 'News of the World' offences! Tomorrow we have to start to disperse them a bit, and thus reduce the disease danger and ease the water supplies.[25]

All this was happening when the Allies were lining up on their respective sides of the Elbe, which is to get some way ahead of the story. But the image of a nation in chaos is accurate enough from the first days after the Rhine crossings. It is simply that the chaos got worse the further into Germany the Allies advanced.

On our long ride to the Elbe we saw scenes hard to comprehend. Thousands of German soldiers were going to the rear, most without even one guard. Some were loaded in huge semi-cattle trucks, others on foot. Thousands of newly-liberated slave laborers headed everywhere. Many French were identified by their tri-color flags they had gotten someplace. They had horses, wagons, wheel barrows, baby buggies and many carried huge packs on their backs. A cry to the French of, 'Viva La France!' brought cheers. Also many German civilians were wandering aimlessly. I saw only two dead Germans and a knocked-out anti-tank gun on the whole ride to attest to the lack of opposition.[26]

Others did encounter opposition but action was sporadic, unpredictable and of varying intensity. Much of it was reflex fighting, carried out with no great sense of purpose but because it was what soldiers did. The futility of spending lives on a war that was almost over made for restraint on both sides.

Wayne Van Dyke was a gunner with Patton's Eleventh Armoured Division.

We were heading south toward Worms, Germany. The platoon was in line when the leading tank came over a rise and stopped. He reported a column of German vehicles passing across his front heading east. The rest of the platoon pulled off the road and deployed along the ridge. It was a long column of German Army trucks, half tracks, cars and horse-drawn wagons. The five tanks immediately opened fire with 75s and machine guns. We continued firing for 20 seconds when without a verbal command, every tank ceased firing. The Germans were not returning fire. Every tank commander sensed that to continue firing would be tantamount to murder and so, we humanely stopped the carnage. We watched as the German column picked up their dead and wounded, abandoned their disabled and burning vehicles, and then continued east. Obviously they just wanted to escape to safety. Our Company Commander called on the radio and asked why we stopped firing. We told him and he agreed we did the right thing.[27]

At Duisberg, where Americans and Germans half-heartedly shelled each other across the Rhine, a telephone link was set up between the opposing commanders. A deal was struck. When one or other decided on some pyrotechnics, advance warning would give plenty of time for those in the firing line to take cover.[28] The surrender of Duisberg, which came in late March, waited only on the construction of a bridge that would carry American tanks across the river. When they did make it, they passed down rubbled streets where walls were daubed with slogans – *Weisse Fahnen Heraus* (put out white flags) or *Schluss Mit Dem Krieg* (end the war).

By now towns in easy distance of the Rhine, many bypassed by the Allied advance, were falling in quick succession, their citizens bewildered by events and uncertain how to behave. Arriving in Iburg, war reporter Wynford Vaughan Thomas found that his was the first Allied vehicle to stop there. The tanks had long since gone and were already many miles ahead.

> All we wanted to do was to ask the way. But the town wanted to surrender and was almost indignant when we wouldn't accept it. A citizen came out and explained that he'd seen to it personally that every house had had its clean white flag. We saw a young girl carrying two rifles and a bayonet. For a moment, we thought we'd at last met that rare phenomenon – the genuine German guerrilla fighter. And we prepared to sell our lives dearly. But there was no need; the Hitler maiden stopped and explained that she was taking the guns immediately to the burgomaster. No one in that town was going to fire them. We had the greatest difficulty in escaping from the burgomaster himself. He, it appears, was waiting patiently in his office to obey our orders. What are you to think of these fantastic people?[29]

At Hamborn, where a military government team was settling in, the bürgermeister was a thoroughly confused man.

> As we entered the wood-panelled office he rose and gave us the Hitler salute, then he suddenly gasped 'Ah!' and turned pale. 'It's an old habit,' he stammered, *'Man muss sich davon abgewoehnert'* (One has to disaccustom oneself).
>
> He was a flustered little bureaucrat, a Nazi by membership and conviction. He knew no other language than *Nazi-Deutsch* and in

his apologetic conversation he constantly and without awareness referred to the Americans as '*Ider Feind*' (the enemy).

Nazism, he said, had been fine. It gave the people social benefits and free trips. Everything would have gone well, he complained, had it not been for the British. The Führer had asked the Poles for Danzig and just as they were ready to grant it, the British intervened and caused the war. Until the last day – only this morning, in fact – the Buergermeister was certain that the Fuehrer would be victorious. But now . . . ! He threw up his hands in a gesture of despair and tears rolled down his fat cheeks. 'Gentlemen,' he appealed to us, 'isn't it terrible how everything is *kaput* in Germany? Do you know the awful news I heard over the radio this morning? *Mein Gott*, I heard that the enemy is already at Muenster. I am speechless.'[30]

Frankfurt fell to the Third Army on March 29th, three days before the First and Ninth Armies linked up at Lippstadt to close the circle on the Ruhr pocket. With the Russians preparing for the decisive blow against Berlin it was impossible to imagine that anything could now be done to save the Reich. Its Führer believed otherwise.

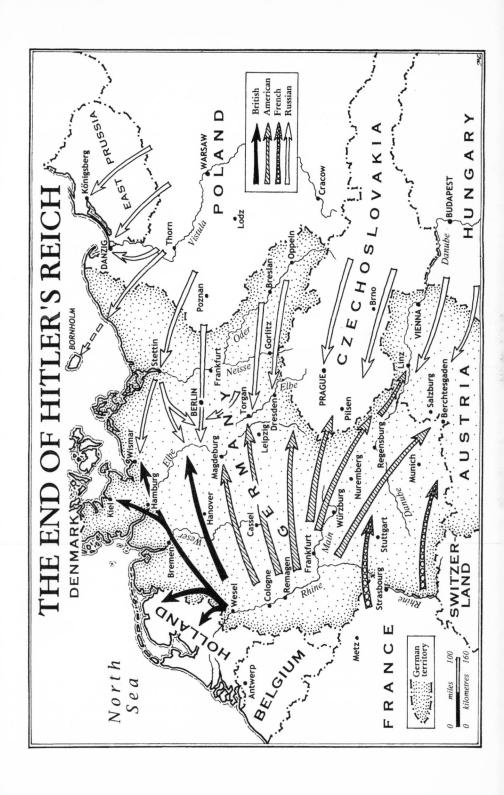

THE END OF HITLER'S REICH

17
End Game

Was it Hitler who gave us the phrase 'bunker mentality'? Encased in his Berlin warren he certainly epitomised all that the bunker mentality implies – a mind closed to rational warnings, primed to self-destruct. Those like armaments minister Albert Speer who were bold enough to speak out were excluded from his inner circle. Papers that told of unpleasant truths were locked away in his safe, unread. But with every rant and rave against the inevitable, Hitler diminished himself in the eyes of even his most devoted followers. If he was not ready to contemplate an end to his struggle, others were.

As early as 1943, the first tentative contacts between the two sides were made in Switzerland where Allen Dulles, head of the European section of American intelligence, was based. Germany's best hope, and one that was kept alive to the last days of the Reich, was to soften the demand for a simultaneous unconditional surrender on both fronts. Initially, the Americans were sympathetic, not least because they feared that if they slammed the door on a separate peace, the same offer would be put to the Russians with maybe a better chance of it being accepted.

But the American position soon hardened. For the western Allies to abandon the Russians at a late stage in the war, after years of cosying up to Uncle Joe and promoting 'our gallant allies', was unthinkable. It was one thing for Churchill to be nervous of Soviet ambitions to replace Germany as the dominant European power, quite another for him to side with a detested enemy to counter the latest threat. In any case, the Americans, ever more optimistic about doing business with Stalin, would not have allowed him the option. It was to be all or nothing. Hitler might have used the same phrase to mean something entirely different. For him it was victory or annihilation. On March 19th, he gave orders for the systematic destruction of all factories, water and electrical installations, railways and bridges before they should fall into enemy hands.

Speer put himself in the firing line by objecting strenuously to a policy that 'implies the elimination of all chance of survival for the German people'. Hitler replied:

> If the war should be lost, then the nation, too, will be lost. That would be the nation's unalterable fate. There is no need to consider the basic requirements that a people needs in order to continue to live a primitive life. On the contrary, it is better ourselves to destroy such things, for this nation will have proved itself the weaker and the future will belong exclusively to the stronger Eastern nation. Those who remain alive after the battles are over are in any case only inferior persons, since the best have fallen.[1]

On March 23rd, the Gauleiters, ironically enough in their capacity as commissars for the defence of the Reich, were told how they were to go about creating a scorched earth. They were to be assisted by the military. Left to their own devices it is likely that most of the Gauleiters would have done as they were ordered. It was to the credit of Speer and the army commanders who supported him that their efforts were frustrated.

With Hitler fixated on mass destruction as the alternative to abject surrender, the only prospect for ending the war short of outright victory on the battlefield, was for one of his hitherto loyal lieutenants to break ranks. In February 1945, an unlikely candidate emerged from the Berlin shadows. SS Reichsführer Heinrich Himmler was so trusted by Hitler that he was seen by many as the Führer's natural successor, an assumption he did nothing to discourage. But while Himmler, the architect of the Holocaust, was as murderously ruthless as any in the Nazi hierarchy, he was not entirely lacking a sense of self-preservation. As the odds shortened on a reversal of Allied fortunes, he gave signs of wanting to talk. The first to discover this was Count Folke Bernadotte, vice-chairman of the Swedish Red Cross and a nephew of King Gustav, who, as a pre-eminent neutral, was well placed to act as an intermediary. He did not start with any grand objectives in mind. His first approach aimed to persuade Himmler to release into Swedish custody those Norwegians and Danes held in concentration camps.

An exploratory meeting on February 17th introduced Bernadotte to Himmler's deputy and police chief, Ernst Kaltenbrunner, who was distantly polite. Late in the session they were joined by Walter Schellenberg, head of foreign intelligence, another of Himmler's close associates but altogether a more accommodating personality. Bernadotte held back on the real purpose of his visit, asking no more than for a face-to-face discussion with Himmler. It took place a few days later in a hospital some seventy miles north of Berlin. Himmler greeted his guest in a green military uniform, without decorations. With his horn-rimmed spectacles, he reminded Bernadotte of 'a harmless schoolteacher from the country'.[2] Their discussion turned on the immediate future of the Scandinavian prisoners. Himmler seemed open to a deal but wanted a reciprocal concession such as a promise to call off the resistance in Norway. It was more than Bernadotte could deliver even if he had wanted it. In the end, Himmler agreed to release the elderly and sick and to gather together the rest of the Norwegian and Danish prisoners where the Swedish Red Cross could look after them. The question of a negotiated peace was touched on tangentially, Bernadotte making the point that while an approach to Eisenhower was feasible it could only bring results if Himmler was recognised as Hitler's successor. Three more meetings followed with Schellenberg pushing the agenda forwards. Both sides were cautious, Himmler because he was risking his standing with Hitler; Bernadotte because he was acting independently of the Swedish government which had no wish to compromise its standing as a neutral.

A lull in the negotiations coincided with news from across the Atlantic that gave delight to Berlin. President Roosevelt, 'the greatest war criminal of all ages' according to Hitler, had died of a cerebral haemorrhage. It was the sign Hitler had been waiting for. Now, his destiny was to be that of his hero Frederick the Great whose defeat in the Seven Years War had been averted by a switch in Russian allegiance brought about by the death of the Tsarina Elizabeth. Goebbels held to the same theme. He managed to convince himself that Roosevelt's successor, his vice-president, Harry S. Truman, would reject the 'Jewish' allegiance in favour of a crusade against Communism. No chance. Roosevelt's dying breath may have brought fresh life to the Reich but the rejuvenation was short-lived. A day later fighting in the Ruhr ended and on April 16th the Red Army struck at Berlin.

Two and a half million men, 42,000 artillery pieces and more than 6,000 tanks encircled the Reich capital. Opposing this military juggernaut were the fragments of an army: old men and boys in ragged uniforms, sick and exhausted Wehrmacht survivors from once proud fighting units. The disaster had long been predicted by Hitler's Chief of General Staff, General Heinz Guderian. Having argued fruitlessly against a strategy that, in his view, made no concessions to reality, he now added his voice to demands for an armistice on the western front. For support he turned to the foreign minister, the duplicitous Joachim von Ribbentrop who professed great surprise when Guderian asked him how he would feel if 'in three or four weeks the Russians are at the gates of Berlin?'

> With every mark of horror Ribbentrop cried: 'Do you believe that that is even possible?' When I assured him that it was not only possible but, as a result of our leadership, certain, for a moment he lost his composure. Yet when I repeated my request that he accompany me to see Hitler he did not dare agree. All I managed to get out of him was a remark made just as I was leaving: 'Listen, we will keep this conversation to ourselves, won't we?' I assured him that I should do so.

But when Guderian appeared at Hitler's briefing that night, he found his Führer in a state of great agitation.

> I must have been a little late, for as I entered the conference room I could already hear him talking in a loud and excited voice. He was insisting that his *Basic Order No. 1* – by which no one was allowed to discuss his work with any man who did not need such knowledge for his own official duties – be exactly obeyed. When he saw me he went on in an even louder voice: 'So when the Chief of the General Staff

goes to see the Foreign Minister and informs him of the situation in the East with the object of securing an armistice in the West, he is doing neither more nor less than committing high treason!'[3]

So Ribbentrop had talked. Guderian experienced a sense of relief. Now, at last, he had got through to Hitler. But he reckoned without the stubbornness of a leader who had lost all sense of reality. Guderian's dismissal, cloaked in an order that he should take six weeks' convalescent leave, was not long in coming. It was another measure of the confusion at Hitler's headquarters that Keitel suggested to Guderian that he should take a long break in Bad Liebenstein. 'It is very beautiful there.' Guderian had to remind him that the town was already in American hands.[4]

Frustrated in their efforts to forestall a Russian drive through Hungary towards Austria, German forces abandoned Vienna after a week of bitter street fighting. That was on April 13th. By now, the Russians had strengthened their bridgehead on the Oder in preparation for the final assault on Berlin which began on the night of April 15th. Backed by unprecedented artillery support, 4,000 tanks of Zhukov's First Belorussian Group crashed the German lines over a fifty-mile sector between Zehden and Fuerstenberg. The following day, Konev's First Ukrainian Army Group launched its main attack across the Neisse River. Berlin was thus caught in a pincer movement which cut off its forces southeast of the city. Events were not quite so dramatic to the west but the impetus of the Allied advance was equally impressive.

Nuremberg, 'the city of the Nazi movement', was under attack day and night from the beginning of April. Gauleiter Holz, who was to be killed in the final raid on the city, was determined to make Nuremberg a fortress, to be defended to the last man. Road blocks were put up but 'it was clear to anyone with even the vaguest of military experience that these measures were inadequate'.[5] There were few fighters and even fewer weapons. 'German planes had long since become a fairy tale. Tanks were something we had only ever heard about and the few wornout flak guns didn't exactly cut the mustard either.'[6] Nonetheless, the city held out for more than two weeks.

The final act was about to begin. What remained of the defence force pulled back to the city centre.

Gustav Bub wandered the streets.

I came across a Hitler youth. He was standing alone and forlorn and didn't know what to do with himself. He said some of his comrades had just shot up an American tank on the Maffeiplatz with a panzerfaust, at 7–800m distance ... as I came to the Befehlsstelle [command office] in the bunker of the transport museum, I couldn't find a soul. After a long search I found another sign of human life – it may have been the caretaker ... Walking through the empty streets in the inner city which lay in rubble was ghostly. The streets and alleys which had once been heaving with people and which I had known since I'd been a child, had completely changed. They all wore the face of death.[7]

From a more objective standpoint, Ed Murrow concurred. Finding little in Nuremberg that was still standing except a few walls and the cathedral spires, he reflected on a nation committing suicide. With Nuremberg wiped out, most of Bayreuth had gone too.

Wagner's piano is still there, but part of the house has been knocked down. Rare books and fine manuscripts are trampled underfoot. There is an empty champagne bottle on top of the piano. The young lieutenant in charge of Military Government has written a letter to Army asking for permission to put a guard on the place.[8]

Murrow was bemused by the determination and sang froid of the looters.

A Russian walked down a street that was under small-arms fire. He carried a huge cheese – it must have weighed 70 pounds. He was interested in that cheese – not in the firing. As a new Burp gun opened up around the corner, an American corporal (in possession of a newly acquired Leica) said: 'Hey, Mack, do you know of any place around here where I can get some films developed?' There wasn't a building standing in the radius of a mile, but he was entirely serious.

And still it was the German watches that were most prized. 'USA became not so much the acronym for a country as for Uhrensammlerarmee or watch collector army.'[9]

In these town-to-town battles it was often the teenage defenders of the Reich, devotees of Nazi ideology, who put most lives at risk either because, in all innocence, they kept the faith, believing that victory could still be achieved, or because, being young, they held to a romantic view of death and glory. At Bad Mergentheim, below Frankfurt, advance units of the Third Army came on an outpost of young paratroopers 'as fanatical as any German soldiers we had fought'. At the height of the fighting, the Americans had faced an old-fashioned charge 'in which an officer stood up and shouting and yelling led his men forward only for them to be cut down and hurled back by our machine guns'. The bloody contest ended with hand-to-hand bayonet fighting. It was then left to the medics to give what help they could with, in one case, a terrifying consequence.

> One of these young Hitler youth had a wound in his leg which prevented his crawling away, and he was sitting under a tree . . . One of the medics started to approach the lad when the boy picked up a 'potato masher', a German hand grenade, so called because it was shaped exactly like an old-fashioned wooden potato masher, with a long wooden handle, for throwing. The medic stopped and pointed to the red cross arm band which he was wearing, then to his medical kit, then to the German. The German stared at him stonily, and as the medic again moved to approach him, he unscrewed the cap of his grenade and the medic hit the dirt, expecting the German to throw it. Instead, the lad held the grenade immediately under his chin until it went off, blowing his head completely and cleanly from his body.[10]

Bad Mergentheim itself, a health resort set in the hills above the Tauber River, offered no resistance. The bürgermeister reported that he had persuaded the remaining German forces to leave town.

> After the arrival of the Americans, life continued normally with only minor restrictions and curfews in effect. The German wounded remained within the hospitals, but German medical officers could be seen moving through the town on their routine check accompanied

by a couple of our medics. In general, the people were very co-operative and quite thankful that their town had been spared the ravages of war.[11]

A not untypical British encounter with a German boy soldier showed how easy it was for false gallantry to spring from naïvety.

> We had gone into a farmhouse and found on a table a loaf of bread which looked rather odd; odd because there were a lot of strange cuts across it. We opened it carefully and found that the inside had been hollowed out to hold an automatic pistol, stripped down into its main components. The only person about was a very frightened boy of about 14 or 15 and we gathered that he had been supplied with the weapon with which to hold at bay the entire British Army (apparently single-handed) while those who had given the order had scarpered.[12]

From mid-April barely a day passed without the Allies notching up another Germany city. In the middle Ruhr, Wuppertal was one of the last industrial centres to submit to a change of regime. Goebbels condemned the city to 'pech und schwefel' (fire and brimstone) when he heard of its surrender which was a little unfair since there was not much the citizens could have done to resist their fate. Writing to his children, who had been evacuated to the countryside, a Wuppertaler, Herr Wenger, conceded:

> It's not exactly cosy at the moment. Since the night before the 14th at around one o'clock Elberfeld and Barmen have been under fire. I mean literally under – much of the shelling screamed over the town and hit Koenigshoehe, the Nuetzenburg or the Hombuechel [hills surrounding the city]. Barmen has been hit even more. The trams have been affected considerably, and now they only go from Sonnborn to Wupperstrasse . . . The air raid shelters are full to bursting – many people sleep in their cellars at night. Yet we can't really see that any defence of Wuppertal is being prepared. Certainly a few road blocks have been put up, and some anti-tank trenches and machine gun hide-aways have been dug, but where are the troops who could defend this town? The Volkssturm are in no position to fight. They have no weapons, no uniforms and no training for modern warfare.

That same day (April 15th) Herr Wenger reported soldiers exchanging their uniforms for civilian clothes before selling off their stores. The following morning, the first Americans were spotted.

> This morning I went into town . . . I saw a lot of the damage from the previous night's shelling . . . Many people were standing before their front doors, others were sweeping the dirt away, some fetched pails of water and others were just wandering around the streets . . . To my regret I came upon Tillmann's house, heavily damaged. The garden side had been badly hit the previous night, the windows and their frames had been ripped out, the doors were completely split apart. The furniture was lying around in splinters. I met him too but he seemed safe and sound. He instantly began to rail against Nazis politics, including their economic policy, which was actually one of their better ones, I thought . . . A few steps further to the corner of Herzog and Bank Street I encountered the front. It consisted of five parachutists and some infantrymen. They didn't seem to be in a hurry or especially tense. They were orderly and prepared for battle.[13]

Opinion weighed heavily against Berlin. As one citizen commented, 'Years ago, as the Nazis won such a big victory at the Reichstag elections, everyone was saying what joy it was to be alive! No one says that anymore, however, you do hear a lot of people saying "'I'd rather be dead."'[14]

Even as Wuppertal shed its Nazi past, there were still those bearing the SS insignia who were intent on hunting out the deserters and saboteurs. As a seventeen-year-old soldier in the Sagan barracks, Karl Schlesier witnessed executions carried out by his comrades who were forced to join firing squads under pain of themselves being put at the receiving end. Post-war, Schlesier emigrated to the States where he became an academic. In the late 1980s, Karl, now Professor Schlesier, returned to Germany where he related his experiences as a young soldier, including having to watch as one of his friends was shot.

> The post was erected before an earth bank and the deserter – actually the boy wasn't a deserter – was tied to it. His hands were tied behind his back and a sergeant (Unteroffizier) was there to give the

shooting order. One order, and the boy's shot. It was awful – they didn't want to shoot him but were forced to, so they shot especially hard. And then the boy who was shot lurched forward. First he was thrown against the post, then he slid forward and fell down. His hands were tied to the post though and held his body up. The sergeant then went up to him and shot him in the head.[15]

The Schlesier revelations led to research by the Wuppertal Stadtarchiv to show that the killings had indeed taken place. Among the documents turned up were a map showing the shooting ground in the barracks, death certificates and letters to families of the dead.

The death sentence given to your husband, former lance corporal Heinrich Sagurna on 13 October 1944 was carried out in Wuppertal today. Should you wish to attend the funeral personally and at your own cost you are required immediately to inform the Wehrmacht-kommandantur Wuppertal – Abt. III – (Tel. 37 344) by noon on Tuesday, February the 20th. The body has been approved for burial. It must be noted that the funeral will take place in absolute silence – no further formalities may take place in Wuppertal.[16]

Hannover and Brunswick fell to the US Ninth Army. In Hannover, less than a quarter of buildings were left standing.

You could walk for miles without seeing a building left with a wall higher than your thigh. Electricity had been cut; the water supply wasn't working; there were no sewers. The city was a gigantic open sore – and crawling about in that sore were not a few thousand, or even a few scores of thousands of people, but a vast population of peoples of all lands and tongues and temperaments.

It was reckoned that there were over half a million people living on the breadline in Hannover – 250,000 Germans, 100,000 foreign workers and over 50,000 released British and Allied prisoners of war. 'They inhabited the ruins of this once prosperous city, and no Wild West town of the last century could compare with the lawless-ness of the life they lived. It was a town of drunkenness and murder.'[17]

This observer saw liberated foreign workers on the rampage, making first for the liquor stores.

They battered down the doors and emerged with cases of schnapps and brandy and wine. They sat in the doorways, breaking off the bottle-necks of Hennessey and Martell and guzzling it down. When they had no liquor they drank bottle after bottle of fine French wines, and hocks and Mosel. When they got hungry they broke into food stores. When the city police tried to protect these places, they fell upon them and hung their bodies from the lampposts and went off with their arms. They stormed dumps of every kind. By the night of April 10 thousands of them were drunk, and thousands of them were marauding the city with guns and knives, on the search for loot or for women. There were fires burning everywhere, and mad screams and shouts coming from every street. Wild shots whistled by from the guns of the drunken foreign slaves, and much more dangerous ones from the Nazi snipers still concealed in some of the ruins.[18]

Order of a sort was restored by the military governor, a Major Lamb, 'an unsophisticated Englishman who believed in treating people as you find them'. With a staff of six British and two Canadian officers, he recruited German officials who were capable of reconnecting essential services while he dealt with the first priority of restoring law and order. Driving with Major Lamb through a street of half-wrecked factories, war reporter Leonard Mosley was startled when the car was halted by a great crowd swarming over the street.

Scores of fights were going on; men and women were rolling in the gutters, tearing at each other's hair, and at the packages they clutched to their bosoms. The Major didn't even seem surprised to see it. 'This is the sort of thing that goes on all day,' he said, as if it were a procession instead of a riot. 'Looting, fighting, rape, murder – what a town!'

Experience had taught him the only possible response.

He brought the car to a halt, got out and took his revolver from its holster. He fired two quick shots in the air. The effect was immediate;

the roar of the crowd died away, the fighting ceased, stolen packages were dropped to the ground. Four or five hundred ugly-looking slave workers and Germans, half of them drunk from stolen wine, turned and looked at him.

The Major waved his revolver and drew in a deep breath. Then in a terrific roar from such a mild and modestly built man: '*Raus*! Go on there – *raus*!' he shouted, 'the whole lot of you, before I start firing lower!'

There was another silence. Then grins began to appear on the grimy faces of the crowd. They nodded their heads, saluted the Major or touched their caps, helped people to their feet whom they had been kicking a few moments ago, and quietly and quickly they dispersed.

The Major did the same thing, with the same effect, four more times before we reached our destination.[19]

This went on all day, every day for nearly two weeks until a civilian police force was recruited. They had neither uniforms nor arms, their only sign of authority being a white armband with 'MG Polizei' written across it. Liberated prisoners of war, British, French and Dutch, helped by setting up mobile patrols to answer alarm calls for murder, theft and rape – a United Nations peace-keeping force before anyone had ever heard of the term.

Ten days after its capture Hannover was beginning to emerge from its anarchy. But, still:

. . . was hardly a city to which you would have taken your maiden aunt. After darkness it was a dark, fearsome, dangerous place, where you faced death or attack at every corner; a place of menace, of mysterious bangs and explosions, of furtive figures among the bomb ruins. Life, if not so lawless as before, was still rough and lusty. The drabs and the slatterns, German and foreign alike, were still doing a roaring trade in the noisome alleys. But there was safety and some semblance of normality again for the citizens; the curfew, which had kept Germans in for all but three hours a day, was lifted until sunset. The shops began to open, as supplies began to come in; new ration cards began to be distributed; factories began to operate again; a skeleton transport service began to function.[20]

This was an occasion when military government actually worked.
Occupied Brunswick was still recognisable as a once attractive
city. The decision to make it the headquarters of the Ninth Army
was preceded by the not unwelcome exit of Bürgermeister Mertens,
a devoted Nazi, who took a pistol to his head. The worst news
was of the fate of some 4,500 prisoners and foreign workers from
the Hermann Goering Steel Works who, on the approach of the
Allies, had been packed into a train moving east. It had come to
a halt for water and coal outside Celle where it was attacked by
what would now be known as 'friendly fire' from the air. As ammunition and petrol began to explode, the occupants of the train made
their dash for safety, only to be mowed down by SS machine-guns
as they hit the tracks. Only 200 survived.[21]

Brunswick itself was quiet, as Saul Padover discovered as he
wandered the city. An American psychologist on licence to explore
the German mentality, he was perhaps too buttoned up to appreciate all that was on offer.

> Everywhere women, some of them beautiful and most of them young,
> accosted us and whispered invitations. They would pass slowly, give
> us a long sideways look and murmur, 'I live all by myself; would you
> like to come up and see me?' Or, 'I know Americans aren't allowed
> to speak with Germans, but would you like to follow me?' This went
> on all the time, on all the streets of Brunswick, and, as I said, the
> women, who were definitely not professionals, were attractive and there
> was not much German male competition. Germany's manhood was
> either in the Wehrmacht or in captivity or in hospitals or underground,
> and the women were starved for men, not to speak of chocolate. Joe,
> who got around, told me that the GIs were having the time of their
> lives. 'Easy pickin',' Joe said. 'You don't even need no chocolate with
> them pussies.'[22]

In cities which were still nominally under direction from Berlin,
the suicide rate for the governing class increased sharply as the
combination of despair and fear pushed many towards the final
exit. A case in point was Leipzig where the town hall revealed a
Wagnerian scene of self-inflicted carnage. Up to a dozen bodies

were strewn about the building, poison bottles beside them. Soldiers of the Third Army were escorted from room to room by a caretaker who listed the victims with bureaucratic precision. In the bürgermeister's office 'a luxuriously furnished, oak panelled room', the occupant was seated at a large desk, his hands on the table, his shaven head tilted back.

> Opposite, in the arm-chair, sat his wife; beside her, in the other armchair, sat his daughter, a flaxen-haired, 20-year-old girl, wearing spectacles. On the desk was a phial, with its stopper lying beside it. They were all dead. The caretaker said he thought they'd committed suicide yesterday, or perhaps the day before . . . On the wall, opposite the dead man, was a large oil-painting of Hitler. There was another locked door, leading out of this room – the caretaker opened it. Here Chief City Treasurer Doktor Lisso lay slumped on his desk. On a sofa, opposite, lay his daughter wearing hospital nurse's uniform. In an armchair sat Lisso's wife. Once again, on the table was an empty, unlabelled phial. By Lisso's side were two automatic pistols – but he had chosen poison.[23]

Of the cities that changed hands in April, Stuttgart earned a certain distinction as the setting for a falling out between the American and French military. The city was taken by the French First Army under General de Lattre de Tassigny whose mostly colonial troops – Moroccan, Algerian and Senegalese – were known more for their fighting spirit than for discipline. Alongside the French First Army was the US Seventh Army led by General Alexander Patch, while in overall command was General Jacob Devers. Responding to what de Lattre described as a 'wholly incorrect' report of unrestrained looting and killing, Devers ruled that the French should evacuate Stuttgart to allow the Americans to take over. He was backed by Eisenhower who, despite his official protestations, distrusted the French close to the point of active dislike. What he and Devers failed to realise was that a regional capital was too important to be lightly handed over by an army that was all out to recover its pride. Knowing that he was on dangerous ground, de Lattre referred the matter to de Gaulle who responded as anyone who had knowledge of that touchy politician might have expected with a direct order to 'keep a French garrison in Stuttgart and to establish a military government there at once'. The let-out for de Gaulle was a firm declaration from the Americans on the handover of the French zone of occupation which was still under discussion. De Lattre passed this on to Devers blandly noting that he 'no longer had any initiative in this matter'.[24]

The standoff lasted almost a week. In that time an American negotiating team who went into Stuttgart felt themselves to be under restraint. It was not that they were compelled to stay, simply that there was no getting away back to their own lines before concessions were made.[25] In the end de Gaulle himself flew in to talk things through with General Patch who now had authority from Eisenhower to threaten a cut-off of equipment and other supplies to French forces. The inevitable compromise was struck. Stuttgart was patrolled by American and French forces with a military government parading all the flags of the wartime Allies. French honour was satisfied. 'You will certainly tell General Devers,' de Gaulle telegraphed de Lattre, 'that this divergence, serious though it might be, modifies neither your mission nor your intention, which is to conduct the fight under his command.'[26] To mark the restoration of friendly relations, Devers attended a Joan of Arc festival in Stuttgart where he heard an 'unforgettable Te Deum'.

Exchanged words of hope and encouragement could still be heard wherever a few Germans were gathered but they were more form than substance.

I think that what kept our belief in victory alive for all those years was our youthful ignorance and our firm belief in what Hitler did and said. We just couldn't accept that, after all this effort, the war could be lost. On my visit to Altomünster, sometime in mid-April 1945, I met a friend of mine on the train and he expressed his doubts to me. 'Well, Rudi,' he said, 'what are you going to do when the war is over? You know it's going to be lost.' 'Berthold,' I responded, 'don't talk so stupid. You know we will win the war.' 'How?' said he. 'Well,'

I said, 'the Führer says that we have a special weapon which he will only use when absolutely necessary to save the German people. I don't think that anyone could lie so much all these years – and us believe in those lies. He must be telling the truth!' 'Well, Rudi,' he said, 'you'll see. There's no sense arguing about it. Maybe you're right, maybe I'm right, we'll see.'

Fifty years later, at a school reunion, the two friends met again.

I mentioned the incident to him and he said, 'I remember that very well, but, you know, it really didn't matter at the time anymore. We, deep down, probably all knew it – that this was the end. How could Germany have possibly won the war when the fronts just seemed to disappear, there was no organisation anymore. Where would we have gotten the "special weapon" from? Where would we have dropped those "special weapons" upon the enemy to destroy him?' . . . We just didn't want to admit defeat to ourselves. I certainly did not want to acknowledge to myself that I didn't do a good job. I and my friends should have helped win the war. We did our best, but what went wrong? Well, the best was not good enough.[27]

The war on the western front was into its last phase. In the third week of April the British Second Army was closing around the North Sea ports of Hamburg and Bremen, and the US First and Ninth Armies were up to and over the Elbe between Magdeburg and Halle. But the news everyone was waiting for was of the beginning of the Russian attack on Berlin. It came on April 20th, Hitler's forty-sixth birthday, when the first shells began falling on the city centre. The distinctive rattle of the guns soon had a name. Berliners called it Stalin's organ which, once it started grinding, would continue its inharmonious tune for hours at a time.

Werner Girling was thirteen when his family abandoned their house to live in the cellar of an old people's home.

'They'll be coming over the Teltow Canal,' my father reckons. I can't help thinking about the Hitler Youth boys on the Kleinmachnower Weg. My friend Kurt and I had been there just three days before and found three or four anti-aircraft guns ready for ground battle on the footpath, 400 metres away from the canal. There was no cover on the marshland. We got talking to one of the operating crew and I remember his words quite clearly to this day. 'When Ivan gets here, it'll be the end of us – there'll be no one left!' Neither of us really knew what he meant at the time. But we realised when we returned, after the Russians had invaded. We could make out the barrels of the anti-aircraft guns jutting up towards the sky from quite a distance. Then we saw five, maybe more of the crew, lying dead beside them.[28]

Taking a rather more mature view of the Berlin defences, journalist Karl Brammer was equally pessimistic.

The Russians are approaching Teltow and a German ground battalion comes out to defend Knesebeck Bridge. A sorry sight. The 'marchers' are taking a breather on the benches before they carry on, many have no weapons at all, most have grey hair. They haven't been fed for 12 hours and have no idea where they are going. They are marching because they have been ordered to march, but all are convinced of the futility of their actions. These last dregs of war don't even have the energy to desert – entrusting them with the defence of Berlin is utter folly.[29]

Later, Karl Brammer went to his local police station where guns were handed out.

Ancient carbines, which none of us has ever used, and Greek ammunition. Great defence, but not for me. Without a word I stash the carbine in the bike shed, along with an ancient revolver. How many times have I told anyone who will listen? – I haven't the slightest intention of dying a hero's death for Adolf Hitler.[30]

Those who had no choice in the matter, the few regular soldiers and others more or less able-bodied, who were under orders lived an unreal life. An anonymous diarist who was in barracks in Hohenzollerndamm found himself organising a concert to celebrate Hitler's birthday.

The Berlin Philharmonic Orchestra was playing, conducted by Robert Heger. I was commissioned to pick up the conductor from the station and keep him amused in the casino until the commander arrived. We sat there, strangers drinking beer, talking of insignificant matters – that times were bad and the weather good . . . Then the party began, with a calm introduction lacking in pathos, followed by a Clausewitz quote read by Paul Hartmann. At the end, Beethoven's Symphony in C-Minor was played.[31]

It was a relief, admitted the diarist, to have something positive to do, however bizarre in the circumstances. His only other order of note was to deliver a message to the deputy Gauleiter whose office was in the cellar of the Hotel Kaiserhof.

I rode my bike along Vosstrasse to Wilhelmplatz and entered the bunker. It was packed with top party functionaries and secretaries. All the doors were open, so one could easily see into the next room. Coffee cups and liqueur glasses littered the desks and the air was so thick with smoke that it stung my eyes. Telephones rang endlessly and everyone was working frantically. I had the impression that they were working to forget, to numb themselves. A functionary without a function is indeed much worse off than the armed soldier at the crucial moment of attack. Death was within reach for us all, and in such moments people see things differently, men and women look at each other differently . . .

I was given a bundle of special permits, which were to authorise me and my colleagues to enter off-limits areas. I had to make immediate use of them. The way back took me along Wilhelmstrasse and through the Brandenburg Gate. Unter den Linden was deserted. A sergeant stood at the main gateway of Gate B, wearing a Ritterkreuz (Knight's Cross) on his uniform. He checked my permit. He was a huge man, and seemed a decent sort of chap. I'd noticed that I had really been 'beside myself' the last few days – I wasn't myself anymore; I felt like I had a split personality. I somehow just got through it all calmly, but all the time felt as though I were watching everything from an observatory far away.[32]

The rumour factory was still churning out messages of hope. Ribbentrop was said to be on his way to London to negotiate a separate peace; freed from the battle in the west, reinforcements were on their way to save Berlin. Speaking in celebration of Hitler's birthday, Goebbels promised that 'Germany will rise again'. Even now the Führer had great plans. If only the citizens of Berlin could hold out for a few more days. In reality, there was to be no separate peace. On April 25th, the Russians and American spearheads linked up at Torgau on the Elbe.

The Americans were there first, much to the surprise of the Russians who had assumed that the western Allies would not get so far so fast. So the men of the First Army paused for two weeks, waiting at Torgau, some thirty miles from Leipzig, as one officer put it, 'for the Russians to climb over the nearest hills'. Not that they were idle – or alone.

18
Looking for the Exit

In the spring of 1945 it seemed that half of Europe was destined to meet at the Elbe. The rush was led by German refugees who wanted to get as far west as their handcarts would take them. Most were disappointed. Bradley had little sympathy for the dispossessed streaming 'tearfully' towards the US lines. 'We turned them back,' he recorded dryly.[1] Possibly he would have been more accommodating had he known what many of them had been through in their vain efforts to reach the American lines.

> Anyone who met the endless trains of people trekking through the ice and snow, who saw how the will to live had simply drained out of these refugees . . . anyone who came across these starving, freezing, dying people, without being able to help them, anyone who was carried along with the tide of refugees when the sirens went off, and later absorbed into the creeping flood of displaced persons, would never attempt to play down or trivialise the misery that was gathered here into one inhumane bundle. But one would also see the gleam in people's eyes, the reoccurring hope when someone volunteered to take on leadership of the group; when he tasted his first soup after days and nights of wandering, the first glass of hot milk for the children, received like manna from the gods, how finally a warm reception in a safe place, in an aid centre especially placed there for them moved them to tears.[2]

Charlotte Zettler, a student nurse in Bavaria who was, as she put it, a 'quartermistress' in a large refugee camp, tried to be positive.

> I think that the German people are gradually ready to face the immense task before us. But whether we will have the chance to fulfil it? And even if it turns out as badly as I fear, there will always be a Germany, which can never be wiped out.

381

But the immediate challenge of caring for the dispossessed without adequate supplies of food and medicine was almost more than she could bear.

I have a room full of refugees to take care of in a school, more children than adults, who are either quartered in the area or being sent ahead. You can imagine what these people have to go through, often it exceeds human capacity. Many of them traded in their last worldly goods at the station in Dresden or Chemnitz, have been travelling for weeks, squeezed into freight trains with no food or sleep or the necessary hygienic conditions. And the poor children almost all have a temperature, colds, stomach problems, cry all the time, are deathly pale and terribly nervous.[3]

German soldiers in retreat were less inclined to take an American no for an answer. If they were able to cross the Elbe, there was a welcome of sorts for them.

Many of them drowned in little boats. It was just too powerful and too wide a river to swim. Those that made it were docile and happy to be in the hands of the Americans. I was one of the three men guarding thousands of prisoners. I was sitting on a roof of a little barn of a farmhouse . . . just sitting there with a rifle next to me. I really didn't need it because there was nothing but happiness on the part of the people who had come over. Most of them looked pretty beat up after a long, hard war but the officers were beautifully turned out, well uniformed, and almost every one of them with his female companion . . . It certainly [was] an astonishing sight.[4]

An attempt was made to ferret out those who might be considered war criminals but most were simply discharged and sent on their way. There were no trains but German army trucks were recalled to service.

The trucks were loaded with as many discharged German soldiers as they could carry, standing like cord wood in the back. The German driver and an assistant driver (mechanic), who were not discharged, had the responsibility of getting the trucks back to the camps. One armed GI was assigned to each truck, to be sure that it, and the drivers, returned. I acted as a truck guard for two different trips returning the Germans to areas close to their homes. There were no complaints among the returnees, even with their cramped conditions. They were going home, after many years of war. I took one truck to Nuremburg, and another to Munich. It was a bit scary on these trips, being the only GI among some 40 to 60 ex-enemies. The trips took two days, with a stay at a hotel over night.[5]

The greatest sympathy, on the west bank at least, was reserved for the liberated prisoners of war who simply wanted to go home. Many of them had been in camps in Poland where they might reasonably have expected to be freed by the Russians. But for reasons that never have been satisfactorily explained, as the Germans withdrew they decided to take their prisoners with them. So began, from January, the great migration better known by the least fortunate as the Death March, in which thousands of POWs were forced to trek up to 400 miles or more, starting in freezing weather, often with not much more to keep them going than a daily ration of two slices of army bread and a bowl of watery soup. Why? If the guards had thought only in terms of personal survival they would have abandoned their prisoners as an unwelcome encumbrance. Perhaps they were motivated by a misguided sense of duty: a bureaucratic fear of being held to account for signing off without permission. Perhaps, at a higher level of authority, there were thoughts of using prisoners as a bargaining counter in peace negotiations. Whatever the driving force, by mid-April the POWs were on the move with the Red Army following close behind. With one of the advance parties was Squadron Leader Campbell.

2130 hours this evening there was consternation, panic, excitement and a general feeling of being upside down. Germans appeared at the doors of huts shouting that everybody was to march from the camp in half an hour . . . This news was very depressing because for the past two days we had heard the gunfire from the Russian advance and were eagerly waiting to be released . . . The only kit that we could take was what we could carry ourselves, as there was to be no transport for prisoners' kit.

After several days of freezing weather, the snow was up to six inches deep. The prisoners wore as much warm clothing as they could get on. Their kit consisted of more clothing and food. As they marched out of the camp they were each given a Red Cross food parcel.

> Many rooms decided to make a large sleigh, ripping wood from the walls and breaking up their furniture, others made small sleighs to pull themselves, but the majority made some sort of knapsack to carry on their shoulders . . . Eventually we were ready, having divided all our rations between us and each having made ourselves a substantial stick to help us along the road.

The march, which eventually started in the early afternoon, was curiously exhilarating for the first few hours. It was a delight simply to be out of the camp. But plodding through the snow was hard going and even with a five-minute rest every half hour, by nightfall the weaker ones were finding it hard to keep up. Survival often depended less on physical endowment than on sheer luck. The temper of the guards, the distribution of Red Cross parcels, the reception from farmers and townspeople along the way who could, if they felt inclined, offer a barn or garage to sleep in – all could make the difference between standing and falling down.

As the march progressed, Campbell observed the edgy but evolving relationship between guards and prisoners. With only six guards to every hundred men, there was a limit to what could be demanded.

> About 1200 hours we reached a small German town and were martialled into a market square. Rumours were rife that we were stopping there for the remainder of the day and night and moving on the next morning. Prisoners became entirely out of hand, bartering cigarettes and chocolate for bread and eggs. Some even gave cigarettes and chocolate for a bath and a few as payment for a night's lodging.

On this occasion the guards managed to reassert their authority.

> The prisoners had taken charge of the town so completely that the local Gestapo got panicky and ordered the German Kommandant to

384

remove us immediately. So at about 1400 hours, after two hours' rest, when we had mostly found some sort of beddown, the orders came to march on.

Ironically, conditions worsened after the prisoners were told that a train had been made available to carry them on. They were put into cattle trucks, thirty to forty to a truck, and locked in.

We were in these trucks for two days, the train travelling very slowly and stopping for long periods at shunting points. Twice a day we were allowed out of the truck under armed guard, to relieve ourselves, and we were given more German rations consisting of bread, margarine and some German sausage. Water was the hardship because only once a day at a stop one person per truck was allowed to get some water in whatever tins we had. During numerous stops when at sidings we were alongside other goods trains which were being loaded by French and Russian prisoners, we managed to persuade them to fill our tin from the engines. This was used to make coffee or cocoa. It was very welcome, but as a result most of us suffered from dysentery.

After a week on road and rail, the reluctant travellers found themselves at a small wayside stop called Tarnstedt Ost.

We were marched a distance of three kilometres in the pouring rain to a German Marine POW camp. Though it was raining and pitch black we had to wait whilst the prisoners were let in ten at a time to be searched and then pushed into the huts. To our horror we found them in a filthy condition, no lights at all and only odd bales of straw to sleep on . . . The huts were not only filthy but very damp, and to top it all the latrines were in a shocking state. We were told the compound had been used for foreign seamen who had been interned, but that it had been condemned and they had been moved elsewhere . . . We were guarded by German Naval ratings, old men who were just about on their last legs. The hut could not be locked so we had the complete freedom of the compound. Although instructions were that we had to remain in our huts after nightfall, they had to give permission to us to go to the latrines. These German Marines were very corrupt and were quite willing to swap eggs and bread for cigarettes, chocolate and coffee, so that after dark quite a large black market went on by the wire.[6]

It was another month before Campbell and his friends were in sight of what now appeared to be their objective. As they approached Hamburg it was to the sound of guns and flashes in the sky as the bombs fell in the latest night raid. By now all semblance of order had been lost. Guards were liable to disappear and those who stayed mixed more or less freely with their prisoners. Civilians too were friendlier. Despite the heavy bombing suffered by the people of Hamburg, those along the route brought pails of water to their gates so that marchers could stop for a drink.

With freedom so close there were two challenges still to be faced. The first was staying clear of friendly fire. Geoffrey Hall, a sergeant navigator with RAF Bomber Command, 427 Squadron, was one of a party welcomed at journey's end with American Red Cross food parcels. Finding a village green they sat in the April sunshine enjoying their treats.

> Then, while we sat there, half-a-dozen rocket-firing Typhoons dived on some target quite close, firing their rockets and machine-guns. I could see the rockets leave the aircraft and hit the ground about a quarter of a mile away with appallingly loud detonations. Later we found that the target had been some of our boys. Thirty-one had been killed, forty-six injured and six guards killed as well. It was a dreadful mistake. It was said that the last machine recognised the boys as prisoners and pulled away without firing. We are now to wear articles of white clothing or towels for purposes of recognition.[7]

The second challenge, at least for those who were left to their own devices, was to find a safe way of crossing the Elbe, preferably with the approval of the Russians or, when they proved difficult, which was often, without them noticing what was happening. This was made all the harder by the discovery that the only bridge across the river within walking distance of Torgau was a pontoon used exclusively by the Russian military. Watching a convoy of tanks approaching the bridge, Gunner Lewis and his two marching companions had a bright idea. 'Why didn't each of us walk between two tanks? Then when reaching the bridge hide behind the side of the tank opposite the bridge sentry. Without much more ado we each selected a tank – to our utter astonishment the ruse worked. We were now over the bridge in the town of Torgau – another obstacle safely negotiated.'[8]

Others made for the wrecked bridges, scrambling over the twisted girders to a welcoming committee on the west bank. James Witte made a precarious crossing by a damaged railway bridge.

> The brick piers only supported badly buckled railway lines which were so distorted that they were arched into 'S' and 'U' shapes. We had to crawl along the sleepers with the water some 75 feet below. One false step and we would have plunged into the river. When we got across at last we saw that the water couldn't have been all that deep in parts as the Americans were making German prisoners-of-war wade through it up to their necks.[9]

Still others preferred to bargain with the Russians – not always with satisfying results.

> We wandered along the banks of the Elbe looking for a crossing point. We heard the grenades exploding before we saw the Ruskies fishing the stunned fish out of the water. We spoke to them in sign language, indicating that we wanted to cross. They seemed quite amiable and allowed us to get into a rowing boat with one oar which a German had nearby. Then they got a bit awkward and wanted to see our papers. We showed them various items of pay books and letters which seemed to mystify them to the extent that they looked at them upside down. Then they intimated that we could go. We stepped into the boat and the swift flowing Elbe carried us down-stream with the one oar and a branch of a tree. Suddenly, for no apparent reason, one of the Ruskies started firing his revolver at us, so we had to crouch in the bottom of the boat until we eventually grounded on the other side of the river.[10]

Finally, there was always the prospect of meeting a friendly boatman. Corporal Barrington was settling down with his friends to one of the best meals they had enjoyed in ages – roasted chicken, peas, potatoes, preserved fruit and cream, all 'liberated' from local farms – when they heard a rumour of a ferry working half a mile upstream.

In five minutes, food, spare clothes, hand wagon and suitcase all left behind, we were heading across the fields. Through my glasses I could pick out a couple of figures on the opposite bank, and a boat. Excitement ran high as they waved back and shouted – in French – wait half an hour! Those 30 minutes were quite tense, we had seen enough of the Russians and their uncouth ways, even though they had liberated us we had no wish to stay as their guests. By a quarter to seven, five more chaps had arrived and we all went down to the water's edge as we saw the Frenchmen putting off. The river was flowing at a good eight m.p.h. and swimming would have been difficult but not impossible. Our chief fear was a Russian bullet. Alf, after so many descriptions of his rowing club days, volunteered as oarsman and within five minutes all had safely landed on the western bank – free men at last!

Once over the river, life for the former POWs was transformed.

Each morning at 11 o'clock an American NAAFI wagon arrived driven by a charming girl who dispensed splendid coffee and doughnuts. We occupied the morning profitably in going round and round scoffing to our hearts' content. The Yanks placed no bar on our movements and we were free to wander round the town at will. Sometimes we made excursions into the nearby countryside to call at farms exchanging cigars for eggs.

However, this Royal Artillery gunner had other pursuits in mind. Meeting some French girls raised his hopes but 'none were very interested in ex-POWs . . . they were far keener on the conquering heroes who had money to spend.' He had marginally better luck with a young German widow.

She appeared to stop for a moment so I stepped gallantly forward and asked her in my best German whether her two delightful children would like some chocolate. Considering that the average

Germans and their kids had had no chocolate for several years she wasn't really in a position to resist my oblique advances. I handed her the chocolate from some K-rations. I promised to return on the next day with more food and some fags.

Back in barracks, the hopeful suitor enlisted the help of a friendly quartermaster. ('I'll say this about the Yanks, they would always help people to get their ends away even if they were not getting any themselves.') But food and wine were not enough. 'And then it came out, she wanted a husband at all costs and unless I promised to marry her I wouldn't get any more.' The story proceeded on its familiar course. 'We had a right old time in bed and then one day we got our orders to stand by for the planes to Brussels. She bade me a tearful farewell but I promised to return to Germany as soon as I could to claim my bride.'[11]

And that, as in so many other cases, was it. Gunner Romeo did not come back. And in the days when the long-distance telephone was the none too reliable prerogative of the wealthy and civilian travel all but impossible, it was easy for an unprincipled lover to cover his tracks. William Blackman, an RAMC corporal, found himself spending more time trying to mend broken hearts than broken limbs. 'There were quite a number of German women enquiring if letters had arrived for them . . . It was my job to explain that there would be no letters because usually the gallant soldier would have a wife and children at home. There would be disbelief and floods of tears as the poor dears departed.' But the anguish was not entirely with the women. 'One of our chap's bed was next to mine, and the night he was due to leave for England in the morning he was sobbing his heart out. It seemed he had fallen dearly in love with a German woman and didn't want to go home to his wife and children in Norwich.'[12]

With the world's press converging on Torgau, the historic meeting of Americans and Russians on the Elbe was stage-managed to present east and west in perfect harmony. The setting was a relatively undamaged medieval town. A central square boasted a statue of Frederick the Great who had made a rather better job of fighting the Russians than his successors. There was little in the way of direct communication between the two Allies on that afternoon of April 25th but the sentiments were clear enough.

I saw soldiers of the First American and the Red Armies throw their arms round each other's necks and kiss each other on the cheeks. I even had to undergo this greeting myself from a burly Ukrainian soldier.

As I stood on a ramp on the west bank of the Elbe, the Russian soldiers in the town fired off mortars and rifles out of sheer joy: this most cordial of welcomes was a wonderful spectacle . . . The whole scene was one of the gayest fraternization. A Russian lieutenant sat on a wall playing an accordion and singing Russian songs and the Doughboys joined in. Drinks were passed round and everyone was happy.[13]

There followed the inevitable victory banquets with the Americans under no illusion that they could outdrink the Soviet revellers. When it came to General Bradley's turn to share the vodka bottle, he prepared himself with 'a heavy breakfast of buttered wheat cakes and a tumbler of canned milk'.[14]

Marshal Koniev's headquarters was at a pleasant country house. Three enormous rooms on the first floor of the house, opening one into the other, had been laid out for a banquet, at the end of which toasts were drunk. Toasts from the high table where Marshal Koniev, a pleasant smiling chairman, sat with General Bradley and their respective staffs, and toasts at the individual tables to fill the interval. The Russians praised the Americans and the British in high terms and General Bradley spoke equally warmly of the Russians. Each side lauded the other's military achievements; they drank to continued co-operation and lasting friendship. The Russians thought of everybody's comfort and, of course, our drivers, who had a banquet all to themselves, and were waited on by Russian officers.[15]

In the afternoon the two commanders exchanged gifts. Bradley gave Koniev a jeep and an American carbine. Koniev presented Bradley with a fine horse and a Russian revolver. General Hodges, whose First Army troops were camped out on the west bank, also enjoyed the princely laudations.

In the spacious grounds of chateau Werdau, an imitation Versailles, a Russian army band played the various national anthems. Over the entrance was an immense streamer – LONG LIVE THE INVIOLABLE AMERICAN-RUSSIAN-BRITISH FRIENDSHIP. Inside, girl sergeants took our coats and helmets and we were ushered into the large banqueting room . . . Sign language was buttressed by individual words from all the European tongues. There was much laughter and little speech.

The guests sat down to a magnificent meal.

All the stuff must have been specially flown in from the Soviet Union, for it was fresh and very Russian. There were infinite varieties of cured meats and fish – fish smoked and boiled and marinated; and a sweet cream cucumber salad; and a borsch that was made by loving hands and an imaginative Russian mind. And before every individual plate stood a full bottle of vodka and a full bottle of brandy and a single glass, not a liqueur glass but a water glass. After the borsch the two bottles were joined by a third, French champagne.

The toasts were knocked back in accelerating succession. Hodges presented an American standard to his 'brave Russian friends'. The Russians responded with thunderous shouts of approval. They drank more toasts.

A wind-instrument orchestra came in and played and then came Cossack dancers and then singers. It was all terrific and we began to float in a haze of love and happiness. Every Russian officer was a veritable Suvorov and every girl sergeant an image of Catherine the Great.[16]

For over a week, every day was party day. 'Night after night, the Russians would come over and drink with our regimental officers, and they would just almost kill them. Part of our job was to help get Colonel Parker to bed.'[17]

According to one observer, the Russians were less concerned for the welfare of their officers.

A Russian major staggered to the centre of the bridge, leaned over the rail, vomited and fell into the water. Nobody from their side did anything to help. He floated down the river, thrashing and yelling. Nobody paid any attention to him. Ted walked to the center of the bridge and asked the sentry there, who had watched the whole thing why no one had tried to help their major. The reply was (in Russian), 'Ah, hell, we got lots of majors.' That was it. I never found out if the officer survived.[18]

By May 1st, the Americans were beginning to pull back from the Elbe which was over ninety miles inside the Russian zone of occupation. This fact has been much touted by Eisenhower's critics who have taken it as incontrovertible evidence that the western Allies sold themselves short in the scramble for Germany. But leaving aside the rights and wrongs of the political case for dealing fairly with the Russians, at the time there were few who would have argued for a bigger share of German administration. A wrecked country with a destitute population did not come under the heading of desirable acquisitions.

Where Eisenhower did go wrong was in Austria where, fortunately for western interests, his mistakes turned out to be self-correcting and in Czechoslovakia where more effort could have been made to frustrate a likely Communist takeover. The problems with Austria started with the mixed messages coming through to Eisenhower from his political masters. As early as 1943, the Big Three had decided to treat Austrian involvement in the war as an aberration deserving of forgiveness. As 'the first free country to fall victim to Hitlerite aggression', Austria was to be re-established as a 'free and independent state'. It was a gesture calculated to stimulate resistance to Berlin but when the expected popular uprising failed to materialise, the future of Austria was again up for discussion. It was accepted that there would have to be an occupying force but its composition remained uncertain. At one point Roosevelt was happy to leave the entire country to the British and Russians to split between them. Wiser counsel prevailed but it was late in the day before Eisenhower had any clear idea of how far he was expected to move into Austria.

In the end it was Patton who made the running with an advance across the Austrian border and along the Danube that was rapid even by his standards. His enthusiastic welcome from the citizens of Innsbruck, liberated by local resistance groups before the arrival of American soldiers, should have dispelled any remaining fears of a Nazi comeback from some Alpine stronghold. It should also have encouraged a stronger American presence in a country that was at the margin of Soviet imperialism. Nonetheless, Vienna was left to the Russians who were encouraged to believe that with their zone of occupation confirmed, another territorial plum was ripe for picking. That they failed to exploit their opportunity was less to do with the determination of the western Allies as with the dissolute behaviour of Red Army troops. When, against all predictions, the elections of November 1945 gave a drubbing to the Communists, it was recalled that 64 per cent of the electorate were women, those who had suffered most at the hands of their Soviet 'liberators'.[19]

Frustrated in his desire to make a triumphal entry into Vienna, Patton focused on Prague as the next best prospect. But here again Eisenhower was over-cautious. Patton's Third Army units were held at the Czech border for two weeks while deference was paid to the strategic needs of the Red Army. Having taken control of the city, resistance fighters in Prague appealed for support from Eisenhower. They were disappointed. So too was Churchill who made a strong plea to Truman arguing that the American liberation of Prague would make a great difference to the post-war situation. Truman held back. Still new to the presidency, he lacked the confidence of his predecessor who, whatever his failings, knew what he wanted. Instead, Truman followed the line favoured by Marshall and adopted by Eisenhower that American lives should not be put at risk 'for purely political purposes'. Or, as Bradley put it, 'we were less concerned with post-war political alignments than with the destruction of what remained of the German army.'[20] So it was that the Russians took Prague and, as Churchill predicted, Czechoslovakia followed Yugoslavia into the Communist camp.

Eisenhower was more sure-footed with his orders to Montgomery.

His forces were moving rapidly into northern Germany to secure the Baltic ports, needed soonest to begin sending American troops and supplies to the war in the east, and to cut off the German military in Norway and Denmark. In crossing the Elbe there was no opportunity for riverside celebrations. The east bank was held not by Russians but by the Germans and they had a different sort of welcome in mind. But before Montgomery could even get to the Elbe, there was a formidable obstacle to overcome. On the River Weser, linked to the North Sea port of Bremerhaven, Bremen was one of the last German strongholds to put up a fight. Looking back on the last week of April, Harry J. Dutton, writing for the *News of the World*, concluded that Bremen was 'different from all other German cities we have captured. Its death agony was more convulsive. It was determined to resist its fate and in consequence it may well have been set back a hundred years as a commercial and maritime centre.' The defenders had certain advantages, notably a surround of low-lying land which was partly flooded, making it impregnable to a conventional tank and infantry assault. But this simply shifted the job of forcing a surrender to the RAF bombers and to the artillery of the British Second Army. As the attack intensified, Himmler paid a flying visit to install a loyalist functionary to coordinate the defences. The city was to be held at all costs. Those remaining of the SS, Gestapo and local police were sent out to recruit to the Volkssturm any boys they could find who were fifteen or older.

> We had military training, although it didn't always make sense to us. However one thing we were drilled in very thoroughly was the use of the Panzerfaust – our task was to destroy tanks. We were provided with few other weapons. The order was 'find them yourselves', which we were happy to do. We managed to get hold of a lot of weapons from abandoned camps and flak batteries, so that most of the company possessed panzerfausts and the rest had a collection of carbines, hand grenades and a few machine guns. Armed with these, we were filled with great confidence.[21]

Not so their parents who spent much of their time in air raid bunkers.

A terrible, claustrophobic squeeze would be an understatement to describe the masses of people herded together in here. These people are unwashed and ungroomed – there is no fresh water – and often the air is barely breathable. Fainting and nausea are common but anything vaguely approaching sanitary conditions is not even talked about anymore. Flu, throat infections and the like are gaining the upper hand on a daily basis.[22]

For reading material there was a steady output of propaganda. 'The German Volk is determined to fight to the last breath' and 'Only cowards surrender'. Any sight of a white flag was to be punished by death. 'The avengers of honour are always prepared.'

Helga Schroeder, her sister and parents spent eight consecutive nights in a shelter.

The generators for fresh air had been broken down for days, the sweat was dripping down the walls. Most of the people inside were women and children, just a few elderly men. We cowered on benches, there was nowhere to lie down. The men stood by the bunker doors for hours watching the air raids and listening to the shelling in Brinkum, which was getting nearer. Of course they gave us running commentaries the whole time. Inside, we were afraid and hoped the whole ordeal would be over soon. But what would the end look like? We young girls were frightened, I was just 19, how would the conquerors behave?[23]

Doctors, lacking even basic medicines, handed out what comfort they could. If there was a shortage of oxygen in the shelter, one said, 'you won't feel that you are suffocating, it will be just like falling asleep.'[24]

In his diary, Albrecht Mertz recorded one of the few occasions when a queue at the food shops brought its reward.

Today was chiefly dedicated to acquiring food, and was doubly difficult for housewives, who have it hard enough as it is. The queues were longer than usual and plenty of things weren't even available at the grocer's. At midday there was a full alarm and endless fighting units flew over us but fortunately weren't aiming at us. In a quieter phase we even managed to eat lunch, a feast such as we hadn't had for ages. In one of the already delicious pea soups there was a thick smattering of fatty pork, which allegedly came from animals killed by bombs and made its way into households as 'substandard meat', exceeding the usual measly ration with half a kilo per head, after queuing up of course. The alarm lasted for six hours and half the day was lost, so to speak, we could only do our necessary work in the evening.[25]

Even as the bombs fell, some attempt was made to maintain the conventions of ordinary life. Helmut Schmidt, a fifteen-year-old who was trying to avoid being called up, went to church to be confirmed on March 22nd.

Father had managed to persuade Pastor Rahn to confirm me . . . I can still remember in the interview that father and the pastor talked about the attempted assassination of Hitler and the pastor said it had been an act of divine providence that Hitler had escaped unscathed. The confirmation was held at 8 a.m. owing to the air raids, and on the way back we only made it as far as the Herdentor before the sirens wailed and we had to rush into the shelter in the city ramparts. Heavy air mines fell, with time fuses, although we didn't know that at the time. At the festive lunch at home – Mother and Grandma had made a big effort in spite of everything – there was suddenly a huge bang, everything shook and rattled, the windows that were left intact fell around our ears. In the park and on Breitenweg a time-fuse bomb had exploded from that morning. We cleared up the mess, swept the glass shards up and then, still wearing my confirmation suit which was much too big for me, I boarded up the broken windows with the hardboard which was always lying around.[26]

Another boy who managed to avoid call-up was Reinhard Groscurth whose father had a high-ranking friend prepared to risk his life.

I was hidden in a cellar and was only allowed out for fresh air once at night. But two days later my father came and allowed me to return home. One of the bosses of the defence department, a Bremen merchant and lieutenant commander whom my father knew well, had given him a certificate saying that I was employed as a courier and therefore may not be called up by the army or any other party sections. On Monday 9th April my father introduced me to my new 'boss' in the 'Haus des Reiches', but I was never requested to actually perform any errands . . . It was only after the war that my father told me how the brave officer N.B. got hold of the army passes as well as seals and writing paper from other sections. In the 'Haus des Reiches' all of the employees had had to leave all the doors open before going into the cellar during air raids. Nobody noticed that N.B. had stayed upstairs and helped himself to the stationery he needed.[27]

The concentration of bombing increased by the day with waves of attacks coming in at twenty-minute intervals.

Our little Hans, who was 18 months old, was sitting on his potty. I was just on the way out to buy some flour when it happened. The sirens weren't working, so the bombs fell without an alarm. Our house literally fell apart, the doors were ripped off. Our little son screamed, the teapot had fallen on him but luckily spilled only cold tea all over him. We had a guardian angel. The child was fine – and had it been one minute later I'd have gone out and been one of the dead outside our front door. We put the baby in the pram, carried it over the dead and made our way to the school in Regensburger Strasse, where there was an emergency shelter. The next bomb attack which followed completely destroyed the house. In the evening we went in search of somewhere to stay. We found accommodation in a shelter for the homeless.[28]

By April 21st most of Bremen was in ruins and British forces were closing in. But still there was no surrender. 'A handful of madmen are in charge,' wrote one disillusioned citizen as he surveyed the wreckage that was once a street of fine houses. 'Everything is covered in a chalky layer of greyish red . . . the road is strewn with tree branches and rubble.' But now the end was near. Irmgard Hagemeyer saw it all through the eyes of a twelve-year-old.

The English and Americans dropped flyers demanding the people of Bremen to surrender. We children were strictly forbidden to pick up or read any of these flyers. A rumour was going around that they were also dropping poisoned sweets, and fountain pens that would explode and blow you to smithereens if you unscrewed them. On the Osterdeich and at the Brommyplatz near us, shelter trenches had been dug. We played hide and seek in them. As the front approached, the people of Bremen hid or buried their last remaining valuables. My father hid his home-brewed potato schnapps, which was an excellent medium of exchange. Everything was in a state of collapse, but the newspapers and radio gave orders to fight to the very last. On the walls of the houses posters were stuck up saying 'Weser-Ems will not give in' and was supposed to spur on the population to hang in there and fight. But most Bremeners yearned for surrender. Their constant hunger, fears for husbands and sons at the front, sleepless nights in the bunker and despair at burned houses had exhausted the population.[29]

The last vestiges of opposition descended into chaos. As a measure of the disorganisation that now ruled, an intelligence officer in Bierden, a village which had been vacated by German troops twenty-four hours earlier, picked up the telephone to find himself speaking to a German staff officer. The caller wanted to know how close were the British. Replying in German, the intelligence officer assured him that the village was secure. The delighted officer promised an early visit, bringing with him his commanding general. The subsequent ambush bagged not only two senior officers but also a fine Mercedes.

In the city itself the last line of defence was left to the young and frightened.

I went into the street and saw boys my age (around 13–15-years-old) had gathered on a street corner to go to war. Of course they had no uniform and no equipment. There was one gun for around ten children. They were ordered to march to Brinkum to hold up and chase out the English army. However, the 'leaders' of these children's corps preferred to stay in Bremen. When they reached the front line in

Brinkum, the English soldiers came, disarmed them and sent them home.[30]

The justification for Bremen holding out against impossible odds for as long as it did was provided by Grand Admiral Karl Doenitz. Now that the ships of the German navy were no longer in serious combat, they were remaining as a coastal ferry service, bringing military and civilian refugees out of east Germany to the Baltic havens, such as Hamburg, that were still under German control and to Denmark. Casualties were high. Early in the year, the 25,000-ton *Wilhelm Gustloff*, carrying some 9,500 passengers, was struck by Russian torpedoes. Fewer than 1,000 were saved in what remains the worst ever sea disaster. But this was no deterrent to those still desperate to get away.

At the harbour, everyone was pushing their way towards the ships. There were some appalling scenes. Humans turned into animals. Women threw their children into the water, just so they could come along. The general confusion was then increased by fully disoriented troops streaming into the town and the houses, mingling with the refugees and pushing their way onto the ships. To get through the barriers to the ships, soldiers snatched children off their mothers, saying they wanted to take their family on board. Others dressed in women's clothing to try and get away on the ships. If they were discovered during the patrol, they were brought on board and after a brief trial were shot by court martial. The first of these deserters were hung from lampposts with signs around their necks to serve as a deterrent to others.[31]

A rather more cheerful image of the evacuation has been left by Martin Bergau who praised the German navy for 'an amazing job . . . thousands were saved at the last minute'. The writer was carried to Rönne on the Danish island of Bornholm.

We got some Danish money, and I bought myself a huge piece of cake with cream. Here it was peacetime, we didn't need to black anything out. We could hardly believe that this was possible. The next day I went down to the beach with some companions. The March sun was warm enough for us to take off our pullovers. I was shocked to see that my lovely marine pullover was almost crawling, it was so full of lice. The others noticed the same thing. The straw camp was obviously seething with lice. I made a fire with dried driftwood and burned the 'lousy pelt' with indignation, thinking to myself: 'If your mother knew that you had lice she'd die of shame.'[32]

Bornholm did not remain a peaceful settlement. In the early days of May, even as the surrender was being signed in Berlin, the Russians bombed the island. The reluctance of the German garrison to hand over its weapons led to widespread destruction.

Knowing what was at stake, Doenitz made an emotional plea for Hamburg to be held. The response from the senior officer, Major General Walz, was to put together an anti-tank battalion consisting of land-locked submarines, grounded air crews and police which carried out several daring commando raids. It could hardly be described as a counter-attack but it slowed the British advance by a few days.

Montgomery's assault across the Elbe was made at night by the Commandos and a battalion of the Forty-Sixth Brigade of the Cameronian Scottish Rifles.

The order, 'Get dressed'. Putting on our packs we moved down the road towards the river, with our weapons, following the small blue lights to our allotted Buffalos. The back ramp dropped and the Platoon marched on with all our gear. The ramp was made secure. With the engines roaring the monster moved forward up a steep flood bank. Then it was over the top and down the bank into the water. The propellers at the rear forced us forward. Most of the noise of the battle was up river, to our right. On reaching the far side of the river the Buffalos could not get out of the water because of the steepness of the bank. So we climbed out of the well, jumping ashore on to a narrow embankment. Facing us, for as far as we could see, was a steep, high bank that went almost vertical. We couldn't see the top. Climbing it was a task in itself with the equipment we were carrying. Getting footholds where we could, pulling on the well-rooted shrubs, it was a good job there were no enemy about. On reaching the top we dug in for the night. Standing to at dawn we had a fine view. Far below us was a troop of amphibious tanks crossing the river. Further up again the Engineers had put a Bailey bridge across during the night. German planes were attacking it, throwing up large sprays of water. That is until some of our fighters arrived.[33]

Edward Loughlin was in the second wave of assault troops, crossing the river in one of a small flotilla of four-man boats. 'We almost swamped the thing half way across where the current was swiftest.' Those ahead had cleared the German positions closest to the river but further inland the small arms fire was still heavy, muffled only by the persistent scream of artillery shells. Loughlin and his comrades moved forward cautiously.

There was a man in civilian clothes running across a plowed field toward a farm house. Being dressed in civilian clothes didn't mean he wasn't a German soldier. I put my rifle to my shoulder and fired one shot just behind his heels – he jumped straight up in the air in the middle of a stride – and then I placed a shot about five yards in front of him. He got the message and stopped immediately, hands raised high over his head . . . We moved on up to the man, guns pointed at him and at the house. We asked if he was armed – he said no – we patted him down, turned his pockets inside out, made him put his hands straight up in the air to forestall any hand signals to the house. We took up concealed positions and hollered at the house. There was a dead silence, no response. So the BAR team fired a burst of 20 rounds through the window, the sergeant ordered 'Shaky' Fraley and myself to rush the house – which we did. I kicked in the front door and Shaky went past me with his Thompson firing into the two rooms we could see – and I fired my rifle around the house. After the deafening sounds of the weapons all that remained was smoke and silence – furniture and clothes chests and other stuff was fairly well damaged by the grenade and the shots. We motioned for the civilian to come on in, putting him in front of us as a shield, looked through a couple more rooms and then noticed a door closed – we made him open the door and precede us down some stairs and there was a sight I'll never forget! There, cowering, were ten or 12 people, men and women, kids to oldsters, all civilians.[34]

As the troops moved on the opposition melted away. There was still Hamburg to win but negotiations with the city's Gauleiter for a peaceful handover were already well advanced. Meanwhile, Montgomery pushed on to Wismar to secure a line that blocked the land route to Denmark. It was here that he at last had his rendezvous with the Russians. Captain William Brown of the Eighth Parachute Battalion was given the job of arranging a formal meeting between Montgomery and a senior Russian commander.

We had no difficulty in finding our way as the Russians had the equivalent of a military policeman at every corner and X road, and as we approached they indicated which direction we should go. We made the arrangements and then the General gave us a large glass of what tasted like vodka and rum and drank a toast. On the way home I could hardly see! I had to explain to Montgomery's Chief of Staff why I was tipsy to say the least. He said I had acted perfectly properly in the circumstances.

But coping with the Red Army was never easy.

We had a lot of trouble with the Russians coming into the town at night and collecting women. When we complained they told us to shoot them! When the armistice was signed they fired all their guns to celebrate, mostly in our direction. They told us to fire ours back at them. They really were impossible.[35]

For the Germans caught east of the line it was harder to take a philosophical attitude towards the strong and unpredictable Russians.

In armed groups of two or more, they broke into homes, raped women and girls of every age, stealing and looting along the way. The first thing they always asked for was watches and the liquor, then they took torches, alarm clocks, shoes, clothes, food and anything else they could find. Although their commander attempted to stop the pillage, the soldiers took no notice, and Ida R and Waltraud G were raped in our house. We shouted a Russian officer for help, and he rapped the soldier on the head with his pistol . . .

The Russians were particularly attracted to a children's home where there were teenage girls.

> The barricaded iron doors offered no protection. They tried to break in, and then shot their way through the windows. They locked up the warden and his wife and set about mass rape of the girls. One of the sisters escaped in spite of the curfew and fetched the nearest commander, who got rid of the drunken soldiers. A poster was put up on the gates of the children's home forbidding soldiers to enter the building, but they ignored it. In despair, many people committed suicide.[36]

It is doubtful that Hitler gave much time to worrying about what was happening to his people in the east. There was more than enough to concern him closer to home. After Zhukov and Konev joined hands west of Berlin it was only a matter of time before the eight Russian armies surrounding the city penetrated the centre. With his forces in the west isolated and impotent and Berlin in its death throes, Hitler all but gave up, telling his entourage that he was ready to take his own life. News of this soon reached Himmler's headquarters where the persistent Schellenberg made yet another plea to his master to assume power and to negotiate peace. For support, he turned again to Count Bernadotte who met Himmler for the last time on April 22nd, at the Swedish Consulate in Luebeck. They had barely started their talk when the lights went out and the bombs fell. The meeting resumed in the cellar by candle-light. The strain on Himmler was all too obvious. He was 'inde-scribably tired and nervous', said Bernadotte, 'and fighting hard to maintain his outer calm'. But he had come to a decision.

> It is very probable that Hitler is already dead and, if not, he very probably will be within the next few days. Berlin is surrounded and it is only a matter of days until it falls. The last three times we three have met you urged me to end the war. I agreed with you that the situation was hopeless, that the war must stop, and that Germany must admit she is beaten. But I have not been able to see how I could break my oath to the Führer. Now the situation is different. I recog-nise that Germany is defeated.

Himmler continued:

> In this new situation I have a free hand. In order to protect as much
> of Germany as possible from a Russian invasion I am willing to capit-
> ulate on the Western Front and to let the Western Powers' troops
> advance as rapidly as possible eastwards. Conversely I am not
> prepared to capitulate on the Eastern Front.[37]

Bernadotte knew it was hopeless but while refusing to contact
Eisenhower, which would have compromised his neutrality, he
agreed to pass on the offer, via his government, to the American
and British representatives in Stockholm. When Bernadotte set off
for home, Schellenberg went with him part of the way. Under orders
from Himmler he was to have one last try at getting Bernadotte
to appeal directly to Eisenhower.

> However, at our parting on the road near Waren in Mecklenburg,
> Count Bernadotte said to me, 'The Reichsführer no longer under-
> stands the realities of his own situation. I cannot help him any more.
> He should have taken Germany's affairs into his own hands after my
> first visit. I can hold out little chance for him now. And you, my dear
> Schellenberg, would be wiser to think of yourself.' I did not know
> what to reply to this.

Schellenberg drove back to Hohenlychen, slept for two hours, and
was then called to Himmler at about 12.30.

> He was still in bed, the picture of misery, and said that he felt ill.
> All I could say was that there was nothing more I could do for him;
> it was up to him. He had got to take some action. At lunch we
> discussed the military situation in Berlin, which was steadily growing
> worse.
>   At about four o'clock, having convinced him that it would be
> unwise to drive to Berlin, we drove towards Wustrow. In Löwenberg
> we were caught in a traffic jam, troops having become involved with
> the unending columns of fleeing civilians which blocked all the roads
> between Berlin and Mecklenburg. As we drove on, Himmler said to
> me for the first time, 'Schellenberg, I dread what is to come.'[38]

Bernadotte duly reported to his foreign minister who passed on the message to the American and British representatives in Stockholm. The response was easily predicted.

Admiral Leahy, the White House Chief of Staff, was with Truman in the Communications Centre of the Pentagon when there was a call from 10 Downing Street. Churchill said he had information from Sweden that Himmler had asked Count Bernadotte to make an offer of the surrender of all German forces on the western front, including those in Holland, Denmark and Norway. Himmler was speaking for the German government because Hitler had suffered a cerebral haemorrhage and was not expected to live for more than a few days.

> Truman told the Prime Minister that America could agree only to an unconditional surrender on all fronts in agreement with Russia and Britain. Churchill was anxious to end the war. Truman said he was too, but we must stand by our commitments.
>
> While we were in the Pentagon, Acting Secretary of State Grew brought in a message from Minister H.V. Johnson in Stockholm, containing the same information just given to us over the telephone by Churchill. This looked definitely like the beginning of the end of Nazism in Germany.
>
> At the President's direction, I sent a cable to Stalin, informing him of the situation and reaffirming our intention to accept only an unconditional surrender to the three powers on all fronts, and that if the Germans would accept these terms, they should surrender at once to our local commanders in the field. Stalin was told that if he was in accord with this arrangement we would direct our Minister in Sweden to so inform Himmler. An identical message was sent to Churchill.[39]

By now, rumours of Himmler's bid to end the war and to create, in effect, an anti-Soviet alliance, were front-page news. Apparent confirmation came with a report on Radio Atlantic, a supposedly 'free German' underground station but in fact operated by British intelligence, which spiced up Himmler's role in the negotiations with claims that his sole purpose was to supplant Hitler. And this was precisely what the Führer himself concluded.

Much has been written about the fall of Berlin, most recently in a monumental work by Anthony Beevor.[40] But in any account of victory over Germany it needs to be said that Soviet revenge for Stalingrad and much else was swift and terrible. The Red Army, said one commentator, 'drove towards Berlin in what can only be called a frenzy, impelled by hatred, vengeance, alcohol and testosterone'. The iron discipline for which the Soviets were famed was not just relaxed but abandoned. Raping and looting were the orders of the day.

It was a free-for-all for some Russians. We managed to chase some away by fetching the commissar. Uri, uri (watch) was their battle cry. With my own eyes I saw one 'comrade' show his left arm, which was full of watches. It was time to plunder. My mother had put all the laundry back in the cupboard, and another one of them would pull it all out again. All the laundry was lying around everywhere. Who would have thought that the Russians would take musical instruments too? It wasn't just a few harmonicas and the mandolin which went, my decent Stradivari fiddle was taken too. Now they were chasing the women. My mother, who was 48, had to jump over three five-foot fences to flee one very keen follower. But they moved on, having heard that lots of women had assembled to find shelter in the air raid bunker on Wilhelmsruger Damm.

We'd hidden my 19-year-old sister – she was safe in a tiny room, lying on a shelf with a wardrobe pushed in front of the door, which was wallpapered. My mother spoke good Polish, which helped to prevent the worse from happening. My 43-year-old father had grown a beard and pretended to be an old man. A patroller pulled down my trousers to see if I was wearing a uniform underneath – my mother had a hard time convincing him that at 15, I was too young to be a soldier. My parents hid me too after that. We only ever moved the wardrobe aside to fetch food and hid again sharpish. How we trembled when a Russian went through my sister's make-up and a pot fell behind the wardrobe! But it was all OK.[41]

Others were less fortunate. If they did not suffer at the hands of the Russians, they were liable to fall victim to their own side.

The snipers fired at everything that moved. On April 24th I went back to the flat for the last time. The walls and furniture had been shot through like Swiss cheese . . . From our cellar you could look out to the factory grounds, where something was moving. A sergeant was sitting in the cellar, firing like crazy in the direction of the factory ground. Before long there were cries, and a man staggered over yelling 'you idiot! You've just shot six comrades – they were all Germans!' He sank down on the stairs, devastated. It's incredible what can happen.[42]

Berliners came to think of their city as the Reichsscheiterhaufen, 'the Reich's funeral pyre'. It was certainly Hitler's. On April 29th, he married Eva Braun, his mistress of twelve years who 'after many years of true friendship came of her own free will to this city . . . to share my fate'. Their suicide took place the following day and their bodies were burned in the Chancellery garden as the Russians shelled the building.

Meanwhile, from Hamburg, Hildegard Wagener sent birthday greetings to her husband Hans, somewhere in the east.

To my dear husband, our birthday boy! On your 31st birthday I wish most of all that you get through the war as well as you have so far, so that you can return home soon to your little family . . . This wish, which we make every year, has to be fulfilled. And I have the feeling that it soon will be . . . We can hardly imagine a calm, peaceful life with daily work, free evenings and Sunday walks. My dear husband, just a short birthday greeting today, but I am thinking more tenderly and longingly of you. A loving embrace, Your Hildegard.[43]

19
Climax

Hitler's last political act was to anoint his successor. Disillusioned with Himmler and equally furious with Goering who, from his hideaway in Bavaria, had telegraphed Hitler asking to be formally acknowledged as the next Führer, his choice fell on Admiral Doenitz. Doenitz saw it as his thankless task to continue to play for time, to give substance to the offer of a wind-down, even surrender, in the west while concentrating what resources he had on saving those of his countrymen who were in the path of the Russians. It may, as he claimed, have been the only strategy open to him but that did not make it workable. Most west Germans who soon got to know of the prospect of an armistice were only too happy to lay down their arms. This was not at all what Doenitz wanted. Without a fight he had nothing to offer in return for an armistice. But his stirring words begging for sacrifices on behalf of comrades in the east went largely unheard.

Setting up his headquarters in a medieval castle in Flensburg in northern Germany, close to the Danish border, Doenitz busied himself creating his 'acting government'. It was not an easy task. He could not ignore the Nazi establishment but at the same time he needed to show the Allies that he was his own man, one with whom they could do business without compromising their pledge never to deal with the Hitler gang.

Assuming ultimate authority to the end, Hitler had drawn up a list of appointees, including Goebbels, Bormann and Seyss Inquart, which Doenitz felt safe in ignoring. Not that he had to worry about Goebbels who had taken his Führer's way out after poisoning his wife and six children. Others, like Ribbentrop, who might have expected a job, accepted their dismissal without much argument. The biggest problem was Himmler. He was already acting as if he was head of state and there could be no certainty that he would accept Doenitz's authority. The admiral decided on a pre-emptive strike.

On the evening of April 30 I told my ADC to telephone to Himmler, from whom I had parted in Luebeck only a few hours before, and ask him to come to Flensburg forthwith. To my ADC he retorted with a blunt refusal, but when I myself spoke to him and told him that his presence was essential, he eventually consented to come.

At about midnight he arrived, accompanied by six armed SS officers, and was received by my aide-de-camp, Luedde-Neurath. I offered Himmler a chair and myself sat down behind my writing desk, upon which lay, hidden by some papers, a pistol with the safety catch off. I had never done anything of this sort in my life before, but I did not know what the outcome of this meeting might be.

I handed Himmler the telegram containing my appointment. 'Please read this,' I said. I watched him closely. As he read, an expression of astonishment, indeed, of consternation spread over his face. All hope seemed to collapse within him. He went very pale. Finally he stood up and bowed. 'Allow me,' he said, 'to become the second man in your state.' I replied that that was out of the question and that there was no way in which I could make any use of his services.[1]

Himmler departed. Knowing the fate that awaited him as the most notorious of Nazi war criminals, he disguised himself as a private soldier but was unable to keep up the pretence when stopped at a routine check by British military police. He was arrested but bit on a poison capsule before he could be interrogated.

Deciding who he did not want alongside him was easier for Doenitz than putting together a viable administration. His first choices had a habit of not being available when the call came or, as in the case of Field Marshal von Manstein, whom Doenitz wanted as Chief of Staff, having already been taken into Allied captivity. With no choice but to fall back on the Berlin old guard, Doenitz called on Keitel and Jodl to join him in shaping the future of Germany.

After the surrender, the Doenitz government was widely judged to have been something of a joke. But for its brief period of office it was taken seriously enough by the western Allies who appreciated the need for a central authority that Germans would accept. Doenitz was not an instinctive politician and he made some bad mistakes, not least his fulsome tribute to the late Führer. But his strategy for ending the war – a gradual withdrawal of the armies on the eastern front to the demarcation line along the Elbe where they could surrender to American or British forces – made, for Germany, the best sense in unfavourable circumstances. It was a policy overtaken by events, as was his maritime rescue operation along the Baltic coast, but over two million soldiers and civilians who did escape Russian captivity had every reason to be grateful to Doenitz.

Hoping to soften Anglo-American demands for immediate and unconditional surrender, Doenitz strengthened the line from the Elbe to the Baltic with the intention of holding Hamburg and Luebeck as bargaining counters. If those two cities were to fall it would be easy enough for Montgomery to move up into the provinces of Schleswig Holstein, taking Kiel on the way to Flensburg itself and, a little way beyond, occupied Denmark. And fall they did, even as Doenitz was briefing Admiral von Friedeburg on a proposed approach to Montgomery for a negotiated surrender.

On May 2nd, British and Canadian spearheads reached the Baltic to take Wismar and Luebeck. Except for a pocket west of Bremen, there was no longer any real opposition on the Twenty-First Army front. Reconnaissance flights showed white flags flying from houses fifty miles behind the enemy line. That night, two German divisions surrendered and hours later General Wolz, commander of the Hamburg garrison, agreed to hand over the city to the Seventh British Armoured Division.

BBC correspondent Wynford Vaughan Thomas watched the German troops coming out of Hamburg to surrender.

> Since two o'clock this morning this endless stream of transport has been pouring through this town, under the white flags hung over the

shattered houses by the inhabitants who are standing in the streets looking dumbfounded at this wreckage of the Wehrmacht that's going past us. For, make no mistake about it, this Army we see going by us is the most curious collection of wreckage you ever saw – improvised cars with people riding on the bumpers, half-track vehicles, thousands of them, going through in a steady stream, and to make matters even more fantastic they've got their own traffic policemen directing them, under British orders, standing on the corner waving listlessly on, as the thing goes steadily by us.

These people are defeated soldiers – you can see it in their eyes. In the middle of them there comes a much more joyous note. We see a charabanc full of R.A.F. released prisoners, cheering as they go by, and the Germans on the half-tracks look glumly on.[2]

An unavoidably triumphant note was struck by British correspondents who discovered the Radio Hamburg studio used by William Joyce, otherwise Lord Haw-Haw, the Fascist propagandist who had defected to Germany to give vent to his vicious prejudices. Joyce's nasal diatribes, heralded by the call sign 'Germany calling, Germany calling', fascinated and repelled listeners in equal measure. Now he was gone, possibly to Denmark or Norway speculated one reporter, and 'in his place, this is the BBC calling all the long-suffering listeners in Britain who for six years have had to put up with the acid tones of Mr. Joyce speaking over the same wavelength that I'm using to speak to you now'.[3] In Joyce's desk was found his radio schedule with 'a pause to collect my wits' written in for April 10th. Well, said the man from the BBC, he and the citizens of Hamburg have now plenty of time to collect their wits as they survey a city of 'blackened walls and utterly burned out streets'.[4]

Some of the few buildings left standing were the tower-block air raid shelters, an example of planners' lateral thinking. While the policy in Britain was to build a large number of shelters which protected against flying debris but were vulnerable to a direct hit, the Germans built huge concrete bunkers above and below ground, designed to protect against any attack. One shelter in Hamburg, called the Holy Ghost for its location in Holy Ghost Plaza, sheltered as many as 10,000 people.

Among the survivors of the destruction of Hamburg was a pregnant girl whose father happened across Corporal Dai Evans.

'Meine Tochter ist schwanger,' he said in an urgent voice. 'Sie muss sofort zum Artz gehen.'

He had me there. I knew his daughter was something or other, and that she must see a doctor at once, but I didn't know what the adjective 'schwanger' meant.

'Augenblick mal,' I said and pulled out my little Collins dictionary. I began to leaf through the pages, but he grabbed my arm impatiently and pulled me to a horse-drawn van that stood nearby. Flinging open the rear door he pointed to a girl who was sitting in the back and one glance told me at once what 'schwanger' meant, as her stomach was hugely distended and her sweat-streaked face told me the matter was urgent.

Using his lieutenant's requisitioned Mercedes, 'a nice one, dark green', Corporal Evans got the patient to a hospital.

The German nurse asked what had happened. The girl's father and I told her in some detail. She thanked me for the part I had played and asked me to thank my officer 'Fur seine Menschlichkeit'. (A quick look at Collins told me the word meant 'humanity', another one for my collection. I always picture the sister-nun when I hear the word.)

Talking to the father, she asked him where the girl's husband was. 'Wir wissen gar nicht von ihm.' ('We know nothing about him.') And he went on to say the girl's husband was a lorry driver with the Luftwaffe on the Eastern Front and they hadn't heard from him or his unit for two or three months. While we were talking, a younger edition of the sister came along to tell us all was well with the girl, but the baby wouldn't arrive for another hour or so yet, so I excused myself, saying I had to return to duty. The older sister held out her hand and, to my great surprise, she said in English, with hardly a trace of accent, 'You are a good man. May God go with you.'

As I stared at her, she laughed and, lapsing into German again, she told me she had as a girl spent some time in Holland with an

English family and there had learned some of the language. She looked forward to learning more in the future.

I drove back in steadier fashion and reported to my lieutenant that all seemed well. I also passed on the message thanking him for his humanity. He grinned broadly.

'It's a strange old world, isn't it? We've spent years trying to kill the bastards, then we go all out to save them. I hope that the little sod we've helped into the world isn't fighting *our* children in 20 years' time.'[5]

As Hamburg succumbed, the Eleventh Armoured Division prepared to enter Neumünster to the north of the city, only thirty miles from the naval base of Kiel. A few hours later, British troops of the Sixth Airborne Division linked up with the Russians near Wismar, while two of the German armies that had opposed Marshal Rokossovsky's Second Belorussian Army north of Berlin declared their readiness to surrender.

As if this was not bad enough for Doenitz, May 2nd brought devastating news from Berlin. After a climactic frenzy of street-to-street and house-to-house fighting, the city had given itself over to the invaders. The death toll was put at over 500,000.

And then there was Italy. Once said by Churchill to be the 'soft underbelly' of Fascist Europe, the Allies had duly plunged the knife but to wound, not to kill. After the liberation of Rome in June 1944, the first Axis capital to fall to the Allies, the offensive slowed as men and supplies were switched to France, seen by American planners as the main field of action.

By now Mussolini was a puppet leader whose strings were pulled by the German military. Tough fighting continued but German forces felt secure behind the Gothic Line, about 155 miles north of Rome, a system of fortifications through the Northern Apennines built, like the Siegfried Line, to be an impenetrable barrier, in this instance, guarding the Po Valley and the cities of northern Italy – Milan, Turin, Genoa and Venice. The decisive action came in mid-April when, aided by Italian partisans, the US Fifth Army and the British Eighth Army broke through into the

Po Valley to take Bologna. This was the signal for a coordinated anti-Fascist rising across northern Italy. The main centres were seized from German control, Mussolini, his mistress and a gang of supporters were captured near the Swiss frontier, tried and executed. General Karl Wolff, the senior German officer in occupied Italy, followed up on earlier tentative proposals for a settlement with an offer to withdraw his troops into Germany. But unconditional surrender was demanded. It came into force on May 2nd and applied not only to Italy but also to a large part of southwest Austria.

Finally, just to make the day for Doenitz and his beleaguered administration, May 2nd marked the end of effective resistance in the south of Germany where the US Third Army had shot off in three directions, driving into eastern Germany, into Czechoslovakia and into the Austrian Alps to take Salzburg. By now nobody worried about the Southern Redoubt where, supposedly, the leaders of the Reich with the SS elite would hole themselves up in a mountain stronghold with the purpose of waging guerrilla warfare. The only discovery of note was the whereabouts of Hermann Goering who gave himself up having decided that American captivity was preferable to the house arrest ordered by Hitler. In the short term he proved to be right. Taking him off drugs, military doctors restored his health and mental agility which he put to effective use at the Nuremberg trials. His life ended with a bite on a cyanide capsule.

The other revelation was the number of high-ranking families that had taken refuge in and around Berchtesgaden, Hitler's mountain hideaway, to escape Allied bombing. It was a pathetic haul but at least it proved beyond doubt that there was no fight left in the Nazi leadership.

Captain William Morgan, an engineer attached to the US Seventh Army in Salzburg, was one who took the opportunity to see Berchtesgaden and Hitler's 'Eagle's Nest' at first hand.

Unfortunately, the US 8th Air Force had done such a complete job on the top of the mountain that access to the summit was barred by rubble. In addition, the departed Nazis had destroyed the elevator system which also looked booby-trapped. However, we managed to reach the SS headquarters, a plush caseme, high up on the hillside, where there had been an elaborate restaurant and living quarters complex. This area had suffered also from air attacks, but there were several lower levels in this structure which escaped including a huge wine cellar with thousands of bottles of wine and shelves holding hundreds of heavy silver-edged plates and other dining utensils. Soon after we arrived, a contingent of the 2nd French Armored Division came up the hill, to savor what to them must have been the sweetest moment in five years, actually standing on the battered remains of Hitler's most hallowed ground. Within minutes, these grubby but excited French soldiers were carrying lighted newspapers as torches down into the pitch dark wine cellars, and emerging with burlap bags full of the choicest vintages. Soon, they were skimming the heavy plates out over the valley towards the little village far below, Colonel Chubbuck and I put several bottles in our jeep for souvenirs, one of which I still have, unopened over the years.

The excursion was memorable for another but sadder reason. Returning to Salzburg, Captain Morgan found a letter waiting for him from his father-in-law. It was to tell him that his wife, Henrietta, whom he had not seen for nine months, had died of cancer a week earlier. A wire sent to him had never arrived. They had been married less than two years.[6]

It was against a backdrop of uniformly bad news for Doenitz and his team that Admiral von Friedeburg and General Kinzel, Chief of Staff to Field Marshal Bosch who commanded the forces opposing the Twenty-First Army Group, met with Montgomery at the field marshal's headquarters on Lüneburg Heath. Following Doenitz's strategy, Friedeburg's opening bid was to offer the surrender of north Germany on the understanding that Montgomery would also accept those troops and civilians who were being driven back into British and Canadian lines by the Russian advance. No, said Montgomery; it was not his business to intrude on entirely Russian affairs. What he was prepared to consider was the unconditional surrender of all German forces on the

Twenty-First Army front west of the Elbe, to include those in Holland and Denmark.

Friedeburg was clearly thrown by this. He had expected a more sympathetic hearing to his plea to save as many as possible of his compatriots from Soviet captivity. But more to the point, he seemed to have closed his mind to the parlous state of German forces on the western front or, possibly, he was simply ignorant of the true state of affairs. In any event, he tried to hold to his objective by suggesting that while he had no authority to end German resistance to the west, he felt that acceptance was likely if allowance could be made for efforts to rescue German forces in Courland, East Prussia and Pomerania. Since this could only be done by sea, Doenitz was not yet prepared to surrender the German navy. But by now Friedeburg knew that his bargaining counters were worthless. At one point, when Montgomery showed him his battle maps revealing the hopeless plight of German forces, Friedeburg broke down. He agreed to go back to Doenitz to propose an unconditional surrender of all forces on the northern and western flanks of the Twenty-First Army Group.

He went away with a small consolation. While Montgomery had rejected a plan whereby German forces would withdraw slowly as British troops advanced – this, argued Friedeburg, was to protect the civilian population – he did agree to discuss the best way of looking after the civilians in the occupied areas. He also gave an assurance that, while he was not able to accept the surrender 'in a body' of forces that had fought only against the Red Army, 'any member of the German Army who arrives in the sector of the Twenty-First Army Group from the east and wishes to surrender will be taken prisoner'. Montgomery added that the surrender of the German navy did not necessarily mean that the evacuation of German troops and civilians over the Baltic had to be stopped immediately.

Friedeburg returned to what must have been a tense discussion with Doenitz and Field Marshal Keitel. All they could do was to play for time. Further delaying tactics would not succeed with Montgomery who had voiced his readiness to continue fighting if

Friedeburg failed to return with a satisfactory answer. On the other hand, a surrender to the Twenty-First Army would raise Allied expectations of a general capitulation which could be dragged out over days, perhaps even weeks.

Friedeburg returned to Lüneburg Heath on the morning of May 4th with power to surrender over a million troops in northwest Europe. Among the war reporters who witnessed the event was Leonard Mosley.

> Montgomery kept the German delegates waiting, standing miserably about in the rain, first while he told us of the events which had led up to the Armistice, and later while he conferred with his *aides* inside the caravan. With their backs towards us, Von Friedeburg and his three companions stood there, on the spot where all of them must, at some time in their careers, have watched German armies manoeuvring on the plain below in the exercises of pre-War days, and where now unending convoys of British troops were moving. Montgomery kept them standing there, letting them watch and think, letting the rain splash over them, until he judged the moment right; and then he sent Colonel Ewart clattering down the steps to round the Nazi generals up and shepherd them to the tiny army tent on the lip of Lüneburg tor, where the Kleig lights were ready, and the microphones, for photographs to be taken and records made of the signing ceremony.[7]

After sitting the German delegates at a plain trestle table with an army blanket serving as a covering, Montgomery read the terms of the surrender.

> 'You will now sign,' he said, and, meekly, one by one, they came. The Post Office pen scraped on the paper; the delegates sat down again, expressionless, and waited. There was a moment, while the last photographs were being taken, when Von Friedeburg turned his full face into the lights, an expression of tremendous anguish in his eyes as he posed for the pictures; and then the flap of the tent dropped and it was over.[8]

But not for Friedeburg. His next mission was to Eisenhower in Reims on May 5th. There his reception was even colder than that given him by Montgomery. Addressing himself to Eisenhower's Chief of Staff, General Walter Bedell Smith, the unfortunate German plenipotentiary pressed for a separate peace. The answer was an emphatic No. What was demanded was the unconditional surrender to all Allies simultaneously of all German forces. Told of this, Doenitz made the curious decision to send Keitel's Chief of Staff officer, General Jodl, to Reims to reinforce Friedeburg's arguments. Of all Doenitz's colleagues, Hitler's former chief of operations, and most devoted of followers, was unlikely to impress the Americans. And so it proved. Various compromises were offered – for example, a surrender in two stages with an end to fighting followed at a later date by an end to troop movements. All were rejected but Jodl's signal to Flensburg, detailing the unpalatable terms, gave time for a warning to German troops in the east that they had less than forty-eight hours to pull back. The response to Jodl came in the early hours of May 7th: 'Admiral Doenitz authorises signature of surrender under conditions stated.'

The simultaneous surrender to the western Allies and the Russians was signed at 2.41 a.m. After the brief ceremony, Jodl rose. First in English, then continuing in German, he said: 'Sir, with this signature, the German nation and the German Armed Forces are at the mercy of the victors. Through this war, which has lasted for five years, both have performed more, and perhaps suffered more, than any other nation on earth. At this hour, we can only hope that the victors will be generous.' There was no answer. Jodl saluted and left the room.

Having presided over the surrender of all German forces on all fronts, Eisenhower telephoned 'Pug' Ismay, Churchill's Chief of Staff. Ismay was in bed asleep when the Supreme Commander put through his call. Though of little significance in itself, sixty years on it tells us something of the problems of communication, even at the highest level, in the pre-digital age.

About 3 a.m. that morning, I was awakened by my telephone bell, and told that the Supreme Commander was on the line. These nocturnal calls had never brought good news and I was afraid that something had gone wrong. But my mind was soon put at rest. 'Is that you, Pug?' 'Yes, Ike. What has happened?' 'They have signed on the dotted line. It's all over.' My wife heard what had been said, and her eyes filled with tears. I too felt a lump in my throat, and could scarcely voice my congratulations. I had got back into bed before it occurred to me that Eisenhower may have intended me to pass the news to the Prime Minister. To be on the safe side, I rang No. 10, but the operators had evidently failed to disconnect me from Reims and my telephone was dead. There was nothing for it but to collect some coppers, put on a dressing gown, and go to the public call-box a hundred yards down the road. I had no difficulty in making contact with No. 10, only to be told by the best switchboard in London that Mr Churchill had already heard the glad news and gone to bed.[9]

There was one more ritual to go through. The Russians wanted their own signing in Berlin. Accordingly, Keitel and Friedeburg were flown by a British transport plane to Tempelhof airport.

A Russian guard of honour had been drawn up for the British and American parties, with a military band; from our landing area we were able to watch the ceremony from afar. A Russian officer had been detailed to accompany me – I was told he was General Zhukov's chief quartermaster – and he drove me in one car while the rest of my party followed in other cars.

We drove across Belle-Alliance-Platz through the outskirts of the city to Karlshorst, where we were put down at a small empty villa not far from the Pioneer and Engineer School's barracks. It was about one o'clock in the afternoon. We were left absolutely to ourselves. Presently a reporter came and took some photographs, and after a while a Russian interpreter came: he was unable to tell me at what time the signing of the Instrument of Surrender was to take place.[10]

It was in fact not before midnight that the now furious Keitel was escorted to the mess hall of the barracks.

As the clock began to strike the hour, we entered the big hall through a side door, and were led across to the long table directly facing us, where three seats had been kept free for my two companions and myself; the rest of our entourage were obliged to stand behind us. Every corner of the hall was packed, and brilliantly lit by spotlights. Three rows of chairs running the length of the hall and one across it were crowded with officers; General Zhukov took the chair with the plenipotentiaries of Britain and America on either side of him.[11]

What Keitel could not bring himself to record was that the French were also there. Alongside Zhukov and Eisenhower's deputy, Air Chief Marshal Sir Arthur Tedder and General Spaatz was General de Lattre de Tassigny. He almost didn't make it. An American Dakota had been promised to take de Lattre and another officer from Mengen to Berlin. It was an hour late in taking off and then, for some mysterious reason, landed at Magdeburg, sixty-two miles short of Berlin. There it was explained that a fighter plane escort had been arranged to take the Allied representatives on to their venue but that, unfortunately, the escort had already departed with the American and British representatives.

> No one seemed to care. I had to remind [the Russians] of the object of my presence. Then two cars came up to take us to Marshal Zhukov's command post. With a Soviet colonel to conduct us, our drivers went off at top speed and plunged towards the ruins of what had been the German capital . . . I saw masses of still smoking and tragically similar ruins, where demining squads were handling their long metal rods and in the midst of which were wretched lines of dazed women, children and old men who had left their cellars and, provided with the most varied receptacles, queued up interminably for a little water at the public fountains and fire hydrants.
>
> At all the crossroads – the only bright feature – young Russian girls, stocky, impeccably neat in their simple uniforms, with bare knees above high boots, were controlling the traffic with great seriousness. They handled their little yellow and red flags with surprising dexterity and cleared the way – then they smartly tucked the flags under their left arms in order to salute our cars.[12]

At the end of a tiring journey de Lattre was welcomed into the band of Allied brothers. But there remained obstacles to French participation in the surrender ceremony. First there was a problem over who should sign the surrender document. Zhukov had been happy to accept an additional signature, though up to the point of de Lattre's appearance he was unaware that the French were involved. However, instructions from Moscow ruled that if de Lattre signed, one of the other participants had to step down. The obvious choice was Spaatz since Tedder was signing on behalf of Eisenhower and his own government. Spaatz was not having that. De Lattre made an emotional appeal to Tedder. 'If I return to France without having fulfilled my mission, that is to say, having allowed my country to be excluded from signing the capitulation of the Reich, I deserve to be hanged. Think of me . . . !'

Tedder went back to Zhukov. A compromise was hammered out. Zhukov and Tedder were to sign as contracting parties, Spaatz and de Lattre as witnesses. But first of all the protocols had to be retyped. No wonder Keitel had to wait so long to be summoned. And there was still another little matter to sort out. In the room where the signing was to take place the sole decorations were three flags upon the end wall: the Red Flag, the Union Jack and the Stars and Stripes. The French colours were nowhere to be seen. De Tassigny declared that France could not be represented at the ceremony without her flag alongside those of her Allies. But where could a French flag be found?

> The Russians decided to make one, with a piece of red stuff taken from a former Hitlerite banner, a white sheet and a piece of blue serge cut out of an engineer's overalls. Alas! our tricolour was less familiar to the young Russian girls than the red flag to many French girls, for when a jeep brought along the flag that had been run up in this way we found a magnificent Dutch flag: the blue, white and red had been sewn not one beside the other but one above the other! It had to be all begun again but the blue was this time too short to go round the staff. Everybody worked with a will. At last, at 20.00, our national emblem was placed between those of Great Britain and the United States in a cluster, surmounted by the Soviet flag.[13]

At ten minutes past midnight Keitel was brought forward, blinking in the glare of the newsreel lights. He clicked his heels

and saluted with his marshal's baton. With the baton still raised
he took in the scene. His eye fell on the French flag and then on
de Lattre. 'Ach,' he growled. 'The French are here too. It only
wanted that!'

No solemn occasion is complete without its element of farce and
this one was set to run with the public announcement of peace in
Europe. The fault line in the management of victory was the news
media. After more than five years of bending the knee to the censor,
war reporters at Reims had been frustrated to find that the best
story any of them were ever likely to have, and entirely good news
at that, was under strict embargo. The thinking behind this was
simple enough. From the political point of view, it was desirable
that the official announcement of the war's end should be made
simultaneously by all combatants. This meant holding off the celebrations until the Berlin ceremony was completed.

Fifteen of the correspondents who witnessed the surrender at
Reims on May 7th accepted the decision. The sixteenth, Edward
Kennedy of Associated Press, did not. Risking the fury of Brigadier
General Frank Allen, SHAEF public relations chief, Kennedy,
described as 'a hardnosed wire service correspondent', telephoned
his report to his Paris office which relayed it to New York via
London. Within the hour, the news was out. At this point bureaucratic inanity took collective hold. Insisting that the embargo stay
in place, SHAEF bullied Kennedy's colleagues into denying the
story. Given the tendency of war reporters to proclaim their responsibility to tell it as it happened, it seems incredible that they
submitted to such pressure and, moreover, failed to warn of the
consequences. Confusion was total. While Germany's collapse was
widely believed to be only hours away, the fact that Associated
Press had once before got it wrong – on April 28th an AP bulletin
said that Germany had accepted unconditional surrender – gave
credence to the official version of events. But this did not deter the
celebrations which were soon in boisterous evidence, most particularly so in London.

Churchill was quickly on his 'secret line' to the White House
asking that the official announcement be brought forward. The

response was unhelpful. Truman would refuse to act 'without the approval of Uncle Joe'. Churchill blustered his objections. 'What is the use of me and the President looking to be the only two people in the world who don't know what is going on . . . It is an idiotic position.'[14] Telegrams had. already been sent to Moscow; now Churchill sent another appeal for cooperation. An hour later he was back in touch with Admiral Leahy. There had been no reply from Stalin. 'I feel I can delay no longer,' said Churchill. Leahy said he understood but could not give the go-ahead for an official announcement 'unless Stalin approves'. Knowing that Stalin was playing power games, Churchill did not feel similarly restrained. Shortly after ending his conversation with Leahy, he wired the Pentagon:

> British Ministry of Information announced that to-morrow, Tuesday, May 8, will be V.E. Day, and a holiday throughout England. The Prime Minister will make a statement at 3 p.m. The King will broadcast at 9 p.m., and Wednesday, May 9 will also be a holiday in England.

Truman continued to hold on for word from Moscow. It came shortly after midnight, Washington time, on May 7th. Stalin wanted the announcement to be postponed until he had given further consideration to the surrender terms. At this, even Truman's patience ran out. Early the following day he held a news conference to announce the German surrender on all fronts to Anglo-American-Soviet forces.

On both side of the Atlantic there was a feeling of anticlimax. 'It all seemed to drift to an end so gradually,' wrote Denis Baron, a medical student at the Middlesex Hospital to an RAF friend overseas.[15] A serving officer recorded a familiar reaction among those who had forged the victory.

> There is no great feeling of elation but mainly a sense of feeling lost. You honestly just do not know how you feel about the whole thing. In a way you feel glad that the whole dirty mess is over, but then again you feel let down. Sort of 'What the hell am I going to do now?' You had been so busy for so long that you had a lost

feeling and wondered what was going to happen now. How soon would you get home? Does my family know about this?[16]

Some who had started early were partied out; others who had waited lost the moment of spontaneity and felt somehow let down. In the States, the celebratory mood was further tempered by the knowledge that Pearl Harbour had yet to be avenged. Japan was heading for defeat but nobody was sure how long it would take. When there was joy in the streets of New York on May 7th, Mayor La Guardia issued a stern admonition: 'I want all the people of the City of New York who have thoughtlessly left their jobs, to go home . . . Maybe there's still some fighting going on. You don't know and I don't know . . . Let's be patient for just a few more hours.' But patience did not bring any reward. In contrast to Britain where VE (Victory in Europe) Day was a public holiday, the US, as indeed the USSR, decided on work as usual. In Washington, the flags were kept at half mast in deference to the late President Roosevelt and in San Francisco, where a United Nations conference was underway, the authorities went into the reverse of celebration by closing all bars for twenty-four hours.[17]

The dampening effect of Mayor La Guardia's words on New Yorkers was short-lived. Up to 30,000 revellers gathered in Times Square and, though disappointed not to hear Truman's victory proclamation (nobody had thought to have it relayed over loudspeakers), they did hear sirens and whistle blasts from the tugs and cargo boats on the Hudson and East River, a refrain taken up by cabbies and other motorists hooting their delight.

> Then the great paper and cloth throwing orgy began. Paper in every possible form and description cascaded from a hundred thousand windows – scrap paper, ledgers, playing cards, torn telephone books, fragments, stationery, streamers, ticker-tape . . . [garment trade workers] threw bale upon bale of textiles into the street: rayon, silk, woollens, prints, foulards, every conceivable remnant in every possible shade and hue turned and squirmed in the thin morning sunlight . . . Within the hour, Sixth, Seventh and Eighth Avenues and Broadway were eight to ten inches deep in multi-coloured fabrics. Thrifty

passers-by forgot their delirium long enough to salvage some of the larger remnants. Passing trucks, pleasure cars and cabs were draped in the material. It clung to ledges, sills and cornices and the wind played with it and tore at it. Men and women in the streets tore it from their hats and shoulders . . . Opposite Macy's women hung from windows waving bottles of liquor and screaming 'Hey soldiers, hey sailors, come on up and get a drink!'[18]

Outside a Broadway hotel, there was a lineup of grinning American, Canadian and British servicemen with a queue of girls waiting to give them congratulatory kisses.

A radio officer in the Merchant Navy, Les Owen, had spent the last year of the war on an oil tanker. On May 6th, his ship anchored off Staten Island.

The local radio stations were agog with the news from Europe. Hourly bulletins told of the final stages of the great drama now being played out in Germany. The atmosphere of excitement was stoked up continually by reports from 'men on the spot over there'. I leaned on the rail that evening, watching the towering dominoes of the New York skyline lit by a million lights. So the war was drawing to a close – at least in Europe.[19]

The following day Les Owen was booked in for a planning session for his next assignment but the conference was postponed in favour of twenty-four hours' shore leave. Early on the 8th Les and his friends made for Manhattan.

Of course, the atmosphere in New York was very much a festive one, and by the evening the great city erupted in a glittering, dazzling, exuberant, singing and dancing party. I can well remember dancing in a 'chorus-girl line' down Broadway singing heartily. The Americans were absolutely marvellous to us. Never could any of us forget their great kindness and friendship. By the time we came to make our way to the Battery to catch the last liberty boat, most of us were feeling quite 'merry' and very tired. Because I knew I would be on watch at 2.30 a.m., I had tried to not drink too much, but I was beginning to feel the strain of two days of celebrations.

I sat in the bow section of the liberty launch, and after loading scores and scores of noisy sailors in various stages of intoxication, we pushed off to deliver them to their ships. We seemed to visit every ship in that vast harbour before eventually nosing towards the familiar outline of the *Voco*. When we were about to sail, I tuned in the receiver for the start of my watch and as I settled in my chair I heard the Mate shouting orders and the anchor chain rattling. The engine room telegraph rang out, orders to the helmsman were shouted, and the great deep throbbing and vibration of the engine meant we were on our way home. I plugged in my extension headphones and poked my head out of the radio room door. We were moving slowly ahead and the wonderful sight of New York at night was slipping away like some gigantic stage set. The towering illuminated blocks slid past in line and I waved a sad and fond farewell.[20]

In Britain, VE Day had a damp start with the rain falling steadily from the early hours. Those who had been out in the cities the night before had searched in vain for the bright lights that would signal that the war was well and truly over. Except for a belt five miles inland from the coast where the lights-out rule after dark stayed in force until May 10th, the blackout had officially ended on April 24th. But street lights had been extinguished for so long, few of them were in working order and quick repairs were out of the question. The same could be said of shop signs and illuminated advertisements. Some householders kept their curtains pulled back to let their living room lights shine out of the windows but this could hardly be described as a festive display. The flag wavers did better. There were Union Jacks everywhere, on poles jutting out from windows, strung across streets and between lampposts and fluttering from the rooftops of every official building. BBC Radio helped to get the national party underway with spirited tunes like 'Victory Parade' and 'Keep Your Sunny Side Up', which in some places were relayed to the streets through loudspeakers. A more common sound was of church bells rung enthusiastically, if not always in harmony.

In London the crowds gathered early, encouraged by a change in the weather from storm clouds to warm sunshine.

The girls in their thin, bright dresses heightened the impression that the city had been taken over by an enormous family picnic. The number of extraordinarily pretty young girls, who presumably are hidden on working days inside the factories and government offices, was astonishing. They streamed out into the parks and streets like flocks of twittering, gaily plumaged cockney birds. In their freshly curled hair were cornflowers and poppies, and they wore red-white-and-blue ribbons around their narrow waists. Some of them even tied ribbons around their bare ankles. Strolling with their uniformed boys, arms candidly about each other, they provided a constant, gay, simple marginal decoration to the big, solemn moments of the day.[21]

By lunchtime it was almost impossible for traffic to get through the masses milling back and forth between Buckingham Palace, Trafalgar Square and Piccadilly Circus. 'This is it – and we are all going nuts,' exulted a *Daily Mirror* reporter.

There are thousands of us in Piccadilly Circus. The police say more than 10,000 – and that's a conservative estimate.

We are dancing the Conga and the jig and 'Knees Up Mother Brown', and we are singing and whistling and blowing paper trumpets.

The idea is to make a noise. We are. Even above the roar of the motors of low-flying bombers 'shooting up' the city.

We are dancing around Eros in the black-out, but there is a glow from a bonfire up Shaftesbury Avenue and a newsreel cinema has lit its canopy lights for the first time in getting on for six years.

A huge V sign glares down over Leicester Square. And gangs of girls and soldiers are waving rattles and shouting and climbing lampposts and swarming over cars that have become bogged down in this struggling, swirling mass of celebrating Londoners.[22]

It was, of course, Churchill's day. His secretary, Elizabeth Layton, was standing a little behind him when he and members of the war cabinet appeared on a balcony overlooking Parliament Square.

Flags and bunting had been put up, and floodlights were directed upon the balcony. A crowd which some estimated at 20,000 stood below, the roar of their cheering seemed almost to lift one off one's feet. It was just a sea of faces and waving arms. As Mr Churchill emerged, the noise increased almost to deafening point. Microphones were ready. He knew so well what to say. He congratulated the Londoners on their fortitude, saying 'I always said "London can take it." Were we downhearted?' The response was overwhelming. He mentioned Japan, and the crowd booed happily. Then he began the first few words of 'Land of Hope and Glory', and the multitude took it up with a will.

The entire nation came forward to show its affection for the man whose courage had been an inspiration in its darkest hours. For the next few days he could not move from the office without being mobbed in every street. He took to driving in an open car, so that he could sit on the back and wave his hat to the crowd, who appeared from nowhere wherever he was to be seen. Letters, telegrams and gifts poured into the office from all over the country.[23]

Churchill was rewarded with an even greater demonstration of gratitude when he went to Buckingham Palace to join the royal family.

Thousands of King George's subjects wedged themselves in front of the Palace throughout the day, chanting ceaselessly 'We want the King' and cheering themselves hoarse when he and the Queen and their daughters appeared, but when the crowd saw Churchill, there was a deep, full-throated, almost reverent roar. He was at the head of the procession of Members of Parliament, walking back to the House of Commons from the traditional St Margaret's Thanksgiving Service. Instantly, he was surrounded by people – people running, standing on tiptoe, holding up babies so that they could be told later that they had seen him.[24]

With the evening of VE Day came the totally unexpected illuminations. Makeshift they may have been but for many it was hard to remember the pre-war London of bright lights.

In Whitehall, the floodlit Houses of Parliament looked absolutely wonderful and inspiring – there were the same quietly cheerful, tired, steadily moving, endless crowds. Back to Trafalgar Square and Nelson and Admiralty Arch were illuminated and the crowds were still there. Then the searchlights came out and formed a vibrating tracery in the sky.[25]

For the young, those teenagers who had felt the heavy hand of official restraint throughout the war years, VE Day was an opportunity to find out what real life – and fun – was all about. Derek Lambert was a fifteen-year-old who came up to London with friends from his school in Surrey.

We hugged ourselves with anticipation as the train trundled through the Claphams and Balhams of London; past boarded windows, clawed roofs, severed spires, playgrounds of rubble, walls still clinging with stairs and chimney flues, craters filled with water, propped up bridges, empty charred houses.

In London they made for a restaurant off Tottenham Court Road where they ate Wiener Schnitzel. There was only one place in the neighbourhood that would serve such a dish and that was Schmidts in Charlotte Street, a cheap and cheerful German restaurant that stayed open throughout the war and on into the 1970s when it fell to the property developers. After a quick meal, Derek Lambert and company made for the action.

The crowds were thickening, dancing, singing, swearing. Girls kissed soldiers and sailors and GIs. One kiss between a girl with a blonde streak bleached in her hair and a hatless GI lasted eight minutes (we counted) before they surfaced, breathless and carmine-chinned, and wandered thoughtfully up a side street. In the pubs girls jived and plump women did the knees-up showing long drawers from which we averted our eyes. Youths struggled up lampposts and split their trousers sliding down, trumpets blew, rattles rattled, tempers flared, heads broke, blood flowed, women cried, bottles smashed, fireworks exploded.

The sight of so many women apparently only too keen to advertise their availability prompted a venture into Soho where the sex business was brisk.

'Go on, man, you first.'

'No, you – you're the oldest.'

'Oh, all right. But you've got to try as well.'

The woman had dark hair, grey near the roots. Lipstick doubled the width of her mouth and powder levelled her craters. She wore ankle straps and a fox fur and radiated desiccated sex, cupidity and Evening in Paris. Effervescing with beer and victory, I approached her.

'Excuse me . . .'

'Bugger off,' she said without removing the cigarette from her mouth, 'Bugger off or I'll tan your backside for you.'

The others were full of admiration. 'What did she say? Did she say you could?'

'We discussed terms,' I said, 'but I told her it was too much.'

'How much did she want?'

'Twenty pounds,' I said.

'Gosh, man,' they said.[26]

Out of London, the celebrations were more subdued. Many families had been saving up a little each week for a big night out in the local pub or for a meal at home. As one housewife put it, 'It is amazing what could be done with dried egg powder.' And then there was the precious bottle of sherry or whisky to be brought out from the back of the larder. Street parties with lots of flags flying were popular with the children who often as not wore fancy dresses made from discarded blackout curtains.

In the evening bonfires were lit and crowds cheered as effigies of Nazi leaders went up in flames.

The chief fire-watcher was invited to light the bonfire at 9.30 p.m. One of the boys handed him a long pole at the end of which was a rag soaked in paraffin. Immediately the bonfire was lit a cheer went up. Hitler started to burn too quickly and there were cries of 'Don't let him end up so soon, let him linger' and the boys promptly doused him with a hose in order to prolong the burning. Soon Goering's chair collapsed and a cheer went up. The children danced round the bonfire yelling at the top of their voices . . . At 9.40 p.m. a piano was carried into the roadway and a lady sat down and played popular songs – 'Roll Out the Barrel', 'Tipperary', 'Daisy-Daisy', 'The Lambeth Walk', 'Knees Up Mother Brown', etc. – and things did really liven up . . . Grown-ups and the young people joined hands and danced and sang and altogether there must have been about 150 people.[27]

For all the pleasure-making, VE Day was a party of mixed emotions. There were those who were just relieved it was all over and many others who were overwhelmed by an awful sadness.

When I heard they'd surrendered I just started to cry and I couldn't stop. I don't know what was the matter with me. I should have been happy, but I was crying my eyes out. I kept thinking of Jack [her husband]. He was killed on D Day. I never knew quite what happened to him, only that he was dead. And I kept thinking, what a waste, what a waste. He was such a lovely man, always laughing and joking. He worked in the docks and needn't have gone in the Army at all, but no, he had to go and do his bit. And for what? He'd never even seen the baby, his baby, sleeping upstairs.[28]

This was twenty-four-year-old Vi Bottomley in Liverpool. Pat Hazlehurst, another war widow, would have sympathised with her.

There was no reason for me to rejoice, first my husband was dead and second because the war in the Far East was still going on. Men were still at risk of being killed, like my husband was killed. I was tied to the office all day and then I went home and put my head under a pillow. There was nothing for me to celebrate. I mean, I was glad for the folks who were coming back home, of course. I didn't feel particularly sad that day, because the sadness never leaves you. You learn to live with it, you cannot live at the same pitch of misery.[29]

There was another sort of sadness brought on by one celebration too many. Elizabeth Denham was a trainee nurse at the Royal Devon and Exeter Hospital.

The night went on quite quietly until the early hours, about 3 a.m., I had to go to casualty because there had been an accident and they were expecting a good many casualties. A Jeep, carrying too many American soldiers and girls had collided with an army lorry. Each of the Americans, except the driver, had had a girl on his lap. We had four girls admitted, one of whom was dead – she'd been in front and gone through the windscreen. Three of the soldiers was dead.[30]

Tom Pocock, one of the youngest war correspondents, had another tragic story.

In Scotland, a young naval officer I knew was in the control-tower of a Fleet Air Arm airfield and broadcast the news by radio-telephone to three young pilots flying over the Highlands on training exercise. Spontaneously, the three flung their aircraft into a display of joyful aerobatics, so exuberant that all three lost control, crashed and were killed.[31]

And there was always the last shot.

I guess one of the saddest things that happened . . . The day the war in Europe ended, I was in some German town that I don't recall the name of, and I was standing there talking to another guy because the war is over and what's going to happen to us now because there's still the war in Japan, etc. When all of a sudden an .88 went off. There was a guy about a block away sitting in a jeep. Whoever fired that, the German that fired that .88, it came and hit that jeep and blew that guy to bits and blew that jeep to pieces, which I thought was very unfair and sad and whatever. The war was over for him and, all of a sudden, some German shoots off somewhere and it just, by sheer chance, it just happens to hit him.[32]

All hostilities should have ceased at just after 11.00 p.m. (Central European Time) on May 8th. In reality, there were pockets of Europe where the conditions of war persisted into the rest of May and beyond. Everywhere, collaborators were at risk. In France it was said that over 20,000 were put to death. In Yugoslavia, a whole army of German sympathisers, up to 30,000 of them, were machine-gunned. Throughout eastern Europe German prisoners of war were shot as a matter of course. And who knows what happened to the thousands of Russian forced labourers who were handed over to the not so tender mercies of the Red Army?

In Amsterdam, rejoicing at the end of German occupation came to an abrupt halt when shots were fired into the crowd gathered in the Dam square. The firing came from the Groote Club, a popular meeting place for the German military. As dead and wounded fell (at least twenty died and 120 injured) there was a panic rush for shelter. At this point two Canadian officers appeared, one of whom was ready to use his carbine to start World War Three. He was dissuaded by Commander Overoff of the Internal Forces, the senior Dutch officer at the scene, who set off on his motorcycle to find a German officer capable of restoring discipline. What followed seemed more associated with the beginning than with the end of the war.

Arriving at German army headquarters, Overoff persuaded Captain Bergmann of the Feldgendarmeri (military police) to go with him back to the Dam.

> He sat in the sidecar while I sat behind the driver. The Hauptmann asked me what had happened and I told him about the shooting that had broken out. He asked me which Germans were firing and I told him that the shots came from the Groote Club. To that, he said: 'Das is natürlich wider die Verdammte Marine, welche eine Schweinerei.' ['Ah, of course, it's those damned marines again. What a mess.'] We drove towards the Dam along the Nieuwezijds Voorburgwal; when we were level with the St Luciensteeg, we found the road completely deserted and every side-street filled with civilians. We left the motorcycle and sidecar behind and the Hauptmann, my driver (a military police sergeant) and I proceeded towards the Dam on foot. In front of us we heard shots from all sides.

Forcing their way into the Groote Club they found all four floors of the building and the roof occupied by marines with rifles and machine-guns; 'men firing and ready to fire'. Shots were now being returned from the streets around the Dam where now three German army vehicles began taking up position to join the action. Overoff and Bergmann braved the bullets to appeal for a ceasefire.

I told everyone to go inside. The Hauptmann ordered the Germans to assemble in the street and the vehicles to retreat. When all was quiet, we walked back to the Dam to collect our motorcycle. We rode back past the Dam again and onto the Damrak. This, too, was deserted; all the civilians stood in the side-streets and alleyways. The Dam itself was a tragic scene. The dead were lying in front of the Nieuwe Kerk and in and around the entrance to the Nieuwendijk. All had been hit by German fire . . . Continuing towards Central Station we heard heavy rifle fire and as we reached the corner by the Victoria Hotel, the motor-cycle rider was hit by a fatal shot. He died instantly and slid sideways off the saddle. Since the last thing he did was to put the motorcycle in neutral, I was able to bring the vehicle to a standstill.[33]

Even though the surrender of German forces in the Netherlands had been agreed on May 5th it was not until VE Day that Allied authority in Amsterdam was established. The makeshift nature of the civil administration was demonstrated by the mayor's secretary who arrived at the town hall on a bicycle without a saddle. In the hard years he had got used to riding on the rear mudguard. Nor did he complain about having to ride on solid tyres, a common enough experience throughout Holland.

A portly Canadian major represented the Allies. Mayor F. de Boer was on hand to witness the major's first encounter with the German city commander.

Lieutenant-Colonel Schröder came in, accompanied by a subaltern officer. Lieutenant-Colonel Schröder tried to shake Major Taite's hand, but the major refused and asked that Schröder listen to what he was going to say very carefully.

'This morning your soldiers behaved like beasts here in Amsterdam and killed a number of civilians. Take note that:

One – I hold you personally responsible for such action and any repeat will have very grave consequences for you indeed.

Two – pointing at a map of Amsterdam – tonight, your troops will be concentrated in this and this barracks.

Three – if the concentration of troops has not been completed by tomorrow morning, you will be held personally accountable, too.

434

You may now go.'

Lieutenant-Colonel Schröder tapped his heels together, saluted, did an about-turn and disappeared with due haste, along with his adjutant.

'Right,' said Major Taite, 'that's that then. He was rather tame, I thought. He probably doesn't know that those two tanks of mine are the only allied force west of Hilversum and that the rest won't arrive until tomorrow.'34

If the German army accepted the inevitable in Amsterdam it seemed less inclined to do so in its garrison at St Nazaire and Lorient on the Atlantic coast and, more curiously, at the Channel port of Dunkirk. Bypassed by the Canadian First Army sweep into Belgium, the German force in Dunkirk had settled in for the duration and now showed no immediate inclination to submit to the Czech, British and French troops laying siege to the town. As a fledgling reporter with a reputation to make, Tom Pocock decided to investigate.

An Army staff car and driver were provided and, accompanied by a news-agency correspondent, I set off for Dunkirk, which had seen the last stand of the British in 1940 and was now, perhaps, the scene of the last battle . . . The countryside was dead and deserted, the fields flooded, or grey with mud where the floods had receded. The road was empty and potholed and the houses we passed deserted and often wrecked. Then suddenly a group of men sprang from a ditch, aimed Sten sub-machine-guns at us as an order to stop. They were Frenchmen of the *Maquis*, wearing civilian clothes together with part of old uniforms, or First World War helmets, but all with an armband bearing the initials 'FFI', for *Forces Françaises de l'Intérieur*. We showed them our papers and they told us that, whatever might or might not have happened elsewhere, no Allied forces had approached Dunkirk by this road. If we wished to continue, that was up to us.

We did so and soon there were signs of activity. Down the road half a dozen men lounged on plush and gilt chairs outside a seaside villa, machine-guns on the grass beside them. They were German soldiers. As we passed, they sprang to their feet and saluted. Farther on, we passed more, who either saluted or stared, and, either side of the road, tangles of barbed wire and black-and-white notices on which were stencilled the skull-and-crossbones symbol and the words *Achtung Minen*! Soon the road was crowded with Germans: non-commissioned officers in high-crowned caps; soldiers cleaning vehicles and equipment; military police, with their Nazi gorgets across their chests, directing traffic. Their uniforms were often patched – they had been under siege for eight months – but they were clean and smart and did not look like a defeated army. But there was nobody about in the khaki battledress of the Allies and now it was the memory of victorious crowds in London that seemed unreal.[35]

The sights seen, the pressmen were directed out of Dunkirk towards Allied lines. It was all perfectly friendly; perhaps too friendly.

There was something ominous about that empty road and our driver, who had been with the 2nd Army since Normandy days and had highly-tuned instincts for survival, opened the door of the staff car and ordered the German to climb in beside him. The sergeant demurred until the driver reached for his Sten. With our hostage aboard, we started down the road until he threw up his hands, crying, '*Nein, nein, nach links*!' Presumably, as our driver had anticipated, the road down which we had been directed was mined.[36]

It was not until May 9th that Dunkirk was taken back into Allied hands. St Nazaire and Lorient were even tardier. It was not until the following day that American troops finally took possession.

Of all the western European cities, Brussels was best equipped to shake off the cares of war. Having escaped serious damage, after liberation the city had become a leave centre with all the facilities needed to revive the spirits of battle-worn heroes. To Private Winifred Banner, an ATS teleprinter operator, Brussels came as a revelation.

After the bombed cities of Manchester, London, Plymouth and Bristol, Brussels was a visual shock. The buildings were whole, there were no jagged spaces nor barriers of rubble, it was all there. The centre of the city was totally unexpected. Though occupied by the enemy until quite recently, the fine streets were lined by shops displaying goods unseen in Britain for years. In a department store were cosmetics, perfume, nail polish, in the windows of the tasteful boutiques lay costly jewellery and fine leather bags.

And the women . . . with their tall, clipped black poodles they sauntered in the boulevards in high-heeled platform shoes, wide shouldered dresses and their hats, piled up confections, rose up in competition with their shoes. The ear-rings they wore, large, lacy, flowery, were an unforeseen delight and their make-up was impeccable, no hint of any shortage there. As they passed by, delicious wafts of Chanel, Houbigant and Coty came in the first warmth of the spring air.

Brussels was well prepared for VE Day. A profusion of Allied flags appeared, hanging from every doorway, window and balcony.

People were clustered in the roads, talking but raised hands to salute 'Les A.T.S.' Here and there stood a repatriated Belgian soldier or civilian, surrounded by a questioning crowd. Approaching the centre, our tram slowed to a crawl. All round us was frenzied movement, laughter, noise, colour, excited relief. Grey, khaki, blue, green uniforms mingled with the tall bright hats of the women, young men and girls clung, calling, to every surface of the slowly moving trams. Jeeps and military cars, laden with all manner of people made an erratic procession.[37]

Colonel Baker recalls there were:

tremendous crowds everywhere celebrating the peace, and I understand most of them have not been to bed for the past two days. They just milled around, plopped down somewhere or other every now and again for a few minutes' rest, and then started whooping it up all over again. They snake-danced all over the place, in and out of buildings, nightclubs, restaurants and so on. Anytime anyone came along with a car or truck dozens of people swarmed all over it and covered every possible inch. I saw some jeeps with at least 15 people on them.

The city was a mass of streamers and flags, and at least half the people were wearing some type of paper hats. There was one old character who had made herself a true V-Day costume. It was in the Belgian colours of red, yellow and black, and her outfit was divided into equal part of each colour. She was happy as a lark and roamed all over the place accosting everyone she met.

All the night spots in town were running wide open around the clock and doing a land-office business. I ran into some friends in the bar back at my hotel and ended up by having a very large evening indeed. We teamed up with a couple of English girls who were in Brussels with one of the services, and during the course of the evening covered quite a lot of territory.[38]

Throughout the night rockets and flares lit up the sky, confetti showered from upper windows and hooting vehicles edged their way along crowded streets.

Entering the Grand Place we were caught up in a crowd of young students, men and girls. A huge ring formed, we sang 'Auld Lang Syne' in a curious mixture of words. (I remember a burly Scot with the right ones.) The ring dissolved into knots and as these processed down the boulevards the Belgian students sang. 'Three Blind Mice' was in their English repertoire. 'My bonny lies over the ocean' their amazing pièce de résistance. We obliged with 'Sur le Pont d'Avignon' and Anne and I brought the house down with the whole of 'Il était une bergère'.[39]

For Mea Allan, a reporter with the *Daily Herald*, another discordant note intruded when she joined the throng on le Grand Place, the famous medieval square with its towered Hôtel de Ville.

A rider came galloping into the square and, reining in his horse, was presented with a red banner emblazoned with the Soviet hammer and sickle – sent, I learned, from Moscow as a gift to the tramwaymen of Belgium. One knew that the Belgian tramwaymen were far to the left in their political views. But somehow the hammer and sickle struck an ominous note. Even then, with the Russians our allies, we were wondering where that hammer and sickle emblem would next appear. Belgium was too near for comfort.[40]

Paris did bear the scars of war – on walls pitted by bullets and on the faces of those men and women lately returned from the concentration camps or from forced labour. Some still had their striped jackets or trousers. 'Like lost souls, they roamed the streets, some homeless, some with a home to go back to but no family.'[41] The queues outside the Red Cross missing persons bureau were longer than for any food shop. Come VE Day, however, 'the bells pealed and cannon roared'.[42] The streets were fully lighted for the first time since 1939. A victory V shone over les Invalides and another in red, white and blue above the Arc de Triomphe. And everywhere the streets disappeared under a surge of humanity.

They started marching on Tuesday afternoon at three o'clock, just after the voice of General de Gaulle announced the great news over the government's street loudspeaker system, and thousands were still marching at dawn the next morning. The crowds marched in the sunshine and on into the night with the collective, wandering rhythm of masses who are not going anywhere but are feeling something which their marching together expresses. VE Day here was like an occupation of Paris by Parisians. They streamed out onto their city's avenues and boulevards and took possession of them, filling them from kerb to kerb. They paved the Champs-Elysées with their moving, serried bodies. Around the Arc de Triomphe the marchers, pouring in from the spokes of the Etoile, solidified into a dangerous, living, sculptural mass which was swayed and pushed by its own weight until the marchers, limping and dishevelled, disengaged themselves to march back down the avenues and boulevards, in the dusty, beautiful spring air . . . All anyone cared about was to keep moving, to keep shouting, to keep singing snatches of the *Marseillaise: 'Le jour de gloire est arrive . . . marchons, marchons.'*[43]

For Susan Mary Alsop, the wife of an American diplomat, it was a night never to be forgotten.

The Arc de Triomphe, Opéra, Place de la Concorde all lit up for the first time and the fountains on everywhere – the Madeleine especially beautiful and flares and fireworks, and the Garde Républicaine riding down the Rue Royale with their helmets gleaming, and sweating police in their blue capes trying to make way for them, and each member of the Guard having at least one girl riding behind him on the horse, clinging to his Napoleonic uniform and screaming.[44]

Paris was Bedlam, agreed the *Herald Tribune* correspondent. 'Pistols were fired into the air from moving cars, planes overhead dropped multi-coloured flares and fireworks boomed in all directions.'[45]

Photographs sent home by Lucia Lawson, assistant to the deputy director of SHAEF public relations in Paris, showed, as she put it, 'a rather shocking record of us all on V afternoon, mostly taken in the flat of a French officer who we picked up somewhere "en route" after we had consumed just a teeny weeny little bit of whisky! . . . You must forgive us all if we look a little "degage" but it WAS VE Day and it WAS Paris.'[46]

In Germany VE Day found many of the occupying forces still in a sombre, reflective mood. For Captain Howard Sweet of the US 908th Field Artillery Regiment, all emotion had been spent.

I suspect that the soldiers back in the rear got more of a lift out of it than we did. Of course we had known for a long time that the thing wasn't going to last much longer – ever since the 200-mile dash from the Rhine to the Elbe. And we had known for several days prior to the V-E announcement that the war in Europe was over, although censorship delayed word to the public. So there were no scenes of wild elation with us. We were thankful, of course, but I believe that most of us felt so war-weary and so wrung dry emotionally from the turbulent ups and downs of the past months that we couldn't get very excited even if we wanted to.

Someone hung an American flag from an upper window of the regimental headquarters. Otherwise it was just another routine day.

For the evening meal we shined our shoes and dressed up as best we could. A couple of bottles of champagne were brought out of hiding and we had a few toasts – to the day of victory, to an early V-J day and, in remembrance, a final toast to our commander who died in Brittany last August. Later there was some singing about the piano

– the usual things: *Tipperary, The Man on the Flying Trapeze, The Caisson Song.* And so the war in Europe came to an end.[47]

The last day was more boisterous and more memorable for James Graff whose Ninth Army Division was based near Hannover. Arms and alcohol, he discovered, make for a dangerous mix.

Simunick started out the door to relieve Christopher on guard when all of a sudden two shots rang out and Simunick stumbled back into the house as white as a sheet. He stammered, 'He tried to shoot me.'

I hollered out, 'Don't shoot, Chris; this is Graff!'

He hollered back, 'I'll kill that Croatian S.O.B.' I went out and Chris was drunker than a lord. I tried to talk him out of his rifle, but he wouldn't give it up and I wasn't about to try and take it away from him.

While we were arguing I saw two men approaching down the street and Chris hollered, 'Halt!' I then recognized them in the moonlight. It was Lt. Hein (2nd platoon) and he was holding up Lt. Cox. Both were pretty well drunked up. They had been to a party over at B company. They did not know the password and Lt. Hein hollered out who they were and as they started forward, Chris shot right in front of them. They stopped dead and I began to lecture them on how much more combat he had seen and how much longer he had been with the outfit. He then let them come in. A hairy situation had passed and fortunately no one was hurt, but three people had had the hell scared out of them. Chris could have shot the officers and I would have testified that they didn't know the password.[48]

As for the British, Major Forrest of the Royal Artillery was concerned that celebrations might get out of hand.

At 'C' troop, Battery Sergeant Major Harding (BSM Fish was then acting RSM) had handed out the rum ration and also set up a Bren allowing gunners to take turns in loosing off tracer. I stopped this practice. The troops captured some German sheep, ewes and lambs, cut V signs on their backs and for greater emphasis painted the Vs black. An invitation, boldly chalked on a three tonner, read: 'Trips to the Ruins – see the Master Race Free'. A tin can band played

'Pistol packing Momma' as it marched up and down the road outside battery headquarters. When I stepped out into the night, it appeared as if all the troops in Rhineland were hell-bent on lighting up the heavens. Very lights swished into space, sizzled and burst, draping the sky in flamboyant baubles of reds and greens. Searchlights mounted beside the Rhine performed evolutions too fantastic even for an Einstein to chart . . . Rifle shots rang out. There was the rat-tat-tat of machine-gun fire, heavier explosions from mortars, detonations from mines and some louder bangs. Such sounds acted as overtones to so much singing, shouting and endless drinking.[49]

It was not to Major Forrest's liking. He wanted to be quiet – and alone.

Ordinary Germans may have felt relief that they could walk in the streets without fear of being shot at but that was about the limit of their emotional response to VE Day. Those who had lost homes and businesses were to be seen wandering dreamily across the bomb sites as if hoping to awake to a new reality. Emergency prefabricated housing shot up wherever materials were available and former army camps were speedily converted to civilian use but even with families sharing homes that were standing there was still a desperate shortage of accommodation and in the spring of 1945 hundreds of thousands were living rough.

In the cities, water from the tap was no longer fit to drink, the sewers overflowed and gas and electricity cuts were frequent and protracted. Families adapted to make the best of a bad job as, for example, getting used to cooking on an upturned electric iron. 'We could even cook pea soup on it. Beetle peas were one of the few things we could get to eat; the peas had to be soaked and then inside every one there was a beetle which had to be removed. This job took ages, but the soup tasted good.'[50]

Processed food such as dried milk and eggs came from army supplies but fresh meat and vegetables depended on knowing a friendly farmer or having relatives out of town. Not surprisingly, the black market thrived. 'You could get anything, and I mean anything, for a block of chocolate, a packet of cigarettes or a bar of soap,' wrote one soldier and another added, 'What have these people to live for? Their dear ones killed, their houses destroyed, tragedy everywhere . . . They thought to rule the world – all the agony, the tears and the suffering have recoiled on them a hundred fold.'

Children who had been let off school for the winter because there was no heating or because their teachers had been called up, now found that their unexpected vacation had been extended indefinitely. There was to be no more school until new textbooks, free of Nazi propaganda, could be written and teachers appointed who had acquired the approved democratic credentials. All this was to take up to a year. Having children running free was just another burden for parents, particularly for widowed mothers and those whose husbands were still held prisoner. Living from hand to mouth, their best chance of earning money was to take advantage of the employment opportunities provided by the military.

One of many careers carved out of work experience with the army was that of the mother of a Cologne teenager whose father had died at Stalingrad. She attached herself to an American barracks as a washer woman. Such was the demand for her services that she soon had a thriving business which her son eventually took over as manager. Interpreters were in demand, so too were secretaries, clerks and drivers. Hobbies were turned to profitable account. An officers' mess in Hamburg hired a pianist and a string quartet to play on alternate evenings. In Krefeld a young man with a passion for photography was such a fixture at army celebrations that, come the early 1950s, he was able to set up his own studio. As military government settled in for the long term funds were released for emergency housing and the restoration of transport links and other services, creating a demand for builders who learned their skills the practised way.

But memories of the top end of commercial enterprise, told now with pride, distort the real pattern of early post-war survival. In the ruins of Berlin dogs were sold for meat and cats for their fur. The sex industry out-prospered every other economic activity. Its none-too-subtle blandishments were the easiest way of parting soldiers from their pay packets or their allocations of cigarettes.

443

The consequences troubled the authorities. On a typical morning sick parade, treatment for sexual diseases was almost as frequent as for the common cold. As VD rates soared, training programmes incorporated illustrated lectures on the risks of casual sex. When that proved ineffective, attempts were made to monitor the distribution of cigarettes and cheap booze both of which were common currency in the red light districts. But by now the black market was too strong to be contained. Efforts to impose discipline foundered on the lack of interest from officers and men in any order that deprived them of supplementary income. The paradox for the higher command was that new rules brought in to impose administrative discipline merely complicated the system still further and thus made it easier to manipulate for dishonest advantage.

Those responsible for army banking made matters worse by a failure to understand basic economics. It would have made sense for occupiers and occupied to share a currency. Instead, in the American zone, for example, troops were paid in army dollars which were given an official exchange rate of ten German marks to the dollar. The real exchange rate was at least double and went even higher when the Russians got hold of the printing plates and started paying their own troops in dollars. The notes soon found their way into the American zone where, used to buy watches, cameras and other highly prized goods, they forced the unofficial exchange rate ever higher. Mickey Mouse would have made a better job of it.

With military rule making its presence felt, an ever larger question mark hovered over the status of the Doenitz government. As soon as the ink had dried on the final surrender document there was little more it could do on its own initiative. But Doenitz and his ministers kept up appearances, meeting at regularly appointed hours to speculate on their future. To resign with honour would seem to have been the only sensible option but Doenitz held off the irrevocable decision when a rumour seeped through of a possible role for his administration as a front for Allied control. Churchill for one thought that the Germans might respond more constructively to military rulers if they were endorsed by their own leaders. But the Russians were suspicious of any move towards reconciliation with the Nazi regime. Popular opinion in America and Britain felt the same way. Enjoying a freedom of expression denied for nearly six years, the press took up the cry for a clean sweep of the old regime. Recognising a public relations opportunity when it was offered, Eisenhower arranged for Doenitz and his associates to make a highly visible exit from the political scene. On May 23rd, Doenitz was summoned on board the liner *Patria* which acted as a SHAEF regional headquarters. There, surrounded by western journalists and photographers, he was told that he was under arrest and that his government was dissolved. While the last defender of the Third Reich was enduring his humiliation, troops of the Cheshire and Hereford regiments and of the Fifteenth and Nineteenth Hussars raided the medieval castle in Flensburg Bay where Doenitz had created, for what it was worth, his power centre. A Reuters correspondent takes up what was left of the story.

They 'held up' all German officers, officials and soldiers whom they found there while squads of searchers removed records, documents and personal belongings. A special guard was placed in charge of General Jodl. As a car drove up to take him away he saluted his hatless Staff, who bowed in reply. Admiral Friedeburg took his last salute when a party of arrested German Marines were being marched down the road, still singing '*Wir führen gegen England*' ('We're marching against England'). Further on the Marines saw Doenitz a prisoner in a car beside the road. They halted and gave a military salute which he returned punctiliously.[51]

As he was being led away, Admiral Friedeburg, made wretched by defeat and convinced that he had failed as Doenitz's chief negotiator first with Montgomery, then with Eisenhower, asked if he might pack some clothes. He then locked himself in the bathroom and took poison. He was dead when they broke down the door.

And so it ended.

For many, and not just for the star turns, the war was the climax of their lives. Nothing ever again could touch their singleness of purpose or even their reason for being, a terrible but nonetheless real indictment of the seductive appeal of war – the great adventure.

I think the word that describes it best is intensity. With the exception of the few periods of brain-deadening boredom, we lived with such intensity, every minute of every day, and you could see what you were accomplishing, you can see the results of what you were doing, and you knew it was right. It gave me a wonderful feeling. It still does.[52]

The other side of the story is given by Sister Georgie Rideout of the Royal Canadian Army Medical Corps:

After listening to Churchill's speech announcing the cessation of hostilities, I took a sponge bath with a ration of water in my steel helmet. Then I went on duty, alone. Most of the unit had moved and being a reinforcement, I stayed behind with patients who could not be moved.

At the start of the duty I went to the bed of one patient with 'Private, the war is over.' He looked straight at me and spoke three most poignant words. 'Sister, who cares!' He was paralysed from the waist down and would never walk again. Sacrifices such as his can never be measured.[53]

Reflections

A party of us visited Berlin one afternoon. It was a depressing experience. The only Germans to be seen were a few old men and women pushing wheelbarrows, perambulators and hand-carts piled up with their pathetic possessions aimlessly about the streets. The part of Berlin that we visited was a shambles with scarcely a house that was habitable. There was a smell of death and decay, and one wondered how many corpses still lay in the ruins. The only building that I entered was the Chancellery. It was smashed to smithereens and the Russians had made no attempt to clear up the mess. Perhaps they had left it on purpose, as an awful warning. In Hitler's study a huge marble-topped table had been blasted into a thousand pieces. I had the feeling of being in the presence of evil. How shameful it was to think that the devil incarnate, whose malignant spirit still haunted the room, had come so near to dominating the whole world. And how tragic it was that the civilised nations of Christendom had been compelled to use such terrible and indiscriminate agencies of destruction in order to preserve their freedom.

I hurried out of the study in disgust, but an adjacent room was almost equally obscene – Iron Crosses and medal ribbons strewn all over the floor in hopeless confusion. Decorations that would have brought pride to brave men seemed in that setting to be a symbol of utter defeat and degradation. I was sorry that I had gone sightseeing, and when, some months later, I was given an opportunity of visiting the Nuremberg Trials, I refused without a moment's hesitation. My first act on returning to Babelsberg was to plunge into a hot bath with a great deal of disinfectant in it; my second was to take a very strong drink to try to get the taste out of my mouth.[1]

*

It is often said that the Germans are unwilling to come to grips with their National Socialist past. I believe this to be a gross exaggeration. In conversations with my fellow Germans I have been struck time and again by the trauma with which the National Socialist period has left them, by their feeling that they are still living in Hitler's shadow. It is true that many of those who were in varying degree guilty still try to repress their feelings of guilt and that many of the innocent are still caught up in complexes induced, even if they reject the thesis of collective guilt, by a sense of collective shame. Nevertheless the vast majority need no prodding to talk about the National Socialist period and show a willingness to bring it out into the open.

In this dilemma, the young people in particular are looking for a new national consciousness free from the old nationalism; they aspire to a united Europe, which most of them believe should include Eastern Europe, and look upon themselves as German Europeans.[2]

*

Everywhere I travelled in Germany, this spring and summer, I found Germans – good Germans, sincere Germans – eager and ready not only to make amends, but to work their passage back to civilisation. They know it will be hard, but they are ready for it. Are we to give them the chance? Are we going to emulate the Russians, and say to the Germans: 'You are the victims. You have been misguided and misled. We will help you to create a just and civilised government'? Or is ours to continue to be a policy of suspicion and repression?

To those who approve of repression, I would say this: there was one of two things to do when we won this war against Germany. We had to decide either that the Germans could never be re-educated, or we had to decide that they could be brought back into the community of nations. We had to decide either to kill them or cure them. I believe, as one with faith in the essential decency of all human beings, that we made the right decision at Yalta when we decided we would cure the Germans. A nation which produced Goethe and Schiller and Heine, Beethoven and Schumann and Mendelssohn, yes, and Wagner too, whose people love music so much that their orchestras are still the best in Europe, cannot be a lost nation. It can be restored.

Germany has been defeated, but she has not gone out of our lives. For my generation, and for the one that follows after, she will continue to play a part in our destinies. No occupation by the Allied armies, no artificial divisions of her land and people, can prevent that. Along the roads in Russian-occupied Germany is a sign which says in small letters: 'It would be ludicrous to identify Hitler's clique with the German people and the German State'. And then in large letters: 'History shows that Hitlers come and go, but the German people and the German State remain'. History has shown, too, that Allied armies of occupation come and go, but the German people and the German State remain. It is no use refusing to fraternise with them. They are a part of Europe and a part of our lives. You can hate them for what has been done in their name, but you cannot get rid of them. By the wrong kind of treatment you can start all the trouble again, create new Hitlers and new Nazi Parties and new wars; but a firm, resolute and unified desire to help her on the part of all those who have a stake in Europe today – Britain, France, Russia, America and the smaller Powers – can make her a factor for peace in the future, a civilised member of the European family instead of its problem and its fear.[3]

*

Perhaps it is inevitable for people, sickened by the destruction and waste of war, to console themselves that out of it will come a better world. Looked at dispassionately, however, it was not reasonable to suppose that six years spent in blowing each other to bits, killing millions and spreading misery and destruction on a scale never before known, could be the preliminary to creating a better world or that armies could fight to and fro across a continent without leaving new problems for those who survived. The war, after all, was not fought to create a better world but to prevent Hitler and the Nazis turning it into a worse one: this we achieved, and let no one underestimate it. The illusion was not victory but what we expected of it.[4]

At our morning conference on May 14, 1945, I advised President Truman that an early meeting with Churchill and Stalin appeared necessary in an effort to settle the troublesome political difficulties in Europe, and to safeguard our plans for defeating Japan.

The misgivings I had after we left Yalta in February, just three months earlier, unfortunately were being realized to a far more dangerous degree than I had imagined in my most pessimistic moments. The great and successful coalition of Great Britain, the Soviet Union and the United States which, with our lesser allies, had vanquished the military might of Hitlerism and Fascism, was coming apart at the seams.

Stalin was suspicious. He appeared to feel that all his allies were 'ganging up' on him. Churchill was bitter. His beloved Empire was weak, not strong, in victory and he faced a domestic political crisis of his own. Chiang Kai-shek wrestled with a growing rebellion. The United Nations Conference at San Francisco was floundering on the shoals of Russian obtuseness. De Gaulle was more cantankerous than ever. And the war was not over. Japan still had to be defeated. The military power of Tokyo's war lords must be broken if the future security of our own country was to be assured.

Victory in Europe had been won, but peace seemed far away.[5]

*

When the war is finally over, the USA will have become a new type of world power. Many men are spending a lot of time overseas who ordinarily might never leave home, in a normal lifetime. American initiative in business will probably be seen in all parts of the world, and not be confined within the territorial coastlines of North America. Perhaps, of necessity, we will be coming of age for the sake of the world's future.[6]

*

There is something terribly depressing about a country defeated in war, even though that country has been your enemy, and the utter destruction of Germany was almost awesome. It didn't seem possible that towns like Hanover and Bremen could ever rise again from the shambles in which the bulk of the hollow-eyed and shabby population eked out a troglodyte existence underneath the ruins of their houses.

Things were better in the country districts, but what struck me most was the complete absence of able-bodied men or even of youths – there were just a few old men, some cripples, and that was all. The farms were almost entirely run by women. How appalling were the casualties suffered by the Germans was brought home to me forcibly when I first attended morning service in the small village church of Eystrop where I lived. The Germans commemorate their war dead by means of evergreen wreaths; and the whole wall was covered with wreaths – dozens and dozens of them. In a similar church in the United Kingdom I would not expect to see more than eight to ten names on the local war memorial. The Germans certainly started the last war, but only those who saw the conditions the first few months immediately after the war ended can know how much they suffered.[7]

*

Germany has started to destroy the giant concrete Siegfried Line, Hitler's defensive wall against an Allied attack, in a gesture of friendship to the French.

Bulldozers and power hammers were at work yesterday smashing a military bunker overlooking the French city of Strasbourg in the first move to destroy the 400-mile frontier fortification.

The Siegfried Line, known as the Westwall in German, was a warren of 20,000 bunkers, hundreds of underground shelters, trenches and tank barricades. Built between 1936 and 1940 by about 400,000 workers, it was supposed to be Nazi Germany's answer to the French Maginot Line. It starts at Kleve on the Dutch border, runs along the Belgian, Luxembourg and French frontiers and ends just before Basle in Switzerland.

Over eight million tonnes of concrete and one million tonnes of steel were used to construct the Siegfried Line. It was a huge effort, compared by some historians with the building of an Egyptian pyramid.

An eight-mile stretch of the wall on the Belgian border has been placed under a preservation order, and some other stretches are being ransacked by museums. The gun pits and underground tunnels are mostly wildlife sanctuaries occupied by bats or rare birds.[8]

*

There was an explosion and screams. A little boy of about seven had found a case of phosphorous bombs and had picked one up which had exploded in his hand. I was on my own as the officer and sergeant had gone to Helmont for some reason. The skin on the boy's wrist had split and was terribly burnt. He kept saying, 'lk kann niet kike.' I knew what he was saying, it was, 'I can't see'. I didn't know what to do and I asked a Dutch nurse who was there what to do. She told me to get him under water. All this was going on in a German barracks and I quickly ran a warm bath and got him in it, pouring water over his face which stopped the burning. When the Medical Officer returned he agreed, and he was wrapped in wet swabs and got away to a civilian hospital in Helmont. I never knew any more of him. That little lad has haunted me ever since.[9]

*

It was Hitler's complete misconception of British mentality, which in no circumstances was prepared to tolerate a further increase in Germany's power, that led to the second war. And so he found himself faced with a conflict which he had wished to avoid, since, to quote his own words, 'it would inevitably result in Finis Germaniae'.

Those who were in Germany in September 1939 know that the people showed no enthusiasm for war. But war nevertheless came and demanded sacrifice after sacrifice. The German soldier fought with unsurpassed devotion to duty. The people and the armed forces marched shoulder to shoulder, in victory or defeat, to the very end.

Every decent German today is ashamed of the crimes which the Third Reich committed behind the nation's back.

REFLECTIONS

To hold the people as a whole responsible for the misdeeds of a small minority is contrary to every canon of justice. Men cannot be condemned for things of which they did not even know.

The assumption that any one people is morally worse than other peoples is, in itself, a false premise, and it comes particularly unjustly from nations who, during the war and after 1945, did things which were an offence against both legal and moral justice and which resulted in the sacrifice of millions of Germans.[10]

*

I would not take a million dollars for my experiences or give a nickel to see it all again. I will always cherish my association with the men in the 3rd platoon. I have made some lasting friendships. You become close to men whose lives depend on you and yours depends on them. The comradeship of combat overshadows the friendships of civilian. I can truthfully say that I enjoyed my experiences and the men I ate, slept and fought with. Of course, there were a few horses-asses, but then there is everywhere. Some were cowards, some were brave and I believe all of us were afraid.[11]

Appendix:
Whatever Happened to:

BRADLEY, GENERAL OMAR NELSON (1893–1981) For two years following the German surrender, Bradley reformed and ran the Veterans' Administration. In February 1948, he succeeded Eisenhower as Army Chief of Staff. The following year he became the first chairman of the Joint Chiefs of Staff in the newly created Department of Defence. Promoted to five-star general in 1950, Bradley was the first chairman of the Military Staff Committee of NATO.

BROOKE, FIELD MARSHAL LORD ALAN (1883–1963) Promoted to field marshal in January 1944, the British Chief of Imperial General Staff was created Baron Alanbrooke in September 1945. After retiring from the army he was a director of Midland Bank.

CRERAR, GENERAL HENRY DUNCAN GRAHAM (1888–1965) The creator of the Canadian First Army, who took command of most of the Twenty-First Army Group forces for the offensive against the Lower Rhine, retired from active service in 1946.

DE GAULLE, GENERAL CHARLES (1890–1970) Leader of liberated France and head of government in the early post-war months, de Gaulle resigned in January 1946 after failing to attract parliamentary support for a strong, American-style presidency. Though remaining at the head of a right-wing group, the Rassemblement du Peuple Français, a national coalition 'above parties', he was out of office until June 1958 when political leaders turned to him to avert the threat of civil war in Algeria. After framing a new constitution, de Gaulle was elected President, serving from January 1959 to 1969. His period in office saw a revival of the French economy and a withdrawal from Algeria and other French colonies. But the last years were beset by social unrest culminating in the riots and strikes of 1968.

DE LATTRE DE TASSIGNY, GENERAL JEAN JOSEPH (1889–1952) A close ally of de Gaulle, the commander of the French First Army continued in

454

service after the May surrender, first as inspector general of the army and then as commander of French forces in Indo-China. He was posthumously created Marshal of France.

DEVERS, GENERAL JACOB L. (1887–1979) After 1945, the Commander of the US Sixth Army Group replaced General Stilwell as Commander of Army Ground Forces. He retired in September 1949.

DIETRICH, SS COLONEL GENERAL JOSEPH (SEPP) (1892–1966) Surrendering to American forces in May 1945, he was sentenced to twenty-five years' imprisonment by a US court but served less than ten. Had he fallen into Soviet hands he would almost certainly have faced the death penalty for war crimes on the eastern front. Having been released from Allied custody, he served a further term of imprisonment having been found guilty by a West German court of having taken part in Hitler's purge of the Sturm Abteilung in 1934. He was freed in 1955.

DOENITZ, GRAND ADMIRAL KARL (1891–1980) Named as Hitler's successor as head of state, he negotiated the surrender of German forces in the west and was arrested at Flensburg on May 23rd. Convicted as a war criminal at Nuremberg, he was sentenced to a ten-year prison sentence in Spandau. He was released in 1956.

DOOLITTLE, LT GENERAL JAMES HAROLD (1896–1993) Commander of the US Eighth Air Force in Europe and the Pacific from January 1944 to September 1945, Doolittle retired from active service as a lieutenant general. A vice-president of Shell Oil from May 1946, he later served on the National Advisory Committee for Aeronautics and the President's Science Advisory Committee.

EISENHOWER, GENERAL DWIGHT DAVID (1890–1969) Ending the war as America's only war hero-rival to General Douglas MacArthur, Commander of US forces in the Pacific, Eisenhower headed German occupation forces until December when he was made NATO Supreme Commander. As the Republican candidate for the US presidency, Eisenhower was elected in 1952 by a wide margin. Fearing that the military build-up on both sides of the Iron Curtain would inevitably lead to war unless efforts were made to reduce tension, he made peace in Korea and tried to persuade Stalin's successors to join in mutual inspection of military hardware. Recovering from a heart attack, Eisenhower was elected for a second term in November 1956.

HARRIS, AIR CHIEF MARSHAL SIR ARTHUR TRAVERS (1892–1984) Promoted Marshal of the RAF after the war, Harris was so compromised by his advocacy of blanket bombing that, while other commanders received peerages, it was not until 1953 that he was awarded a baronetcy. Retiring from active service immediately after the war, Harris went to South Africa where he set up a shipping firm. He returned to Britain in 1953.

HODGES, GENERAL COURTNEY HICKS (1887–1966) Commander of the US First Army which took the bridge at Remagen, Hodges was preparing to take his forces to the Pacific when the war ended. He continued to command the First Army, retiring in 1949.

JODL, GENERAL ALFRED JOSEF (1890–1946) Having signed the unconditional surrender at Reims on behalf of the Doenitz government, Jodl was found guilty at Nuremberg of planning an aggressive war and hanged.

KEITEL, FIELD MARSHAL WILHELM (1882–1946) Chief of Staff of the German High Command, Keitel signed Germany's surrender in Berlin on May 8th, 1945. He was found guilty of war crimes at Nuremberg and hanged in 1946.

KESSELRING, FIELD MARSHAL ALBERT (1885–1960) The successor to Field Marshal von Rundstedt as C-in-C West, Kesselring surrendered to American forces on May 7th, 1945. In 1947 a British court found him guilty of ordering the execution of 335 Italian civilians and he was sentenced to life imprisonment, a conviction that was thought to be unsound by many jurists and participants in the Italian campaign. Kesselring was released in 1952 and became president of Stalhelm, the German ex-servicemen's association.

KONEV, MARSHAL IVAN STEPANOVICH (1897–1973) Having played a leading role in the battle for Berlin, he commanded Soviet troops in Austria and Hungary before being appointed deputy defence minister. His last appointment in 1961 was as commander of Soviet troops in East Germany. He retired in 1962.

LEAHY, ADMIRAL WILLIAM DANIEL (1875–1959) After the death of Roosevelt, Leahy was asked by Truman to continue to serve as the President's Chief of Staff, a job he held until 1949. As a White House adviser, Leahy opposed the use of atomic weapons against Japan.

MARSHALL, GENERAL GEORGE CATLETT (1880–1959) Having served as Roosevelt's Chief of Staff, he was made Secretary of State (1947–49) by President Truman, the only career army officer to hold that post. In September 1951, three months after the outbreak of the Korean War, he was appointed Secretary of Defence, a job he held for a year. He was awarded the Nobel Peace Prize in 1953 for his contribution to the recovery of Europe with the aid programme known as the Marshall Plan.

MONTGOMERY, FIELD MARSHAL BERNARD LAW (1887–1976) Created Viscount Montgomery of Alamein in 1946, Montgomery was made chief of British occupation forces in Germany and, subsequently, Chief of the Imperial General Staff. From 1948, he served as Chairman of the Western Europe Commander in Chiefs Committee and, from 1951, as Deputy Supreme Allied Commander in Europe (NATO) until his retirement in 1958. Increasingly dotty political views damaged his reputation, a fate avoided by his rival George Patton who died at the height of his military powers.

PATTON, GENERAL GEORGE (1885–1945) Of all the Allied generals, Patton was the least likely to retire quietly. Less than two months after the German surrender, he was in the news with some ill-advised comments that were judged to be anti-Semitic. Relieved of his Third Army command, Eisenhower ordered him to take over the Fifteenth Army, whose task it was to collect material for the official US army history. Thoroughly frustrated and in dangerous mood, it was probably fortunate for Patton's long-term reputation that his life was cut short by a car accident near Mannheim in December 1945.

QUISLING, VIDKUN (1887–1945) After the surrender of German forces in Norway, Quisling gave himself up to the restored Norwegian government, was tried as a collaborator and executed by firing squad.

RUNDSTEDT, FIELD MARSHAL KARL RUDOLF GERD VON (1875–1953) Having commanded the last Ardennes offensive (Battle of the Bulge) he was retired from active service in March 1945. Captured by US troops at Bad Tolz in May 1945, he was held by the British for war crimes but he was sufficiently well regarded as a professional soldier to avoid arraignment. He was freed in 1949.

SEYSS INQUART, ARTHUR (1892–1946) Repenting after 1945 the 'fearful excesses' of Nazism, the Reichskommissar for the Netherlands was nonetheless sentenced to death at Nuremberg and hanged on October 16th, 1946.

SPAATZ, GENERAL CARL (1891–1974) After commanding the USAAF in Europe, Spaatz led the US Strategic Air Forces in the Pacific (1945–46), directing the final stages of the bombing offensive against Japan which culminated in Hiroshima and Nagasaki. Present at all three signings of unconditional surrender by the Axis powers, at Reims, Berlin and Tokyo, he was promoted to major general and, in February 1946, appointed to command the Army Air Forces. In September 1947 he was made first Chief of Staff of the new US Air Force. He retired in June 1948.

SPEER, ALBERT (1905–1982) Hitler's armaments minister from February 1942, he became disenchanted with Nazism but remained in his job until April 1945. Arrested at Flensburg in May, he stood trial at Nuremberg, pleading guilty to war crimes for which he was sentenced to twenty years' imprisonment. He was freed in 1966. His autobiography, *Inside the Third Reich*, was published in 1969.

ZHUKOV, MARSHAL GEORGI KONSTANTINOVICH (1896–1974) Having launched the final offensive against Berlin, he commanded Soviet occupation forces in Germany until 1946 when he was demoted by Stalin. After Stalin's death in 1953, Zhukov became Soviet minister of defence but was dismissed in October 1957 by Khruschev who accused him of 'Bonapartism'.

Notes

1. Misreading Hitler (pp.1–26)

1. Frank Gillard, BBC, in *On the Air – War Report*, Oxford University Press, 1946
2. Captain Athol Stewart, NBC, ibid.; p.266
3. Captain Howard Sweet, US 908 Field Artillery Regiment, Imperial War Museum; 95/33/1
4. Ed Cunningham, *The Battle of the Bulge*, taken from *Reporting World War II: Vol. 2, American Journalism 1944–46*, Library of America, 1995; pp.591–2
5. Wayne van Dyke, Eleventh Armoured Division, US Third Army, Second World War Experience, Leeds; 2001/892
6. Julian Thompson, *Victory in Europe*, Sidgwick & Jackson, 1994; p.210
7. Captain J.J. Moore, First Battalion Oxfordshire & Buckinghamshire Light Infantry, *Local Minor Patrol Activity*, Imperial War Museum; 95/19/11
8. Richard Hough, *Other Days Around Me*, Hodder & Stoughton, 1992; p.116
9. Sergeant Richard Greenwood, Imperial War Museum; 95/19/11
10. ibid.; 95/19/11
11. Julian Thompson, op. cit.; p.203
12. Rudolf Semmler, *Goebbels – the Man Next to Hitler*, Westhouse, 1947; p.169
13. Milton Shulman, *Defeat in the West*, Secker & Warburg, 1947
14. General Hasso von Manteuffel, *The Fatal Decisions*, Michael Joseph, 1956; p.217
15. Milton Shulman, op. cit.
16. Danny S. Parker, ed., *Hitler's Ardennes Offensive*, Greenhill Books, 1997; p.18
17. *The World War II Years: The Memoirs of Jack W. Brugh*, Hoskins Library, University of Tennessee, Knoxville
18. Hanson W. Baldwin, *Battles Lost and Won: Great Campaigns of World War II*, Harper & Row, 1966; p.354
19. Noel Annan, *Changing Enemies. The Defeat and Regeneration of Germany*, HarperCollins, 1995, p.131

20. Gerald Astor, *A Blood Dimmed Tide*, Dell, 1992; pp.125–6
21. Gene A. Curry, Hoskins Library, University of Tennessee, Knoxville
22. George Nicklin, *The Bulge Bugle*, Feb. 1991, Hoskins Library, University of Tennessee, Knoxville
23. Gene A. Curry, op. cit.
24. ibid.
25. ibid.
26. Harry Martin, *The Bulge Bugle*, Vol. X, No. 2, May 1991, Hoskins Library, University of Tennessee, Knoxville
27. *The World War II Years: The Memoirs of Jack W. Brugh*, op. cit.
28. Leon Setter, *The Bulge Bugle*, op. cit., Nov. 1991
29. Joe Tatman, *The Bulge Bugle*, op. cit., May 1991
30. *The World War II Years: The Memoirs of Jack W. Brugh*, op. cit.
31. Charles B. MacDonald, *The Battle of the Bulge*, Weidenfeld & Nicolson, 1984
32. James Cassidy and Robert Barr, in *On the Air – War Report*; p.298
33. Jack Belden, *Time*, January 1, 1945
34. *Yank*, March 2, 1945
35. Gerald Astor, op. cit.; pp.125–6

2. Comeback (pp.27–44)

1. General Sir Brian Horrocks, *A Full Life*, Collins, 1960; p.240
2. Alan Moorehead, *Eclipse*, Hamish Hamilton, 1945; p.215
3. Ed Peniche (www.nhmccd.edu/contracts/lrc/kc/peniche.html)
4. David C. Laing, *Battle Experiences in Belgium*, Hoskins Library, University of Tennessee, Knoxville
5. Frederick Fox, Third Army signals officer, Hoskins Library, University of Tennessee, Knoxville
6. Dan Shine (www.xs4all.nl/~hulsmann/accountbotb2.html)
7. Michael Moynihan, *War Correspondent*, Leo Cooper, 1994; pp.128–30
8. www.geocities.com/Pentagon/5233/4armdiv.html
9. Ed Peniche, op. cit.
10. Kenneth Kayen, *The Fourth Armoured Division from the Beach to Bavaria*, http://216.239. . . ./beachtobavariabook.htm+manure+heap +in+bigonville&hl=e n&iie=UTF-
11. Martha Gelhorn, quoted in *The Mammoth Book of War Correspondents*, ed. Jon E. Lewis, Robinson, 2001; p.381
12. Captain Rudolf Schueppel, Kempowski Archive, Nartum
13. General McAuliffe in *On the Air – War Report*, Oxford University Press, 1946; p.305

14. Harold H. Martin, *Soldier: The Memoirs of Matthew B. Ridgway*, Harper, 1956
15. http://freespace.virgin.net/hart.ofeuro/bulgeinc.html
16. Belgian War Crimes Commission Report, Liège, 1945
17. www.clandavidsonusa.com/wac/panzergruppe/aug96/aug96.html
18. General Edward Bautz in Rutgers Oral History Archives of World War II
19. Roy Brown in Rutgers Oral History Archives of World War II
20. Michael Moynihan, op. cit.; p.136
21. Horst Lange, *December 1944 Bigonville* (translated by Bruce Burdett). Website: www.bigonville.com
22. 'Milk' (copyright Josef Schroeder) taken from a collection of stories entitled *Journeys*. Website: www.bigonville.com
23. Michael Moynihan, op. cit.; p.134
24. Major General Sir Francis de Guingand, *Operation Victory*, Hodder & Stoughton, 1947; p.431
25. James Graff, *Memoirs of the 134th Infantry, 35th Division, Ninth Army*, Hoskins Library, University of Tennessee, Knoxville

3. The Best of Enemies, the Worst of Friends (pp.45–61)

1. Albert Speer, *Inside the Third Reich*, Weidenfield & Nicolson, 1945; p.419
2. The United States Strategic Bombing Survey, Summary Report, September 1945
3. Tom Pocock, *1945: The Dawn Came Up Like Thunder*, Collins, 1983; p.60
4. Peter Haining, *The Flying Bomb War*, Robson, 2003; p.195
5. William A. Buckley, Captain 117th Infantry Personnel Officer, April 5, 1945, Hoskins Library, University of Tennessee, Knoxville
6. Walter G. Denise in Rutgers Oral History Archives of World War II
7. Robert E. Sherwood, *Roosevelt and Hopkins: An Intimate Portrait*, Harper, 1950; p.815
8. ibid.; p.812
9. Roy Jenkins, *Churchill*, Macmillan, 2001; p.786
10. General Edward Bautz in Rutgers Oral History Archives of World War II
11. General Sir David Fraser, *Wars and Shadows*, Allen Lane, 2002
12. Field Marshal Montgomery of Alamein, *Memoirs*, Collins, 1958; p.313
13. Horst Bergmeier and Rainer Lotz, *Hitler's Airwaves. The Inside Story of Nazi Radio Broadcasting and Propaganda Swing*, Yale, 1997; p.229

14. Field Marshal Lord Alanbrooke, *War Diaries*, eds. Alex Danchev and Daniel Todman, Weidenfeld & Nicolson, 2001; p.628
15. Major General Sir Francis de Guingand, *Operation Victory*, Hodder & Stoughton, 1947; pp.434–5

4. Bleak Midwinter (pp.62–74)

1. Lester Atwell, *Private*, Simon & Schuster, 1958; p.151
2. R.M. Wingfield, *The Only Way Out*, Hutchinson, 1955; p.140
3. Noel Ryan, *A Life of His Own*, http://www.3.ns.sympatico.ca/laird.niven/public. html/ryan.htm
4. *War Diary, 1st Bn. Black Watch (Royal Highland Regiment) of Canada*, National Archives of Canada, Ottawa
5. William B. Morgan, Captain Corp of Engineers, US Army, Hoskins Library, University of Tennessee, Knoxville
6. Wynford Vaughan Thomas, BBC, in *On the Air – War Report*, Oxford University Press, 1946; p.290
7. Lieutenant Russell W. Cloer, Seventh Infantry, in Rutgers Oral History Archives of World War II
8. Wynford Vaughan Thomas, op. cit.; p.290
9. David Eisenhower, *Eisenhower at War, 1943–45*, Random House, 1986; pp.644–5
10. Lester Atwell, op. cit.
11. Edwin Kolodziej in Rutgers Oral History Archives of World War II
12. James Graff, *Memoirs of the 134th Infantry, 35th Division, Ninth Army*, Hoskins Library, University of Tennessee, Knoxville
13. ibid.
14. James Essig in Rutgers Oral History Archives of World War II
15. Harold H. Martin, *Soldier: The Memoirs of Matthew B. Ridgway*, Harper, 1956; p.122
16. General Sir Brian Horrocks, *A Full Life*, Collins, 1960; pp.251–2
17. Milton Shulman, *Defeat in the West*, Secker & Warburg, 1947

5. United in Hate (pp.75–101)

1. Robert E. Sherwood, *Roosevelt and Hopkins: An Intimate Portrait*, Harper, 1950; p.847
2. Jim Bishop, *FDR's Last Year*, William Morrow, 1974; p.268
3. Roy Jenkins, *Churchill*, Macmillan, 2001; p.764
4. Fleet Admiral William D. Leahy, *I Was There*, Gollancz, 1950; p.329
5. Robert E. Sherwood, op. cit.; p.849
6. Fleet Admiral William D. Leahy, op. cit.; p.334

7. Michael Beschloss, *The Conquerors*, Simon & Schuster, 2002; p.23
8. David Eisenhower, *Eisenhower at War, 1943–45*, Random House, 1986; p.653
9. Richard Overy, *Why the Allies Won*, Cape, 1995; pp.250, 254
10. Joan Bright Astley, *The Inner Circle*, Hutchinson, 1971; p.175
11. ibid.; pp.177, 178
12. ibid.; p.180
13. General the Lord Ismay, *Memoirs*, Heinemann, 1960; p.386
14. Joan Bright Astley, op. cit.; p.184
15. Albert Speer, *Inside the Third Reich*, Weidenfeld & Nicolson, 1945; p.421
16. General Heinz Guderian, *Panzer Leader*, Michael Joseph, 1952; p.387
17. Robert E. Sherwood, op. cit.; p.848
18. Field Marshal Lord Alanbrooke, *War Diaries*, eds. Alex Danchev and Daniel Todman, Weidenfeld & Nicolson, 2001; p.653
19. Robert E. Sherwood, op. cit.; p.849
20. Harold Nicolson, *Diaries and Letters 1939–45*, ed. Nigel Nicolson, Collins, 1967; p.435
21. General the Lord Ismay, op. cit.; p.386
22. David Eisenhower, op. cit.; p.650
23. Sir Alexander Cadogan, O.M., *Diaries, 1938–1945*, ed. David Dilks, Cassell, 1971; pp.706, 708
24. General the Lord Ismay, op. cit.; p.387
25. Martin Gilbert, *Winston S. Churchill, Vol. VII, Road to Victory, 1941–1945*, Heinemann, 1986; p.1218
26. General the Lord Ismay, op. cit.; p.387
27. *The Gallup Poll Cumulative Index. Public Opinion 1935–97*, eds. Alec Gallup, George H. Gallup
28. Martin Gilbert, op. cit.; p.415
29. Robert E. Sherwood, op. cit.; p.593
30. Martin Gilbert, op. cit.; p.471
31. Churchill to Eden, March 25, 1945, Martin Gilbert, ibid.; p.1265
32. Robert E. Sherwood, op. cit.; p.871
33. Fleet Admiral William D. Leahy, op. cit.; p.381
34. ibid.; p.382
35. ibid.; p.382
36. Daniel Litvin, *Empires of Profit*, Texere, 2003; p.188
37. Fleet Admiral William D. Leahy, op. cit.; pp.218, 219
38. Daniel Yergin, 'Gulf Oil', *Financial Times*, March 22, 2003
39. Fleet Admiral William D. Leahy, op. cit.; p.266
40. ibid.; p.382

41. Robert E. Sherwood, op. cit.; p.872
42. Fleet Admiral William D. Leahy, op. cit.; p.383
43. ibid.; p.384

6. War in the Air (pp.102–20)

1. Quoted in *The Faber Book of Reportage*, ed. John Carey, 1987; pp.608–9
2. ibid.; pp.611–12
3. Nicholas Rankin, *Telegram from Guernica*, Faber, 2003; p.121
4. ibid.; p.124
5. John Peyton, *Solly Zuckerman: A Scientist Out of the Ordinary*, John Murray, 2001
6. Sir Arthur Harris, *Bomber Offensive*, Greenhill Books, 1990; p.73
7. Shirley Williams, *God and Caesar*, Continuum, 2003; p.82
8. Chris Hodges, *War is a Force that Gives us Meaning*, Public Affairs, 2002; p.3
9. Flight Lieutenant George Millington, Imperial War Museum; 92/29/1
10. *The Army Air Forces in World War II*, eds. W.F. Craven and J.L. Cate, Vol. 3, University of Chicago Press, 1965; p.767
11. Richard Dimbleby, BBC, in *On the Air – War Report*, Oxford University Press, 1946; p.279
12. Richard Dimbleby, ibid.; p.281
13. Vergessen kann Mann nicht, Köln Stadtarchiv
14. ibid.
15. Charles E. Cope, Hoskins Library, University of Tennessee, Knoxville
16. ibid.
17. ibid.
18. Flight Lieutenant George Millington, op. cit.
19. UN General Assembly Special Session on the World Drug Problem, 8–10 June 1998
20. Ian McLachlan, *USAAF Fighter Stories*, Patrick Stephens, 1997; p.19
21. Ian McLachlan and Russell J. Zorn, *Eighth Air Force Bomber Stories*, Patrick Stephens, 1991; p.153

7. The Unstoppable War Machine (pp.122–47)

1. Heilbronn Stadtarchiv
2. Wilhelm Steinhilber, *Heilbronn – die schwersten Stunden der Stadt (The City's Toughest Hours)*, Verlag Heilbronner Stimme, 1961
3. ibid.
4. Heilbronn Stadtarchiv

5. Stuttgart Staatsarchiv
6. ibid.
7. ibid.
8. Taken from 'Bonn im Bombenkrieg'/Bonner Geschichtsblaetter, Band 38 Herausgegeben vom Bonner Heimat-und Geschichtsverein und dem Stadtarchiv Bonn
9. Helmut Vogt/Anneliese Barbara Baum, Bonn 1994
10. Marianna Pross, *Die Einschlälge kommen Naher.* Aus den Tagebüchern 1943–5 von FAK, 1945–7 Oberbürgermeister der Stadt Pforzheim, Kempowski Archive, Nartum
11. Max Gaupp, reported in *Pforzhem 23 Februar 1945. Der Untergang einer Stadt in Bildern und Augenzeugenbreichten, Herausgegeben und bearbeitet von Esther Schmalacker-Wyrich*, Verlag J Esslinger, Pforzheim, Kempowski Archive, Nartum
12. Henry Probert, *Bomber Harris: His Life and Times*, Greenhill Books, 2001; p.320
13. *To the Bitter End: The Diaries of Victor Klemperer 1942–45*, abridged and translated by Martin Chalmers, Phoenix, 2000; pp.497–500
14. David Irving, *The Destruction of Dresden*, Focal Point Publications, 1974
15. Helmut Schnatz, *Tiefflieger über Dresden? Legenden und Wirklichkeit*, Böhlau, 2000
16. Martin Gilbert, *Winston S. Churchill, Vol. III, The Challenge of War, 1914–1916*, Heinemann, 1986; p.1219
17. Herman Rosenberg, *Haagsche Courant*, March 2, 1995
18. Churchill papers, March 18, 1945, D75/5 20/209
19. Churchill papers, D85/5
20. *The War in the Air 1939–1945*, ed. Gavin Lyall, Hutchinson, 1968
21. Richard Overy, *Why the Allies Won*, Cape, 1995; p.20
22. ibid.; p.125
23. The United States Strategic Bombing Survey, 1945
24. ibid., Summary Report
25. Sir Arthur Harris, *Bomber Offensive*, Greenhill Books, 1990; p.144
26. ibid.; p.147
27. ibid.; pp.176–7
28. ibid.; p.242
29. Jörg Friedrich, *Der Brand, Deutschland im Bombenkrieg, 1940–1945*, Gebundene Ausgabe, 2002; W.G. Sebald, *On the Natural History of Destruction*, translated by Anthea Bell, Hamish Hamilton, 2003
30. Ibid.
31. W.G. Sebald, op. cit.
32. *Daily Telegraph*, November 25, 2002.
33. *Spectator*, September 22, 2001

8. The Little Guys Fight Back (pp.148–70)

1. Richard Petrov, *The Bitter Years*, Morrow, 1974; p.41
2. *Expressen*, March 22, 1945
3. Knud J.V. Jespersen, *No Small Achievement: Special Operations Executive and the Danish Resistance 1940–45*, University of Southern Denmark; pp.390–2
4. Sir Basil Embry, *Mission Completed*, Methuen, 1957; p.245
5. ibid.; pp.251, 252
6. ibid.; p.273
7. Danish Resistance Museum
8. Jørgen Haestrup, *Secret Alliance, Vol. 3*, Odense University Press, 1977; pp.228–59
9. John Oram Thomas, *The Giant Killers*, Michael Joseph, 1975; pp.287, 288
10. Jørgen Haestrup, op. cit.; p.462
11. Knud J.V. Jespersen, op. cit.; pp.462–3
12. John Oram Thomas, op. cit.; p.295
13. Sir Basil Embry, op. cit.; p.278
14. Robin Reilly, *The Sixth Floor*, Leslie Frewin, 1969; p.175
15. ibid.; p.176
16. ibid.; p.251
17. Aage Trommer, *Railway Sabotage in Denmark During the Second World War*, Odense University Press, 1971, English summary; pp.303–15
18. Group Captain Johnnie Johnson, *Wing Leader*, Chatto & Windus, 1956; p.311
19. Gunnar Sonsteby, *Report from #24*, Barricade Books, 1965; pp.153–5
20. Tore Gjelsvik, *Norwegian Resistance 1940–45*, Hurst, 1979; pp.191–3
21. Gunnar Sonsteby, op. cit.; pp.172–4
22. Tore Gjelsvik, op. cit.; p.211

9. Advance to the Rhine (pp.172–94)

1. Lord Lothian, quoted in W.S. Churchill, *The Second World War, Vol. I, The Gathering Storm*, Cassell, 1948; p.176
2. Colonel C.P. Stacey, *The Canadian Army 1939–45: An Official Historical Summary*, Ottawa, 1948; p.240
3. Lieutenant Colonel H.M. Baker, Second Canadian Corps, Imperial War Museum; 87/44/1
4. Colonel C.P. Stacey, op. cit.; p.239
5. History of the Lowland Division
6. ibid.

7. Major Desmond Flower, *History of the Argyll and Sutherland High-landers, 5th Battalion, 91st Anti-Tank Regiment: 1939–45*, Nelson, 1950
8. Captain J.J. Moore, First Battalion Oxfordshire and Buckinghamshire Light Infantry, *First Into Germany*, Imperial War Museum
9. Corporal Dai Evans, Royal Welsh Fusiliers, Imperial War Museum; 92/37/1
10. Lieutenant General Sir Brian Horrocks, *A Full Life*, Collins, 1960; p.248
11. A.E. Baker, Wireless Operator, 4th Squadron, Seventh Royal Dragoon Guards, Imperial War Museum; 88/34/1
12. John Foley, *The Mailed Fist*, Mayflower, 1975
13. Lieutenant General Sir Brian Horrocks, op. cit.; pp.248–9
14. ibid.; p.249
15. Brigadier C.N. Barker, Second World War Experience Centre, Leeds, 1999/04
16. Martin Lindsay, *So Few Got Through*, Collins, 1946
17. Corporal Dai Evans, op. cit.
18. ibid.
19. ibid.
20. A.E. Baker, op. cit.
21. Captain J.J. Moore, op. cit.
22. General Sir Brian Horrocks, op. cit.; p.250
23. *War Diary of the First Battalion, Black Watch (Royal Highland Regiment) of Canada*, National Archives of Canada, Ottawa
24. Lieutenant Colonel H.M. Baker, op. cit.
25. General Sir Brian Horrocks, op. cit.; p.251
26. James Graff, *Memoirs of the 134th Infantry, 35th Division, Ninth Army*, Hoskins Library, University of Tennessee, Knoxville
27. Captain Howard Sweet, US 908 Field Artillery Regiment, Imperial War Museum; 95/33/1
28. Howard Brodie, March 1945. Quoted in *Reporting World War II: Vol. 2, American Journalism 1944–46*, Library of America, 1995
29. James Graff, op. cit.
30. Corporal Dai Evans, op. cit.

10. Hanging Out the Washing (pp.195–224)

1. A.E. Baker, Wireless Operator, 4th Squadron, Seventh Royal Dragoon Guards, Imperial War Museum; 88/34/1
2. ibid.
3. General Sir Brian Horrocks, *A Full Life*, Collins, 1960; pp.253–4
4. http://www.multipointproductions.com/heroes/loren/hochwald.htm *Canadian Heroes* – Private Loren Nelson

5. ibid.
6. http://www.multipointproductions.com/heroes/loren/veritabl.htm
7. ibid.
8. Field Marshal Lord Alanbrooke, *War Diaries*, eds. Alex Danchev and Daniel Todman, Weidenfeld & Nicolson, 2001; pp.667–8
9. Major General Sir Francis de Guingand, *Operation Victory*, Hodder & Stoughton, 1947; p.440
10. Saul K. Padover, *Psychologist in Germany*, Phoenix, 1946; p.218
11. Marie Therese Fuegling, *Die Heimat*, Summer 1954
12. Saul K. Padover, op. cit.; p.231
13. Letter dated March 4 1945. Düsseldorf Historisches Archiv
14. Diary of the Wilhelm family, published in the *Nordrheinische Zeitung*, November 17 1954
15. Captain Howard Sweet, US 908 Field Artillery Regiment, Imperial War Museum; 95/33/1
16. History of the 94th Infantry, Düsseldorf Stadtarchiv
17. ibid.
18. Otto Greve, Cologne Historisches Archiv
19. Karl Juesgen, Cologne Historisches Archiv
20. ibid.
21. Josefine Heinrichs, Cologne Historisches Archiv
22. Gertrud Geimer, Cologne Historisches Archiv
23. Ingrid Schampel, taken from 'Bonn im Bombenkrieg'/Bonner Geschichtsblaetter, Band 38 Herausgegeben vom Bonner Heimat-und Geschichtsverein und dem Stadtarchiv Bonn
24. Kriegsende (The End of the War), Bonner Geschichtsblaetter, Band 41 Herausgegeben vom Bonner Heimat-und Geschichtsverein und dem Stadtarchiv Bonn/ Anneliese Barbara Baum/Reiner Pommerin, Bonn, 1991
25. Diary of Lucie Lecoq, quoted in *General Anzeiger*, Bonn newspaper, 1979 (Gisela H. Williams)
26. Chaplain William S. Boyce, 22nd Infantry, Hoskins Library, University of Tennessee, Knoxville
27. ibid.
28. ibid.
29. George M. Patton, *War As I Knew It*, Houghton Mifflin, 1947
30. Lester Atwell, *Private*, Simon & Schuster, 1958
31. Wallace R. Cheves, *Snow Ridges and Pillboxes*, Hoskins Library, University of Tennessee, Knoxville; p.223
32. ibid.; p.235
33. ibid.; p.242

34. ibid.; p.249
35. ibid.; p.246
36. ibid.; p.247
37. John Foley, *The Mailed Fist*, Mayflower, 1975; p.164
38. Corporal Dai Evans, Royal Welsh Fusiliers, Imperial War Museum; 92/37/1
39. Lieutenant Colonel H.M. Baker, Second Canadian Corps, Imperial War Museum; 87/44/1

11. The Hunger Winter (pp.225–45)

1. Netherlands State Institute for War Documentation, Amsterdam
2. ibid.
3. Major General Sir Francis de Guingand, *Operation Victory*, Hodder & Stoughton, 1947; p.438
4. Netherlands State Institute for War Documentation, Amsterdam
5. *Dagboekfragmenten 1940–1945*; pp.500–1. Netherlands State Institute for War Documentation, Amsterdam
6. ibid.; pp.510–11
7. M.R.D. Foot, *SOE in the Low Countries*, Little Brown, 2002
8. Joyce Hibbert, *Fragments of War: Stories From Survivers of World War II*, Dundurn Press, 1985; pp.178–9
9. *Dagboekfragmenten 1940–1945*; p.565
10. ibid.
11. Cornelia Fuykschot, *Hunger in Holland*, Amherst, NY: Prometheus Books, 1995; pp.132–3
12. *Dagboekfragmenten 1940–1945*; pp.599–600
13. ibid.; pp.560–4
14. http://www.multipointproductions.com/heroes/loren/delden.htm *Canadian Heroes* – Private Loren Nelson
15. *Dagboekfragmenten 1940–1945*; pp.520–1
16. ..../veterans_searchdetail.cfm?VeteransContentID=D58EB87E-D56C-4999-A918-763976BEF228&StoriesContentID=A7E60F02
17. ibid.
18. Mathew Holton, CBC, in *On the Air – War Report*, Oxford University Press, 1946; pp.376–7
19. Major General Sir Francis de Guingand, op. cit.; pp.446–9
20. ibid.; p.449
21. Hal E. Wert, 'Military Expedience, the Hunger Winter and Holland's Belated Liberation', from *Victory in Europe 1945*, University Press of Kansas, 2000; p.134
22. Major General Sir Francis de Guingand, op. cit.; pp.451–2

23. Henry van der Zee, *The Hunger Winter. Occupied Holland 1944–45*, University of Nebraska Press, 1982; pp.276, 277
24. *Dagboekfragmenten 1940–1945*; pp.613–14
25. ibid.; pp.614–15
26. Resistance Museum Archive, Amsterdam

12. The Bridge at Remagen (pp.246–64)

1. Milton Schulman, *Defeat in the West*, Secker & Warburg, 1947
2. New Brunswick History Dept. Rutgers Oral History Archives of World War II. Interview with Edwin Kolodziej (http://fas-history.rutgers.edu/oralhistory/kolodziej2.html)
3. Karl Hechler, *The Bridge at Remagen*, Pictorial Histories Publishing Coy., 1957; p.112
4. ibid.; p.113
5. ibid.; p.114
6. http://www2.gasou.edu/facstaff/etmcmull/REMAGEN.htm
7. Karl Hechler, op. cit.; p.121
8. Omar N. Bradley, *A Soldier's Story*, Holt, 1951; pp.510–11
9. Rolf Pauls, quoted in *Voices from the Third Reich: An Oral History*, eds. Johannes Steinhoff, Peter Pechel and Dennis Showalter, Grafton, 1991; p.408
10. Field Marshal Kesselring, *Memoirs*, William Kimber, 1953; pp.238–9
11. ibid.; pp.243–4
12. Alexander McKee, *The Race for the Rhine Bridges*, Souvenir Press, 1971; p.344
13. ibid.; p.343
14. Flight Lieutenant John McAlevey, quoted by Ian McLachlan, *USAAF Fighter Stories*, Patrick Stephens, 1997; pp.53–4
15. Report of Captain James B. Cooke (http://humber.northnet.org/488thengineers/Remagen.html)
16. Alexander McKee, op. cit; p.347
17. Omar N. Bradley, op. cit.; p.521
18. ibid.; p.522
19. Charles M. Province, *Patton's Third Army: A Daily Combat Diary*, Hippocrene Books, 1992; p.226
20. Russell W. Cloer in Rutgers Oral History Archives of World War II
21. Nigel Hamilton, *Monty: Life of Montgomery of Alamein: The Field Marshal 1944–76*, Hamish Hamilton, 1986; p.405
22. Field Marshal Kesselring, op. cit.; p.238
23. ibid.; p.239

13. A Set Piece Battle (pp.266–92)

1. Alan Moorehead, *Eclipse*, Hamish Hamilton, 1945; p.228
2. Lieutenant (later Captain) Tom Flanagan, Fourth King's Own Scottish Borderers, Imperial War Museum
3. ibid.; pp.36–7
4. General Sir Brian Horrocks, *A Full Life*, Collins, 1960; p.257
5. Lieutenant Tom Flanagan, op. cit.; pp.39–40
6. *Eyewitness War*, Marshall Cavendish, 1995; p.221
7. General Sir Brian Horrocks, op. cit.; p.258
8. ibid.; p.259
9. Wynford Vaughan Thomas, BBC, in *On the Air – War Report*, Oxford University Press, 1946; pp.323–4
10. http://www.thedropzone.org/europe/Germany/hashway.htm
11. Major Gerald Ritchie, Sixth Airborne Division, Parachute Regiment, collection of letters, Imperial War Museum; p.182
12. Colonel John Kormann, Second World War Experience Centre, Leeds, 2002/1480
13. ibid.
14. A.E. Baker, Wireless Operator, 4th Squadron, Seventh Royal Dragoon Guards, Imperial War Museum; 88/34/1
15. Major Gerald Ritchie, op. cit.
16. Colonel John Kormann, op. cit.
17. Major Desmond Flower, *History of the Argyll and Sutherland Highlanders 1939–45*, Nelson, 1950
18. Captain Tom Flanagan, op. cit.
19. Major General Sir Francis de Guingand, *Operation Victory*, Hodder & Stoughton, 1947; p.441
20. General the Lord Ismay, *Memoirs*, Heinemann, 1960; p.393
21. Major General Sir Francis de Guingand, op. cit.; p.441
22. Alan Moorhead; op. cit.
23. Kirk B. Ross, *The Sky Men: A Parachute Rifle Company's Story of the Battle of the Bulge and the Jump Across the Rhine*, Schiffer Military History, 2000; p.290
24. Major Gerald Ritchie, op. cit.
25. Kirk B. Ross, op. cit.; p.297
26. ibid.; p.296
27. ibid.; p.297
28. *Eyewitness War*, op. cit.; pp.218–19
29. Major Gerald Ritchie, op. cit.
30. Lieutenant Colonel J.C. Watts, *Surgeon at War*, Allen & Unwin, 1955
31. http://www.thedropzone.org/europe/Germany/hashway.htm

32. Harold H. Martin, *Soldier: The Memoirs of Matthew B. Ridgway*, Harper, 1956; p.133
33. Major Desmond Flower, op. cit.
34. ibid.
35. *Colliers*, May 1945. Quoted in *Reporting World War II: Vol. 2, American Journalism 1944–46*, Library of America, 1995
36. Sir John Rupert Colville, *Footprints in Time*, Collins, 1976; p.185
37. Staff Sergeant Peter Secretan, Sixth Airborne Division, Imperial War Museum; 67/22/1
38. Lieutenant Colonel J.C. Watts, op. cit.
39. ibid.; p.122
40. Major Desmond Flower, op. cit.
41. Colonel John Kormann, op. cit.
42. Kirk B. Ross, op. cit.; p.310
43. *On the Air – War Report*, op. cit.; p.328
44. P.R. Devlin, Royal Ulster Rifles, Sixth Airborne Division, Imperial War Museum; 89/13/1
45. Lieutenant Tom Flanagan, op. cit.
46. Richard Hough, *Other Days Around Me*, Hodder & Stoughton, 1992; p.119
47. Harold H. Martin, op. cit.; p.133

14. Into Germany (pp.293–318)

1. Louis Albrecht, Second World War Experience Centre, Leeds; 2000/640
2. Major A.J. Forrest, Royal Artillery, Imperial War Museum; 91/13/1
3. Major John Stirling, Eighth Armoured Brigade, Royal Dragoon Guards, Imperial War Museum; 96/12/1
4. Major Roland Ward, Second World War Experience Centre, Leeds; 2000/382
5. A.E. Baker, Wireless Operator, 4th Squadron, Seventh Royal Dragoon Guards, Imperial War Museum; 88/34/1
6. Lieutenant (later Captain) Tom Flanagan, Fourth King's Own Scottish Borderers, Imperial War Museum
7. Corporal Dai Evans, Royal Welsh Fusiliers, Imperial War Museum; 92/37/1
8. Major P.J. Hurman, Imperial War Museum; 99/85/1
9. Sergeant Richard Greenwood, Ninth Battalion Royal Tank Regiment, Imperial War Museum; 95/19/1
10. Corporal Dai Evans, op. cit.
11. Chester Wilmot, BBC, in *On the Air – War Report*, Oxford University Press, 1946; pp.341–2

12. http://victorian.fortunecity.com/finsbury/764/ryan.htm
13. Captain Maurice Jupp, Imperial War Museum
14. Stephen Cassell, War Diary, Hoskins Library, University of Tennessee, Knoxville
15. Sally Peters, quoted in *The Doughnut Girl* by Alan A. Richardson, Imperial War Museum; 93/18/1
16. James Graff, *Memoirs of the 134th Infantry, 35th Division, Ninth Army*, Hoskins Library, University of Tennessee, Knoxville
17. Captain Maurice Jupp, op. cit.
18. Frank Danster, Rutgers Oral History Archives of World War II
19. *On the Air – War Report*, op. cit.; pp.356–7
20. Charles M. Province, *Patton's Third Army*, Hippocrene Books, 1992; p.253
21. Marshal de Lattre de Tassigny, *History of the French First Army*, Allen & Unwin, 1952; p.421
22. ibid.; p.428
23. Dr Kurt Morhard, Stuttgart Stadtarchiv. Taken from *Amtsblatt der Landeshaupstadt Stuttgart Nummer 16, 20.4.95. Kriegsende 1945*
24. Nuremberg Stadtarchiv
25. Dr Julius Kober, printed in Rudolf Albart, *Vom Hakenkreuz zum Sternembanner*, Bamberg, 1979, Kempowski Archive, Nartum
26. Robert Ipsmann, Nuremberg Stadtarchiv
27. James Graff, op. cit.
28. A.E. Baker, op. cit.
29. Corporal Dai Evans, op. cit.
30. Corporal William Blackman, RAMC, Imperial War Museum; 99/85/1
31. Crandon Clark, Rutgers Oral History Archives of World War II
32. Field Marshal Kesselring, *Memoirs*, William Kimber, 1953; p.253
33. ibid.; p.262
34. Harold H. Martin, *Soldier: The Memoirs of Matthew B. Ridgway*, Harper, 1956; p.139
35. Lieutenant General Walter Bedell Smith, SHAEF Chief of Staff, quoted in Forrest C. Pogue, *The Decision to Halt at the Elbe*. http://www.ibiblio.org/pub/academic/history/marshall/military/wwii/command.decisions/contents/contents.txt
36. Winston S. Churchill, *The Second World War, Vol. VI, Triumph and Tragedy*, Cassell, 1954
37. Stephen E. Ambrose, *Eisenhower and Berlin, 1945*, Norton, 2000; p.97

15. Meeting the Enemy (pp.319–40)

1. Saul K. Padover, *Psychologist in Germany*, Phoenix, 1946; p.82
2. ibid.; pp.180–2, 200
3. ibid.; p.211
4. Leonard O. Mosley, *Report from Germany*, Gollancz, 1945; pp.14–15
5. Corporal Dai Evans, Royal Welsh Fusiliers, Imperial War Museum; 92/37/1
6. Leonard O. Mosley, op. cit.; pp.96–7
7. Corporal William Blackman, RAMC, Imperial War Museum; 99/85/1
8. Uschi Lacey, correspondence with the author
9. Kempowski Archive, Nartum
10. Corporal William Blackman, op. cit.
11. Alan Moorehead, *Eclipse*, Hamish Hamilton, 1945; p.240
12. Noel Ryan, *A Life of His Own*, http://victorian.fortunecity.com/finsbury/764/ryan.htm
13. Werner Carl Sturm, 114th Infantry Regiment, Rutgers Oral History Archives of World War II
14. A.E. Baker, Royal Dragoon Guards, Eighth Armoured Division, Imperial War Museum; 88/34/1
15. Lieutenant (later Captain) Tom Flanagan, Fourth King's Own Scottish Borderers, Imperial War Museum
16. Henry Kimberly, US Quartermaster, Second World War Experience Centre, Leeds; 2002/1550
17. Robert Inglis, Rutgers Oral History Archives of World War II
18. Corporal Dai Evans, op. cit.
19. Leonard O. Mosley, op. cit.; p.29
20. Lieutenant (later Captain) Tom Flanagan, op. cit.
21. ibid.
22. Guy le Grand, Battalion Sergeant Major, 290th Engineer Combat Battalion, Hoskins Library, University of Tennessee, Knoxville
23. Captain Howard Sweet, US 908 Field Artillery Regiment, Imperial War Museum; 95/33/1
24. Stadtarchiv Düsseldorf
25. Alfons Houben, *Düsseldorf Stunde Null*, Hornung Verlag
26. Arnold Gehlen, *Nordrheinische Zeitung*, November 1954
27. Gauleiter Florian, Stadtarchiv Düsseldorf
28. Willi Kallbach, Stadtarchiv Düsseldorf
29. Hildegard Kleinfeld, Stadtarchiv Düsseldorf

16. On the Way to the Elbe (pp.341–60)

1. Ed Murrow, in *Voices from Britain*, ed. Henning Krabbe, Allen & Unwin, 1947; pp.262–3
2. Quoted in Tom Pocock, *1945: The Dawn Came Up Like Thunder*, Collins, 1983; p.81
3. Richard Dimbleby, BBC, in *On the Air – War Report*, Oxford University Press, 1946; pp.401–2
4. Captain William Morgan, Corps of Engineers, Hoskins Library, University of Tennessee, Knoxville
5. Kempowski Archive, Nartum
6. M.E. (Mea) Allan, Imperial War Museum; 95/8/3
7. Dr David Bradford, Imperial War Museum; 86/7/1
8. Rutgers Oral History Archives of World War II
9. Dr Arnold Horwell, Imperial War Museum (no ref. given)
10. *History of the 94 Infantry*, Düsseldorf Historisches Archiv
11. Eva Lilly, Kunran, near Salzwedel, Kempowski Archive, Nartum
12. Leonard O. Mosley, *Report From Germany*, Gollancz, 1945; pp.93–4
13. Quoted in *Belsen, The Liberation of a Concentration Camp*, Joanne Reilly, Routledge, 1998; p.74
14. Tom Pocock, op. cit.; p.88
15. ibid.; p.89
16. Lieutenant (later Captain) Tom Flanagan, Fourth King's Own Scottish Borderers, Imperial War Museum
17. James Stern, *The Hidden Damage*, Chelsea Press, 1990; p.144
18. *On the Air – War Report*, op. cit.; p.359
19. Uschi Lacey, letter to the author
20. Major Gerald Ritchie, Letters, Imperial War Museum; p.182
21. http://www.eliteforcesofthethirdreich.com/German%20Veterans/Gert/memoirs.htm
22. Hugo Stehkämper, quoted in *Voice from the Third Reich: An Oral History*, eds. Johannes Steinhoff, Peter Pechel and Dennis Showalter, Grafton, 1991; pp.491–2
23. Bill Downs, CBS, in *On the Air – War Report*, op. cit.; p.363
24. Corporal Dai Evans, Royal Welsh Fusiliers, Imperial War Museum; 92/37/1
25. Captain C.T. Cross, Imperial War Museum. By kind permission of the Worshipful Company of Armourers & Brasiers in the City of London
26. James Graff, *Memoirs of the 134th Infantry, 35th Division, Ninth Army*, Hoskins Library, University of Tennessee, Knoxville
27. Wayne Van Dyke, Second World War Experience Centre, Leeds; 2001/892
28. Douglas Botting, *In the Ruins of the Reich*, Allen & Unwin, 1985; p.5

29. Wynford Vaughan Thomas, BBC, in *On the Air – War Report*, op. cit.; p.354
30. Saul K. Padover, *Psychologist in Germany*, Phoenix, 1946; p.271

17. End Game (pp.362–80)

1. Quoted at the Nuremberg trials, June 25
2. Ralph Hewins, *Count Folke Bemadotte: His Life and Work*, Hutchinson, 1948; p.118
3. General Heinz Guderian, *Panzer Leader*, Michael Joseph, 1952; pp.404–5
4. ibid.; p.429
5. Gustav Bub, Nürnberg Stadtarchiv
6. ibid.
7. ibid.
8. Ed Murrow, CBS, in *On the Air – War Report*, Oxford University Press, 1946; p.387
9. Nürnberg Stadtarchiv
10. William S. Boyce, Twenty-Second Infantry, Hoskins Library, University of Tennessee, Knoxville
11. Captain John Amsden, Seaforth Highlanders, Imperial War Museum; 87/23/1
12. Nürnberg Stadtarchiv
13. Sammlung Christian Wenger, Wuelfrath, Stadtarchiv, Wuppertal
14. Stadtarchiv, Wuppertal
15. Dr Uwe Eckhardt, Deserteure in Wuppertal, Stadtarchiv, Wuppertal, 1992
16. ibid.
17. Leonard O. Mosley, *Report From Germany*, Gollancz, 1945; p.72
18. ibid.; p.72
19. ibid.; p.69
20. ibid.; pp.81–2
21. *On the Air – War Report*, op. cit.; pp.391–2
22. Saul Padover, *Psychologist in Germany*, Phoenix, 1946; p.295
23. *On the Air – War Report*, op. cit.; pp.382–3
24. Marshal de Lattre de Tassigny, *The History of the French First Army*, Allen & Unwin, 1952; p.490
25. Lewis Bloom, in Rutgers Oral History Archives of World War II
26. Marshal de Lattre de Tassigny, op. cit.; p.492
27. http://www.feldgrau.com/interview6.html – © 1996–2004 Jason Pipes
28. Werner Girling, taken from *Zehlendorfer Chronik 9(94)*, *Das Ende des Krieges in Zehlendorf*, ed. Kurt Trumpa, Heimatverein Zehlendorf, Berlin

29. Karl Brammer, April 23, 1945, taken from *Zehlendorfer Chronik* 9(94), op. cit.
30. ibid.
31. Heimatsmuseum Tiergarten Archive, Berlin
32. ibid.

18. Looking for the Exit (pp.381–407)

1. Omar N. Bradley, *A Soldier's Story*, Holt, 1951; p.544
2. Herbert Hahn, quoted from Erich Kuby *Das Ende des Schreckens*, Listbücher 1961, Kempowski Archive, Nartum
3. Charlotte Zettler, student in Schwandorf (Bavaria), *Grüss dich Deutschland, aus Herzensgrund I – das kann ja nicht vergehen Kriegsbriefe gefallener Studenten*, ed. Rainer Wunderlich, Kempowski Archive, Nartum
4. Ray W. Brown, Rutgers Oral History Archives of World War II
5. William Louis Meissner, *Life as a GI*; p.33, Hoskins Library, University of Tennessee, Knoxville
6. Squadron Leader C.N.S. Campbell, DFC, Imperial War Museum; 86/35/1
7. Geoffrey Hall, *Kriegie: The Diary of a Prisoner of War in Germany 1943–45*, Imperial War Museum
8. W.A. Lewis, Imperial War Museum; 88/60/1
9. James Witte, *The One That Didn't Get Away*, Imperial War Museum; 87/12/1
10. N.L. Francis, Imperial War Museum; 88/58/1
11. James Witte, op. cit.
12. Corporal William Blackman, RAMC, Imperial War Museum; 99/85/1
13. Edward Ward, *On the Air – War Report*, Oxford University Press, 1946; p.418
14. Omar N. Bradley, op. cit.; p.549
15. Frank Gillard, BBC, *Voices From Britain*, ed. Henning Krabbe, Allen & Unwin, 1947; p.266
16. Saul Padover, *Psychologist in Germany*, Phoenix, 1946; pp.308–9
17. Roy W. Brown in Rutgers Oral History Archives of World War II
18. William Louis Meissner, op. cit.; p.33
19. Gordon Brook-Shepherd, *The Austrians*, HarperCollins, 1996; p.383
20. Omar N. Bradley, op. cit.; p.528
21. Dr Werner Ellerbeck, Bremen Stadtarchiv
22. Albrecht Mertz, Bremen Stadtarchiv
23. Helga Schroeder, Bremen Stadtarchiv

24. Margot Rotman, Bremen Stadtarchiv

25. Albrecht Mertz, Bremen Stadtarchiv

26. Helmut Schmidt, Bremen Stadtarchiv

27. Reinhard Groscurth, Bremen Stadtarchiv

28. Bremen Stadtarchiv

29. Irmgard Hagemeyer, Bremen Stadtarchiv

30. Bremen Stadtarchiv

31. Lieutenant Commander Dr Arnold Schoen, Pillau (East Prussia). Taken from Bundesarchiv – Lastenausgleichsarchiv Bayreuth. Seedstadt Pillau – *Stadt und kriegsgeschichtliche Aufzeichnungen*. Bd. 1: 1944–45. Bd. 2: 1945 und Nachkriegszeit, ed. Hugo Kaftan, Stadtbürodirektor in Pillau, Kernpowski Archive, Nartum

32. Martin Bergau, *Der Junge von der Bernsteinküste Erlebte Zeitgeschichte 1938–1948*, Heidelberger Verlagsanstalt, 1994, Kempowski Archive, Nartum

33. http://www.iwmcollections.org

34. Edward Loughlin, *Crossing the Elbe*, Hoskins Library, University of Tennessee, Knoxville; 2012/Box 8/Folder 16

35. Captain W.C. Brown, Eighth Parachute Battalion, Imperial War Museum; 97/19/1

36. Gustav Schulze diary, taken from *Zehlendorfer Chronik* 9(94), *Das Ende des Krieges in Zehlendorf*, ed. Kurt Trumpa, Heimatverein Zehlendorf, Berlin

37. Ralph Hewins, *Count Folke Bernadotte: His Life and Work*, Hutchinson, 1948; p.118

38. *The Schellenberg Memoirs: A Record of Nazi Secret Service*, ed. and trs. Louis Hagen, André Deutsch, 1956

39. Fleet Admiral William D. Leahy, *I Was There*, Gollancz, 1950; pp.415–16

40. Anthony Beevor, *The Fall of Berlin 1945*, Viking, 2002

41. Wolfgang Sturn, Heimatsmuseum Tiergarten Archive, Berlin

42. Fran K., born 1927, Heimatsmuseum Tiergarten Archive, Berlin

43. Kempowski Archive, Nartum

19. Climax (pp.408–46)

1. Karl Doenitz, *Memoirs*, translated by R.H. Stevens, Cassell, 2002; pp.443–4

2. Wynford Vaughan Thomas, BBC, in *On the Air – War Report*, Oxford University Press, 1946; p.421

3. *On the Air – War Report*, op. cit.; p.425

4. ibid.; p.426

5. Corporal Dai Evans, Royal Welsh Fusiliers, Imperial War Museum; 92/37/1
6. Captain William Morgan, Corps of Engineers, Hoskins Library, University of Tennessee, Knoxville
7. Leonard O. Mosley, *Report From Germany*, Gollancz, 1945; p.101
8. ibid.; p.102
9. General the Lord Ismay, *Memoirs*, Heinemann, 1960; p.394
10. Field Marshal Keitel, *Memoirs*, translated by David Irving, William Kimber, 1965; pp.230–1
11. ibid.; pp.231–2
12. Marshal de Lattre de Tassigny, *The History of the French First Army*, Allen & Unwin, 1952; p.515
13. ibid.; pp.518–19
14. Fleet Admiral William D. Leahy, *I Was There*, Gollancz, 1950; pp.421, 423
15. Professor D.N. Baron, Imperial War Museum; 01/01/1
16. Lieutenant Colonel H.M. Baker, Second Canadian Corps, Imperial War Museum; 87/44/1
17. Norman Longmate, *When We Won the War: The Story of Victory in Europe 1945*, Hutchinson, 1977; p.136
18. *New York Times*, May 8, 1945
19. L.O. (Les) Owen, Imperial War Museum; 83/4/1
20. ibid.
21. Mollie Panter-Downes, *London War Notes 1939–45*, ed. William Shawn, Longman, 1972; pp.368–9
22. *Daily Mirror*, Tuesday, May 8, 1945
23. Elizabeth Nel (née Layton), *Mr. Churchill's Secretary*, Hodder & Stoughton, 1958; pp.176–8
24. Mollie Panter-Downes, op. cit.; p.374
25. Professor D.N. Baron, op. cit.
26. Derek Lambert, *The Sheltered Days: Growing Up in the War*, André Deutsch, 1965
27. Reproduced from *Ten Days in May* by Russell Miller (Michael Joseph, 1995) by permission of PFD on behalf of Russell Miller; pp.180–1. Mass Observation Archive: Report of Victory in Europe, FR 2263
28. Russell Miller, op. cit., pp.69–70
29. ibid.; p.146
30. ibid.; p.191
31. Tom Pocock, *1945: The Dawn Came Up Like Thunder*, Collins, 1983; p.100
32. Edwin Kolodziej, Rutgers Oral History Archives of World War II
33. Centraal Archievendepot, Ministerie van Defensie, Doc. O.D., inv. Nr. A-53. *De Dam 7 mei 1945*, Flip Bool & Veronica Hekking, Uitgeverij

Focus, Amsterdam, 1992
34. Netherlands State Institute for War Documentation, Amsterdam; KBII 651
35. Tom Pocock, op. cit.; pp.110–11
36. ibid.; pp.111–12
37. Mrs W. Lane (Private Winifred Banner), Imperial War Museum; 89/19/1
38. Lieutenant Colonel H.M. Baker, op. cit.
39. Mrs W. Lane, op. cit.; 89/19/1
40. M.E. (Mea) Allan, Imperial War Museum; 95/8/1
41. ibid.
42. Catherine Gavin, *Liberated France*, Cape, 1954; p.85
43. Janet Flanner, *Paris Journal 1944–45*, Atheneum, 1965
44. Susan Mary Alsop, *Letters to Mariette*, Weidenfeld & Nicolson, 1960
45. Quoted in Russell Miller, op. cit.
46. CSM the Hon. Lucia Lawson, Imperial War Museum; 87/19/1
47. Captain Howard Sweet, US 908 Field Artillery Regiment, from a letter written on May 9, Imperial War Museum; 95/33/1
48. James Graff, *Memoirs of the 134th Infantry, 35th Division, Ninth Army*, Hoskins Library, University of Tennessee, Knoxville
49. Major A.J. Forrest, Royal Artillery, Imperial War Museum; 91/13/1
50. Marianne Beier, Düsseldorf Historisches Archiv
51. Private collection of cuttings
52. Russell W. Cloer, Rutgers Oral History Archives of World War II
53. Quoted in *Fragments of War*, Joyce Hibbert, Dundurn Press, 1985; p.84

Reflections (pp.447–53)

1. General the Lord Ismay, *Memoirs*, Heinemann, 1960; p.402
2. Jürgen Neven-du Mont, *After Hitler – Report from a West German City*, translated by Ralph Mannheim, Allen Lane, 1970; p.14
3. Leonard O. Mosley, *Report from Germany*, Gollancz, 1945; pp.124–5
4. Alan Bullock, *Spectator*, May 14, 1965
5. Fleet Admiral William D. Leahy, *I Was There*, Gollancz, 1950; p.429
6. Captain William B. Morgan, Corps of Engineers, US Army, 27.11.44, Hoskins Library, University of Tennessee, Knoxville
7. General Sir Brian Horrocks, *A Full Life*, Collins, 1960; p.268
8. Roger Boys, 'Friendship Washes Over Siegfried Line', *The Times*, January 18, 2003
9. Corporal William Blackman, RAMC, Imperial War Museum; 99/85/1
10. Karl Doenitz, *Memoirs*, translated by R.H. Stevens, Cassell, 2002; p.477
11. James Graff, *Memoirs of the 134th Infantry, 35th Division, Ninth Army*, Hoskins Library, University of Tennessee, Knoxville

Acknowledgements

My first debt of gratitude is to my friend and colleague Brian MacArthur who had the idea for the book and was generous enough to pass it on to me. My second debt is to my assistant Jill Fenner who keeps me sane, though she would not necessarily concur with that judgement. I have been blessed with outstanding researchers – Samantha Wyndham, Constance Wyndham and George Wyndham in London, Nicola Varns in Berlin, Mark Boulton in Tennessee, Robin Glendenning in Amsterdam and Lennart Oldenburg in Stockholm. Uschi Lacey was kind enough to share with me memories of a childhood in post-war Germany, Joan Bright Astley gave a vivid recall of the Big Three conference at Yalta and Linda Ippolito came up with some remarkable pictures of the bombing of Germany. My thanks to them and to others, too many to mention by name, who helped with contacts and introductions. Of the libraries and archives consulted, my special thanks go to Roderick Suddaby, The Imperial War Museum, London, Professor G. Kurt Piehler, Center for the Study of War and Society, Hoskins Library, University of Tennessee, Knoxville, Walter Kempowski, Dr Dirk Hempel and Kirsten Hering, Kempowski Archive, Nartum, David Barnouw and René Kruis, The Netherlands Institute for War Documentation, Amsterdam, Ivar Kraglund, Norges Hjemmefrontmuseum, Oslo, Esben Kjeldbaek, The Museum of Danish Resistance, Copenhagen, Shaun Illingworth, Rutgers Oral History Archives, Dr Peter Liddle, The Second World War Experience Centre, Leeds, Brigitte Holzhauser, Köln Historisches Archiv and to the curators of the Bonn Stadtarchiv, Bremen Stadtarchiv, Düsseldorf, Historisches Archiv, Fotografien aus den Sammlungen des Landesarchivs, Berlin, Heilbronn Stadtarchiv, Heimatsmusem, Tiergarten Archiv, Berlin, Nürnberg Stadtarchiv, Stadtarchiv Wuppertal and Stuttgart Staatsarchiv.

For permission to quote from documents held by the Department of Documents at the Imperial War Museum, I am grateful to the copyright holders of the papers of: Major J.D.P. Stirling, Eighth Armoured Brigade, Royal Dragoon Guards; Major P.J. Hurman; Corporal Dai Evans, Royal Welsh Fusiliers; the Hon. Lucia Lawson; Dr David Bradford; Geoffrey Hall, RAF Bomber Command, 427 Squadron (extract from *Kriegie. The Diary of a Prisoner of War in Germany 1943–45*); James Witte (extract from *The*

One That Didn't Get Away); letter from Sally Peters, taken from Alan Richardson's BBC Radio programme, *The Doughnut Girl*; N.L. Francis; Captain Maurice Jupp; Major A.J. Forrest, Royal Artillery; L.O. (Les) Owen; Corporal William Blackman, RAMC; Captain John Amsden, Seaforth Highlanders; Private Winifred Banner; A.E. Baker, 4th/7th Royal Dragoon Guards; Professor D.N. Baron; M.E. (Mea) Allan; Staff-Sergeant Peter Secretan, Sixth Airborne Division; Lieutenant (later Captain) Tom Flanagan; Squadron Leader C.N.S. Campbell, DFC; Captain J.J. Moore, First Battalion Oxfordshire and Buckinghamshire Light Infantry (extract from *Local Minor Patrol Activity*); Dr Arnold Horman. Extract from the letters of Captain C.T. Cross, held in the Department of Documents at the Imperial War Museum, by kind permission of the Worshipful Company of Armourers & Brasiers in the City of London.

It was not possible to contact all owners of copyright of papers held by the Department of Documents at the Imperial War Museum but we would be pleased to hear from any who might wish to make themselves known.

For permission to quote from published sources, I am indebted to the copyright holders here listed:

1945: The Dawn Came Up Like Thunder by Tom Pocock, Collins 1983.
After Hitler: Report from a West German City by Jürgen Neven-Du Mont, translated by Ralph Mannheim, Pantheon Books 1969, Allen Lane 1970. Copyright © Nymphenburger Verlagshanglung, 1968.
The Army Air Forces in World War II, Vol. 3 edited by W.F. Craven and J.L. Cate, The University of Chicago Press, 1951.
Belsen, The Liberation of a Concentration Camp by Joanne Reilly, Routledge, 1997.
A Blood-Dimmed Tide by Gerald Astor, Donald I. Fine, an imprint of Penguin Group (USA) Inc.
Bomber Harris: His Life and Times edited by Henry Probert, Greenhill Books 2001.
Bomber Offensive by Sir Arthur Harris, Greenhill Books.
The Bridge at Remagen by Karl Hechler, Pictorial Histories Publishing Co. 1957.
Count Folke Bernadotte: His Life and Works by Ralph Hewins, Hutchinson.
Defeat in the West by Milton Shulman, Secker & Warburg.
Eisenhower at War by David Eisenhower, HarperCollins Publishers Ltd and Random House Inc 1986.
Eyewitness War, Marshall Cavendish Ltd 1995.
Footprints in Time by Sir John Rupert Colville, Collins (permission granted by Lady Margaret Colville).

Fragments of War: Stories from Survivors of World War II by Joyce Hibbert, Dundurn Press 1985.

A Full Life by General Sir Brian Horrocks, HarperCollins Publishers Ltd, 1960.

Hitler's Ardennes Offensive edited by Danny S. Parker, Greenhill Books 1997.

The Hunger Winter: Occupied Holland, 1944–45 by Henri A. van der Zee, University of Nebraska Press 1982.

Hunger in Holland by Cornelia Fuykschot, Amherst, NY: Prometheus Books 1995.

The Inner Circle by Joan Bright Astley, Random House, (reproduced by permission of the author).

London War Notes 1939–45 by Mollie Panter-Downes, Longman 1972 (reproduced by permission of Pollinger Limited and the proprietor).

The Memoirs of General the Lord Ismay, Heinemann.

Monty: Life of Montgomery of Alamein: The Field Marshall 1944–76 by Nigel Hamilton, Penguin Books.

Mr Churchill's Secretary by Elizabeth Nel, Hodder and Stoughton Limited.

Norwegian Resistance 1940–45 by Tore Gjelsvik, C. Hurst & Co. 1979.

On the Natural History of Destruction by W.G. Sebald, translated by Anthea Bell, Penguin Books 2003, Random House Inc. 2002.

Operation Victory by Major-General Sir Francis de Guingand, Hodder and Stoughton Limited.

Other Days Around Me by Richard Hough, Hodder and Stoughton (permission given by Judy Taylor Hough).

Panzer Leader by Heinz Guderian (Michael Joseph, 1952) , copyright © Heinz Guderian, 1952.

Patton's Third Army. A Daily Combat Diary by Charles M. Province, Hippocrene Books, 1992.

Private by Lester Atwell, by permission of Harold Matson Co.

The Race for the Rhine Bridges by Alexander McKee, Souvenir Press Limited 1971.

Report from #24 by Gunnar Sonsteby, Barricade Books.

Roosevelt and Hopkins: An Intimate History by Robert Sherwood. Copyright © 1948, 1950 by Robert Sherwood, copyright renewed © 1975, 1978 by Madaline Sherwood.

Ten Days in May by Russell Miller (copyright © Russell Miller, 1994) reproduced by permission of PFD on behalf of Russell Miller.

To the Bitter End: The Diaries of Victor Klemperer 1942–45, Weidenfeld & Nicolson.

Voices From the Third Reich: An Oral History edited by Steinhoff, Pechel and Showalter, Grafton Books 1991. Permission granted by Bobbe Siegel Literary Agency.
The War in the Air by Gavin Lyall, Hutchinson.
Wing Leader by J.E. Johnson, Chatto & Windus.

Every reasonable effort has been made to acknowledge the ownership of the copyrighted material included in this volume. Any errors that may have occurred are inadvertent and will be corrected in subsequent editions provided notification is sent to the author. All attempts at tracing the copyright holders of the following were unsuccessful:

Reporting World War II: Part Two: American Journalism 1944–45 Library of America
Mission Completed by Basil Embry, Methuen, 1957
I Was There by Fleet Admiral William D. Leahy, Gollancz, 1950
Report from Germany by Leonard O. Mosley, Gollancz, 1945
Memoirs of Field Marshal Kesselring, William Kimber 1953
Surgeon at War by Lt Col J.C. Watts, Allen & Unwin 1955
Voices from Britain edited by Henning Krabbe, Allen & Unwin 1947
History of the French First Army by Marshal de Lettre de Tassigny, Allen & Unwin 1952
The Fatal Decisions by General Hasso von Manteuffel, Michael Joseph 1956
History of the Argyll & Southern Highlanders by Major Desmond Flower, Nelson 1950
Soldier: Memoirs of Matthew B. Ridgway by Harold H. Martin, Harper 1956
The Only Way Out: An Infantryman's Autobiography of the North-West Europe Campaign August 1944 – February 1945 by R.M. Wingfield, Hutchinson 1955
So Few Got Through by Martin Lindsay, Pen & Sword Books/Leo Cooper
Changing Enemies by Noel Annan, HarperCollins 1995
War Correspondent by Michael Moynihan, Pen & Sword Books/Leo Cooper 1995
Victory in Europe. The North-West European Campaign 1944–45 by Julian Thompson, Sidgwick & Jackson & Imperial War Museum 1994
The Mailed Fist by John Foley, Mayflower 1975
The Sixth Floor by Robin Reilly, Leslie Frewin 1969
Alfons Houben *Düsseldorf Stunde Null*, Hornung Verlag
Paris Journal 1944–65 by Janet Flanner, Atheneum 1965
Heilbronn – die schwersten Stunden der Stadt by Wilhelm Steinhilber, Verlag Heilbronner Stimme 1961

Index

INDEX